FIGHTING WITH FOOD

FIGHTING WITH FOOD

*Leadership, values and social control
in a Massim society*

MICHAEL W. YOUNG

*Assistant Lecturer in Social Anthropology in the
University of Cambridge*

WITH A FOREWORD BY
PROFESSOR W. E. H. STANNER

CAMBRIDGE
AT THE UNIVERSITY PRESS
1971

Published by the Syndics of the Cambridge University Press
Bentley House, 200 Euston Road, London NW1 2DB
American Branch: 52 East 57th Street, New York, N.Y.10022

© Cambridge University Press 1971

Library of Congress Catalogue Card Number: 72–158549

ISBN: 0 521 08223 4

Printed in Great Britain
at the Aberdeen University Press

To Maribelle

CONTENTS

TABLES

FIGURES

GENEALOGIES

MAPS

PLATES

FOREWORD

Having been privileged to watch the development of Dr Michael Young's researches in Goodenough Island from their inception, and having read his field-reports with intense interest, I am now gratified to be invited to write a Foreword to the completed book.

Dr Young prepared himself with care to study one set of problems only to find on arrival in the field that they seemed less significant than others which began to force themselves on his notice. It is never easy, and it may be inadvisable, to jettison a well-prepared plan of work and to try to devise another to meet the apparent demand of unexpected facts and situations. How can one be sure that what one came to study may not turn out in the longer run to be as significant as it has seemed, on good grounds, from afar? It would have been defensible for Dr Young to persist with his predetermined study: as yet, there are no canonical specifications for anthropological fieldwork and, under the rule of the scholar's sovereignty of interest, he might justifiably have said that *his* interest lay in things more fundamental than the passing parade. But as Salisbury did in the same situation among the Siane, Dr Young responded positively, and with rewarding results. He saw that the passing parade can *itself* be a true subject of anthropological inquiry and that *within* it what is fundamental to the process of a society's life is tested as well as revealed. This stance called for intellectual flexibility, technical ability, and theoretical insight. In my opinion, the account of 'the bitter-sweet life of intensive sociality' in the westernmost D'Entrecasteaux Archipelago is a more significant contribution to social anthropology than the study of political development with which a less perceptive or more timorous scholar might have persisted.

The work of Seligman, Jenness and Ballantyne, Malinowski, Fortune and others left us with at best an outline of some possibilities of Goodenough culture and society. Dr Young's book removes most of the ethnographic obscurity which had hung over the western Massim. It also makes possible for the first time some controlled comparisons with other Massim societies and with some in the wider Melanesia. It provides as a basis a careful but vivid analysis of the inwardness and outwardness of a somewhat isolated society in marked contrast with others, adjacent to it, which have been long familiar, and have had much to do with shaping our expectations of Melanesian studies. In my opinion *Fighting with food* should earn its author place in the front rank of specialists in that region. His clear and often felicitous writing is not the least of the book's attractions.

xi

In spite of some good taxonomic and synoptic essays in recent years, it is still difficult, for some of us at least, to see Melanesian sociality as an overall pattern. This book could strengthen an impression of a divided mosaic made up of strongly figured local identities. Almost every element of any local piece has a shape and quality reminiscent of those within other pieces. The difficulty lies in typing and comparing the ensembles so as to make the mosaic coherent.

It is, then, almost with expectation that one hears that Goodenough society is composed of a large number of small political units in rivalrous or friendly alliance, and of clans intricately arranged in traditional enmity or amity. That the physical scene is one of coastal and inland villages following somewhat different styles of life and responding differently to alien influences. That there is a dominant ideology of agnatic descent, inheritance and succession; that the pattern of residence is tightly patrilocal and patrivirilocal, and at times fratrilocal; that shallow patrilineages are anchored by symbols and magic to the villages or their constituent hamlets; that villagers have a potent sense of community and a pride in the persistent uniqueness of clusters of people, in spite of some ambiguity about identities; that networks of kinship, friendship and mutual interest cross-cut intra-village and inter-village life so as to formalize enmities and enjoin amities; that the villages are functions of social rather than ecological or demographic factors; and that mobility is low. Or that matrikin are warm, friendly, uncompetitive and unpossessive, affines friendly but somewhat embarrassed, and patrikin competitive, quarrelsome and prone to violence in some situations while sentimentally well-disposed in others. Or that men are timorous in love, prudish in sex, disposed to regard courtship as a title to later adultery, and capricious in their choices of wives from among the unlaughing, unfaithful, rather predatory girls; and that marriages are brittle and unstable, and divorce has no stigma. Or that there are no ritualized initiations into adulthood. And so on. All these features, and even collations of some of them, are familiar. The same might be said of some features of the rivalrous food exchanges which in this island have been developed almost to the stage of efflorescence. But not all. Goodenough's title to identity and uniqueness probably lies here if anywhere.

Dr Young's description and analysis of the exchanges, following on the account of the structure and organization of the society from the contrasted viewpoints of two villages, are thorough and thoughtful. The title *Fighting with food* is an apt description of a system in which clan-leaders seek with fanatical zealotry to gain renown for themselves and for their supporters by prestations of food, the main valuable, on rival groups, daring the not uncommon disaster of a greater return prestation. The methods are coercive in a variety of forms which intended victims can hardly – and because of their own zeal, hardly want to – evade. The purpose, at least the nearer purpose, is to requite or redress a real or fancied injury by inflicting humiliation, the shamefulness of a publicly revealed inferiority in food wealth. Dr Young make it readily understandable that valuations, through symbolisms of extraordinary subtlety and range, should concentrate on food in an island where drought, food-shortage and famine were familiar, where pigs and shell-goods were not a store, standard and symbol of wealth as in so many parts of Melanesia, and where external trade had not developed strongly. He considers the fact of rivalry to be a complex function of the structure and organization of the society, and the expression of the function a regulative, restitutive and integrative mode of social control, in the all-prevailing symbolic idiom of food. He demonstrates a persuasive 'fit' between environment, subsistence, settlement pattern, social structure, social control and leadership on the one hand and the sumptuary and redressive aspects of the food-exchanges on the other. He is able to suggest, further, on convincing grounds, that the main external causes of change – steel tools, Government administration, the suppression of warfare, and mission teaching – far from loosening the 'fit' have, so to speak, tightened it by allowing and even inducing an evolution of the traditional system. The product, at least where people cling to the old ways, and above all to the old symbolic idiom, has been something like a hyperbolic version of the system of rivalry.

Satisfying and fascinating as the account is, Dr Young accepts that he has left some questions unanswered and no doubt some unasked. Such candour inclines a reader to put the greater reliance on the positive findings. It is perhaps only a puzzle of formulation rather than of fact that, in a society where one of the canonized moral values is 'an uncompromising egalitarianism', a main and continuing enthusiasm of life should be to shame one's fellows into a public status of permanent inferiority, not equality. If I have understood Dr Young's thesis aright, it is that the Goodenough Islanders have enlarged the redressive element of the institution. Could it be, rather, or additionally, the punitive element? So that it is to the jural aspect that theoretical analysis might progressively turn?

One aspect of *Fighting with food* of which the author modestly makes little is its revelation of the dynamism capable of persisting in a Melanesian society under the worst conditions of external power. That the people of this island, poor in resources, but for long the prey of the external re-cruiter, and for longer still almost totally neglected by the Administration, should have retained the will to go on being themselves, and to preserve their animated and enthusiastic scheme of life, has much political import for those who are now concerned with the future of Papua–New Guinea. Dr Young's insightful account of that life in the dynamic round, and not just in the flat of its plan and structure, is a very notable contribution to a larger purpose than social anthropologists are yet encouraged to assist.

W. E. H. STANNER

The Australian National University
Canberra

1 June 1971

ACKNOWLEDGEMENTS

The field research on which this book is based was carried out whilst I was a Scholar of the Australian National University. For its generous financial support and many facilities, I owe this body a considerable debt of gratitude. I am grateful to the members of the Department of Anthropology and Sociology, both for their intellectual stimulation and their friendship. I would like to thank particularly Professor A. L. Epstein and Professor W. E. H. Stanner for their counsel and encouragement, and Dr A. Chowning for her patient and painstaking supervision of my research and writing. Professor J. A. Barnes, Mr A. Forge, Dr H. I. Hogbin and Dr P. M. Kaberry read the manuscript in its earlier thesis form, and offered many helpful suggestions for its improvement. No one but myself, however, is responsible for the defects of argument and presentation which still remain.

Members of the Administration of the Territory of Papua and New Guinea who helped me in so many ways deserve my warmest thanks. In particular, I am grateful to Graeme Baker, John Boulderson, Terry Bourke, Barry and Marion Downes, Peter Hill and Graham Mathews for their hospitality and assistance. I owe special thanks also to those European residents of Goodenough – Ailsa Hall and Clem Rich, Margaret Hooper, Pat Mylrea, Margaret Walker and Fr Kevin Young – who helped migitate some of the Island's hazards and discomforts.

The greatest debt of an ethnographer is inevitably to the people he studies. I thank all those Goodenough Islanders whose lives in some small part I shared. If I found some aspects of their culture distasteful, this does not diminish the respect and affection in which I hold them. Despite their initial suspicions of a white alien, they showed me tolerance and friendliness, and in time paid me the compliment of trust. It would be invidious to list those to whom I owe most, but I must mention my dearest friends and most conscientious assistants: Manawadi, Velowalowa and Kawanaba of Kalauna, and Tomokivona of Bwaidoga. Without these men my knowledge of Goodenough culture would be very much the poorer.

Finally, with pride as well as gratitude, I acknowledge the untiring assistance of my wife, whose resourcefulness in the field was an inspiration to me.

M. W. Y.

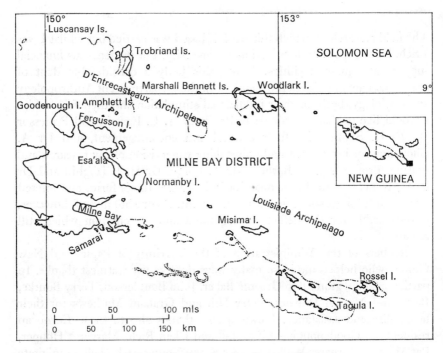

150°
Luscancay Is.

Trobriand Is.

SOLOMON SEA

D'Entrecasteaux Archipelago

Marshall Bennett Is.

Woodlark I.

153°

9°

Goodenough I.
Amphlett Is.

Fergusson I.

Esa'ala

MILNE BAY DISTRICT

NEW GUINEA

Normanby I.

Milne Bay

Louisiade Archipelago

Misima I.

Samarai

Rossel I.

Tagula I.

| 0 | 50 | | 100 mls |
| 0 | 50 | 100 | 150 km |

Map 1. The Massim: Southeastern Papua

PREFACE

This book, an amended version of a doctoral thesis, is based on fieldwork carried out during 1966–8 under the auspices of the Australian National University. My research plans, drawn up in Canberra early in 1966, were for an investigation of traditional and modern leadership in Goodenough Island, Papua. I intended to study the recently-established local government council as an emergent political institution, and to try to detect the processes by which the leaders of hitherto separate political units might bring about a form of centralized authority structure through modes of co-operation beyond the village level. Such an investigation would demand a familiarity with the socio-cultural framework, and the institutions and processes therein which could be regarded as political. This could best be achieved by that time-honoured technique of social anthropology: participant-observation in the life of a community. For purposes of comparison it would be necessary to study in depth at least one other community on the island, selected to bridge the apparent range of social and cultural variation.

The project was still-born. The council was immature, its role in village affairs was insignificant, and local leaders were for the most part unconcerned with its existence. It took some weeks to discover this, of course, and by that time I was beyond regret, having already become immersed in affairs of greater moment to villagers than mere council matters. I mention my original research plans because they largely determined my choice of a field base. A further consideration was that my wife and infant son were to join me once I had established a home, and I wished to be no more than a day's journey from competent medical help should it ever be required. Moreover, there seemed to be no virtue in isolation as such, and my initial patrol of the sparsely populated northern and western portions of the island convinced me that poor communications would hinder rather than help my research. The eastern side of the island is served by a vehicular track, and about 60% of the island's population lives within an hour's walk of it. It was also desirable to be within reasonable walking distance – no more than half a day – of the patrol post and local government council headquarters, to enable me to keep at least a light finger on the pulse of events of political moment. My range of choice was thereby reduced to less than a dozen villages.

The largest of these was Bwaidoga, which recommended itself by its size, the fact that it was the home of the council President, its documented language (Jenness and Ballantyne 1928) which I had already begun to learn in Canberra, and the fact of its also being the scene of an early ethnographic study by Diamond Jenness and the Rev. A. Ballantyne (1920). As the site of my first community study, however, I rejected Bwaidoga. I feared, rightly as it proved, that as the headquarters of the Methodist Overseas Mission on the island, missionaries had dominated the life of the community to such an extent that traditional leadership patterns would be exceptionally difficult to reconstruct. I decided to return to it, however, as my choice for the second, comparative community study.

Rejecting other coastal villages, therefore, and all hill communities of less than 300 people, I was left with only two choices. Mataita seemed suitable but for its unusual degree of hamlet dispersal, whereas Kalauna appeared favourable from every point of view. It was half an hour's walk from the road at Belebele and an hour by cross-country path to the patrol post. It was of above-average size and the most highly nucleated settlement in Goodenough. Since the compactness of Kalauna was apparently a function of its physical environment rather than of some centripetal social principle which would almost certainly have been atypical for the culture area, I had no reservations about welcoming the advantages which accrue to the ethnographer in a densely settled village.

Kalauna people seemed prepared to welcome, or at least to tolerate, my residence among them, and with the help of the councillor I commissioned eleven young men to build me a house. Since living space is at a premium in Kalauna, I was obliged to accept a site in a marginal hamlet which, however, commanded a view of the main path into the village. A few days after my appearance and before work on my house had begun, a village meeting was called at which I was the main item on the agenda. Speaking through an interpreter I put across my case for wanting to live there, and scotched the vague cargo rumours which had accompanied my baggage up the hill. These were no trouble to me subsequently, although a few individuals remained unshakeable in their belief that I was a 'spy' for the ancestors.

I spent thirteen months in Kalauna altogether, from September 1966 to May 1967, plus a few weeks in August 1967; then again from mid-January 1968 until the end of April, with a final fortnight there in June 1968. I tended to work intensively through a small number of informants, finding that close and personal relationships with a few friends were more productive, as well as more satisfying, than dependence on a wide range of acquaintances. Although I became fairly proficient at 'hearing' the language my speaking knowledge of it remained unimpressive. On the positive side, this probably did something to undermine my Goodenough friends' racist belief that all Europeans are innately more clever than all Papuans.

Two field periods were spent in Bwaidoga: from May to July 1967 and from May to June 1968, a total of five months. The contrast between Kalauna and Bwaidoga was stimulating, and the study of the latter provided valuable correctives to the perspectives I gained through the study of the former. Impressionistically, there was a brooding quality about the atmosphere of Kalauna, which was partly due to the position of its sombre, tree-shaded hamlets beneath towering mountains, and partly due to the existence of sorcery fears and the occurrence of frequent quarrels. By comparison, Bwaidoga had a sea-freshness, a brilliance of light and a sense of spaciousness. Its people seemed less prickly in their relationships with one another; they were untroubled by sorcery and showed more relaxed attitudes towards food – the source of so much competition in Kalauna. Clearly, a transformation of values had occurred in Bwaidoga which gave it a 'progressive', but rather dull and Apollonian air. Kalauna had retained an exciting Dionysian quality which seemed almost anachronistic in a long-contacted and heavily missionized area of seaboard Melanesia.

Social values are given an important place in this book. It seemed to me that I could not adequately account for the behaviour, institutionalized or 'spontaneous', which I observed in Goodenough without a fairly detailed understanding of these – particularly those relating to food. In gradually relinquishing my prepared research topic and in taking up one which the daily preoccupations of Kalauna people thrust at me, I discovered that although leadership remained a major focus of my study, it was articulated to something better categorized as 'social control' than 'political process'. The phrase *vemunumunuya au'a aiya'aine*, 'hitting/fighting/killing with food', was reiterated in my presence for a long time before I grasped the fact that it referred to a regular form of punitive sanction as well as to a conventional form of status-acquisition. It was first brought home to me, perhaps, when Wakasilele's friend from another village presented him with a large pig. Wakasilele is a 'big-man', a tough, stony-faced leader with a ferocious temper and a haughty pride, who on occasion even managed to intimidate me. His friend was not a 'big-man', but he left Wakasilele speechless with emotion when he gave him the pig. 'Why is he being given the pig?' I asked. 'Because his friend is angry with him', I was told. I learned that the friend had earlier brought Wakasilele some shell-fish from the coast, but the latter had churlishly spurned the gift. The giver was shamed, insulted and indignant. To point out to Wakasilele in the most humiliating way possible that he had committed a breach of good manners, his friend presented him with the most valuable asset he possessed – a pig. The emotion Wakasilele was struggling with was shame and presumably contrition. There was no 'political' element that I could discover in this incident. The act of giving the pig was purely punitive and redressive.

In general terms this book is about social control: the ways in which
Kalauna people coerce, manipulate, and sometimes manage to control
each other, and the reasons why they use certain means rather than others.
'Sanctions' is the operative word, perhaps, for this does not attempt to be
a definitive ethnography of social control in Kalauna. I do not deal with
processes of socialization, nor do I treat exhaustively modes of conflict
resolution. I am concerned, however, with those mechanisms or instruments of social control which Berndt would classify as 'coercive' and
directed towards the 'deliberate regulation of conduct' (1962, pp. 10–11),
and which Pospisil (1958) would presumably regard as 'legal' – although it
seems to me preferable to avoid the use of those question-begging terms
'law' and 'legal' in this non-didactic context.[1] In so far as I do elucidate
processes of conflict resolution and dispute settlement in Kalauna, this
monograph is some small contribution to the anthropology of law; though
the reader may well feel that here the opposite of Nader's stricture applies
(1965, pp. 17–18), and that my account of Kalauna's 'legal system' leaves
it too deeply embedded in the socio-cultural matrix to be of much use for
comparative purposes beyond a range of similar Melanesian societies.

More specifically, then, this book is concerned with the regulative aspects
of competitive food-giving. In order to demonstrate the role, functions and
consequences of such behaviour, it has been necessary to analyse it within
a context of specific social, cultural, environmental and historical conditions.
Thus, Chapter 1 sets the scene of modern Goodenough and looks briefly
at its contact history, especially the changes which have occurred in settlement pattern and local grouping. Chapter 2 introduces Kalauna by
describing its environment, settlement and residence patterns, and by
giving a short history of the community. In Chapter 3 the institutions of
kinship and marriage in Kalauna are briefly examined, mainly as providing
bases for community integration, but also as providing sources of conflict.
Wider institutional modes of integration are described in Chapter 4, which
is concerned with the ideology of clanship and the general structure of the
community. Chapter 5 identifies leaders, considers their attributes and
discusses the structural and cultural restraints on bigmanship. In Chapter 6
I attempt a limited quantitative analysis of instruments and agencies of
social control in Kalauna, considering in turn the redressive and regulative

[1] I agree with Gulliver (1969, pp. 12–13) that: '... it should be possible to ignore
some of the older, and bitterly contested, controversies: does "law" necessarily entail the
possibility of the use of force, or the practice of adjudication, or the existence of a court?
For example, do conciliation processes, duels, song contests, and various types of self-help
come within its realm? It is more desirable to analyze these kinds of phenomena in their
own contexts, in order to understand the social processes and ideas at work and to perceive
the comparable factors and the significant variables at both the intra- and the cross-
cultural levels.'

value of a variety of sanctions. The social values associated with food are the broad subject of the following two chapters, while in Chapters 9 and 10 I deal with competitive food exchanges: 'fighting with food'. The significant part they play in social control is considered, and the course and consequences of their development during the post-contact era are also discussed. In the final chapter I pull together the several themes of social values, leadership and social control in the analysis of their most dramatic institutionalized expression – the festival. In a brief Conclusion, I restate my general model of the development of competitive exchanges on Goodenough, consider the reasons for their demise in Bwaidoga, and finally indicate some problems which require more investigation.

The ethnographic base of my general topic is of necessity broad, and several chapters are therefore concerned with laying it down firmly. A historical dimension has also been essential, for not only are Goodenough Islanders themselves highly conscious of what traditions and institutions they have retained, modified, adopted or lost, but the early study by Jenness and Ballantyne (1920) invites the frequent backward glance. Despite its shortcomings as a systematic treatise, and its total neglect of the problems anthropology is concerned with today, their monograph provides useful background for a crucial watershed in the islanders' history. The social and cultural changes undergone in Bwaidoga during the fifty-five years between Jenness and Ballantyne's fieldwork there and my own are, in their own way and on their own scale, just as profound as those which have affected our own culture during the same period – with the difference, perhaps, that the Bwaidogan's standard of living has not altered substantially since 1911. Bwaidoga receives scant attention in this work, however, for its main focus is on institutions which that community has renounced.

A final word on method and scope. On one level the book is an attempt to integrate the general and the particular. I have flirted with the 'extended case method' but stopped short before the point where tedium begins to replace enlightenment. In giving illustrative case material I have tried to use the same *dramatis personae* whenever possible, so that not only may the reader trace analytic and sequential continuities between certain events, but that he may also become familiar with a number of individuals, grasping something of their personalities and life-styles. The behaviour, coercive techniques, and 'careers' of several leaders, for instance, may with the help of the index be traced through case material in the text.

In his attempt to convey the quality of life in an alien culture, the anthropologist is defeated ultimately by the nature of his medium. For although Goodenough Islanders stand in rigid postures when a camera is pointed at them, their social life is flux and movement, and any description of even those aspects of it which are 'salient' must proceed, as Gregory Bateson noted (1936, p. 3): 'not with a network of words but with words in linear series'.

M. W. Y.

Cambridge, 1971

1

THE ISLAND AND ITS PEOPLE

Goodenough Island is the westernmost of the D'Entrecasteaux Group, an archipelago of mountainous islands which curls above the eastern tail of Papua. These islands were first sighted as early as 1782 by the French navigator Bruni D'Entrecasteaux, but it was Captain Moresby in 1874 who was the first European explorer to name and set foot on them (see Moresby 1875).

Administered first from Samarai as part of the Eastern Division of British New Guinea, they came under Australian rule with the transference of the Crown colony to the Australian Commonwealth in 1905. Today the D'Entrecasteaux are administered as a sub-district of the Milne Bay District, and carry a population of about 33,000. The sub-district office is situated at Esa'ala, on the northerly prong of Normanby Island. Since 1963 Goodenough Island has been served by a patrol post at Bolubolu on the east coast. Bolubolu is eight road miles from a large air-strip (laid down during the Second World War), which currently receives a weekly DC3 flight from Port Moresby, the administrative capital of the Territory of Papua and New Guinea. Esa'ala, however, is six to eight hours from Bolubolu by government boat.

A native local government council was proclaimed in 1964, giving the island for the first time in its history a substantive political unity. The council became multi-racial in 1968 (though the non-indigenous population was less than 15), and in the same year there was discussion of the possibility of amalgamation with the neighbouring council of West Fergusson. The indigenous population of Goodenough numbered 10,375 in 1967 and it is this well-defined geographical, linguistic and cultural unit which forms the maximal ethnological focus of this study.

ENVIRONMENT

The island, which is shaped like a tilted egg, is approximately 300 square miles in area. The bulk of it consists of a dissected massif which rises to over 8,500 feet above sea level, but this extremely rugged and densely-forested interior is uninhabited. Clear, fast-flowing watercourses plunge

steeply from the centre of the island. Geologically, most of the island consists of acid igneous rocks which occur in areas of relatively recent volcanic
activity, and these basalts provide the richest soils on the island. Generally
speaking, however, the soils are thought to be poor. The violent tropical
rainfall and the precipitous topography of the island together cause
excessive drainage, so that everywhere soils tend to be shallow (Cole
1958).

Few rainfall statistics are available for the island, and none that are
entirely reliable. Fig. 1 presents two sets of averages based on my own

Map 2. Goodenough Island

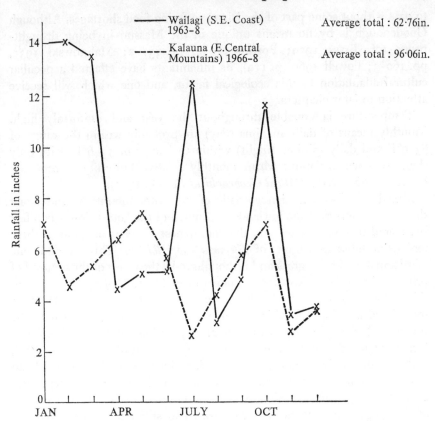

Fig. 1. Rainfall distribution on Goodenough

figures for Kalauna and those recorded at a mission school in Bwaidoga. Predictably, the mountain site is wetter than the coastal site; even so, for most of the inhabited areas of the island, precipitation would be under 100 inches for any 'average' year. Generally speaking, the southeast season dominates the climatic year, bringing cool, breezy weather, and owing to its partly sheltered position in the lee of the mountainous mass of Fergusson Island, somewhat unpredictable rains. The northwest monsoon period, lasting approximately from October to March, is humid and moist but even then good rainfall is not entirely dependable. As far as the records go, serious droughts with crop failures and human privation of famine proportions occurred in 1899–1901, 1911–12, 1946–7 and 1957–8.[1] In addition, innumerable local droughts have been recorded and scarcely a year seems

[1] *British New Guinea: Annual Reports* 1899–1900, 1900–1, 1902–3. *Papua: Annual Reports* 1911–12, 1949–50. *Patrol Reports* 1946, 1947, 1957, 1958. Jenness and Ballantyne 1920.

to pass without some part of the island suffering food shortages. Although Goodenough is by no means unique in the Massim in being drought-prone (cf. Brass 1959; Fortune 1932, pp. 131–2; Malinowski 1935, pp. 160–3; Powell 1960, p. 119), its inhabitants have effected a peculiar cultural adaptation to this ecological factor, and one which will receive attention in later chapters.

Temperature is equable throughout the year and uniformly high. Monthly means of daily maxima (day) are probably within the range of 83–9°F and daily minima (night) within the range of 73–6°F, with only slight seasonal variation. Mean monthly relative humidity is probably between 75 and 85% (*Allied Geographical Section* 1942).

Mixed rain forest is characteristic of the lower mountains and along the stream courses of the lowlands, but much of the land below 1,000 feet is covered in rank grasses and the commonest plant association in these regions is the savannah one of *Themeda* and *Albizzia*. This lowland zone of savannah and open grassland is thought to be the result of the removal of primary forest for cultivation purposes (Van Deusen 1957). The area of this zone is believed to be increasing yearly through inadvertent or intentional burning off, which in unexpected ways poses a threat to the future ecological viability of the human population. In 1966–7 a series of locust plagues devastated the coconut crop of practically the entire island, and, but for timely – and costly – administrative intervention by aerial and ground spraying, the food crops too would have been seriously depleted.[1] Since this event, the Administration has repeatedly warned the islanders of the long-term dangers of burning-off, and stiffer penalties have been introduced for causing fires which get out of control.

LINGUISTIC AND CULTURAL VARIATION

Culturally and perhaps linguistically Goodenough, together with the northwestern portion of neighbouring Fergusson Island, forms a relatively homogeneous area (see Jenness and Ballantyne 1920, p. 27). Despite some highly distinctive features, the most prominent of which is patriliny, this broad culture type can probably be regarded as a variety of the Southern Massim.[2]

[1] Entomologists maintained that the species (similar to *Locusta migratoria* of Biblical times) reached plague proportions due to exceptionally favourable breeding conditions produced by dry weather and burnt grasslands (Mr T. V. Bourke, personal communication; *South Pacific Post* 14 Dec. 1966).

[2] Since Seligman (1910, p. 9) appears to regard matrilineal descent as diagnostic of the Southern Massim, there are good grounds for excluding the Northern D'Entrecasteaux altogether. However, in several other respects, particularly in the indigenous material culture, including art, the region well qualifies for inclusion. It is not my intention here to propose a more satisfactory classificatory label.

The Island and its people 5

With one exception,[1] all communities speak dialects of a single Melanesian (Austronesian) language which is referred to in the literature as Bwaidogan. The earliest authorities seem to have minimized the linguistic divisions while the latest appear to have maximized them. Thus while Jenness and Ballantyne (1920, p. 56) maintained that 'there are several dialects spoken on Goodenough Island and North Fergusson, no one of which differs very greatly from the rest', a survey conducted in 1965 by a Summer Institute of Linguistics team attributed Goodenough with no less than four distinct languages.[2] I would be inclined to argue for a much lesser degree of specificity, since it is probable that the dialects were mutually intelligible indigenously as they are today. The islanders are still acutely conscious of their dialectical differences, however, since they serve them as badges of village allegiance; and in Kalauna for instance, there is a conscious resistance to the adoption of Bwaidogan words and phrases. Jenness and Ballantyne were nevertheless correct when they predicted that Bwaidogan, as the medium of Methodist teaching throughout the island, would become its *lingua franca* (1920, p. 56).

Although minor cultural variations coincide with linguistic distinctions, the most conspicuous and profound cultural division is that between inland and coast dwellers, which is reflected in native stereotypes of *kwana oyaoya* (people of the mountains) and *kwana imolata* (people of the littoral). The former are cast as hunters and snake-eaters who are afraid of the sea; the latter as fishermen and snake-loathers who are afraid of the high bush. Additionally, some influences from Fergusson Island are evident along the adjacent east coast of Goodenough, so there is a broad cultural distinction also to be made between the eastern and western parts of the island. In the east, for example, there has been a relatively recent adoption of some Fergusson forms of mortuary ceremony and food distributions. A more traditional impulse from the same general source is the 'canoe complex'. From Belebele to Wagifa canoe builders send their new vessels to neighbouring villages to solicit gifts of food, pigs and, indigenously, shell valuables. In earlier times the adjacent coast of Fergusson from Fatavi to Kukuya formed part of this gift-exchange circuit associated with the launching of new canoes.[3]

[1] Buduna or Budula is a tiny enclave of later migrants whose speech differs quite markedly from the other speech communities on Goodenough. Their own myths of origin derive them ultimately from a site in Mud Bay in the south of the island, from whence they sailed to the Amphletts and thence to a succession of settlements on the north coast of Goodenough, where they remain at present. Their language may have some affinities to that of the Amphletts. It is also notable that they are one of the few peoples on Goodenough who still make pottery.

[2] Personal communication from Miss J. Huckett of the S.I.L.

[3] See Chowning 1960, for an account of this practice in Molima, on the south coast of Fergusson. In contrast to Molima, the gift-exchange and canoe-building complex on

Despite local cultural differences, however, basic structural principles, the major social institutions and the value systems associated with these, appear to be uniform throughout the island. A broad definition of Good-enough Islanders would characterize them as a light-skinned, Oceanic negroid people[1] with a subsistence economy based on the cultivation of yam, taro and banana, dwelling in what Hogbin and Wedgwood (1953) would describe as discrete multi-carpellary parishes, the carpels of which are locally-anchored patriclans. Pig husbandry and, on the coast, fishing, are important subsidiary economic activities. A system of leadership by 'big-men' and hereditary ritual experts is articulated with a value system which centres on food production and distribution. Food exchanges are a major preoccupation and an expressive feature of almost every kind of institution and social event. Otherwise, public ceremonies are few and art (nowadays) virtually non-existent. The world-view is pervaded by belief in the efficacy of magic in most areas of human action, the social aspect of which is a preoccupation with sorcery. The most salient contrasts between Goodenough and what is known of other Southern Massim cultures appear to be the presence of patrilineal descent groups and an agnatic ideology, a puritanical attitude towards sex, absence of belief in female witches and relatively undeveloped trade relations with neighbouring societies.

Mention should be made, finally, of perceptible differences to be found today between communities on Goodenough which have been unequally exposed to missionary influence. Although this is essentially a continuum of acculturation, villages which represent the extremes, such as the two which I studied, manifest some striking contrasts. It is fortunate from this point of view that the study by Jenness and Ballantyne was completed before social and cultural changes had got far under way. Their mono-graph, while entirely lacking a sociological orientation, provides a valuable compendium of indigenous customs, thereby preserving a base line from which may be gauged changes occurring in the intervening generations. Many of the usages which they describe for Bwaidoga are scarcely re-membered there today; others from Fergusson or elsewhere have taken their place. Yet even in Bwaidoga, the community most intensively influenced by the Mission in its midst, there is a tangible continuity of tradition and a certain pride in its uniqueness and persistence.

Goodenough is not associated with mortuary feasts or memorials to the dead. Further, Goodenough was never a link in the *kula* chain which bound many other islands of the Massim; although some villages constructed sea-going canoes, they were used for war and short trading trips rather than for the long *kula* voyages characteristic of the Dobuans and Trobrianders (Malinowski 1922). Shell valuables were obtained (principally from Amphlett Islands traders) by barter for pigs and yams.

[1] Physical type in the Southern Massim is described in Seligman (1910, pp. 3–8) and Malinowski (1922, p. 36).

CONTACT EXPERIENCE

The pacification of Goodenough Island was effectively complete by the middle of the second decade of the century, and there are few old people alive today who can recall either the taste of human flesh or their villages being in a state of war with their neighbours. For the most part, the government had imposed its rule without need for violence, though there are two or three ugly exceptions in the record (Monckton, 1921 pp. 95–103; *British New Guinea: Annual Report* 1897–8; *Patrol Reports* 1910). Once homicide and cannibalism had been suppressed, the influence of the government became secondary in importance to that of the Methodist Mission, and except in the matter of resettlement, perhaps, until quite recently the government's role has been almost entirely restricted to the somewhat negative one of imposing and enforcing regulations.

As indicated by the number of recorded patrols, few Goodenough villages would have seen a government officer more than once a year until the 1960s. Just before the Second World War a patrol post was established at Mapamoiwa on Fergusson Island, and from this base two patrols a year were made on Goodenough. During the war there was considerable ANGAU (Australian New Guinea Administrative Unit) activity in the area, associated with a large bomber base on the island; and later a police camp was established by the Department of Native Affairs at Bolubolu for a few years. This was abandoned about 1950 and the post at Mapamoiwa re-opened and closed again twice in the following decade. The current revival of Administration interest in the island dates from 1958 when a series of agricultural and medical surveys discovered a sick, hungry and apathetic population. This state of affairs had been the result of the inter-related factors of prolonged drought, over-recruitment of male labour for work abroad and inadequate gardening by those who remained. Labour recruitment was closed for almost two years, seed yams were widely distributed, and the situation improved as adequate rains returned. A patrol post was opened at Bolubolu in 1963 and since then a series of energetic officers have helped to effect more economic development than was probably evident during the whole of the previous period of European administration.[1] Since 1964 the local government council has brought the

---

[1] In 1958 one officer could write: 'Economically and socially these people have shown practically no development since the arrival of the Administration 50 years ago.' He attributed this situation to (1) the fact that the island is one of the 'prime sources of labour in the Territory', (2) neglect by the Administration, and (3) 'lack of ability of the people to help themselves' (*Patrol Report* 1958). The remainder of the D'Entrecastreaux had apparently fared little better. Another officer referred to it in 1957 as 'the dead heart of Milne Bay District' (*Patrol Report* 1957).

direct participation of the people into the problems of their future development. To date, however, the council has few substantive achievements to
its credit, and in 1967 it was rated by an experienced official (in a private
communication) as among the most inefficient in Papua.

Mission influence, although unevenly spread in space and time, has
thoroughly permeated Goodenough culture. The Methodist Overseas
Mission has been based at Wailagi, on land purchased from Bwaidoga,
almost continuously since 1898. For a long time most villages on the
island have had a resident native teacher, usually a Bwaidogan, sometimes
a Dobuan, whose task it is to preach on Sundays and teach children during
the week. The educational attainments of these men are generally very
limited, as is their grasp of Christian doctrine. Their teaching, however,
with its curious blend of Biblical stories, ethical precepts and categorical
restrictions, has over two or three generations been more or less passively
assimilated. An often incongruous syncretism has resulted in which
Christian values are commonly expressed in word, though less commonly
in deed, where an older stratum of values is still dominant. Except in
Bwaidoga, Church sanctions against the use of magic and the practice of
polygyny, for example, are generally weak and inoperative. Again, except-
ing Bwaidoga, it would be true to say that mission leaders have notably less
influence than traditional leaders. There have been no mission representatives at all in Kalauna since 1964, other than informal 'prayer leaders' who
hold poorly attended 'services' in the villages each Sunday. (The last
resident teacher, a Bwaidogan, fled Kalauna after his wife had been
seduced by a Kalauna man.)

For Kalauna and neighbouring communities at least, my general
impression was that the high point of mission influence had been passed a
generation or more ago, and that if anything it is now in decline. The
sharp edges of the pagan culture have been worn down by the ubiquitous
Methodism, but the indigenous growths of materialism, pragmatism and
individualism remain firmly rooted in the people's subsistence and society,
and until these are radically altered the culture will probably remain proof
against further Christian subversion.

Sixty years after the Methodist Mission settled at the Dobuan heart of
the D'Entrecasteaux, the Roman Catholic Sacred Heart Mission entered
the area, and about 1950 a station was established at the northern end of
Goodenough. There was initially considerably acrimony between the two
missions, particularly so on the part of the Methodists, who regarded the
Catholics as intruders. But where there are no zealots there can be no
heretics, and the majority of Goodenough Islanders were passive and
bewildered spectators of the confrontation. The Catholic Mission intro-

duced considerably higher educational standards in the schools it was able
to establish, which had the salutory effect of prompting the Methodists
to take formal education more seriously than they had done hitherto.
English was taught for the first time in the 1950s. Government legislation
in 1952 brought all schools under the control and direction of the
Administration, which eventually had the effect of raising standards of
teaching in those schools the Administration recognized. By 1967, however,
there was still only one government (i.e. non-mission) school on Goodenough, and this, like the handful of mission schools recognized by the
Administration, was only of primary standard. The very small number of
Goodenough children who had received any secondary education at all by
1967 had acquired it at mission schools elsewhere in the District. Probably
no other single factor has contributed as much to the present state of
political ignorance and apathy among Goodenough Islanders as the
long-term neglect of their basic education (see Gostin *et al.* 1971).

  Two other influences of the post-contact period should be mentioned.
The war years brought considerable disruption for a large proportion of
the population. The Japanese assault on Milne Bay in 1942 resulted in a
force of 360 Japanese soldiers being marooned upon the west coast of the
island. After some months they were driven off by an Australian task force,
and for the remainder of the war a large air base was maintained on the
flat plain in the north east of the island (McCarthy 1959, pp. 347–9;
Odgers 1957, p. 32). The native population of several villages close to the
base was evacuated to the adjacent coast of Fergusson Island to make room
for several thousand Australian and American air-force personnel. Those
islanders who were able to remain recall this brief era as one of novel
tinned foods and unexpected perquisites in money and material objects.
But when the armed forces withdrew, all materials and supplies that were
not considered useless were taken away, leaving the indigenes to salvage
what they would of the air-strip matting, the empty oil drums and the tons
of rusting scrap iron.

  For as long as a decade after the war, patrolling officers were apt to
blame the effects of the war (including the Military Administration,
ANGAU) for the unhappy state in which they claimed to find Goodenough
Islanders. There were pockets of discontent which provoked small-scale
cargo cults. There was a succession of droughts which seriously hindered
the attempts of the people to recover from the disruption of war. There was
an increasing flow of willing recruits for labour abroad, yet there was a
passive resistance to government attempts to interest young men in
apprentice training. Finally, officers found cause for complaint in the
'apathy' and 'surliness' of the people, of which they found evidence in the

untidy villages, the unkempt roads, the ramshackle houses, the shiftless village constables and the unwilling carriers.

Although, as far as is known, there were very few native casualties during the war, its psychological impact was probably considerable. Other forms of European enterprise have been minimal by comparison, and their impact correspondingly less. There have been fewer than a dozen commercial coconut plantations in the history of the island and all have been small. Currently there is but one. There is also a moderately profitable, European-owned trade-store which supplements its income by recruiting labour for employers in Samarai and Port Moresby. Indigenous enterprises are on a very much smaller scale. The people of Goodenough give only covert value to successful entrepreneurship. Accumulation of native wealth and the manipulation of capital were not such conspicuous features of their political system as they appear to have been elsewhere in Melanesia. Sorcery was, and still is, greatly feared by those who would display an uncommon talent or a conspicuous degree of wealth, whether this be counted in gardens, pigs, shell valuables or cash, and the D'Entrecasteaux islanders as a whole affect an uncompromising egalitarianism. These are probably important factors in the weak personal incentives of would-be entrepreneurs.

Copra is the most immediate source of income, but co-operatives have yet to be tried on Goodenough. Production is on an individual or family scale, and either sold at low prices to the local European traders or personally taken on an expensive expedition by boat to the Copra Marketing Board in Samarai. For a brief period the local government undertook the responsibility of sending copra into Samarai on behalf of local producers, but the plan was ill-administered and failed to win their confidence. A generous estimate would put the number of people on Goodenough earning more than $A30 a year from this source at about 200.[1]

Cash crops other than coconuts have been experimentally grown from time to time under the direction of administration agricultural officers, but none has proved notably successful. Chillies, coffee, cocoa, peanuts and rice have all been tried but are nowhere on the island a significant source of income. Timber resources are considerable but they remain unexploited. One or two saw-mill ventures by local entrepreneurs have failed through lack of capital and technical knowledge. Cattle projects have been mooted at intervals for the grass plains in the north east, and the council has finally, in 1968, set aside a fund for a small herd. In sum, the island – and

---

[1] I would estimate the per capita income of Goodenough Islanders at about $15 in 1967. Of this figure copra production would account for about $3 and income from wage labour for the remainder.

one may include the D'Entrecasteaux as a whole – is economically under-developed and without any immediate prospect for development. The cash needs of the people continue to be met, as always, by migrant labour.

Since the earliest days of European contact the D'Entrecasteaux Islands have provided employers elsewhere in the Territory with a supply of sturdy, industrious and relatively tractable unskilled labourers (see Mair 1948, pp. 122–3). '*Gosiagos*', as D'Entrecasteaux men are sometimes called (after the Dobuan term for 'my friend'), have done much over the years to build up the local economies of other areas of Papua at the expense of their own, and European traders in the area continue to find it more profitable to recruit men for labour abroad than to buy copra from them. It is, indeed, a not unreasonable charge that the Administration has, unwittingly or otherwise, preserved this area as a vast pool of unskilled labour.

Clearly, the volition of the people themselves has been a considerable factor in perpetuating this situation, and some three generations of migrant labour experience have had an ineradicable effect on local cultures. On Goodenough, while it is hard to find a woman who has been further than Fergusson, it is impossible to find a man who has not at some time in his life worked in another District. A spell of labour abroad is regarded as an essential *rite de passage* which every young man must undergo before he can marry and achieve adult status. (Indigenously, however, there were no puberty rites or abrupt ceremonial initiations into manhood.)

While migrant labourers invariably return to their villages for good once they approach middle age, they spend some of their best working years away from home – often to the detriment of their communities. Currently, the local government council is encouraging men to stay and earn their money at home, but since it can provide no more than a handful of jobs itself, since its annual tax demands are inexorable, and since certain European goods are now regarded as necessities (steel tools, tobacco, and men's shorts, in particular), there are no alternatives open to the man with few cash crops other than to seek money abroad. Nor is it desirable, of course, that men be prevented from leaving the island to work. An aftermath of the highly unpopular ban on recruitment in 1958 was a cargo cult centred on Wagifa in the south of the island, but which seriously affected a number of other village areas. This cult was more or less effectively quelled by prompt government action, and although there were some minor recrudescences, no serious manifestations have appeared for at least ten years. Cargo beliefs are still held by many individuals, however, and a fresh catalyst could well provoke another mass cult (see Young 1971).

SETTLEMENT AND LOCAL GROUPING IN THE PRE-CONTACT ERA

Nothing factual is known of the original human settlement of Goodenough, and I do not intend to speculate on the islanders' origins nor document their affinities with other Melanesians. In eschewing these problems of ethnology, I am reconciled to being unable to answer satisfactorily some fundamental questions concerning the pattern of settlement over the island as a whole. Thus, for example, there can be no final agreement as to the validity and significance of the distinction which islanders make between *kwana oyaoya*, 'people of the mountains', and *kwana imolata*, 'people of the coast'. Do the stereotypes associated with these categories refer exclusively to differential cultural adaptation to habitat, or do they also hint at distinct migratory strata, peopling the island from different homelands at different times? I am inclined to the former view, for there is no clear linguistic, ethnic or cultural evidence to warrant a genetic separation of the sub-cultures of the mountains and the coast (cf. Jenness and Ballantyne 1920, p. 37). Today many communities are composed of inextricably mixed contingents from both zones, and in these much of the force of the colloquial stereotype is lost. However, I happened to work in two communities of unmixed composition: one proudly *kwana oyaoya* and the other no less proudly *kwana imolata*. In these villages the stereotypes were apt and meaningful, and being Lamarckian in thought, informants would offer inheritable, 'genetic' factors to account for such things as the coast-dweller's inept bushmanship and the mountain-dweller's incompetent seamanship, but without, it must be added, surrendering the doctrine of the common origin of all Goodenough Islanders and the essential unity of their cultural heritage. This doctrine takes a mythical form.

Situated mid-way along the east coast of the island and some three miles from the sea is a mountain called Yauyaba. In a moist glade within a few feet of the summit there is a vent in the rock from which a faint draught issues. This hole, according to universal Goodenough legend, is the point of emergence of mankind from beneath the ground. The Yauyaba origin myth has as many versions as there are groups with an interest, for whatever purpose, in the past. Questions of ethnology, culture history, the content of customary behaviour and the form of institutions – even the still undigested problems of culture contact – all converge, in Goodenough Islanders' thinking, at Yauyaba. As well as the locus of all mysteries, it is a dogma which provides answers to the ultimate questions of existence. Of course, not all islanders believe in raw mankind's appearance at Yauyaba; but it is widely accepted in the same way that the Garden of Eden is believed in by fundamentalist Christians. To ask a question about traditional life is to invite an answer couched in a traditional idiom.

Yauyaba, then, is the Goodenough Islanders' answer to the problem of their origin, their cultural and linguistic differences and their dispersal and settlement over the island. Stripping the myth (or rather, one full version of it) down to its baldest theme, it states that after the surface of the earth had been discovered from below, and the people had settled it and found it good, they were forced to flee a man-devouring monster which was later killed by two brothers. Calling the people back to Goodenough, the brothers distributed the monster's heart for them to eat, but after doing so the people found that they all spoke different 'tongues' so they went off to settle in different places.[1] No version of this myth that I am familiar with, however, concerns itself with the distinction between mountain and coastal populations nor, to anticipate the following paragraphs, does it suggest why the spread of settlement on Goodenough has been so uneven.

If the clue to the first question posed lies in ecological adaptation, it is less easy to offer ecology as the key to the problem of why, in the past no less than in the present, greater population densities occur in the south and east of the island than in the north and west. Over 50% of the population resides in what may be called the 'foot' of Goodenough, with approximately 15% of the total area. The density here is over 100 persons per square mile, while for the remainder of the island it is about 20.[2] Dividing the island down the middle along its axis of greatest length, the average density of the eastern half with 70% of the population would be some 46 per square mile; that of the western half (with 30% of the population) some 20 per square mile.

This imbalance in the distribution of population points up one important fact: that the size of an indigenous political unit was not a correlate of the size of its territory, or the amount of land to which it laid claim. Writing of a period when the effects of pacification had yet to be felt, Jenness and Ballantyne state:

The island is divided into a number of districts varying greatly in size, but each with a distinctive name. Mud Bay carries a considerable population and its

---

[1] The myth contains readily identifiable elements belonging to the vast pool of mythological themes to which all Massim peoples appear to have had access. Only the ordering, combination and relative stressing of these elements are unique to local cultures.

[2] These calculations are my own, based on the latest census figures. In an early report, Vivian (1921) calculates that the coastal fringe of the 'foot', 'having a coastline of some score miles and an area of about nineteen square miles, has 4,584 natives, or at the rate of 240 people to the square mile'. There is no evidence to suggest that this area is any more fertile than elsewhere on Goodenough, or that it otherwise provides a habitat in some way more congenial to human settlement (Cole 1958).

districts are numerous and small; Malitauya [i.e. Moratau], on the other hand, and Belebele cover several square miles of country (1920, pp. 39–40).

These 'districts' (which Hogbin and Wedgwood (1953) would call parishes, Goodenough Islanders call *melala*, and I propose to call villages) were the nominal political or war-making units in the past, within which marriage was preferred and fighting discountenanced. The optimum size of these units was clearly a function of sociological rather than ecological or demographic factors.

Another feature of the general settlement pattern on Goodenough was noted by Jenness and Ballantyne: 'At the present time [i.e. 1911] at least half the population dwells on the hills and mountain slopes from 600 feet to 2000 feet above sea level' (1920, p. 29). These authors raise the question of why, if there are such extensive plains on the island, populations adjacent to them prefer to live in the hills? They suggest firstly that since local subsistence crops are equally if not better suited to drained slopes, and since the hills are less susceptible to the shrivelling droughts which frequently afflicts the plains, then there are sound economic reasons for avoiding the latter. They conjecture secondly that in the era of endemic warfare 'the weaker villages, oppressed by constant raids, migrated for refuge to the hills' (1920, pp. 28–9).

Plausible though they are, both hypotheses can be controverted. In the first place, proneness to drought notwithstanding, a far larger proportion of the population now lives on the plains and littoral; I would estimate that less than one third remains above 600 feet, though it is true that drained slopes are retained for gardens where possible. In the second place, as Jenness and Ballantyne admit (*ibid.* p. 29), apart from the occasional harassment of coastal populations by Dobuan raiders seeking victims for cannibal feasts, there are no concrete examples to support their conjecture that weaker groups were driven into the hills. Early patrol reports and the oral history of several villages tend to suggest the opposite: that weaker groups were driven *out* of the hills and onto the plains. This, certainly, was the pre-contact experience of sections of present-day Belebele, Yauyaula, Mataita, and many of the villages which make up the Kwaiaudili 'tribe', which is the largest and most dispersed dialect and sub-cultural group on the island.

Whatever the reasons, the fact remains that a large proportion of the pre-contact population preferred to dwell in the mountains, despite an abundance of land at lower altitudes. Certain consequences have followed. There is the differential ecological adaptation which has been mentioned above and which, to take the extreme viewpoint of the stereotype, has created and perpetuated a cultural distinction between hunters and fishermen. There is the historical significance of the fact that by dwelling in the interior a large proportion of the population was denied even the possibility of inter-island trade and cultural contacts such as the *kula* provided for other insular societies in the Massim. Finally, a present-day corollary of the relative isolation of those mountain-dwellers who still remain is the tenacity with which they have maintained their hold on traditional ways by comparison with those communities which have been more accessible to non-indigenous influences.

SETTLEMENT AND LOCAL GROUPING IN THE POST-CONTACT ERA

Three broad trends characterize the seventy years of European influence on indigenous settlement patterns and local groups. The first is the general shift of populations from isolated upland settlements to more easily accessible lowland sites;[1] the second is the tendency of dispersed hamlets to become nucleated; the third is an increase in the overall size of communities. Obviously, not all villages on Goodenough have undergone these processes to an equal extent, and it would doubtless be possible to find a present-day community which, by various historical or demographical accidents, exemplified the reverse of them. But exceptions do not invalidate general trends which are discernible for the majority, and it seems true to say that most Goodenough communities which were self-contained, viable entities seventy years ago are today closer to the coast, more concentrated in settlement and larger in size. While there is some functional relationship between these trends, the most significant fact about them is that they stem directly or indirectly from the pressures and influences of an alien government. Discounting the changes introduced in the economic sector, the government's influence on Goodenough Island society can be seen as principally affecting the political sphere. By banning warfare and providing a superordinate justice, by investing selected individuals with powers of coercion which were foreign to the traditional context, and by express directives to alter certain modes of grouping, the colonial government has significantly altered many aspects of the indigenous political system.

The people of Goodenough currently dwell in twenty-three census groups, locally referred to as 'barracks' (see Table 1). This term is in itself a memorial to the specific mode of government contact with three generations of Goodenough Islanders. The earliest patrols, dating from

[1] Jenness and Ballantyne (1920, p. 30) hint at initial resistance to this process: 'Many of the hill villages are so inaccessible that the Government has attempted to induce their inhabitants to migrate down to the plains, but hitherto its efforts have not been crowned with much success.'

Administrator MacGregor's visit of 1888, found 'quiet, friendly and undemonstrative' people who were disinclined to trade and refused to accept twist tobacco[1] (*British New Guinea: Annual Reports* 1888–9; 1891–2).

TABLE I *Goodenough Island villages and their populations*

Census group village or 'barrack'	Present location	Present composition by origin (hill, coast or mixed)	Population at November 1967 (Official Census)
Abolu	Coast	Mixed	312
Awali	Coast	Coast	272
Belebele	Coast	Mixed	361
Bwaidoga	Coast	Coast	1,087
Eweli	Hill	Hill	312
Faiava	Coast	Coast	500
Idakamenai	Hill	Hill	286
Kalauna	Hill	Hill	475
Kalimatabutabu	Plains	Hill	639
Kilia	Coast	Hill	571
Lauwela	Coast	Mixed	598
Lower Wataluma	Coast	Coast	159
Mataita	Hill/Coast	Mixed	677
Moratau	Coast	Mixed	525
Ufaufa	Coast	Hill	485
Ufufu	Hill	Hill	707
Utalo	Hill	Hill	418
Vivigani	Plains	Hill	318
Waibula	Coast	Hill	123
Upper Wataluma	Hill	Hill	400
Wagifa	Coast	Coast	754
Wakonai	Hill	Hill	269
Yauyaula	Coast	Hill	127
Total			10,375

Within a few years, the first village constables had been appointed (probably at Bwaidoga and Wagifa), and by the year 1921 there were sixteen (Vivian 1921). The procedure of 'bringing under government control' followed a pattern. The year 1898 marked both the establishment of the Methodist Mission on the island, and the institution of fairly regular government patrolling. Few patrols took longer than a month, as it was rare for every inland or mountain settlement to be visited by each patrol. Coastal or accessible lowland communities were quickly provided with village constables, who were also given nominal jurisdiction over inland groups in their vicinities. Each community was instructed to build a rest

[1] It is a conventional joke among the thoroughly addicted islanders of today that their ancestors rejected tobacco. Some are said to have believed it was pig excrement; others love-magic. Yet others are said to have planted the sticks.

house for the use of itinerant officers, and a 'barracks' for the armed native police who accompanied each patrol.

Barracks (as rest houses also came to be called) became a symbol of government influence and authority, just as the village constable was intended to be their agent. In a procedure which has scarcely changed down to the present, the patrolling official would expect to be met by the village constable at the boundary of his district and escorted to the barracks. There, the officer would hear the village constable report on local matters, and investigate complaints, the state of houses, coconut plantings and the cleanliness of the village. He would arbitrate disputes brought before him, have his police arrest offenders of the Native Regulations Ordinance, and in a speech to the assembled community exhort them to plant more coconuts, improve the tracks between villages, build better houses and generally obey the village constable. If they were a hill-dwelling group he would also instruct or 'invite' them, as one patrol officer quaintly put it, to move down to a more accessible settlement site.

Thus, over a period of two decades or so the concept of 'barrack' was being formed: meaning a neighbourhood under the official authority of a village constable and charged with a collective responsibility to build and maintain rest houses for the use of government patrols. When the first detailed census was conducted in 1921 for the purpose of introducing taxation, the field officer, while guided by the form of the indigenous 'district' or village in determining boundaries, grouped an enumerated thirty-three of them into sixteen census units, each of which was represented by a village constable.[1] These contained from one to four indigenous political units. It is important to stress that they were not the creation of this one officer; his role was merely to fix (and in one or two cases to alter) by entering in tax census books, the form of grouping that had been created over a period of more than twenty years. The number of indigenous villages included in a 'barrack' in this initial census varied according to such factors as their size and accessibility. The hill communities, for instance, generally lacked village constables and therefore forfeited their 'independence' by being included in census units based on, and named after, their nearest lowland neighbours. Since 1921 there have been some re-alignments and further subdivisions as the number of village constables was gradually increased to twenty-three, and as differential growth or decline occurred in individual village populations. There has been a

[1] There were probably a good deal more than 33 indigenous political units at the time of contact. Jenness and Ballantyne (1920, pp. 210–16) list 32 but they appear to have included some 'districts' under the headings of others. From all of the available data I would estimate the number to have been nearer 50. Mr Peter Lauer has supplied me with historical information about the communities at the northern end of Goodenough.

tendency, too, for villages which remained in the foothills or the mountains to regain their 'independence' by being granted the status of self-contained census units.

The significance of the development of 'barracks' on Goodenough lies in the extent to which local groupings, political organization, and even political behaviour, have been adapted in phased response to what was initially an alien model. In many of those instances in which the 'barrack' was constituted of a number of indigenous political units, its members have now come to regard themselves as belonging to a single, discrete community. A major, if relatively recent development in this process was the establishment of the local government council. An extra 'barrack' was created prior to proclamation by the division of an unwieldy one; otherwise no changes were made in these groupings which now form electoral wards. The proclamation, by naming and defining the units from which twenty-five councillors were to be elected,[1] effectively fixed the existing configuration of 'barracks' and gave yet further impetus to their development as self-conscious political units.

[1] On account of its size, Bwaidoga 'barrack' was granted the right to be represented by two councillors. Unlike Mataita, the 'barrack' which was subdivided, Bwaidoga lacked a convenient political fault-line.

2

PROFILE OF KALAUNA:
SETTLEMENT AND RESIDENCE

The second, and perhaps most important, reason why increase of population tends to the creation of new parishes is that the political organization of most Melanesian parishes, dependent as it is for stability on a network of kinship ties, is unsuited to groups with a population of over 350 persons.

Hogbin and Wedgwood 1953, p. 71

The community of Kalauna, which is to be the principal social unit of study in this work, is in at least two respects atypical of other Goodenough Island villages. It is unusual for its physical compactness and in that it constitutes a single indigenous political unit. So far as I am aware, the hamlets of no other village are so highly consolidated, and only two other 'barracks', both considerably smaller than Kalauna, are also co-extensive with a single indigenous polity. In other respects Kalauna is not unusual. There are ten other 'barracks' with larger populations, though only two of these are also mountain settlements. It is neither the highest village on Goodenough nor the most isolated, though it shares with other mountain groups the distinction of being among the most tradition-oriented.

ENVIRONMENT AND SETTLEMENT PATTERN

The main village, comprising sixteen hamlets, is situated between 900 and 1,000 feet above sea-level. Behind the village the forest-clad mountains rise precipitously to the island's spine at a mean of some 5,000 feet. For several hundred feet above the village some of the more accessible slopes are utilized for taro gardens. The prospect inland is of a steep mountain wall clothed in dense primary forest, etched in places by rocky scars overhanging narrow valleys down which race wild torrents, and occasionally broken by grassy spurs which mark the site of old gardens. The higher forests are entered sometimes by hunters in search of game; lower down they are exploited for their timber for building materials. Generally, however, hunting parties prefer to scour the grasslands below the village for pig or wallaby, while men building houses prefer to collect what materials they require on the way home from their gardens.

The undulating spurs and foothills below Kalauna are mostly covered with coarse grasses and stunted *Albizzia*. Along the watercourses and in hollow pockets there is denser vegetation: mixed forest with pandanus, clumps of coconut, and the occasional edible nut tree. Yam gardens are made on these gentler slopes; lower down are the yam gardens of neighbouring Belebele. At the bottom of the foothills is the vehicular road, built during the war, which connects the patrol office at Bolubolu to the air-strip at Vivigani. The road runs through the village of Belebele, beyond which are the coastal flats, some two miles deep at this point. Towards the sea the alluvial soils provide for good banana gardens and stands of coconut trees, but about a mile from the sea the forest grows denser as the soils become moist from seepage, and sago and beach pandanus are the most notable species. The narrow beach along this stretch of coastline, like much of the strand around Goodenough, is backed by mangrove swamps which in places, instead of giving way to the sago forest, open out into extensive salt flats. Here there are hot springs and boiling mud pools, active remnants of the island's volcanic past, and, according to local belief, the home of malignant dwarfs. Kalauna has little to do with the sea. Although many of its men enjoy fishing, they are less skilled than their coast-dwelling neighbours, and they possess neither nets nor canoes.

The site of the village itself is an approximately level platform some few acres in area. This natural shelf is bounded on two sides by ravines which plunge 200 feet to the cold torrents which provide Kalauna with its water. On a third side the village is backed by the mountain wall and on the fourth by another steep drop to a smaller stream, and thence to the undulating foothills and plains. The main path into the village meanders up this fourth slope to the platform, around large boulders and up crude rock stairways. It is a path which none but the fittest of young men can climb without a breath-catching pause.

Twelve of the sixteen Kalauna hamlets occupy the flattest part of the tiny plateau, each hamlet separated from its neighbours by a line of stones or a low wall, and sometimes by a different physical level. Three other hamlets, Mulina, Ukevakeva and Buveta, are separated from the rest and from each other by stands of betel nut, patches of *Alocasia*, small banana gardens, tangled undergrowth and some tall forest treees, as well as breadfruit, coconut and native chestnut (*Inocarpus fagiferus*). These three hamlets are situated on sloping ground. Most of Ukevakeva is physically higher than the rest of Kalauna; Buveta and Mulina are lower, for their land falls down to the third stream. The remaining and most recently established hamlet is Wakulava, a colony of Ukevakeva.[1] It is the most exposed, being separated by a low ridge from the rest of the village and lacking even the shelter of trees. Only from Wakulava can the sweeping plains, the towering peak of Mt Madawa's, the massive blue-green bulk of northern Fergusson and the sharp distant pyramids of the Amphletts, be seen in uninterrupted

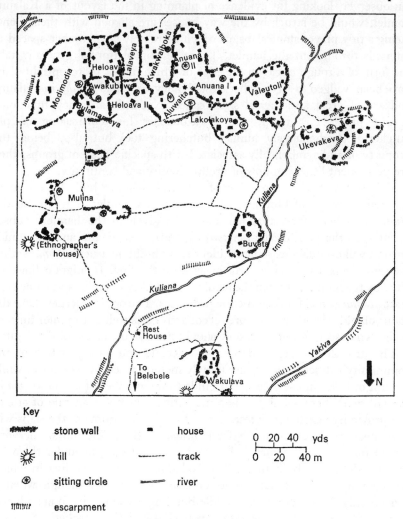

Key

stone wall		house	
hill		track	
sitting circle		river	
escarpment			

0 20 40 yds
0 20 40 m

Map 3. Kalauna Village

[1] There is a seventeenth hamlet belonging to Kalauna which was also founded in recent years by an Ukevakeva patrilineage. This is Daulu'u, which is also the site of a Sacred Heart Mission school. It is situated near the vehicular road, some two miles below Kalauna and on land adjacent to Belebele.

view. Approaching the village, only the houses of Wakulava betray the
presence of human settlement; the rest is nestled on its sheltered platform
beneath shady trees and lowering rocks.

THE HAMLET: SIGNIFICANCE OF THE 'ATUAHA'

An observer, looking for evidence of planning in the layout of a Kalauna
hamlet, would be struck by the way houses are aligned with their fronts
facing a tidy pile of stone slabs, of which there may be a number spaced at
intervals throughout the hamlet. These 'sitting platforms' generally take
the form of a rough circle on the edge of which one or more upright slabs
have been wedged to serve as backrests.[1] They are called *atuaha* in Kalauna
and are of great sociological significance. Not only are they functional
seating places for gossip, and work-benches for tool-making or pig
butchering (indigenously human butchering too) but also, being the
property of and symbolically associated with specific descent groups, they
are permanent lithic symbols of group identity and continuity.

This is manifest in a number of ways. *Atuaha* are built by the men,
generally a group of brothers, who settle a new hamlet. They name the
atuaha and henceforth that name may be given to the hamlet. Subsequently, as the patrilineage (*unuma*) expands, it segments and the junior
portion will establish its separate identity by building a new *atuaha* within
the same hamlet but some yards away from the first. Immigrant lines invited by the founders to join the hamlet would likewise build and name separate *atuaha* as foci for their members' houses. The original settlers have the
status of 'elder brothers' to more recent arrivals as well as to junior lines of
their own descent group, and they should provide the leader of the hamlet.

The growth and segmentation, the decline and amalgamation of the
community's descent groups are mutely memorialized by its *atuaha*, while
a count of those in use gives a fair guide to the number of extant *unuma* in
the village. Where a line has become extinct, an unkempt pile of stones
overgrown by vegetation is testimony of its demise. Some of the slabs will
have been removed to make fresh *atuaha*, others left out of nervous
regard for the magic which is believed to have been put under them by
the ancestors who built them. The Kalauna hamlet of Mulina in which
my own house stood had no fewer than five *atuaha*, though when I
arrived only three were in use. While building my house in an abandoned
corner of the hamlet, my workers uncovered an adjacent *atuaha* to serve
as my 'marker'. Subsequently my landlord, who had been living for some

[1] Structures of this kind have a wide distribution in the Massim (see Seligman 1910,
pp. 463–6).

years in a garden hamlet near Belebele, returned to Mulina and erected a house near my own. His widowed sister and her son built another small house alongside. I was thus the unwitting stimulus of a minor re-settlement which focussed itself on the *atuaha*.

Another expression of a man's identification with the *atuaha* of his patrilineage is the practice of laying out, or more accurately, sitting up, his corpse on the *atuaha* when he dies. His brothers may proclaim a period of mourning (to culminate in a festival or a large food distribution) by putting a taboo on the *atuaha*, and it may be crudely fenced off with vines as a form of memorial. Although such taboos are not done for women, and although it is rare for a woman's body to be seated on her *atuaha*,[1] the following incident indicates the extent to which even long-married women continue to be identified with their natal *atuaha*. After a village-wide feast at which pots of cooked food were exchanged randomly, a man discovered when he went in search of his pot next day that it had been set on the *atuaha* of his dead wife's *unuma*. As a widower, it is his lifelong obligation to avoid contact with the food – or any other intimate posses-sion – of this *unuma*. Although his avoidance is a conventional expression of respect for his ex-affines rather than a taboo backed by any supposed supernatural force, the widower declared that he could never again eat food cooked in that pot, and he exchanged it for his brother's. The man's dead wife had not been laid on the *atuaha* before her burial, and the notion of contamination of the pot through its physical contact with the *atuaha* was mediated entirely by the fact of the woman's 'mystical' association with it. Had the pot been placed on the ground of the hamlet instead, or even in her brother's house, it would not have been 'spoilt' thus.

Many *atuaha* in Kalauna were built by unremembered ancestors, although to make a connection more personal and a claim more secure a man will at first say that his own grandfather built it. A factor in the relative stability of settlement emerges: the ancestors who built an *atuaha* are believed to have put a special kind of 'anchoring magic' (*bakibaki*) under the uprights.[2] This magic is meant to 'look after' the group and its descendants by protecting their bodies from sickness and their gardens from ruin. These general benefits are assured only as long as the *unuma* resides near its *atuaha*. To abandon it is to forego them. There may even

[1] Jenness and Ballantyne record an instance of this occurring (1920, p. 117). A woman is generally mourned inside her husband's house prior to being carried back for burial in her natal hamlet.

[2] Another form of *bakibaki* is put under one of the posts during the construction of a new house. It is clear from the words of the spell that this is intended not so much to make the structure secure, as to keep the owners dwelling there.

be a negative aspect to the magic, which then inflicts illness or worse on those who abandon their *atuaha* to dwell elsewhere. It was suggested by some informants that the many deaths which occurred during the unhappy sojourn on Fergusson Island, whence Kalauna people had been evacuated during the Pacific War, were due to the magic in the *atuaha* meting out punishment for the abandonment of their homes. Yet another form of magic which is sometimes said to reside in *atuaha* is a variety of love-magic intended to evoke an irresistible nostalgia in those who leave their hamlets.

Despite these rationales for dwelling a lifetime on the same piece of ground, some men do in fact move; not only within the village, but also to set up or join other communities elsewhere. In so far as the magic in the *atuaha* is a sanction which encourages permanent agnatic co-residence, its power may be waning even in conservative Kalauna. At Belebele, two miles down the mountain, where there are fewer *atuaha* than there are *unuma*, where oil drums and steel matting are sometimes used in their construction, and from whence several groups have migrated during the last two generations, these beliefs are now disregarded.

THE HAMLET: SOCIAL COMPOSITION

A Kalauna hamlet, then, contains one or more minimal descent groups (*unuma*) which are associated with stone sitting circles. Although the latter are named, they do not usually give their name to the *unuma* which own them. More commonly, where there are more than one *unuma* in the same hamlet, they are referred to by the names of their leaders, or they may simply be called *Aina'onina* ('First'), *Minafaneya* ('Middle'), or *Ainamulina* ('Last'). These terms refer to their genealogical ranking if they are known to belong to the same wider descent group, or to their historical order of settlement in the hamlet if their origins are diverse. This naming system of the *unuma* of a single hamlet points up the significance of the hamlet itself as a reference group. Indeed, hamlet rather than descent group names provide people with their readiest means of self-identification. Asked in the most neutral way possible, what is his 'group' (*yo'o*), a man will invariably give the name of his hamlet (*melala*) first, his clan (*yabu*) second, and his *unuma* only if specifically asked for it. Except in the context of food exchanges and distributions when clan and *unuma* names come into their own as defining political units and sub-units, they are used sparingly.

For some purposes it might be convenient to regard the descent group composition of certain hamlets as sub-clans. I avoid doing so here, however, because the term creates a precise taxonomic distinction midway between patrilineage (*unuma*) and clan (*yabu*) which is not given formal recognition by the people themselves, and which, furthermore, appears to be of social significance in some cases only. Thus, some hamlets are occupied by only one *unuma*; that is, all male members can trace agnatic descent from common grandparents or great-grandparents. Other hamlets are occupied by single clans; that is, all male members, although belonging severally to discrete *unuma*, share a common myth of origin and acknowledge other criteria of common clanship (see Chapter 4). Clearly, to state that 'some' hamlets are occupied by sub-clans, in those cases in which a clan is spread over more than one hamlet, and then to define sub-clans in terms of the membership of certain hamlets, would be to add confusion to the ambiguity with which Kalauna people themselves handle the terms *unuma* and *yabu*. For those cases in which there are more than one patri-lineage but less than one clan associated with a single hamlet, people may speak of either *unuma* or *yabu* when referring to its members; or they may evade the taxonomic issue altogether by using the general term *yo'o* (group).

TABLE 2   *Descent groups and hamlets in Kalauna*

Clans (*yabu*)	Hamlets	Number of patrilineages (*unuma*)	Hamlet population (1967) including absentees
Ainaona	Kwakwaiboka	2	24
Lulauvile I	Aluwaita	2	19
,,	Anuana I	2	34
,,	Heloava II	3	25
Lulauvile II	Heloava I	2	28
,,	Anuana II	4	29
Malabuabua	Modimodia	4	51
,,	Awakubawe	1	12
,,	Bulamameya	1	8
Foloyai	Lalaveya	1	11
,,	Lakolakoya	1	12
Iwaoyana	Ukevakeva	2	59
,,	[Ilobelobe]	1 (females only)	abandoned
,,	Buveta	2	22
,,	Wakulava	2	37
,,	Daulu'u	1	20
,,	[Edu'edu – a single isolated household]		10
Nouneya	Valeutoli	3	35
Mulina	Mulina	4	34
8 clans	17	38	470

Fighting with food

Table 2 will demonstrate better than further description and qualification the taxonomy and group composition of Kalauna clans and hamlets.

RESIDENCE NORMS

The importance of the patri-virilocal rule in Goodenough is that it underwrites agnatic solidarity, ensuring that the co-resident group of men, which is the principal co-operative group, is also the patrilineal descent group. Table 3 compares residence statistics for six villages, and demonstrates the high degree of conformity to the patrilocal norm.

TABLE 3   *Residence of adult males in six Goodenough villages: 1967*[a]

Village	Married men				Widowers/bachelors			Total	Percentage living patrilocally
	Patrilocal	Avunculocal[b]	Uxorilocal	Neolocal	Patrilocal	Avunculocal	Neolocal		
Belebele	28	2	2	2	12	1	2	49	81·6
Bwaidoga	32	7	2	1	4	2	—	48	75·0
Kabune (Bwaidoga 'barrack')	35	3	1	4	10	1	—	54	83·3
Kalauna	75	3	—	17	17	4	3	119	77·3
Ukuna (Bwaidoga 'barrack')	39	5	3	3	11	4	—	65	76·9
Wailolo (Belebele 'barrack')	16	1	1	2	3	—	—	23	82·6

[a] Men who were absent from the villages during this year are included in the table, classified according to their residence at the time they left their homes.
[b] By 'avunculocal' I mean residence with mother's *unuma*.

The environmental factor in these six villages is not a constant; some of them, like Belebele, enjoy abundant village land and others, like Kalauna, suffer an acute shortage. Yet the proportion of men living patrilocally is consistently high in all villages. Where living space is limited by steep hillsides, large boulders or the seashore, patrimonial land might be expected to be more highly valued than where settlement area is not thus constrained. But instead of junior members of a hamlet being encouraged to break away from a cramped site, they are prevailed upon to stay, or if they have left, to return. Under such circumstances there may be another expression of agnatic solidarity: a man who feels the necessity to seek less congested living conditions is usually accompanied by one or more brothers. They set up neolocal residence together, perhaps in a roomy hamlet at the invitation of its leader, but more commonly on a new site altogether. Since there are nine such men in Kalauna (four sets of brothers) who fall into the neolocal category of married men in Table 3, they could well be re-classified as dwelling 'fratrilocally' (a term used in a somewhat different way by Chowning 1966, p. 496). By this I mean to imply, firstly that the changes of residence from patrilocal to neolocal of these nine men were partly a result of population pressure; and secondly that in the next generation their children are likely to remain where their fathers raise them, i.e. in patrilocal residence. The fratrilocal phase, then, can be seen as one intermediate between two patrilocal generations. From this point of view it is no less an expression of agnatic solidarity than patrilocal residence. Whereas the latter expresses a diachronic dimension of agnatic group strength, fratrilocal residence expresses a synchronic dimension. The figures for Kalauna in Table 3 can be adjusted accordingly as shown in Table 4.

TABLE 4 *Residence of adult males in Kalauna: 1967*

Residence	Married Men	Widowers/ bachelors	Total	%
Living patrilocally	75	17	92	77·3
Living avunculocally	3	4	7	5·9
Living neolocally				
(1) fratrilocally	9	2	11	9·2
(2) non-fratrilocally	8	1	9	7·6
Total	95	24	119	100

The total number of adult males living patrilocally and fratrilocally is thus 103 (86·5%), which gives a crude index of agnatic solidarity as expressed in residence patterns.

To clarify the effectiveness and strength of the residence norms further, it will be useful to consider briefly the exceptions to them. The fathers of all seven men who are living avunculocally are dead. In five cases the men, as children, had accompanied their mothers when the latter were obliged by custom to return to their natal hamlets following their husbands' deaths. None of these five men have true brothers. Two of the three married men intended to return to their natal hamlets when the houses they are currently occupying become unserviceable. Two of the four unmarried men expect to return to their own hamlets when they marry, if not before. The other two are likely to stay with

their mothers' brothers, as is the remaining married man, since their natal
unuma are weak in strength and none have close living agnates. In short, if all
these men do as they say only three of the original seven will be living avunculocally a few years hence.

Some cases of neolocal residence have been referred to already. Three brothers
and their families established the hamlet of Daulu'u near the Catholic Mission
school, some two miles from the village. They left their natal hamlet Ukevakeva
as a result of a series of quarrels with other *unuma* living there. Subsequently,
six more men left Ukevakeva, encouraged to do so by further quarrels. Two sets
of siblings founded the hamlet of Wakulava (about 1963) where there were
more quarrels, causing one individual to take his family and make a new home in
relative social isolation at Edu'edu (see Table 2). The other founders of Wakulava
attracted to themselves two sisters' sons, and later more individuals joined the
'refugee' hamlet temporarily to escape bad relations with agnates in their own
hamlets. Another major focus of 'neolocal' resettlement in recent years has been
Kimaola, a Lulauvile clan leader. Having no close male agnates of his own, he
has induced five men (including two pairs of brothers) to join him from an
overcrowded hamlet belonging also to Lulauvile. This case is analysed in more
detail in Chapter 5.

Finally, there are a handful of individuals, most of them married, who have
left their natal hamlets after quarrelling with their brothers. Most will probably
return in time, unlike those who have founded new hamlet sites and created, in
their *atuaha*, attestations of establishment.

It is unlikely that the already high percentage of agnatic co-residence
(86·6) could ever be, or have been, much higher; there will always be
children forced to leave their natal hamlets with their widowed mothers,
and men who seek, whether temporarily or permanently, refuge in isolation
or with distant kinsfolk.

The wonder, perhaps, is that so few men do *not* conform to the patrilocal norm, for flexible rules of residence and high mobility appear to be
more usual than not in Melanesia (see e.g. Barnes 1962; Epstein 1964;
Langness 1964). Kalauna is not untypical of other Goodenough Island
communities in that it displays a tight residence pattern and low population mobility. Men tend to stay put. Obviously, the pressure of population
on an acutely delimited settlement area is a factor, for men have full
residential rights only in their fathers' hamlets. However, not all the villages
of our sample in Table 3 are as pressed for living space as Kalauna, so a
more general problem is indicated. Even if some of the force behind the
patrilocal norm were to be derived from scarcity of village land, the broader
problem is still raised as to why Goodenough Islanders, and Kalauna
people in particular, should consider it so desirable to live together in
highly nucleated settlements. While there would appear to be no simple
historical, ecological or sociological answer, by considering the relevant

factors for Kalauna we shall be in a better position to assess the significance of stable nucleation.

In common with other Goodenough Islanders, Kalauna people claim to have emerged from beneath the ground at Yauyaba. According to contemporary belief, the clan ancestors appeared in the order in which I listed the clans in Table 2, bringing with them the customs and competences by which these maximal descent groups are still identified (see Chapter 4). In this beginning, Kalauna people called themselves Nibita, the name they bore until European contact. Nibita peoples also included clans or clan fragments which are now dwelling elsewhere. Wailolo, Awaiya and part of Belebele, for instance, are said to be Nibita people like Kalauna; their 'tongues', meaning their dialects, are the same.

Nibita peoples are said to have dwelt together initially at a site called Kwabua, a dank and gloomy place atop the 2,000 feet ridge which separates the territories of Kalauna and Mataita. A man of Lulauvile clan was 'bossman' or 'chief' of this settlement and most of the subsequent legendary accounts of Nibita are myths which are the exclusive possession of Lulauvile. This clan exercised supremacy because it alone had the magic 'secrets' of food; not only were its leaders the 'food-bringers' but since they had the monopoly of productive magic, they were also the 'food-growers'.

Nibita was split asunder when Kedeya, the 'chief', became angry with some fellow-villagers for lewdly peeping at his wife whilst she was bathing. A battle of coconut husks ensued, after which Kedeya ordered the subdivision of Nibita. Different segments were sent to different places with instructions to specialize in certain crops or commodities. Awaiya was sent to the coast for salt and 'tree-cabbage' (*baoka*); Mianiva (now part of Mataita village) was sent over the ridge to produce lime-gourds; I'amulina (now part of Eweli) was sent around the mountain for medicinal leaves (*dibila*); while Lulauvile declared that it would stay in Kwabua and exchange yams and taro for these commodities. It is not clear at this point whether what were to become the other clans of Kalauna remained behind with Lulauvile in Kwabua. The Lulauvile myths make no mention of them, although in answer to specific questioning the elders think that they did.

From Kwabua the remaining Nibita peoples moved down to a number of other sites, somewhat closer to present-day Kalauna, though what prompted their move is unknown. It is perhaps significant, however, that the abandonment of Kwabua is mythically associated with the partial 'sharing out' by Lulauvile of some of the food 'secrets' to which it had hitherto held exclusive title. It is said that Kedeya and other Lulauvile ancestors were warned by a Belebele friend that unless they distributed some of their 'power', they would soon die from sorcery. They gave banana, plantain, sugar cane and *Saccharum edule* (and, some maintain, sweet potato) to other Nibita clans, but managed to retain control of the more important crops (yams, taro, coconut) themselves. The abandonment of Kwabua is thus associated with the granting of concessions to other clans, which may well symbolize a surrender of supremacy on the part of Lulauvile.

Shortly before the arrival of the first Europeans (*c.* 1900), the leader of the Nibita clan which occupied the present site of Kalauna (sent there by Kedeya from Kwabua) invited the other clans to come together and dwell there, as he was taking his group down to the plain near Belebele. The rationale for this move was the leader's anger over the murder of his son, a philanderer who had been speared by jealous kinsmen. The other Nibita clans obeyed his behest and descended from their separate sites on the mountain behind to settle together on the tiny plateau which later came to be known as Kalauna. The move was a partial one; for more than a generation afterwards the clans are said to have retained dwellings on the mountain sites as well as in the village itself. Why the move was made at all, however, remains a puzzle. The legends ascribe no motives to the new settlers, while modern commentators state merely that the Kalauna site was 'good' and the people moved in to claim and 'look after' it.

The first documentary reference to Kalauna appears in a patrol report of 1903, in which the Resident Magistrate mentions visiting 'Kalona' and finding the people friendly. The nucleated settlement was probably in existence at this time, although the officer estimated a population of only 100. During the next few years a number of other visits were made by government officers; one to investigate a complaint by Belebele that Kalauna had threatened to raid them, another to investigate a 'murder' that had resulted from a quarrel over food-sharing at a 'feast', and one to caution an old man who was rumoured to have encouraged Kalauna people to attack the police next time they came to the village. None of these visitors refer to the demography of Kalauna.

Jenness and Ballantyne are the next chronological source, and the first to offer any description of the village. They probably visited it during the year 1912, and in their monograph make two references to it: the first concerning its nucleated settlement pattern, and the second in their list of Goodenough 'districts', hamlets and their associated totems (1920, pp. 43, 214). From the first reference we learn that: 'To all outward appearances it [i.e. Kalauna] consists of one unusually large hamlet with about 150 houses; in reality there are four hamlets fused together'. If we suspend disbelief and accept the authors' rather improbable estimate of 150 houses (there were fewer than 130 in 1967), together with their curiously low 'probable average of from two to three inmates' for houses on Goodenough as a whole (*ibid.* p. 42, also p. 47), then Kalauna's population in 1912 could have been between 300 and 450. The lower figure is more acceptable, for a proportion of houses in any village are likely to be unoccupied (*ibid.* p. 47), while the higher figure jibs with later reports. The 'four hamlets' that the authors mention under 'Kelauno District' (*ibid.* p. 214) are Livauga, Ulavila, Malabuabu and Dodoma, which respectively refer to the clan names Iwaoyana, Lulauvile, Malabuabua and Mulina. Only Dodoma is a hamlet name. Three clans are missing from this list: Ainaona and Foloyai, which are small enough to have been mistakenly included in adjacent Lulauvile during a hasty census, and Nouneya, which some older informants still lump with Iwaoyana under the 'old name' of Livauga. It may be assumed then, that the clan structure of the community in 1912 was essentially what it is today, and that Kalauna's existence as a consolidated village was well under way by then.

The first official house-count of the area appears in a patrol report dated 1920. At this time Kalauna, together with the neighbouring villages of Wailolo and Eweli, was under the nominal authority of a Wailolo village constable, the unit thus constituted being officially referred to as Bolubolu District. A total of 249 houses was recorded for this District, ninety-nine of them for Kalauna.

A year later, in 1921, the first census of the island was completed by an officer who, more than any other European except Dr Bromilow (the pioneer of the Methodist Overseas Mission), has become immortalized in local legend. Mr Vivian, or Misibibi as he is recalled in Kalauna and numerous other villages, is variously attributed with the resettlement of whole districts, the seduction of native women on an orgiastic scale (on the pretence of teaching them to plant coconuts!), and the 'shooting' of spearmen with a fountain pen. It is asserted in Kalauna that Misibibi was the first white man to visit the village, that it was he who renamed it (improbably because 'Nibita is too hard to say'), and that it was he who first lined up the people for census. On the last point only are they likely to be correct, but the tales are instructive for what they teach about the tendency to telescope 'lines' of European visitors as well as native genealogies. Misibibi, in other words, represents all the government officers that the grandparents of today's maturing generation had ever known; he is a composite symbol of Kalauna people's early experience of government power. Strangely, there is a fund of awed affection for Misibibi and amused pity for the fumbling attempts of their forebears to cope with 'him'.

The 'real' Mr Vivian, who spent longer among and wrote more words about Goodenough Island people than any previous officer had done, counted 392 Kalauna people in what he describes as 'the largest village on the island' (Vivian 1921, p. 12). He would be deeply endeared to Kalauna people if they knew of the complimentary things he had written about their yam gardens: 'The rich, chocolate soils of the undulating uplands are cultivated in a manner reminiscent of ploughed areas in civilized countries. The yams are huge' (*ibid.* p. 13).

TABLE 5   *Population of Kalauna: 1903–67*

Year	House count	Population	Source
1903	—	Est. 100	*Patrol report*
1912	Est. 150	Est. 300	Jenness and Ballantyne 1920
1920	99	—	*Patrol report*
1921	—	392	Vivian 1921
1947	—	318	*Patrol report*
1949	—	362	*Patrol report*
[Official census made almost annually from this point on]			
1954	—	359	Official
1959	—	387	Official
1964	—	446	Official
1967	—	475	Official
1967	120–30	470	Ethnographer

The next documents to refer to Kalauna belong to the 1940s and their intrinsic interest is less. Table 5 synthesizes the gross population counts of the village from all sources down to the present.

SOME INTERPRETATIONS

Several points emerge from this survey of Kalauna's legendary and sparsely documented past, the most important being: (1) that the village has been in existence as a consolidated community for at least 60 years and probably longer; (2) that the legend of its settlement by the Nibita clans is not contradicted by anything in the documentary record, so it can be safely assumed that Nibita people came together for their own reasons and without government prompting; (3) that since 1921 and perhaps as early as 1912 the population of the village has never been less than 300. Two principal problems still remain, however: whether or not Nibita clans dwelt together in the original settlement of Kwabua; and why they came together in Kalauna after being (temporarily?) separated during the middle phase.

There is convincing evidence, in the existence of four or five abandoned settlements sites, of the dispersal of the larger clans prior to their convergence on Kalauna. All these sites are within a mile of each other, and closer to one another than to the pre-historic sites belonging to neighbouring political units. Whatever the significance of the legend which recounts the 'invitation' to settle Kalauna by the retiring Belebele group, it is clear that the Nibita clans who did so 'willed' the event, and have since shown no signs of wishing to break up or migrate any further themselves. There was, however, a period of adaptation during which many people appear to have maintained houses in both Kalauna and the sites from whence they had immediately come. Some of my middle-aged informants were born in these hamlets on the mountain-side (in, say, the 1920s), though they insist, and all sources confirm, that the nucleated settlement of Kalauna existed at the same time. For as long as a whole generation, perhaps, many people appear to have practised a form of dual residence. Some of these mountain hamlets were in use until the Second World War as garden bases, and Malabuabua clan maintains one even today, though not on the exact site of its predecessor. Indeed, people associate the abandonment of these 'garden hamlets' with a shift in yam planting practices by which, as nowadays, the whole community makes its yam gardens in the same general area and there is considerable intermixture of clans in the formation of co-operative gardening groups. Previously, it is asserted, clans planted separately on their own land, and the only co-operative groups were those composed of members of the same clan.

Any basic re-organization of co-operative gardening groups, however, and any basic changes in subsistence patterns following the introduction of steel tools, would have post-dated the settlement of Kalauna and therefore cannot be adduced to explain its occurrence. Nor can the suppression of warfare, for Kalauna's settlement preceded effective government control of this part of the island by quite a number of years. In the terrible famine of 1900–2 the community was temporarily dispersed (see Chapter 8), and the legendary accounts of the period make it clear that fighting and cannibalism were rife (cf. also Jenness and Ballantyne 1920, p. 82). There remains the possibility that Kalauna was formed in response to the need for mutual defence or the desire for collective aggrandizement. Too little is known about the nature of indigenous warfare at this period to be certain, but it seems to offer the most plausible explanatory factor for the consolidation of Nibita clans.[1] This proposition is ultimately unsatisfactory, however, in that modern informants deny its truth. For them, it is enough to say that their ancestors merely 'wanted' to 'join together' to make one big *melala*; and those legends which deal with the history of Nibita clans and the settlement of Kalauna do seem curiously unconnected with those others which commemorate inter-community warfare.

If we are unable to determine exactly why Kalauna people consolidated their community, what reasons can be adduced for their staying together? The centrifugal forces appear to be derivative, generated by the frictions and short-circuits of high-pressure community life. But it is despite these – the apparent overcrowding, the constant quarrelling, and the prevalent sorcery fears – that Kalauna people prefer to dwell together as a community. There are, of course, structural reasons why they should do so. The clans are intricately bound together by innumerable ties of kinship, affinity and other institutionalized bonds. Even without the need for defence against outsiders or for co-operation on a village scale, the sense of community is potent. People speak of the clans as 'branches of the Kalauna tree' – evidence in a single phrase of a bond of common origin felt by Kalauna people for each other.

The social value of *melala*, community or sociality, is one that people stress untiringly, and they do so even while worrying about sorcery, thereby expressing disguised fear and hatred of their neighbours. A man thoroughly shaken by a sequence of deaths proclaimed his intention of going to live in his gardens, away from the sorcerers, but he added wistfully: 'it would be better if the government would just separate the bad men from the good'. Needless to say, he did not leave the village, for those few who do live in isolation are regarded with contempt, pity or fear. The gardens and the bush are places where people live in times of famine, when the sense of community is subordinate to the sheer struggle for individual survival. In a later chapter I shall examine the values relating to food in this culture,

---

[1] My own data on traditional warfare are broadly consistent with Jenness and Ballantyne's account (*ibid.* pp. 82–9) though there is probably a tendency for present-day informants to offer somewhat exaggerated pictures of the scale and intensity of indigenous fighting. Certainly, raids rather than pre-arranged battles, ambushes rather than open attacks, were the norm. Even so, there can be no doubt that safety lay in numbers and that a large community was better equipped for survival than a small one. In all Kalauna's history there is no mention of an external attack on the village itself, nor on any of its hamlets. Belebele, on the other hand, with less than half the adult male strength of Kalauna, was raided by the latter as recently as the 1950s.

and one of the points to emerge will be the extent to which Kalauna people associate the good life of abundant food with the bitter-sweet life of intensive sociality. It is in their socializing experiences, after all, that values are formed and reinforced, and if among them there is a strong sense of the 'goodness' of close community, then it adds little to explanation to invoke, for example, notions of *atuaha* magic for remaining on patrimonial hamlet ground. Such magic is to be seen as an expression of the sentiment 'home is best', rather than the cause of its inculcation. Men who really want to leave their homes do so, without undue fear of the punitive sanction in the sitting circle.

Yet ambivalence remains, and with it much of the problem. Sociality is good, but it is also dangerous because it produces frictions which may in turn unleash forces (the anger which raises a spear-arm or the envy which provokes sorcery) which are the very negation of sociality. This ambiguity in social life is at the root of Kalauna people's ambivalence, and is implicit in the response of an informant to my question: 'Why do you like living so close together?' He answered, not entirely frivolously: 'Because when there is a fight we can be there quickly and join in'! All arguments on this problem are perhaps bound to be circular, but I hope to have indicated, like my informant, the need for a system of social control.

3

KINSHIP AND MARRIAGE

The Arapesh father does not say to his son: 'I am your father, I begot you, therefore you must obey me' . . . Instead he says 'I grew you . . . I laboured for the food that made your body . . .'

Mead 1935, p. 77

This chapter presents, in the briefest compass, descriptive data on the form and content of those relationships – principally consanguineal and affinal – which constitute the basis of Kalauna society. In addition to giving a short account of this primary level of community integration, my intention is also to indicate the major sources of tension in such relationships as background to the subject of my main study.

KINSHIP STATUSES[1]

In the previous chapter the residential basis of patrilineal kinship was briefly examined, and it was seen how each hamlet contains one or more named sitting circles which are the focus of identification for shallow patrilineages called *unuma*. An *unuma* is composed of the patrilineal descendants of a male ancestor and is typically four to five generations in depth. Occasionally members are recruited through adoption. There are 38 *unuma* in Kalauna with a range of from 1 to 33 members and an average size of 12·3 persons (i.e. 3·1 men, 3·4 women and 5·8 children under 16 years). Besides forming the core of the most significant residential unit, the *unuma* has corporate status within the community as a form of minimal political group. It possesses a leader, generally the senior male member, and contributes to food exchanges on a corporate basis. Unless it is of recent formation, it possesses exclusive rights to special customs and usages which distinguish it from other *unuma*, while it places its members in certain permanent relationships *vis-à-vis* other like groups. Most notable among these, with respect to *unuma* belonging to different hamlets and clans, are exchange partnerships and traditional enmities (see Chapter 4). In everyday life, *unuma* 'brothers' (male members of the same generation)

[1] Kinship terminology is of the generational ('Hawaiian') type. Although I do not discuss it here, Jenness and Ballantyne do so briefly in their monograph (1920, pp. 64–6).

interact and co-operate with each other more than with any other category of kinsmen.

Patrilineal descent confers the most important attributes of social identity. A person is generally defined as being the child of a particular father, as being identified, therefore, with a particular stone sitting circle within a particular hamlet which is itself associated with a particular clan. A child takes his father's totemic food taboos, which may number from two to half a dozen, and though he is likely to respect his mother's totems also, he does not transmit these to his own children. Through his father he also acquires the right to use and be identified by his *unuma*'s and his clan's *dewa*, or distinctive customs, including membership of one of the ceremonial moieties. An eldest son succeeds to his father's exchange partnerships and to his other political statuses within the broader community. Furthermore, he inherits his father's debts and credits.

Although there is a hierarchy of nominal corporate land rights from the sibling group through the *unuma* to the clan, it is the sibling group which is the most important operational land-holding unit. An only son inherits personal rights to all his father's land and trees. An eldest son will normally divide such patrimonial land and trees among his siblings, including sisters. This may be done before their father dies, for as a man's gardening activities slacken with advancing age, his eldest son generally takes over the executive decisions of the family, subject of course, to the father's advice. Sometimes the subdivision of patrimonial land is not made at all by the inheriting generation, though this is seen to cause difficulties in time. Where joint rights are thus exercised one tends to find the strong leadership of an eldest brother.

Although women gain land rights by inheritance, children can only use their mothers' land or exploit their trees if certain conditions, to be mentioned below, are met. While a man may use his wife's land during her lifetime, this right automatically lapses if she dies. A man's right to patrilineally inherited land (*babivagata*) never lapses, as its name (*babi* – land, *vagata* – forever) implies. In some circumstances, however, there is customary provision for the transfer of land outside the *unuma* and even outside the clan. The dozen or so men who bury a dead man are generally recruited from among his close agnates, though more distant clansmen, maternal kin and even unrelated friends may request to join the burial group. The reward for the services of those who are not close agnates is frequently a piece of land, and the trees it carries, given in perpetuity. The proposition holds that the more uncertain the continuity of an *unuma*, the more likely it is that when a member dies distant relatives will bury him, and the greater the probability that they will be paid for their services in land and trees. An equitable distribution of land is maintained thereby. Should the declining *unuma* begin to burgeon again, its members may reobtain their own or other land in the same fashion.

Inheritance of traditional valuables (*lokoloko*) is also patrilineal. Some of these items (arm-shells, necklaces, boar's tusk pendants, etc.) along with other movable property which a man acquires during his life-time (pots, tools, weapons, etc.) are appropriated at his death by various kinsmen and friends for his 'remembrance'. To circumvent the utter depletion of his wealth in this way, a man commonly transmits his shell valuables to his eldest son's keeping long before death; the latter in theory holds them in trust for his younger siblings to use for marriage payments, curers' fees and other contingencies.

A man generally teaches his sons garden magic, sorcery and other spells when he considers they are old enough to benefit from them, but again, it is the eldest son who almost invariably receives the bulk of his father's ritual property. While it is felt that an eldest son should not divulge all his father's spells to his brothers (for their value resides largely in their secrecy, and the fewer people who know them the less likely they are to be alienated), it is also felt that a 'good' brother should not deny his younger siblings the benefit of them. The situation appears to be far more flexible than that described by Fortune for Dobu (1932, pp. 16–17), and enmity between blood brothers does not seem to occur over the inheritance of magic. Jealousy, and the possibility of sorcery, is present only when a father teaches some of his magic to his sister's sons; that is, when he jeopardizes the rights of his true heirs. This happens infrequently, however, and even when it does, sisters' sons have to pay cash or valuables for the magic they receive in this way.

A man calls those kin who constitute his mother's *unuma* by the term *susu*. They call him *tubuya*. Intermarriage between *tubuya* ('sister's child') and *susu* ('mother's brother's child') is strongly discouraged and would be exceedingly shameful should it occur. Although they are not *susu*, a man considers other women from his mother's clan to be unlikely mates, though such marriages do occur from time to time. In some parts of Goodenough it is the practice for *susu* to bury their *tubuya*, but this is the exception rather than the rule in Kalauna,[1] where, however, the *susu* cry for a sister's son and can expect to be given a pig as compensation for their loss. This gift is also the final prestation in the series which began with the dead man's father's marriage. 'They gave our group a woman', it is

---

[1] It is noteworthy that in those communities where maternal kin do perform burial services, the transfer of land as payment does not occur. They receive instead gifts of uncooked food from the patrikin. (Cf. Chowning 1962, pp. 97–8; Fortune 1932, pp. 193–6; Seligman 1910, pp. 610–29, for similar practices elsewhere in the Southern Massim.)

said of the recipients of the death-payment, 'and now her son is dead, so it is finished.'

Tubuya are expected to help their *susu* when the latter initiate food exchanges, and in certain circumstances, to be discussed in later chapters, they may even adopt the duties and privileges of agnates. *Tubuya* have no rights to their mother's land, however, unless a transaction called *foya* has taken place. Essentially, *foya* is the gift of a pig and vegetable food made on behalf of the children of a fruitful marriage by their father to their mother's patrilineal kin. It is quite distinct from brideprice payments, in which a pig, food, cash and other valuables also pass from the husband's to the wife's *unuma*. *Foya* is paid several years later, and it secures for the man's children the right to use a specified parcel of their *susu*'s land for the duration of their lives.

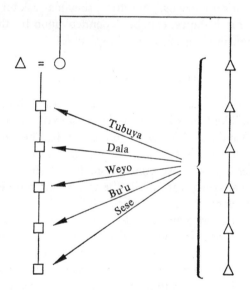

The network of kinship is cast widely by a system of classifying the descendants of women who marry out from one's *unuma*. In the first generation, as we have seen, the woman's own offspring are called *tubuya* (ZS, FZS, FFZS etc.) by members of her *unuma*. Children of *tubuya* are called *dala* by the same *unuma*, and should male *dala* wish to retain the use of the land secured by *foya* for their father, they can renew it by a further gift of a pig to their father's mother's *unuma*. The children of *dala* are called *weyo*, and male *weyo*, too, may renew the contract for land usufruct by paying *foya* to the same group: their father's father's mother's *unuma*. The transaction is unlikely to be sustained beyond this point, although two more generations are classified, *bu'u* and *sese*. It is uncommon to find persons who are quite certain who falls into these last categories, since in a fairly small intermarrying population other and more important kinship relationships are established which obscure this system of classification. For those who can identify their *bu'u* and *sese*, there is no bar to marriage with them, whereas it is considered 'bad' to marry one's *dala* or *weyo*.

Since what is being stressed is, in effect, the extension of the patrilineal group through out-marrying women, there are no true reciprocals to these terms, save for the *susu* reciprocal of *tubuya*. All of them can be acknowledged uniformly by the term *eda* (road or way), indicating that assistance or safe treatment may be expected from those relatives who call one *dala*, *weyo*, *bu'u* or *sese*. Such relatives are particularly useful in other villages. As one informant put it: 'We go to our *eda* for betel nut and food, for we know they will not sorcerize us.' In return, they may ask for small services. *Dala* and *weyo*, for instance, can be depended upon by their *eda* to give material assistance in competitive food exchanges.

IDIOM AND IDEOLOGY

Indigenous theories of conception stress the roles of both sexes in producing children. The foetus is formed from a mixture of male and female secretions (*molo*) and blood (*daiyaya*) in the womb. The mother is credited also with giving it 'breath' (*yawai*).[1] Intercourse over a period of months is believed necessary to cause conception, but it should cease once the woman is obviously pregnant. While the role of the mother in producing a child is self-evident, the father must reinforce his own role by feeding his wife during her pregnancy. This is explicitly seen as nurturing the foetus, and it is a principal element in the ideology of agnatic descent. A man who does not sustain his child, either before or after its birth, is merely its genitor, *to'etoheya* (a term used also of a man who spears a wild pig then leaves it in the bush to decay). It follows that a man who divorces his wife while she is pregnant has no claim to the child she bears if she is fed by someone else during her pregnancy. On the other hand, if he had fed her and then divorces her after she has given birth, it is she who lacks rightful claim to her child. The difference is one of 'feeding' or 'giving food' (*au'a vele*) to the child through the mother. Even after birth, although a mother feeds her child with her own milk, it is her husband who is said to feed her and thus sustain the milk-flow. Widows are sometimes obliged

---

[1] Although 'breath' is associated with 'spirit' (*maiyau*) a child does not owe its *maiyau* to its mother. Some form of mystical agent (collectively, *giduwa*) is thought responsible for providing this, though the influence of both parents can be detected from the ways in which the child resembles them. Notions of reincarnation are quite absent.

to feed their children without a man's help but it is axiomatic to a Good-enough Islander that such children cannot 'grow properly' and may even die. Custody of children, in short, is phrased almost entirely in terms of the rights and duties derived from the fact of having fed them and caused them to thrive.[1]

Within the nuclear family and ideally within the *unuma* food is given freely. Generosity is highly valued and negative sanctions against stinginess include sorcery – even between kinsmen. A general reciprocity holds between those who feed and those who are fed. An old man, for instance, will tell a youngster that he fed him when he was small in order to demand some small service of him, such as cutting firewood or climbing a coconut tree for nuts. The fact that it might not be true that the man fed the boy simply demonstrates what a coercive moral argument it is held to be. There is a range of customary expressions which underline heavily the duties that are owed to those responsible for one's nurture, and these can be used as effective shaming devices, as when a father is angered by his child's disobedience. Grown children, in return for the nurture they themselves received, have the unquestioned duty to provide for their aged parents.

Within the overall pattern of what Sahlins (1965) calls 'generalized reciprocity' there are, however, some special emphases with regard to the idiom of 'feeding'. Thus, unusually sympathetic relationships may be established between particular siblings in which the elder 'feeds' and 'looks after' the younger. I have seen a brother provoked to fury by his brother's action in striking their sister, who was bonded to the first brother by a 'feeding' relationship. When a brother feeds a sister, he creates for himself the right to distribute (or appropriate) her brideprice when she marries. In the case of a sister who feeds a brother, she can expect to receive regular gifts of food from him after she has married and moved to another hamlet. Since her children will also eat this food, their mother's brother by this means gains a future claim on their services. This is sometimes mentioned as a further rationale for the death payment made to his *susu* by a dead man's *unuma*.

FOSTERAGE AND ADOPTION

Fosterage is an important institution in Kalauna, and is wholly conceived in terms of feeding. (This statement is really tautologous since the identifi-cation is buried in our own language: Old English 'foster' means 'food'.)

---

[1] See Mead (1935, p. 77); also Bell (1948–9, p. 53) re the Tanga: 'The natives believe that the food becomes an integral part of the mother's milk and that the child, by drinking the milk, participates in the gift.'

Of the 119 adult men in Kalauna, 42% acknowledged men other than their fathers as having fostered them. This figure breaks down as follows: 18% were fostered by other agnates (brothers, father's brothers, etc.); 14% by maternal kinsmen (mother's brothers, mother's brothers' sons, etc.); and 10% by other categories of male relative (mother's husband, father's mother's brother's son, etc.).

True adoption, in which a child is assimilated to the descent group of his adopter and relinquishes full rights in his natal group, is unknown in Kalauna, and I am not sure that it is possible, save in the unlikely event of a child being ritually cursed by its parents. There is, however, a conspicuous gradation in the degree of adoption: from partial assimilation through permanent residence with one's adopter, to a form of fostering which involves no changes of status with respect to one's natal group.

According to the practice of simple fostering, a child will continue to reside with and be reared by his or her own parents, but another man (more rarely a woman) will single out the child to feed as his *kwamana* (lit. 'child', in the sense of young person). A warm, nurturant bond is established between the adopter (*faiyeya*) and his *kwamana*, and it may eventually come to be stressed at the expense of the true parent–child relationship. In cases where the adopter has no children of his own, he may declare his *kwamana* heir to his personal property, and in the absence of agnates with stronger claims, may even transfer land to him by testament. To some extent the relationship endures into the following generation. Thus, the son of a man who 'fed' a girl who marries after her adopter has died may receive her brideprice in his father's stead, though her own brothers would also expect a share. In sum, in this form of fostering the true parents continue to hold rights over the child, but they are modified by the rights held by another which were created by regularly feeding it.

Closer to the extreme of genuine adoption, is the case in which the adopter acquires almost full rights over his *kwamana*, who continues to reside in his adopter's hamlet even after the latter is dead. Although it is usual for the children of a dead man to remain in their natal hamlet and be reared by their father's brothers, it sometimes happens, as we saw in the previous chapter, that they accompany their widowed mother on her return to her own group, and are reared by her brothers. When such a child reaches maturity he must decide whether to bring his bride to live with him in avunculocal residence, or to take her to his natal hamlet and claim his rightful land inheritance there. Which course he follows will depend upon a multitude of factors, a not inconsiderable one of which is his obligation towards the man who brought him to manhood, his maternal kinsman. But the latter would need to have some inducements to offer to counter the likely pull of his *kwamana*'s agnates, which most men in this situation appear not to resist, since the most common course of action for those men reared in hamlets other than their own is for them to return at, or shortly after, marriage. In this case the adopter, or his son, will demand a pig and a considerable amount of food from the *kwamana*'s brothers, as compensation for having fed him and brought him to maturity.

Even if the *kwamana* stays, however, and though he may have spent the greater part of his life in his mother's hamlet and begun to raise his own children there, he would not be exempt from the obligations, nor excluded from the rights, associated with his continued formal identification with his father's *unuma* and clan. Thus, he would still be expected to assist his agnates in accumulating food for an exchange, as he would likewise expect to share in the distribution of the return. But by the fact of his residence with his mother's agnates, and having been fed by them, he would also be closely involved in their food exchanges. The process of assimilation to mother's *unuma*, or to that of any adopting group with which a man chooses to live, can be regarded as one of gradual disengagement from the activities of his agnates – made considerably easier by physical distance – and by a reciprocally increasing involvement in his adoptive group's activities. If they remain with him, his children will complete the process, so that they would be able to assert that they were members of their father's adoptive descent group.

STRESSES AND STRAINS IN THE SYSTEM

Kalauna people quarrel frequently, and while it was scarcely possible to determine with absolute precision those categories of persons who quarrel the most, a crude reckoning would put agnatic kinsmen high on the list. Certainly, of a man's three main groups of relatives – paternal kin, maternal kin and affines – he is most likely to encounter strife with the first. A rough index of this is the fact that the incidence of sorcery accusations within the clan approaches 40% of all recorded cases (see Chapter 6).

The tenor of a man's relationship with his *susu* may broadly be characterized as warm, friendly, unpossessive, and uncompetitive. His relationships with affines are unequal ones and although they may develop warmth and friendliness too, they are never entirely free from elements of shame and embarrassment. Patrilineal kinsmen, on the other hand, are equals, yet burdened with the most demanding obligations towards each other, the neglect of which can create much bitterness. They are also the most competitive relationships, and seem to be those most subject to sudden changes of temper. Patrikin are capable of the most affectionate and sentimental bonds, and the most violent mutual hatred. Close residential contact is clearly an important factor here, but there are others.

We have seen that the most binding obligations in the society are created by 'feeding'; it is also true that the customary modes of production and distribution are primary foci for competition and conflict. The extent to which they are, or become, political matters will emerge in later chapters; here I merely indicate them as a source of tension within the patrilineal descent group, whether this is defined at the level of *unuma*, hamlet or clan. Less common than quarrels over food in this sphere are disputes over inheritance, over land demarcation, over cash, and over women, but with the exception of the last, quarrels concerning these are more frequent between close agnates than any other category of persons (see Chapter 6).

Iyahalina's first and second sons, Bunaleya and Adiyaleyale, had made adjacent banana gardens in which they had also planted manioc. There was no clear division between the plots, and one day Bunaleya's wife complained to her husband that she had seen his brother's wife take manioc from Bunaleya's garden. Bunaleya mentioned this to Adiyaleyale's wife, but she strongly denied having done so. Adiyaleyale overheard their conversation and declared that he would make a 'marker' to separate the plots so that there could be no more dispute. He did so, but some weeks later saw that Bunaleya's wife had planted manioc right on the boundary he had indicated. He pulled up the plants and threw them inside Bunaleya's plot. Bunaleya's wife saw them there and told her husband, who went to his brother's house in a rage and threatened to fight him. A fight did ensue in which Adiyaleyale drew blood and was the tacit victor. After avoiding each other for several weeks, Bunaleya made friendly overtures by offering Adiyaleyale a bunch of ripe bananas from his plot. Adiyaleyale refused them on the grounds that he had no children whereas Bunaleya had two. Almost a year later the two brothers had still not eaten together (which would signalize the resumption of normal relations), although they were now on speaking terms with one another. Kalauna people say: 'We do not fight over manioc.' They should perhaps add: 'Except when the dispute is between brothers.'

Kaulubu, leader of Mulina hamlet and clan, had named his first son after his dead father's brother's son. Talukava, the dead man's brother and thus also Kaulubu's father's brother's son, had reared a pig to 'honour' the name, and the pig was to be killed and shared amongst Mulina clan members. When he had butchered it, however, Talukava distributed it also among his *susu* and his *dala*. Among the latter was Uyavaiyava, a Lulauvile man whom Talukava had 'fed' as a child and regarded as his principal heir, for he lacked children of his own. At the distribution of his pig Talukava had grudgingly given a small portion to Enowei, a Mulina agnate belonging to a different *unuma*, with the comment that he (Enowei) had 'never killed a pig for Mulina'. Enowei was ashamed and insulted, and although he took the pork home he threw it away behind his house. Before it was light next morning, Uyavaiyava stole up to Talukava's house and deposited his portion of pig inside the door. When Talukava awoke and found it there he began to wail in distress. (So dirge-like was his crying that my first thought on waking was that someone had died.) After a while Daudia (Kaulubu's brother and Talukava's father's brother's son) stepped onto the *atuaha* outside his own and Talukava's house and began a long harangue. Although he addressed Talukava, who could be seen crouching inside his doorway, his voice and gestures reached the whole hamlet.

> It's your fault your *kwamana* [i.e. Uyavaiyava] sent that pig back. You told many other people to come for your pig, but that pig was just for Mulina people. You should have called only us. You talked badly to Enowei, our brother, and said he never killed a pig himself. You made him ashamed. You called him 'elder brother' but you didn't treat him like one. You treated him like a bastard or a rubbish man. He plants gardens. He works. He's not a good-for-nothing. You can't talk to your brother like that. It's your fault if everyone is angry with you . . .

Daudia went on in this vein for twenty minutes. Talukava remained motionless but his wife had begun packing things into her basket. As soon as Daudia finished speaking he went into his house and the hamlet was silent. Talukava's wife, her head laden, left the house and descended the path, followed a few moments later by Talukava, carrying his spear, sleeping mat and hurricane lamp. Immediately they were out of sight, both Kaulubu's wife and Daudia's scampered across to the abandoned house and took the firewood which was lying beneath it. Daudia's wife even climbed into the house through the window and threw out more firewood from inside! Talukava and his wife went to live in their garden hut, and they were to be gone from the village for three months.

Although no curse had been uttered on this occasion, a previous quarrel between Talukava and Daudia over their gardens had resulted in their being unable to speak to each other for several years, owing to the ritual pronouncement by one of them of their clan's *talahaiyi* curse (see below).

Full siblings are prone to the most destructive quarrels since they share, or should share, the same inheritance, and for them the ideals of amicable and harmonious co-operation are most unequivocal. A breach between brothers is the most blatant, and perhaps because there are few possible mediating roles (a parent or third sibling), it is often the most violent and prolonged. Some sibling sets appear to be more congenitally disposed to quarrel than others, a point which is recognized by Kalauna people when they attribute such tendencies to *dewa* – in this context, personal idiosyncrasies which are conceived as having some inherited basis. Thus, with reference to the second case given above it is known to be Kaulubu's and his two brothers' *dewa* to bicker chronically over property: a characterization which is reinforced by their own expectations, for they believe themselves to have been 'spoilt' by their *unuma*'s powerful war-magic. Although the three brothers have fought seriously with each other several times over land boundaries and tree ownership, observers maintain that the original distribution of the patrimonial land by Kaulubu was equitable, and that there is no question of land shortage in their *unuma*.

Of the twenty married men who were not, in 1967, conforming to the patrilocal norm, eleven were residing elsewhere because of quarrels with their *unuma* agnates. Several of these are likely to return, however, for just as children who are discontented with the treatment they receive at home may take temporary refuge with their mother's brothers, so do adults follow a similar if more protracted pattern. Some, too, are living separate from their kinsmen because a form of curse, *talahaiyi*, had been uttered during their quarrels.

Each clan has two *talahaiyi* totems, a 'big' and a 'small' one. If the name of the former is spoken in the appropriate ritual formula by one of the parties to the quarrel, they may henceforth communicate with each other only at the risk of sickness sent by their *talahaiyi*. The 'small' imprecation is a lesser curse of the same kind, which can be revoked by a small ceremony involving a shared pot of food, permitting the restoration of the relationship. Although *talahaiyi* may be invoked by husbands in divorcing their wives,[1] or by fathers to prevent their daughters from breaking their marriages by returning home, the most frequent use of *talahaiyi* is between full brothers. Even though I recorded only one instance of 'big' *talahaiyi* being used by brothers as against several 'small' ones, the drastic nature of a sanction which uncompromisingly severs the relationship for a period is some indication of the bitterness which may infect the sibling bond.

EATING COMPANIONSHIPS

It is instructive to contrast with these tense, ascriptive relationships one which Kalauna people invest with great value, seemingly because it is unencumbered by obligations and thereby represents an ideal of easy informality. Again, however, its referent is food. In this society of acutely sensitive attitudes towards food, eating is not a seemly public activity. There are some occasions when a group of unrelated men will sit down to eat together, but it is not done without some embarrassment. In most contexts the family is the only commensal unit, and even visiting friends are generally fed separately. The exceptions to these are a man's *aveyau*, of which each mature man acquires several in different hamlets of the village. They are either unrelated or distantly related, and the custom serves to

---

[1] Jenness and Ballantyne (1920, p. 68) document an instance of this, but mistakenly interpret the husband's utterance of his '*talagi*' to mean that he had bestowed the totem on his wife.

extend the intimacy of commensality characteristic of close kin to other areas of the community.

The importance of *aveyau*, or eating companionship, lies not in its structural significance, for this is minimal, but in the manner it is stressed by Kalauna men as representing their ideal of a fully satisfying and tension-free relationship. *Aveyau* symbolizes informal sociality, unmotivated friendliness, and the kind of mutual giving which can only be enjoyed when there are no advantages to be gained or obligations to be met. *Aveyau*, in short, are equals in status who have few, if any, additional mutual ties to complicate their relationship. It is significant that in this highly structured and covertly competitive society, men should seek to form personal relationships which involve little more than the freedom to climb into another's house and share the food on his plate.

THE SOCIAL RANGE OF MARRIAGE

Although it is the women who must leave their natal hamlets when they marry, they do not thereby relinquish membership in their own agnatic descent groups. In the matter of food exchanges, for instance, although they are expected to provide produce from their gardens to assist their spouses, they may also be called upon to help their brothers in the same way, even if it means supporting both sides in a single competitive exchange. Women, therefore, have an important role to play in the establishment and maintenance of links between nominally opposed political units within the community. Most marriages indeed take place within the community (see Table 6). Men are generally disdainful of the women of other villages, suspecting them to be slothful, improvident and reluctant bearers of children.[1] Women are wary of marrying too far from the protection of their brothers, who in turn actively discourage them from alienating their productive capacities – economic and sexual – to other communities. In 1967 there were fourteen Kalauna women married to men of other villages and thirteen non-Kalauna women married to Kalauna men.

The preference for marriage within the village is nevertheless severely constrained by a number of rules restricting choice of partner. The most all-embracing rule forbids marriage of persons who can trace genealogical relationships to each other (e.g. the offspring of cross-cousins). This subsumes the two axioms that one cannot marry into one's own (father's)

---

[1] Although the numbers are too small to be statistically significant, in-marrying women do have fewer children than Kalauna wives. This fact is attributed by some men to the contraceptive devices (mainly magical) which they believe in-marrying women to have been given by their fathers. The latter are assumed to want to prevent Kalauna's population from expanding at the expense of their own villages.

unuma nor into that of one's mother. But the personal kindred, so defined, is usually extended to take into account the other *unuma* (if any) in one's own and one's mother's hamlets, so that a courting youth shuns all the girls of these two hamlets as 'sisters', claiming that he cannot marry them even though genealogical links cannot be traced. Unions do occasionally occur which breach this general rule, but they are still subjects of some shame to those involved. There is no rationale for the interdict; it is simply thought 'bad' to marry someone who falls thus easily into the category of 'sister'.

TABLE 6   *The spatial and social range of extant marriages of Kalauna men (August 1967)*

Provenance of spouse	Total	Sub-total
A. Contracted within Kalauna		
Within the hamlet	—	
Within the clan	6	
Within Kalauna	74	80 (86%)
B. Contracted outside Kalauna		
Belebele (½ hour distant)	4	
Wailolo (¼ hour distant)	1	
Eweli (½ hour distant)	1	
Mataita (3 hours distant)	2	
Kuyakwaiakwaiana (3 hours distant)	2	
Bo'owa (5 hours distant)	3	13 (14%)
Total	93	

There is no term for 'incest', nor is clan exogamy a categorical rule, for much depends upon the size of the clan. Lulauvile, for instance, is composed of two sections which in many circumstances have the status of discrete clans.[1] Intermarriage has occurred over at least four generations between these two sections. Iwaoyana is another large clan which has grown to the extent of occupying four hamlets, and genealogies show several cases of marriage between clan members, though there was but one existing in 1967. Nevertheless, the norm is clearly that one should seek a mate outside one's own clan and, if one is obedient to expressed norms, one should also avoid marrying those females one classifies as *dala* (e.g. FFZSD), and *weyo* (e.g. FFFZSSD), whether or not one can place them with genealogical certainty. Bearing in mind all these restrictions the number of marriage choices available to a girl or youth are few indeed, even in a village the size of Kalauna. Sampling half a dozen

[1] I regard Lulauvile as a single clan only because Kalauna people represent it as such when they discuss it *vis-à-vis* other clans (see next chapter).

adolescents on the matter, only one considered that she had more than five potential spouses in the community, while most had three or four and one had only two. This factor influences courtship, as we shall see below.

It would be reasonable to expect that, given the same and perhaps more rigidly observed exogamic restrictions in the past, and before 1900 at least, given also a somewhat smaller community, out-marriage would have been considerably more frequent than it is today. Genealogies reveal that this is indeed true of the earliest generations (grandparental or great-grand-parental) remembered by mature living informants. Thus, by counting back three generations from the present cohort of young adults, of a total of 66 marriages 30 (45·4%) were with women from villages beyond Kalauna.[1] (The current out-marriage rates for men of Belebele (pop. 170) and Wailolo (pop. 99), the two villages closest to Kalauna, are 36·1% and 63·3% respectively. With a rate of out-marriage of some 45% three generations ago, Kalauna's population might therefore have been little more than 150. Genealogies show that the rate of out-marriage in the following generation (say 1900–25), which was the first to live in peaceful conditions, had already dropped to the present level of 14%, suggesting that a marked growth in Kalauna's population had occurred about the time of European contact.)

Under what conditions intervillage marriage took place in the pre-contact era can only be surmised. Jenness and Ballantyne say nothing more about it than that it occurred (1920, pp. 37, 66). Courtship in villages other than their own is even today a hazardous undertaking for Goodenough youths.[2] It must have been so much more so in the past that it was probably kept to a bare minimum. Apparently, some females captured in war were married instead of being eaten (*ibid.* p. 66), and there is at least one old man in Kalauna whose mother fled her own distant village to be captured and claimed in marriage by a Kalauna man.

Neighbouring villages were not permanently hostile to each other, however, and as we shall see in the following chapter, traditional enemies (*nibai*) were formed on an *unuma* basis, so that not all the segments of a community were at enmity with all the segments of another. Indeed, friendship was institutionalized between some of them through a relationship which is complementary to *nibai*. Whereas *nibai* were created by killing, *solama* were created by protecting. According to informants the

[1] Another expression of the high frequency of out-marriage in this generation is the fact that 14 (37%) of a total of 38 apical ancestresses of extant *unuma* were from villages other than Kalauna.

[2] A few years ago two Kalauna men were beaten up in Belebele while wooing girls in that village. For their part, Kalauna youths guard the girls of their own village jealously, and the only occasions I observed youths from elsewhere in Kalauna were intervillage food exchanges, festivals, and my own farewell parties.

formula was almost invariant: an ancestor in danger of being killed and eaten by members of another community was saved by one of their number, who hid him, helped him to escape, or pleaded for his life. Thenceforth, the protector and the person he saved were *solama*, their patrilineal descendants inheriting the relationship. Each *unuma* has several, usually one in each neighbouring village, though many also have *solama* in other parts of the island. Thus, the picture of intervillage political relations in the pre-contact era was considerably complicated by the segmented structure of each polity. The current distribution of *nibai* and *solama* linkages show that patterns of hostile and friendly relations cross-cut the nominal political boundaries of each village. Under such circumstances, a flow of women between communities would have been permitted, though the evidence does not suggest that intervillage marriages were exclusively between those who were *solama*. The main function of *solama* at the present is to provide food and shelter when visiting one another's villages, but some trade flowed between them in the past, and it is highly probable that women were occasionally exchanged also. Of the fourteen Kalauna women and thirteen Kalauna men who are currently married to outsiders, no more than four took spouses who were *solama*; though the proportion of such marriages might be expected to have been somewhat higher in the past.

COURTSHIP

Youths do not marry until they have undergone an 'initiatory' period of work abroad. They begin courtship at about the age of sixteen, and by the time they leave the village a year or two later they will each have betrothed a future wife. Within the narrow range of permissible choices there may be keen competition for the same girl, or of girls for the same boy. Yet when the youths leave to seek work in Samarai or Port Moresby, the results of seemingly secret courtships will be evident in the tacit public recognition given to the betrothal of particular partners. The girl who tries to change her boy-friend while her acknowledged partner is absent meets with general disapproval.

Courtship itself, like the early months of marriage, is a timorous affair characterized by the mutual shyness of the couple. In contrast to the attitudes found in most Massim societies, premarital intercourse is held to be morally reprehensible.[1] It is also supposedly damaging to a youth's

[1] Puritanical attitudes regarding premarital chastity certainly pre-date mission contact (see Jenness and Ballantyne 1920, pp. 94, 100, 200). The sexual laxity of other Massim peoples is notorious (cf. Malinowski 1929; Seligman 1910, pp. 499 *et seq.*; Chowning 1969; Fortune 1932, pp. 241–9). However, while Dobuans enjoy 'complete pre-nuptial freedom' (Fortune *ibid.* p. 248), they appear to be even more prudish than Goodenough Islanders.

subsequent chances of marriage, for it is believed to spoil his complexion and render his love-magic useless. Without effective love-magic a man is believed to be condemned to permanent bachelorhood.

When a youth has returned from his first working tour abroad he will resume the courtship of his girl-friend, chewing betel nut with her one or two nights a week in her father's house. He makes new gardens, and waits for her to propose marriage to him. If she does not he may take another trip abroad, after making persuasive gifts to her father or brothers so they will further his suit during his absence, or at least discourage her from chewing betel with other youths. Mutual jealousy among the youths induces them to encourage each other to leave the village at the same time, and the worst is suspected of unattached ones who insist on remaining behind.

A girl may not even wait for her boy-friend to return, but may move into his parents' house to begin the marriage in his absence. Whether he is there or not, the period of trial marriage is much the same for the bride. She practices living with her affines rather than with her husband. She soon learns to eat without shame in front of the former, but although she cooks for her husband, they eat separately for a few months, being as ashamed of eating in each other's company as they are of sleeping together. The groom usually sleeps in another house during this period. To beget a child during the first year of marriage is considered shameful, since it betrays inordinate sexual desire, which is held to be incompatible with ideals of good gardening. As well as testing the temperaments of her affines, the bride is on trial herself. Her industriousness, gardening skill, cleanliness, child-minding aptitude and general demeanour are keenly gauged by her husband's family. In particular, she must refrain from laughing too often, which is the mark of the wanton and would bode ill for her future fidelity; and she must refrain from eating too much, which is the badge of the prodigal and would bode ill for her husband's future gardening efforts. However, while parents-in-law may be influential in the acceptance or rejection of a new bride by measuring her against certain standards of behaviour, they have little or no say at the present in the actual choice of a wife for their son. This point will receive further comment below.

BRIDEPRICE AND BRIDESERVICE[1]

Several exchanges take place between the *unuma* of the couple during the early months of marriage; the groom's kin give cooked food and game, the bride's reciprocate with uncooked vegetable food. The couple are forbidden

---

[1] A more detailed account of marriage exchanges is in preparation, and will appear in a projected volume of the series Cambridge Papers in Social Anthropology.

to eat of any of these. There is no single point at which the trial period of the marriage becomes a bona fide union. There are no ceremonies (other than the occasional food exchanges), and an outsider is not in a position to determine when cohabitation begins; though for the couple concerned it presumably would be marked by the first shared pot of food and the first shared sleeping mat. Depending upon age and temperament, the marriage may need anything from a week to half a year to get under way, three months probably being an average.

By the end of six months or so, it is assumed that both parties to the marriage have found each other acceptable and it is about then that the major portion of the brideprice is generally paid, although small instalments will have been given at the inception of the marriage and at intervals subsequently, as cash became available. Today the groom bears the burden of providing the brideprice, although he will usually do this indirectly by soliciting it from 'brothers' recently returned from working abroad. He will pay them back by performing the same service, if indeed he had not already done so before he himself married. Money, like food, is socially invested by giving it away almost as soon as it is obtained. It is the younger men of the community, therefore, who tend to sponsor each other's marriages.

Until quite recently, the sums involved were not large. Indigenously, several items of *lokoloko* – shell valuables, or pots – and perhaps a pig were all the brideprice necessary. In 1964 a local government council rule was adopted setting the brideprice at £A20 for first marriages, but by 1968 only one man in Kalauna had paid that amount in cash, and it appeared quite uncertain whether more would ever do so, as general opinion in the village was that £A20 is far too much. It is not uncommon for a bride's kin to refuse to accept a great amount. There are a number of reasons for this: they may fear that if she divorces they will be unable to recoup the money paid for her; they may suspect that more of her services are being alienated than they are prepared to allow; they may fear that the traditional, and still desirable ascendancy of 'wife-givers' over 'wife-receivers' would be jeopardized by an over-generous marriage payment; and finally, they may realistically prefer to retain a call on the groom's services, a right which they would suspect of being abrogated by a large brideprice.

Brideservice is indeed practised to a lesser extent than formerly, and in individual cases this appears to be correlated with the payment of a large brideprice. It is still incumbent upon a young man, however, to work several days a month for his affines during the trial period of his marriage. Just as his bride must demonstrate her homely virtues to his own family, so must he demonstrate to her kinsmen his energy, strength and willingness by untiring work – without food – in their gardens. He labours in turn for all those men to whom his wife gave his betel nut whilst they were courting. According to custom, for every nut they chewed together she will have saved half to give to one of her kinsmen. Once the marriage is under way brideservice obligations are fewer, though in a sense, today as well as previously, a man's brideservice is never complete, for he is under perpetual obligation to those who gave him a woman in marriage. A 'wife-taker', a daughter's or sister's husband, is *tomovaiva*, a word which carries a mild connotation of 'menial', for he can be called upon to do various tasks for his affines whenever they require help. Thus, the major formal objection to the high brideprice set by the council, and the main reason for it having been largely ignored to date, is that it is seen as subversive of the traditionally unequal relationship between 'wife-givers' and 'receivers'.

ADULTERY

Paradoxically, young married men are better placed to pursue sexual adventures than unmarried youths, who, besides being filled with the shame of adolescence, are conscious of the possibility of spoiling their marriage chances. Adultery is viewed seriously and sexual jealousy is a common cause of marital disharmony and divorce. Adultery is punishable at law, a fact of which most Goodenough Islanders approve, and is one of the few offences that cause Kalauna people to bring court charges against their fellows. Yet there is commonly an element of tragedy in adultery cases, for the parties to it are often at the mercy of cultural forces which their society does not entirely expect them to be able to resist. Thus, the most common pattern is for a man to seduce a woman with whom he chewed betel nut as a youth and whom he had bespelled with his love-magic. There is much native speculation on the subject, and a common theory is that the last man to put love-magic on a girl whom he then marries, takes the risk of his love-magic being washed out of her by the afterbirth of her first child. Earlier love-potions are thought to remain, and the husband is faced once again with the competition of her previous suitors for whom his wife's affection is once more revived. Most adultery cases which I investigated in Kalauna were between men and women who, in accordance with this pattern, had shared a period of courtship during their late adolescence.

In addition to the serious social disturbances it creates, adultery is also supernaturally damaging to those involved. Sexual intercourse is held to be generally inimical to the growing crops, so an adulterer risks spoiling his gardens. A female adulterer not only jeopardizes her own and her husband's crops, but also poses a danger to his physical health (see Chapter 10). As a general rule, men who return from wage-labour abroad neither cohabit nor eat with their wives for a month or two, or until they are otherwise certain of their wives' fidelity and their own safety. It is for fear of their adultery that men prefer to go abroad when their wives are pregnant; for a year at least they can be reasonably sure of their wives' sexual continence. It is for the same reason that women who are sexually unattractive are deemed the 'best' wives; those disfigured by ringworm (*tinea imbricata*) are valued for their potential fidelity. In short, men are chronically jealous of their wives, and while adultery is probably no more common than in the next society, it gives rise to a great deal of bitter quarrelling. Disputes between men concerning women are second only to disputes concerning food in frequency of occurrence.

Yet, as in most other Massim societies, the overall status of women is high. Sexuality is not considered to be contaminating nor dangerous in itself, only when it is exploited by men as in adultery. There are no menstrual taboos, and unlike in many areas of the Massim, men do not attribute malevolent supernatural powers to women. There are no witches on Goodenough Island. (Cf. Chowning 1959; Fortune 1932, pp. 150–3; Malinowski 1929, pp. 39–40; Roheim 1948; Seligman 1910, pp. 640 *et seq.*)

DIVORCE

In Kalauna, one marriage in every three ends in divorce. Frequencies based on the calculations recommended by Barnes (1949, 1967) are given in Table 7.

TABLE 7   *Divorce ratios: Kalauna*

$$\text{Ratio A} = \frac{\text{Marriages ended in divorce}}{\text{All marriages}} \times 100 = \frac{8500}{258} = 33 \cdot 0$$

$$\text{Ratio B} = \frac{\text{Marriages ended in divorce}}{\text{All completed marriages}} \times 100 = \frac{8500}{151} = 56 \cdot 3$$

$$\text{Ratio C} = \frac{\text{All marriages other than those ended by death}}{\text{Marriages ended in divorce}} \times 100 = \frac{8500}{192} = 44 \cdot 3$$

Since divorces occurring in the 'trial' phase of marriage (i.e. within the first three months) account for about a quarter of the total, if these are discounted, the frequencies are modified as follows:

Ratio A: 26·4%
Ratio B: 48·4%
Ratio C: 36·7%

The justification for excluding them is that full brideprice will rarely have been paid and full cohabitation will rarely have commenced when the divorce occurred. Kalauna people, however, make no conceptual distinction between the early and later phases of a marriage, and as soon as a bride takes up residence with her in-laws she is married (*nayi*). Similarly, as soon as she decides to return to her own hamlet she is divorced (*violili*). In extreme but not uncommon circumstances, this entire sequence may occur without the 'husband's' knowledge if he is away working. In giving their marital histories women would recall these abortive marriages whereas their 'spouses', not having experienced them, would not.

Even by the exclusion of unions which end in divorce within the first three months, the figures given justify the description of marriage in Kalauna as brittle and unstable. Other than in the 'trial' period, divorce is not characteristic of any particular phase of marriage; nor is childlessness a correlate, for although divorce tends to be rare where couples have more than two children, the existence of one or two need not prevent it.[1]

Several reasons may be given for a particular divorce and, not surprisingly, both spouses may offer strikingly different, if not discrepant, causes for the dissolution of their marriage. I recorded details of some 36 divorces in Kalauna, over half (19) of which were initiated by the female partner. Crudely classified, the principal reasons given by those spouses who took the initiative were as follows:

	No. of cases
A. Women divorced their husbands	
Desire to marry someone else (usually disguised by the accusation that her husband did not bespell her with his own love-magic)	8
Quarrels with co-wife in polygynous union	4
Quarrels with mother-in-law	4
Beating by husband	1
Neglect by husband	1
Overworked by husband	1
B. Men divorced their wives	
Adultery or suspected adultery of wife	8
Laziness in gardening	3
Bad housekeeping (including taking food from the wrong gardens)	2
Nagging and intransigence	2
Desire to marry someone else	2

Unless they are encumbered by many children, divorced persons carry no stigma, and their prompt re-marriage is usual. Henceforth they suffer from 'divorce shame' only in relation to their ex-spouses whom they scrupulously avoid, and to a much lesser extent their ex-spouses' close kin, whose food they avoid eating.

[1] The problem of the relationship between divorce rate and brideprice level will be dealt with elsewhere (see n. 1, p. 51, above).

CHOICE AND CHANGE

It will be apparent from what has been said so far that personal choice plays a considerable part in the selection of a marriage partner, and that conversely, the authority of the *unuma* or any larger descent group in disposing of women is minimal. This at least is the case today, although there is much evidence to suggest that marriage choices in the past were not the capricious affairs they now appear to be. Formerly, a type of betrothal (*wabuwabu*) was common, by which a man selected a wife for his son during their early adolescence and sent regular gifts of food to her.[1] Such marriages were believed likely to endure, being based on a food-created bond. But they are ill-favoured today, as men are sensitive to the charge that they won their wives by gifts of food rather than by love-magic. Women also object to early betrothal, and a fair proportion of divorces initiated by wives were partly rationalized by a desire to marry one whose love-magic was active inside them, leaving behind husbands who had 'only fed' them. Restitution to such a husband is generally paid by his successor, and involves not only the brideprice, if any, but also what the husband and his kin regard a just reimbursement for the food the ex-wife had eaten over the duration of the couple's betrothal and marriage.

Along with a number of other changes, the decline of the incidence of *wabuwabu* is clearly a correlate of the increased independence of the young.[2] Personal choice of marriage partner is certainly the norm today, and I recorded very few cases of girls having been obliged to marry against their wishes. Such girls usually managed to get their own way eventually by employing techniques of passive resistance and non-co-operation, and if these did not work, by fleeing the village for a period of months and staying with kinsfolk elsewhere. In other villages (but not in Kalauna), some cases were known of girls committing suicide rather than marry the partners chosen for them.

The effects of wage-labour on marriage are too many and too complex to deal with in detail here. In general, however, the greater economic independence of young men goes a long way towards explaining the pattern of change that the marriage system in Kalauna appears to have undergone over the last two or three generations. In addition to greater personal

---

[1] The idea is similar to that expressed by Mead for the Arapesh (1935, p. 80). 'As a father's claim to his child is not that he has begotten it but rather that he has fed it, so also a man's claim to his wife's attention and devotion is not that he paid brideprice for her ... but that he has actually contributed the food which has become the flesh and bone of her body.'

[2] The direct interference of government and mission can be discounted as there was nothing in traditional Goodenough marriage practices – with the exception of polygyny – objectionable to Europeans.

freedom of choice, the following trends can also be attributed to the direct or indirect influence of the important economic status of young men: earlier marriage and reduced period of courtship, experimental polygyny, larger brideprice and shorter brideservice, more stress on love-magic and less on betrothal, and possibly increased adultery and divorce rates. All are interrelated and all contrast with the picture of traditional marriage evoked by older informants.

It must not be assumed that there is acute intergenerational conflict, for in general there appears to be a remarkable lack of it. Despite what the elders say about the morals and the new 'customs' of the younger generation, the latter is still prudish about sex, respectful to its elders, and acquiescent in the principal values of the culture (cf. Oliver 1955, p. 203). Certain material constraints have vanished, however, for although there is no evidence to suggest that leaders in the past found a source of support in sponsoring marriages, it is likely that without access to considerable garden resources, pigs and the necessary shell valuables, young men could not easily marry. These things are now available to them more freely than hitherto; gardens are larger, pigs more numerous and shell valuables of secondary importance to cash. But the importance of brideprice must not be overestimated, for it was apparently never very large. The significant point, perhaps, is rather that the young men gain, through the cash and goods they bring into the community, an influence which permits them to decide for themselves whom and when they shall marry. This can be seen clearly in the highly unstable polygynous unions contracted by young men under the age of thirty. There were several such marriages in Kalauna during the period 1966–8, and they presented a striking contrast to the stable secondary unions of much older men. Traditionally, polygyny was a privilege only of the latter (see Chapter 5).

There remain the systemic social constraints. It has been already noted that the range of marriage choices is still narrow; village in-marriage is preferred but a youngster's choice of partner is severely limited by a number of exogamic restrictions. Some of these appear to have weakened but they have yet to be overthrown. The marriage system as a whole, although it involves 'wife-givers' and 'wife-takers', is not one of 'general exchange'; indeed it could hardly persist as such with a high divorce rate. Neither clans nor *unuma* exchange women systematically, and there is no evidence to suggest that they never did so. If the sizes of clans are standardized, the frequency of intermarriage with each other is found to be the same for all clans, and while sister exchange is a not uncommon occurrence, it forms part of no grander design of alliance groupings.

In a sense, the general rule that one cannot marry into one's mother's descent group safeguards the egalitarian ethic of clanship, for it obviates the danger of certain clans gaining ascendency over others by becoming instituted 'wife-givers'. A crude balance is achieved by the apparent randomness of intermarriage; at least, analysis of marriage frequencies between particular groups reveals no pattern, and if an obscure one does exist my informants were quite unconscious of it. With these considerations in mind, it is not so surprising that a minimum of authority is exercised by the *unuma* over the question of whom its daughters shall marry. Nor is it surprising that the freedom to choose their own partners should have been granted to the young if it did not thereby jeopardize the social system.

4

CLANSHIP AND CUSTOM

Yabu se'iyina se'iyina,
melala se'iyina se'iyina,
yadi dewa tulidi tulidi.

[Each and every clan,
each and every village:
their customs are different and diverse.] – Kalauna saying

In formal terms a Kalauna clan may be defined as a named, localized, ideally exogamous, corporate descent group, the members of which claim common agnatic kinship, and differentiate themselves from members of like units by appeal to diacritical customs and validating origin myths. It will be the task of the present chapter to examine briefly the system of clanship in Kalauna with a view to understanding the institutional bases on which these groups cohere to form a unified community.

Despite its importance there is no unambiguous term for 'clan' though there is some consensus among the older men that *yabu* is the proper term.[1] But just as *unuma* may be used to refer loosely to all the members of a hamlet as well as to the patrilineage, so may *yabu* be used to refer to a personal kindred as well as to the group I have designated a clan. '*Unuma*' and '*yabu*' are for the pedants of the tribe, but even they frequently lapse from the consistent usage I have here proposed for them. Indeed, not satisfied with the vagueness of their own terms for descent groups, Goodenough Islanders have seized upon a number of foreign ones ('family' and 'group' from English, and '*boda*' from Fergusson) all of which may, on occasion, be used interchangeably with the indigenous *unuma*, *yabu* and *yo'o* (see also Young 1968, pp. 334–5). This ambiguity in the terminology of structural units may reflect their untidiness on the ground, though it is also possible that it indicates structural ambiguity or taxonomic confusion arising from social change.

The preamble above is a reminder that particular structural units are

---

[1] Jenness and Ballantyne were given some clan names (1920, pp. 43, 211) but they appear to have failed to recognize clanship. They define *yabu* (*gabu* in Bwaidoga) as 'the people belonging to the same group of hamlets' (1928, p. 235).

impermanent and that the relationships between them, as well as those which create them, are fluid over time. The ethnographer notes a particular configuration, which his informants encourage him to believe is the ordained and determinate social order. For these pre-literates, myth rather than history explains the present in terms of the past. Similarly, 'customs' are as important as genealogies in providing Kalauna people with evidence of the continuity of their descent groups, for they are perceived in terms of the customs which differentiate them as readily as they are in terms of genealogical reckoning.[1] It is necessary to give at least equal recognition to the cultural dress of the structural units, not simply because the native model of the social system does so, but also because a good deal of behaviour in Kalauna can only be adequately interpreted by reference to it. To paraphrase an actual case, when a Kalauna man says that A fought with his brother B over land apportionment, we may suspect a structurally-determined source of tension. But when he adds that A and B belong to a descent group whose 'custom' is fighting, and that X and Y belong to another descent group whose 'custom' is different and would therefore not fight under the same circumstances, then we may suspect that there are predispositions and reinforcing expectations at work which have no *a priori* relation to social structure.

KALAUNA CLANS AND THEIR 'DEWA'

The operative word in any discussion of clanship in Kalauna is *dewa*, which is perhaps the most general and oft-used explanatory concept in Goodenough thought. In most contexts *dewa* can be translated as 'custom', if this is given its widest sense of regular, patterned behaviour.[2] Thus, it is possible to speak of the *dewa* of a group ('traditional usages') and the *dewa* of an individual ('habits' or 'idiosyncracies'). *Dewa*, as one informant put it, are what make people different from one another: Papuans from Europeans no less than one Kalauna man from his neighbour. *Dewa* also carries the connotation of 'proper', 'right' or 'correct', since it forms the stem of the commonest evaluative word *dewadewana*, 'good'. There is in addition a non-behavioural application of the term, for *dewa* are also things: what an earlier anthropology might call artifacts, cultifacts and mentifacts. A drum, a design, a spell and even a natural species, a dog, a pig or a bird, may all be referred to as *dewa* if they form part of a descent group's heritage.

---

[1] 'Variation in custom or in ideological emphasis is regarded by the natives as one of the most significant indices of group differentiation' (Fortes 1945, p. 21).

[2] Jenness and Ballantyne define it as 'manner of life, custom, habit' (1928, p. 230).

In its application to clanship the notion of *dewa* is all-important; indeed, while in the field I found it more helpful to adopt the native viewpoint in regarding clans as 'custom groups' than to abide by a structural concept of clan as a maximal unilineal descent group. But there are problems of description whichever view is taken. One of the difficulties of generalizing about clans in Kalauna stems from their being in different phases of expansion or contraction. Another arises from their presenting different images to the world. There is, in short, no 'typical' Kalauna clan, a description of which would serve as a model for the rest; all have some anomaly which defies reduction to a simple principle. It seems worthwhile, therefore, to say something about each clan in turn in the light of their differentiating *dewa*; to work, as far as possible, from the particular to the general. This method of presentation will provide the opportunity to discuss some of the main problems associated with clanship in Kalauna: ceremonial moieties, rank, structural opposition and mythical validation.

TABLE 8 *Clan membership in Kalauna: 1967*

	Men	Women	Children (16 and under) male	female	Total	*Unuma*
Ainaona	3	7	6	3	19	2
Lulauvile I	20	20	20	14	74	7
Lulauvile II	18	22	12	13	65	6
Malabuabua	19	12	18	15	64	6
Foloyai	7	8	5	4	24	2
Iwaoyana	29	30	37	34	130	8
Nouneya	13	18	12	8	51	3
Mulina	10	11	9	9	39	4
Total	119	128	119	100	466	38

The order in which the clans are introduced is the sequence in which they are represented as having emerged from the ground in the respective myths of origin. These myths (*nainiya*) have concise 'public' versions and comprehensive 'private' or secret versions. The former purport to state and explain the appearance of the clans' ancestors, their pairing in food exchange partnerships (*fofofo*), and the principal distinguishing customs and competences which the ancestors brought with them or soon afterwards acquired. The secret versions of the myths are comprised mainly of magical formulae, which are intended to be for the ears of clan members only. The general term for these spells is *sisikwana* and they are among the most highly valued items of property. It is the public versions of the myths which concern us here, however, since they help to define clanship according to the indigenous model, being mainly charters for descent group individuation. It should be noted also that in addition to clan myths which are subscribed to by all the component *unuma* of a clan, some *unuma* have accessory or supplementary mythical charters which are distinct from those of other *unuma* within the same clan. These too have exclusive, secret versions. Thus, group charters for *dewa* may sometimes be found at both the *unuma* and the clan level; the myths of the former are subsumed under the myths of the latter.

1. *Ainaona*

The first Nibita man to emerge from beneath the ground at Yauyaba was Adikunuwala, whose descendants were henceforth called Ainaona ('Foremost'). Since he appeared with only a dog, Adikunuwala's descendants are attributed with no other important *dewa*; since he appeared alone he was unable to form a food exchanging partnership; and since he appeared before bearers of Fakili and Modawa, he belonged to neither of the ceremonial moieties.[1] His descendants today occupy a single hamlet and number only 18 persons. The senior patrilineage is led by Yaneku who claims to trace direct patrilineal descent from Adikunuwala. Yaneku's *unuma* still has no moiety affiliation, although in the last generation it acquired exchange partners in Malabuabua in order to be able to participate more fully in the major food exchanges. The junior *unuma* of Ainaona is led by Awakili, the sole surviving male member of his line. Although Awakili, too, claims descent from Adikunuwala, his grandfather purchased *modawa* (drum) paraphernalia from the village of Awaiya, thereby admitting his agnatic descendants to the drum moiety. Even though they dwell in the same hamlet, Yaneku and Awakili continue to distinguish themselves, and are carefully distinguished by others, by reference to their different *dewa*, dog and drum respectively.

2. *Lulauvile*

The next clan ancestors to emerge from the ground were those of Lulauvile, which in many respects is the most anomalous clan of all. Its uniqueness is something that its members hold to be self-evident, and in spite of the vehemently egalitarian ideology of the culture, one is obliged to entertain the concept of rank when discussing Lulauvile. As a clan, it possesses the most elaborate and coherent myths which collectively give mandate to the most comprehensive and significant body of *dewa* to be found in Kalauna.

Structurally, Lulauvile is composed of two sections with somewhat different traditions. One section, sometimes referred to as Lulauvile Number One, contains seven *unuma* grouped into three hamlets; the other section, Lulauvile Number Two, comprises six *unuma* unevenly distributed between two hamlets. The sections are exogamous but can and do intermarry with each other. They

[1] It should be noted at this point that Modowa and Fakili are mutually exclusive 'custom groups' which partition the majority (but not all) of Goodenough Islanders. Although they are not moieties in the strict sense (since they are non-exogamous) it will become clear in this and later chapters that it is convenient to label them as such.

also form mutual *fofofo* pairs. Lulauvile is unique in having branches in neighbouring villages, and to Lulauvile belong the traditions of the foundation of Nibita, the prehistoric Kalauna (see Chapter 2).

According to some versions of its origin myth, Lulauvile ancestors appeared in pairs: Didiala and Matalaukonina of Lulauvile I, and Kedeya and Uyavaiyava of Lulauvile II. These men brought food as their *dewa*: coconuts, yams, taro and pigs respectively; also (though who brought which is uncertain) bananas, sugar-cane and (some now add) sweet potato. In other versions, Didiala and Kedeya alone appeared and carried the food between them. All versions agree that it was Didiala who 'invented' the *fofofo* institution of food exchange partnerships which is so integral to the social system. He split a spray of betel nut and gave half to Kedeya, declaring that henceforth they must 'help' each other and eat each other's food. He advised all subsequent arrivals from the world underground to pair off in the same fashion with those immediately behind them. The Lulauvile ancestors also brought with them the customs of Fakili: the long combs, the large lime gourds, the decorative apparel and songs of this moiety.

It will be recalled that Lulauvile people, who claim to have been 'boss' of the Nibita clans in Kwabua, were obliged to distribute some of their 'power' (*abavemeiya*) by relinquishing their ritual control over some of the food crops. Thus, they gave bananas and plantains to Iwaoyana, sugar-cane and *Saccharum edule* to Mulina, and sweet potato to Ainaona,[1] but managed to retain the more important staples – notably yams and taro – for themselves.

Whatever their former, pre-contact status, it is true that present-day Lulauvile leaders enjoy, through the magical techniques they control, considerable prestige and not a little authority. Just as the Lulauvile myths are the central documents of the community's oral history, so does this super-clan appear as the king-pin in the village structure, and its leaders as 'guardians' (*toitavealata*) whose task and prerogative it is to 'look after' the community's food supply. No other clan possesses members who can cause or revoke famine by 'chasing away' or prospering the crops. Under the prevailing ideology of egalitarianism,[2] however, its leaders receive no tokens of special respect – beyond a wariness of offending them – than are accorded to other leaders. While it is freely acknowledged by non-Lulauvile people that of all the *dewa* owned by descent groups, those concerning food are the most important and desirable, no-one would denigrate his own status or that of his clan by saying that Lulauvile people are deserving of most prestige. Yet, almost intangibly, and in despite of the ethic of egalitarianism, they possess it. The clan has what might be called 'submerged rank', which will be more readily understood when the role of food in the system of values is considered (see Chapters 7 and 8).

[1] This is probably an anachronism, since sweet potato was apparently introduced by Europeans (see Jenness and Ballantyne 1920, p. 28, also Malinowski 1935, pp. 161, 181, with regard to the Trobriands).

[2] Although I use the term 'egalitarianism' here and elsewhere to refer to what is a fairly explicit ideal of equality between men, it is for want of a more precise word. The 'ethic of egalitarianism' which Goodenough Islanders profess is perhaps better understood as a moral justification for 'levelling'. Thus, the main imperative of the doctrine would seem to be individualistic rather than social: 'no-one shall be seen to be bigger or better than me'.

(Although some analogy with sub-clan ranking in the Trobriands is invited, there are considerable differences of degree. Lulauvile's status in Kalauna is but a faint shadow of Tabalu's status in Kiriwina, and far from 'the existence of rank and social differentiation' being 'one of the main sociological features [which] at once strikes an observant newcomer' [Malinowski 1922, p. 52], it was fully a year before I was prepared to concede the existence of this feature in Kalauna. For this reason I am unable to state categorically whether or not other Goodenough villages have clans which can be attributed with 'submerged rank'. I am fairly satisfied that neither Belebele nor Bwaidoga have such clans, but for the remainder I cannot be sure.)

3. *Malabuabua*

Malabuabua people claim descent from a single ancestor, Tomolaulawa, who brought from Yauyaba the paraphernalia of the Modawa moiety: drums, certain shell valuables, dances and songs. This clan demonstrates, in its comprehensive genealogies and its clear traditions of hamlet formation, the simple processes of growth and segmentation. In 1967 Malabuabua was composed of six *unuma* which shared three adjacent hamlets, though during the following year a fourth was being established by Wakasilele (the clan's *de facto* leader) and his brothers.

As 'owners' of Modawa, Malabuabua are stereotyped as a peaceful clan. Among the valuables brought out of the ground by Tomolaulawa was *nimakabubu*, a bracelet of spondylus discs which is an emblem of peace. It is impossible at this stage to be sure of the peacemaking role of the Modawa moiety during the era of endemic warfare; modern informants state that Modawa people fought as willingly as anyone else when necessary, but that they were ritually prohibited by their *nimakabubu* from initiating fights. Again, in semi-legendary instances I recorded of intra-community fighting which were mediated by Modawa people, their peacemaking role was attributed to the 'power' of their *nimakabubu*. At all events, Modawa people contrast themselves favourably with the 'fighting' moiety of Fakili. It is said for instance that Fakili people 'do not eat properly' because they are 'always jumping up to go to war' – or nowadays to quarrel. Ideology notwithstanding, there are few men in Kalauna more violent and quarrelsome than Wakasilele of Malabuabua. When this contradiction is pointed out to Kalauna people, his un-Modawa-like traits are attributed to personally acquired, idiosyncratic *dewa*.

4. *Foloyai*

The symbolic opposition which is deemed to exist between the ceremonial moieties is heightened in Kalauna by another anomaly; for the clan which followed Malabuabua out of Yauyaba, thereby becoming their *fofofo*, belongs to neither Modawa nor Fakili. Adimaniutu, the ancestor of Foloyai clan, brought with him a spear and hunting magic. He emerged from the hole prancing in the stiff-legged manner of a warrior. He had many names which he called out one after the other in order to trick hearers into believing that he was an army of men – a practice which frightened people away until his *fofofo*, Tomolaulawa, made Adimaniutu desist by giving him his drum to hold. Today Foloyai are still said to 'carry the drum' for Malabuabua, though their 'true' *dewa* is said to be Hiyo, or spear. Some comments are necessary on this point.

Throughout Goodenough the Modawa ceremonial moiety is found as a constant, but in complementary opposition to it one finds (in the majority of villages) Fakili, or (in the minority of villages) Hiyo. However, where Hiyo is said to be the opposite moiety, there are frequently also traces of the customs associated with Fakili; signs, that is, that Fakili has been (or is still in process of being) assimilated to Hiyo. The reverse arrangement, too, appears to be fairly common. Two of the *unuma* in Mulina clan of Kalauna, for instance, claim to be both Hiyo and Fakili, but they gave me the latter as their moiety when first asked.

The simplest historical hypothesis, suggested by an intelligent informant, is that Hiyo and Modawa were the original ceremonial divisions and that the former came to be replaced by Fakili in recent generations. Certainly, according to my own interpretation, Fakili has received functional emphasis during the fairly recent era of elaborate festival cycles based on the Modawa/Fakili moiety system (see Chapter 11). The possibility that there was a tripartite division indigenously cannot be ruled out, however, for just as there are Hiyo clans (like Foloyai) which deny any connection with Fakili, so one may find Fakili clans (like Lulauvile) which deny any past equation with Hiyo.

Too much significance should not be attached to this conundrum. The divisions, whether dual or tripartite, are largely ceremonial and emblematic; they neither regulate marriage nor (with the possible exception of the supposed peacekeeping functions of Modawa) directly affect the political organization. They appear to be principally badges of identity for individuals and groups, though they also thereby provide the basis for stereotyping. Foloyai people, for instance, are regarded as violent, quick-tempered, boastful and deceitful; and true to the type of Adimaniutu, his ancestor, Foloyai's leader Tabwaika complained to me once about government peacekeeping and lamented the passing of local warfare.

5. *Iwaoyana*

The ancestors of Iwaoyana, the most burgeoning and scattered clan, brought fish nets and fishing magic as their principal *dewa*. But they also emerged with a duplication of the Fakili paraphernalia which Lulauvile claim to have brought first. This contradiction in the mythical charters is the rationale of a quarrel between the ancestors of the two clans, a quarrel which was never resolved. To this day Lulauvile and Iwaoyana are 'enemies from the ground'. Being the two largest clans in Kalauna, and for other reasons we shall consider below, their mutual antagonism reflects the most fundamental political cleavage in the community.

6. *Nouneya*

Nouneya, which occupies the single hamlet of Valeutoli, is subsumed by some old men under the clan name of Iwaoyana, although nowadays these are clearly distinct units which claim descent from different apical ancestors. It is possible that a few generations ago Nouneya and Iwaoyana were 'one group' in the same sense that the two Lulauvile sections are said to be today. The Nouneya myth of origin declares that its clan ancestor became Iwaoyana's *fofofo* and brought forth betel nut from Yauyaba as its main *dewa*. His descendants retain the ritual power to increase or banish the community's supply. Initially, it is said, Nouneya people belonged to the Fakili moiety, but they saw and admired the 'good', peaceful ways of Modawa and so acquired for themselves a drum and other Modawa customs from the village of Belebele.[1]

7. *Mulina*

The last Nibita clan to emerge at Yauyaba was Mulina (which means 'Hindmost'), and with none to follow it was obliged to divide itself into *fofofo* pairs. More detailed traditions suggest that at least two of the four Mulina *unuma* were at one time part of Lulauvile, having been driven away for appropriating the wrong share of food during a distribution. Despite their possibly diverse origins, Mulina ancestors are represented collectively in the current public versions of the Yauyaba myths as bringing forth as their *dewa* potent war magic, a heavy fighting spear, a stone axe and a war emblem. There is no mythical explanation as to how Mulina came to 'own' Fakili. Informants simply assert that it is the 'same' as Lulauvile's, which is to say that their ancestors somehow acquired the minutiae of Lulauvile's Fakili paraphernalia.

THE SOCIAL VALUE OF 'DEWA'

The identifying 'customs' mentioned so far are the principal ones in the sense that they are the first to spring to a Kalauna person's mind when he is asked what are his or another's *dewa*. They can be designated for each clan by a word: Ainaona – dog; Lulauvile – food (or comb); Malabuabua – drum; Foloyai – spear; Iwaoyana – fish-net (or comb); Nouneya – betel nut (or drum); and Mulina – war magic. But there are in addition many categories of *dewa* which every clan possesses: bird taboos, personal names, pig names, houseboard designs, planting magic, some types of sorcery, yam planting techniques, lullabies, hunting techniques, curses, death portents, mortuary observances, as well as, of course, stories and myths. Some of these *dewa* may be more accurately described as *unuma* property. Pig names, houseboard designs and certain magical techniques, for instance, are usually exclusive to the *unuma* rather than to the clan.

Whatever the group level at which *dewa* are claimed, however, exclusive rights to them are protected by certain sanctions. If a person practises a usage which is the property of another the latter may demand compensation in the form of traditional wealth from the transgressor. Ancestral spirits are conceived vaguely as protectors of *dewa*, and the breach of privilege respecting them is thought to invite supernatural retribution. For this

[1] According to Kalauna informants, Belebele acquired its Modawa by stealing it from the ghost of Tomolaulawa, the founding ancestor of Malabuabua.

reason I was unable to induce men to draw for me houseboard designs belonging to *unuma* other than their own. On the whole, however, actual instances of misappropriation of *dewa* seem to have been quite rare; in two years I encountered only three minor altercations arising from this, and in none of them were the transgressors fined or 'hit' by avenging spirits. I myself unwittingly provoked several breaches of privilege by asking for myths, spells, songs and details of particular *dewa* of those who were not fully entitled to tell, sing or give them. Umbrage and sometimes anger were the responses of the true owners of such *dewa*.

With more prerogatives to guard than the members of most clans, Lulauvile men could be peculiarly sensitive to what might appear to be trivial breaches of privilege. Kimaola, for instance, was irate with me on one occasion for playing to a small audience a tape recording of a song he had sung to hasten a woman's childbirth. The recording was made with his permission, but I did not think to secure this again when I played back the song in his absence. Another Lulauvile leader, Iyahalina, likewise resented and took great pains to correct the impression given to me by an Iwaoyana man who claimed his own *dewa* to be the growing of good taro. As a descendant of Kedeya, the Lulauvile ancestor who brought taro from Yauyaba, Iyahalina was infuriated by what he regarded as a false claim.

Why should *dewa* be valued to the extent that they are? There is little problem with those which are seen to confer specific advantages. Much traditional magic is of this class, for it not only 'ritualizes optimism' with regard to an inadequate technology (Malinowski 1948, p. 70), but also provides tools (and frequently weapons) in the competitive struggle between men for limited resources, whether these be yams, pigs, women or prestige. Magic is highest on the list of important property precisely because its many forms may be held exclusively (cf. Fortune 1932, pp. 96–7, 129). Magic which is known to all is of no value, being merely folklore; indeed, to a Goodenough Islander magic is almost by definition something exclusive, secret, and therefore to be protected from appropriation by others. (It is significant that the English word 'secret' – *sikeleti* – has been adopted on Goodenough as the general term for 'spell'.)

There would appear to be little practical utility or value, however, in many of the other classes of *dewa* which are also jealously protected. Consider, for example, the prerogative of planting yams in mounds grouped in a circular pattern, which until the present generation was said to have been the practice followed by an Iwaoyana *unuma*. It neither produced better yams nor conveyed any tangible benefit to the planters. On the contrary, it was abandoned because it was disadvantageous, requiring the preparation of more garden land than usual for its execution.

Why then was it done? Goodenough Islanders give the clue to the significance of such *dewa* when they call them, in English, 'markers', for it would appear to be precisely their function to signify identity by 'marking' social boundaries. If there is such a construct as the 'social personality' of a descent group, what better way to define and express it than by behavioural signs and symbols, which can be as diacritical as more obvious emblems such as names and totems?

If *dewa* demarcate the corporate, social personalities of clans in Kalauna, one might expect to find also the phenomenon of behavioural stereotyping. The range of these is indeed considerable; though not all are mutually consistent and, needless to say, they are frequently contradicted by observed conduct. To mention but a few, Lulauvile people are said to 'take things for nothing'; Malabuabua 'work too hard' and 'don't like to fight'; Foloyai 'tell lies' and are 'always getting angry'; Iwaoyana 'never give you what you ask for'; Nouneya 'boast about their food'; Mulina are 'always fighting' and 'wasting food'.

Such stereotypes may produce and reinforce behavioural expectations. The following incident illustrates both the positive and the negative application of this principle:

Before setting off to watch the climax of a festival in neighbouring Wailolo, Manawadi of Mulina chewed a leaf of the *cordyline* plant which grows on his *unuma*'s sitting circle. Each clan has its own named type of *cordyline* which is associated with exclusive war-magic. Mulina's, however, is believed to be the most potent in Kalauna, since this clan possesses the mythical charter for most things concerned with war. In addition to inspiring bravery, arrogance and recklessness, as do the *cordylines* of other clans, Mulina's plant is believed also to induce behaviour called *vetayakulo*, which may be rendered 'hooliganism'.[1] Manawadi's act, in snatching a leaf of the potent war-plant to prime him for the tense excitement of a large gathering of people, was about to be emulated by his companion, Adiwai, when he was stopped by Enowei, Manawadi's father. Adiwai, of Iwaoyana clan, was dwelling in Mulina with his widowed mother and her brother but this did not give him the right to adopt Mulina usages. Enowei berated Adiwai for plucking the *cordyline*, then went on to warn him that *vetayakulo* was not his *dewa* either, and if he attended the festival and committed destructive or violent acts he would receive no understanding from others. They would be angry with him and take punitive action. On the other hand, Manawadi and other Mulina men might behave with less than the customary

---

[1] English-speakers offered me the label 'cowboy' to describe a person who does *vetayakulo*. Deriving from the urban labour context, 'cowboy' in Port Moresby is used of smartly dressed young men who affect laconic, 'cool' and tough attitudes (personal communication, Mr A. Rew). On Goodenough the word has additional connotations, and is used of a man who is unreasoningly violent, amoral and given to anti-social trickery. The Goodenough concept subsumes the Port Moresby one, but appropriately in face-to-face communities, gives it a social dimension.

decorum of visitors to a neighbouring village – indeed, it would be expected of them by those who knew of their *dewa* – and they would be accorded a measure of tolerance for their conduct.

COMMUNITY STRUCTURE: 'FOFOFO'

At the sociological level the phenomenon of clan individuation by means of distinctive *dewa* and stereotype can be interpreted as an expression of clan solidarity and an assertion of segmental autonomy. It is perhaps to be expected that in the evolution of a compact community of clans their differentiation would be stressed by the elaboration of 'cultural dress'. The process is presumably what Bateson would call 'symmetrical schismo-genesis' (1936, pp. 183–6). This concept is a useful one in picturing what might have occurred to Nibita clans during the history of their association with one another. Since clan rivalry did not result in the break-up of the community, at least since its consolidated existence as Kalauna, it may be supposed that a state of 'dynamic equilibrium' was reached. This Bateson defines as 'a relationship between the groups in which the tendencies towards schismogenesis are adequately restrained or counteracted by other social processes' (*ibid.* p. 186). It is these 'other social processes' which are among the main concerns of this book, and we must now turn to a consideration of some of the principal institutionalized ways in which clans interact with one another.

In addition to cross-cutting kinship ties which help to bind the solidary clans together, many *ad hoc* relationships (such as the *aveyau* eating companionships mentioned previously) are formed across clan boundaries between men of approximately the same age. These relationships are not institutionalized at the group level, and although they produce networks which serve to enmesh the clans, they are formed by individuals acting for themselves in the pursuit of their own rather than their clans' interests. There are, however, two important and complementary institutions which tie clans together through relations of formalized opposition and enjoined co-operation. Since they involve corporate descent groups which survive the deaths of individual members, these relationships are prescribed and in theory immutable.

As we saw above, the formation of *fofofo* or food exchanging partnerships is attributed in myth to the clan ancestors at the very inception of society. Informants define their *fofofo* as 'those who eat our *niune*'. *Niune* is the term for food or pork which is received in formal exchanges between political groups, and implicit is a prohibition on the consumption of that food by the direct recipients. Reciprocity governs the relationship between *fofofo* pairs. In addition to eating each other's *niune* or prohibited food, they assist each other to provide for their own external exchanges. This is the crucial political aspect of the institution, as the term *fofofo*, which means 'to carry on the back', suggests. Furthermore, by the use of an alternative term, *kwamana*, speakers imply that the relationship is characterized by the succour and dependence, expressed by food giving and receiving, which obtains between a man and his adoptive child. The contexts in which the *fofofo* institution plays a part will be examined in later chapters where additional aspects of the relationship will be introduced.

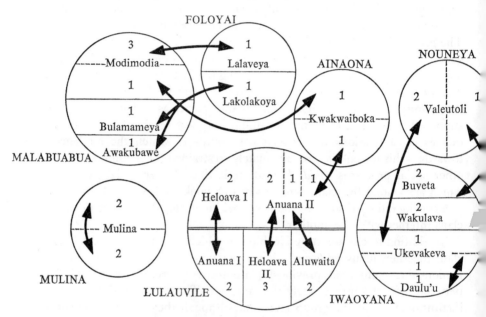

Fig. 2. *Fofofo* partnerships in Kalauna. (Clans are circled; hamlet names and number of *unuma* are given within segments)

There is an individual correlate of the *fofofo* partnership between groups. Certain major distributions, feasts and exchanges require that *fofofo* give each other cooked food. Since cooking has to be done in individual pots on individual hearths and is eaten in individual houses, each man must have a partner with whom to exchange cooked food. *Venima'abi* perform this reciprocal task. This relationship is formed when a man takes his place in adult society; that is, when he has a wife and adequate gardens, and when he has begun to contribute to the food exchange activities which constitute such a large part of the political life of the community. He will select a young man of similar age and status from his *fofofo*'s group – ideally the son of his own father's *venima'abi* – and following a small ceremony they will henceforth 'clasp hands' (*ve*–causative, *nima* – hand, *abi* – to clasp).

Figure 2 maps the community structure of Kalauna in terms of *fofofo* partnerships between *unuma* and clans. According to the Yauyaba origin myths, four of the seven clans were paired in this relationship, two partnered themselves, and one, the first arrival, stood alone without *fofofo*. We have noted that empirically, however, Lulauvile is composed of two sections which for some purposes can be regarded as discrete clans, while Mulina is apparently an amalgam of clan fragments. Finally, Ainaona has quite recently acquired partners in Lulauvile and Malabuabua. There is more detailed evidence at the *unuma* level of Iwaoyana and Nouneya clans to support a contention that *fofofo* partnerships are re-aligned periodically to balance differential growth, segmentation or extinction of *unuma*. The important point here, however, is that *fofofo* partnerships link descent groups at the most inclusive segmentary level, and that with the exceptions of Ainaona's and one of Ukevakeva's *unuma* partnerships (which are the result of fairly recent adjustments), the component *unuma* of any clan are symmetrically allied in parallel partnerships. The implied model is fairly clear: that the segments (*unuma*) of two clans partner each other.

COMMUNITY STRUCTURE: 'NIBAI'

The model of *fofofo* partnerships is considerably complicated by the complementary institution of *nibai*, 'traditional enemy'. In contrast to *fofofo*, *nibai* may belong to different villages as well as to Kalauna, though we are concerned here only with the structure of relations within the community. The rationale for *nibai* formation is usually as follows: an ancestor of *unuma* A1 of clan A was killed, and generally eaten, by the ancestors of *unuma* B1 of clan B. Whether there was vengeance killing (*miwa*) or not, the descendents of these two *unuma* A1 and B1, regarded each other as *nibai*, perpetual antagonists.

Most *unuma* in Kalauna have at least one *nibai* in one or more of the neighbouring villages, but less than half have one or more *nibai* within the village. The remainder, however, claim *nibai* by assimilating themselves to other *unuma* of their clan which do have 'true' *nibai*. Thus, *unuma* A2 and A3 will consider *unuma* B1, and in some cases the whole of clan B, to be their *nibai*. 'Adoptive' *nibai* of this kind are usually distinguished from 'true' *nibai* by calling them 'food enemies' (*au'a ana nibaina*). These may also have been chosen from within the village or beyond within relatively recent times, in some cases because pre-existing 'true' *nibai* had died out. This indicates clearly that *nibai* are as necessary to the food exchange system as *fofofo*. A diagrammatic model will make this plain. Thus, clans A and B are traditional enemies and give each other food competitively, either simultaneously or in delayed exchange, depending upon the ceremonial context. Clans C and D do likewise. Clan A cannot eat B's food, however, as it is their *niune*, so their *fofofo*, clan C, takes it for its own consumption. Clan A similarly takes C's *niune*, from C's enemy D. The arrows in the diagram represent food flows, and '*unuma*' could be substituted for 'clan' in certain empirical instances.

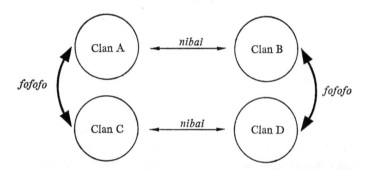

Since most *nibai* relationships were caused by what may be regarded as historical or contingent events, the total pattern of such links is less tidy than that of *fofofo* partnerships. Nevertheless, there is some regularity in that the majority of *nibai* relationships within Kalauna link two clan clusters in roughly parallel fashion, as can be seen from Fig. 3.

The most conspicuous opposition is that between Lulauvile and Iwao-yana, and it will be recalled that a *nibai* relationship at the clan level was formed between them following their quarrel over the possession of Fakili *dewa*; but under this legendary rationale are subsumed a number of *nibai* relationships between *unuma* of both clans, and these are said to derive from mutual killings in the past. Since they are the two largest clans in Kalauna, the traditional antagonism between Lulauvile and Iwaoyana has implications for the political stability of the whole com-munity. This is even more apparent when the pattern of *fofofo* pairings is superimposed on the map of *nibai* relationships.

The simplified representation in Fig. 4 indicates that the community is crudely divided into two opposing blocs, leaving only Mulina unaligned. This arrangement is probably fortuitous rather than contrived, though there is little doubt that the basic opposition has been reinforced in fairly recent times by the formation of new *fofofo* and 'food enemies'. That is to say, partners were apparently selected with a view to perpetuating the cleavage rather than bridging it. However, it would be erroneous to assume

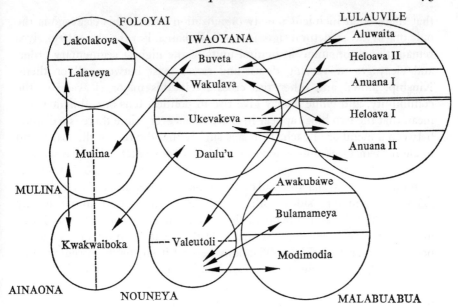

Fig. 3. *Nibai* relationships in Kalauna

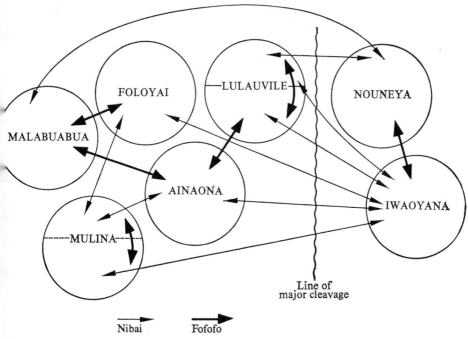

Nibai ——▶   Fofofo ━━▶

Fig. 4. *Fofofo* and *nibai* relationships at clan level. (Spatial relationships of clans in this figure approximate to actual settlement pattern in Kalauna)

that there is an incipient moiety organization or that this cleavage is the only one of any structural significance in Kalauna. For the clans themselves remain the autonomous structural units of the highest segmentary order, and cleavages of varying depth and stress exist between all of them. Kinship, affinal and other ties cross freely this major cleavage in the community, and while it may give rise to political tensions, this does not mean that the two blocs appear in sharp focus every time there is a dispute between a member of each. It means simply that the rest of the clans tend to align themselves thus whenever there is a confrontation, expressed in a competitive food exchange, between the two major antagonists in the community, Iwaoyana and Lulauvile. Thus, since Nouneya is Iwaoyana's *fofofo*, Malabuabua sides with Lulauvile in opposition to its enemy Nouneya. Foloyai and Ainaona, being Malabuabua's *fofofo*, are also drawn in to oppose Iwaoyana and Nouneya. Mulina, with traditional enemies in both camps, and no *fofofo* obligations beyond itself, tends to remain 'uncommitted', which effectively means helping both sides. This is a gross interpretation of the pattern of clan alignment in such a confrontation; in practice, the situation is almost infinitely complicated by the fact that individuals and not clans decide whom they are going to assist and in what degree (see Chapter 9). The resultants nevertheless demonstrate that clan alignments are determinate rather than fluid, and confirm the impression that there is a general balance of power to be found between the clans of Kalauna.

5

LEADERSHIP

To begin with, just to identify the holders of authority in the indigenous political hierarchies is not a simple matter. They wear no special insignia. Their standards of living are not markedly different from other men's. And in the presence of white visitors many of them tend to be purposefully unobtrusive.

Oliver 1955, p. xviii

Most approaches to the study of leadership in Melanesia are faced initially with the problem of identifying the leaders and secondly with determining their attributes. In this chapter I introduce Kalauna leaders through a discussion of the terminology of leadership, briefly consider their authority and functions, then compare their empirical attributes with the indigenous stereotype. Among the attributes examined are renown, wealth, knowledge of sorcery, polygyny and personal support. To illustrate modes of achievement and succession I present several short case histories. Finally, I consider the structural correlates of the overall pattern and the determining or limiting factors which shape the form of leadership characteristic of Kalauna society.

IDENTIFYING THE LEADERS

With the exception of the elected local government councillor and the Administration-appointed village constable, current leaders in Kalauna are such by virtue of indigenous qualifications and criteria. While there are several terms for such leaders they do not necessarily refer to distinct types; and although the various terms connote role variations, some of them may be applied at different times to one and the same leader. The use of these terms, therefore, tends to reflect the situational context in which a given leader is acting rather than role or status differentials between leaders.

Kaliva lakaina (lit. big-man) is perhaps the most common general term for a leader, though it may be applied to anyone of above average wealth or influence, including Europeans. In the plural it usually refers to the old men of the community, whatever their status as individuals may be; and when tradition and customary behaviour are being discussed it may also be used in the sense of 'ancestors'. As a gently flattering form of address *kaliva lakaina* conveys esteem, respect for age, wealth or dignity, but does not necessarily imply a relationship of super-subordination. However, when comparisons between leaders are being drawn, the pre-eminent ones are referred to as 'real' or 'true' big men (cf. Oliver 1949a; Salisbury 1964, p. 236).

Kaiwabu has a more restricted connotation. As a title rather than a descriptive term it defies translation. It bears considerable and significant connotations of rank; although appropriately in an egalitarian society, rank is not a fixed status but an attribute of certain persons in certain social – usually ceremonial – situations. The primary referent of *kaiwabu* is the man (or woman) who sits on a raised platform at the food and pig distribution which marks the climax of a Fakili festival (see Chapter 11). Strictly speaking, the Modawa counterpart of *kaiwabu* should be called *kuyau*,[1] but the latter term is less favoured and *kaiwabu* usually serves to designate both Fakili and Modawa 'leaders'. What may be regarded as secondary referents of *kaiwabu* have developed, to the extent that the term may be applied to any leader who is ostentatiously, by dress or demeanour, 'lording it' over others. This expression is not inappropriate, for the Catholic priest who translated the Creed into Bwaidogan saw fit to render 'Lord' by the term *kaiwabu*.[2] Furthermore, in my first efforts to define the word, I was offered the translation 'king' by an ex-schoolteacher with a fair command of English, and by extension of the analogue he claimed that since his father was a *kaiwabu*, his family was 'royal'.[3] However, not even those Lulauvile leaders whose status in the community exceeds that of all others are entitled to be called *kaiwabu* at all times. The term thus implies a context in addition to defining a status and a role. The primary usage is a ceremonial one, and while not entirely limited to ceremonial contexts now, the broader applications of the term imply some ceremonial element in which the notion of hierarchy is evident. *Kaiwabu*, then, do not possess authority and rank in a structure of social relations, though as we shall see in the final chapter, they appear to symbolize or objectify these elements.

Native conceptions of authority emerge most clearly in the wide use of

[1] In Molima *kaiwabu* is the leading man of a community (Dr A. Chowning, personal communication). Cf. Kiriwina *guyau*, translated by Malinowski as 'chief' or 'chiefly'; also *gulau* ('headmen or chiefs') of Bartle Bay (Seligman 1910, p. 455).

[2] The Methodist Mission on the other hand, translates 'Lord' by *kauvea*, a Bwaidogan term for 'elder' which is never heard in Kalauna. Jenness and Ballantyne (1928, p. 240) define it as 'the head man of a hamlet', and it is the only term they give for 'leader' in their monograph (1920).

[3] This remark did not entirely deserve the scorn with which I treated it. The informant belonged to Lulauvile, which, as I indicated in the previous chapter, has what I called 'submerged rank'.

the English word 'boss', which as noun or verb has become an integral expression in Kalauna speech.[1] 'Boss' and its derivative 'bossman' are doubtless borrowed from the wage-labour situations – plantation work, wharf labour, storeman jobs and so forth – with which all mature Kalauna men are thoroughly familiar. 'Boss' is used in expressions which have the force of dicta, and they are frequently uttered with a sententious air of wisdom which leaves no doubt but that they are held to be incontrovertible statements of authority relations. Thus, *kaliva hi bos* (man is boss) is a reference to a fundamental aspect of the marriage partnership. *Tawana hi bos* is used to explain an elder brother's right to make certain decisions on behalf of his siblings; while *Kaunsil hi bos* is an oft-repeated, though somewhat sardonic reference, to the elected councillor's right to demand the performance of certain communal tasks such as road-clearing. Finally, folk-wisdom has distilled into the phrase *moni hi bos* the recognition of the increasing cash needs of the community.

TABLE 9 *Kalauna 'bossmen', their hamlets, ages and genealogical status (1967)*

Name	Hamlet	Approximate age	Senior member of senior *unuma*	Relationship to previous 'bossman'
Yaneku	Kwakwaiboka	40	yes	son
Siboboya	Aluwaita	60	yes	son
Didiala	Anuana I	65	yes	FBS?
Kimaola	Heloava II	50	yes	son
Iyahalina	Heloava I	55	no	FFFBSS
Malawidiya	Anuana II	35	no	classif. son
Wakasilele	Modimodia	35	no	son
Awatula	Awakubawe	50	yes	son
Tabwaika	Lalaveya	55	yes	son
Neailena	Lakolakoya	40	yes	son
Bwanakovi	Ukevakeva	55	no	brother
Ilukwalukwa	Buveta	40	no	son
Nadeweya	Wakulava	45	no	son
Silowai	Daulu'u	50	yes	son
Kafataudi	Valeutoli	40	no	FFBSS
Kaulubu	Mulina	45	yes	son

Within the village, every hamlet is said to have its 'bossman'. There is little difficulty in eliciting the names of 'bossmen' in Kalauna, for informants simply enumerate the hamlets and offer a leader's name for each; in fact it is common to refer to a hamlet, or the members which compose it,

[1] Curiously, it has not had the same success in Bwaidoga, where the native usage *vemeiya* continues to be preferred. On the other hand, it might be noted that the English 'leader' is heard in Bwaidoga (but not in Kalauna), though it refers exclusively to church leaders.

by naming its 'bossman'. The preceding table gives the names of Kalauna 'bossmen', their hamlets, and their genealogical status. The 'bossman' of a hamlet is ideally the senior male member of the genealogically senior patrilineage. As the last column in the table indicates, this is by no means always the case in practice, and I shall be concerned to show why when I turn to consider modes of achievement later in the chapter.

The main political function of a 'bossman' is to direct and co-ordinate his hamlet's external food exchanging activities. Outside this context his authority is not much in evidence, and in matters of land and other forms of property it does not normally extend beyond his own *unuma*. Members of the same hamlet who belong to other *unuma* may resent any interference by the 'bossman' in matters which do not directly concern the political affairs of the hamlet. It is not for him, they will say, to tell them when or where to plant their gardens or instruct them to raise more pigs (unless they are sponsoring a festival); to mediate disputes within the hamlet (unless they also concern his own *unuma*); or to supervise the distribution of bridewealth and death-payments (unless his own *unuma* is a party to the transaction). While his authority in these and other matters is not held as of a right, it may be won by influence and persuasion, so that in effect a 'bossman' may *encourage* hamlet members to plant more gardens, *suggest* the best uses to which their pigs may be put, *conciliate* quarrelling members by appeals to the 'good name' of the hamlet, and *advise* in the distributions which concern other *unuma*.

I have described a hypothetical mode and outlined a set of possibilities. Some 'bossmen' in Kalauna exploit these and are thus able to direct many activities within the hamlet and, more so than lesser leaders, are said to 'look after' it. Such men tend to be of 'real big-man' fame.[1] But others may not take the opportunities offered for maximizing their authority, and may be lax in performing adequately the political role that is expected of them.

It might seem curious that a non-indigenous term should be adopted for what is apparently a traditional and fairly well-defined position. The answer, I suggest, goes to the heart of an issue to be considered in later chapters, namely, the development in post-contact times of major food exchanges as a surrogate for warfare. Present-day informants do not remember when or why the term 'bossman' came into use, but they readily

---

[1] The process seems to be identical to that described for the Choiseulese 'manager' by Scheffler (1965, p. 186): 'His authority is confined to his own group, but his reputation and a respect for his abilities, or . . . a fear of them, spreads to others and then exercises a sort of feed-back upon members of his own group who give him greater deference as his more general reputation grows. The amount of influence a manager exercised within his own descent group was, therefore, directly dependent upon his influence in intergroup affairs.'

offer *toveimeya* as the vernacular equivalent. Indeed, in colloquial speech 'boss' is frequently substituted for *veimeya*, which carries the additional meanings of 'law', 'rule', 'instruction' or 'authority'.[1] Thus a *toveimeya* is a man who possesses some right to exercise authority over others, a man who lays down rules of conduct and gives instructions. As we shall see, however, the social range of this authority is normally quite small, embracing on average about seven adult men. His sanctions, moreover, tend to be informal and contingent: shaming by harangue, the withdrawal of support, cursing by the invocation of a special totem, and temporary banishment (see Chapter 6).

Traditionally, there was another term for the hamlet leader in war-time. This was *tonagona* (lit. man who goes in front), a term which has all but passed from memory, for the circumstances of local warfare in which the *tonagona* was pre-eminent belong to the distant past. The *tonagona*, however, may be seen as the antecedent of the modern hamlet 'bossman',[2] and just as the latter today co-ordinates the activities and resources of his group in relation to extra-hamlet (i.e. political) food exchanges, so the *tonagona* used to co-ordinate and direct the group's activities in war-time: consult allies, plan raids, perform war-magic, and lead his followers in the fighting. As chief strategist he was expected to be the most courageous, agile, powerful, and reckless warrior. Following a battle or raid he supervised the distribution of the bodies of captured enemies for consumption in cannibal feasts. As the major food exchanges came to replace intervillage warfare and inter-clan feuding as the dominant expression of political relations, the *tonagona*'s warrior role came to be transformed into the 'bossman's' role of food manager for the group (cf. Oliver 1955, chap. 12).

While this development probably called for a different array of skills and strategies it did not necessarily demand an entirely different set of qualities in the leader. Among the most successful 'bossmen' of the present, those who bear the stamp of 'real' big-men, are those who have inherited or emulated some of the most distinctive personal attributes of the renowned *tonagona*: physical prowess, stamina, self-discipline, courage, and in some circumstances, aggressiveness. From the point of view of his followers, however, it is preferable that a 'bossman' should not be *tonuakoyo*, an angry man, but gentle (*bikabika*) in word and deed to set them an example of 'good' conduct; although the influence of Christianity is to be suspected

---

[1] Jenness and Ballantyne (1928, p. 259) define *veimeya* even more forcefully: 'rule, command; to rule, govern, command'.

[2] The 'war leader' was not a different functionary to the usual hamlet leader as, for instance, was the case in Molima (Dr A. Chowning, personal communication). Cf. Jenness and Ballantyne (1920, p. 131) who state that it was 'the head man of the hamlet . . . who led the war-party on its expeditions'.

here. Such men are Yaneku, Bwanakovi, and until his death in 1968, Malawidiya. However, there are also foul-mouthed, assertive and irascible leaders who chivvy their kinsmen, like Kimaola and Wakasilele, and these tend to be more prominent in village affairs.

Who then are the biggest men in the community? There is no consensus as to the ranking of the sixteen hamlet leaders; indeed, most informants find this kind of comparison invidious. 'They are "bossmen" of their hamlets', one informant said, 'and sometimes we call them all big-men, but some of them – their names are not big'. A big name (*eyana lakaina*) is a reputation in other villages. Twelve or thirteen were confidently offered as being known from Kalimatabutabu to Bwaidoga, or most of the east coast of the island. Three of these (and opinion was unanimous on this) are known and respected all over the island, and wherever I enquired I found this to be true. 'They are given food, betel nut and a house to sleep in wherever they go', it is said. These three men, Didiala, Iyahalina and Kimaola, are the Lulauvile leaders who have hereditary claims to special ritual competences concerned with the prosperity of the community. The respect accorded them, their generally pre-eminent status, and a measure of their authority derives principally from their magical knowledge. This is a double-edged weapon: a power for prosperity or a power for famine. An informant said of them: 'If they did not look after us we would have to search in the bush for our food. If we make them angry they can send the food away to punish us for our pride.' The implications of this statement for the sanctions wielded by these leaders will emerge later; here I am concerned only to delineate crudely their status and roles.[1]

There is no special term for these men, save the cumbersome phrase *melala ana toitavealata* (lit. 'man who looks after the village'). *Toitavealata* (lit. 'man who looks after or is responsible for') is commonly used to apply to them and also to others who perform garden magic on behalf of their kinsmen. More commonly than any other leaders, one hears them spoken of as *kaiwabu*, *kaliva lakaina*, *tovemeiya* and 'bossmen' of the village (i.e. not simply of their hamlets). As the other 'bossmen' are food managers of their hamlets, so these three men are seen as food managers for the whole of Kalauna. More than any other leaders in the community they are worthy of the description 'chiefs' by which my early informants, using English as a medium, sought to define them. 'We respect them', 'we are

---

[1] Once again analogy is invited with Kiriwina, where the possession of potent magical powers by the 'chiefly' sub-clan is an important key to an understanding of its rank (see Powell 1960, pp. 128–9). Once again, however, I must stress that the incipient or 'submerged' rank of Lulauvile and its leaders bears little similarity to the vigorous principle of rank in Kiriwina, which is, in Powell's words, 'an inherent element in the kinship and marriage system' (1969, p. 601).

afraid of them', 'they look after the people', 'they known well how to look after the food', 'we obey them because they know food secrets'; such were the reasons given to me as justification for calling them chiefs. They receive no tribute or remuneration for their ritual services to the community, however, and they perform them with only prestige (and a measure of political power) for reward. They have no insignia nor any right to claim extraordinary privileges. The chiefly metaphor which my informants thought fitting proves to be apt only in that these men possess more than a usual amount of authority, and reciprocally, are charged with more than a usual amount of responsibility.

It is necessary to mention briefly what these responsibilities are. Tasks with which they are associated may be divided into two categories: regular magical rites which accompany the normal rhythm of the annual gardening cycle, and contingent magical rites which are designed to counter periodic ecological crises, especially drought. The Lulauvile myths (see Chapter 4) validate the possession of these magical controls over three of the most important crops. The distribution of these competences within Lulauvile itself is not tidy, and there is sharing and overlap of functions. Didiala, Kimaola and Siboboya, leaders of the three hamlets of Lulauvile I share the knowledge of yam and coconut magic. Iyahalina of Lulauvile II 'looks after' taro and also the coconuts. Didiala also knows the taro secrets, and both he and Iyahalina know the ritual of *manumanua* to prosper all the crops and banish hunger. There is a division of labour in practice, however. For the past few years Kimaola has initiated the various phases of the yam gardening cycle and has taken on the general responsibility for 'looking after' the yam gardens of the community. In years past he is said to have alternated with Didiala and Siboboya in performing these tasks, but both of these men are now elderly and infirm. Iyahalina alone initiates and prospers the taro gardening; aging but still agile, he wanders from garden to garden singing his spells. With respect to the contingent rituals, Iyahalina and Didiala consult and divide the tasks between them or perform them simultaneously. Thus in 1966, following the devastation of many coconut trees by the locust plagues of the previous year, both men co-operated in setting a taboo and performing increase-magic on the community's crop in the areas worst affected.

Although it was suggested to me that the three *toitavealata* of Lulauvile could limit the amount of food available to the village by imposing taboos on the crops of their speciality, I recorded no concrete case of their ever having done so either individually or in concert. At a village meeting in 1966 an Iwaoyana man accused Iyahalina of 'spoiling' the manioc, bananas and sweet potatoes in the general area where the coconuts had been tabooed, offering his children's sickness as proof of the charge.[1] Iyahalina strongly denied it, saying that it was not within his power or competence (*abavemeiya*) to 'spoil' these crops by his taboos. There seem to be no circumstances, in fact, under which the Lulauvile *toitavealata* might publicly proclaim universal taboos for any of the food crops, though my informants insisted on the theoretical possibility. It emerges rather, that the most effective sanctions of these men lie in their being believed able to banish the food supply altogether, or more literally, to 'chase it away' (*au'a hi kwavina*) by means of crop sorcery and weather magic. This is the negative aspect of their ritual competences, and one I shall have cause to discuss more fully in Chapter 8. The extent to which the Lulauvile *toitavealata* may use their powers coercively or to make political capital is illustrated by the following case material.

Didiala's sun magic

I observed none of the events described in this case, most of which I obtained from Adiyaleyale, Iyahalina's son. I have edited his tape-recorded text considerably, but given a minimum of explanation to allow his (Lulauvile) view of the affair to come across. There is no doubt that he, as well as everyone else in Kalauna, fully believes in Didiala's ability to control sun and rain by means of his *valeimu'imu* magic (cf. Jenness and Ballantyne 1920, p. 128).

Tabwaika, 'bossman' of Lalaveya and nominal leader of Foloyai clan, is known for his argumentative disposition, independent-mindedness and trouble-making. These traits are popularly explained by his clan's *dewa*. In 1964 he is reported to have said in conversation with a group of men and women:

> I don't respect Kimaola's *vemeiya* (rule). I don't obey him when he says we are to harvest our yams. He doesn't sing his magic over my yams, but they still grow well. Everyone has his own secret spells.

Others present said:

> But it is Lulauvile's custom to do this for our yams. If we have bad seeds they can make them grow well. They help us to find big yams.

Tabwaika still scoffed at his brother-in-law Kimaola, who was not present. Tabwaika's sister heard him speak but was ashamed to tell her husband. Wakasilele, who is Tabwaika's *venima'abi* (food exchange partner), but with whom he often quarrels, reported to Kimaola instead. He said:

> Your *vemeiya* is that we wait for you to say before we dig our yams, but Tabwaika says he can do it when he likes.

Kimaola said:

> Enough! He wants to be *tovemeiya* himself. He doesn't want to obey me.

[1] Crop taboos (*tabu*) are believed to operate by magically 'spoiling' (*kivekoyo*) and rendering unfit for consumption the crop on which the taboo has been put. The operator defines in his spell the area to which the taboo shall apply and the type of sickness which its transgression will inflict. He warns the community of his act both by public announcement and by signs on the paths to the area affected.

His way is like this. I can't say anything to him, because I married his sister.

But he told Didiala who got angry and shouted across the village to Tabwaika:

You, only you, every year disobey us. You think we are going to believe you can make yams big yourself? Everyone has their own spells but they still respect us because yam is our custom from Yauyaba. Yam belongs to Lulauvile not Foloyai. Your ancestors brought only spear and anger – no food. You cannot do this by yourself.

Tabwaika answered:

If it is as you say that only Lulauvile make big yams, you Didiala, or Kimaola, then we cannot know the value of other people's magic. I want everyone to try his own magic alone then we can see who finds the biggest yams in his gardens each year.

Didiala replied:

Enough! I can't say more. I want to tell you our yam story but you cut my speech.

This quarrel was remembered the following year when there was a drought, for Didiala alone in Kalauna possesses sun magic. But people were uncertain whether to attribute it to Didiala's anger with Tabwaika or with the unknown sorcerer who had killed Didiala's youngest son the same year. No one dared speak openly about it for fear of strengthening Didiala's resolve (*kuluwana kuyana*, lit. 'hard head' i.e. intransigence, determination). Later the story was pieced together as follows:

After the quarrel with Tabwaika Didiala waited. But Kimaola said to his heir Kiyodi:

You go and help that old man. I can't do anything because Tabwaika is my brother-in-law. But I want to test him. Is he really strong like he says? Will he stay in the village when there is no food?

But still Didiala waited. Then his son died and he was angry. He said to Kiyodi:

Now you can help me. Now I cannot feel sorry for Kalauna people. They can think I make sun magic because my son died, but I can teach Tabwaika to respect us.

Kiyodi helped him perform the rites because Didiala is nearly blind.

After four months of sun Iyahalina, Lulauvile's third leader, went to see Didiala, his *venima'abi* and classificatory brother-in-law, for many people had petitioned him to approach Didiala about the drought. Iyahalina said:

O my brother-in-law, can you make this thing better? Think of our children. When we die people will remember the trouble we gave them and they will make sorcery against our children, and they will die too.

But one of Didiala's sons had already died and he didn't listen to Iyahalina.

At length, however, a meeting was held in the village. Neailena the councillor asked the assembled people:

Who can tell me who is giving us this big sun? Already the ground has dried up, we can't plant our taro and we eat only manioc. We try to find bread-

4*

fruit and chestnuts but they have already gone away, and many men have gone to work on plantations because there is no food in the village. You must tell me why we have this big sun.

Wakasilele said:

It's because we don't respect Lulauvile. We never obey their *vemeiya* but do our yam spells ourselves. We want to be *tovemeiya*, or we say 'We are strong men, we can find our own big yams.' This is why we have a big sun now.

Neailena replied:

Yes truly, the big-men of Lulauvile made it.

Then he asked Iyahalina:

I think you helped your brother-in-law [i.e. Didiala]. First you made a *bolimana* [southeast wind], then he made the sun strong. You see, already people went away into the bush to find food, or to the sea to fish.

Iyahalina replied:

No, I didn't do it. Maybe Siusiu made it.

But Siusiu [an albino with a formidable battery of sorcery techniques inherited from his father Tobowa] said:

No, I did it before when my father died, because I was angry. But I didn't make the wind come this time.

Adiyaleyale, Iyahalina's son, said:

You blame these people for nothing. This is *bolimana* time. Every year the wind comes like this. Soon it will stop.

Neailena said:

But still the sun is burning up the ground. I want everyone to agree to give Didiala a present, then he can make rain come and we can plant our gardens and food will grow again.

Didiala spoke for the first time:

No, you can give presents to my *venima'abi* Iyahalina. Then he can bring the coconuts back and the breadfruit, and he will help you to plant your taro. Some *lokoloko* [i.e. material goods, valuables] you can also give to Wa'afui [of Nouneya] and he will bring back the betel nut. Some you can give to me and I will stop the sun. Then you can plant your food. But first you must go to Wailolo people and give them *lokoloko*, too, so they can bring rain.

(Wailolo people, being also afflicted by the dry weather, had already tried to make rain but failed. Their rainmakers, Yadivana and Kadikalina, had come to Kalauna a few weeks before to see Didiala. They knew the rumours that he was causing the drought. They brought their rainstone in its basket and gave it to Didiala and said:

We know you are making this sun. You are stopping our rain-spells, so here, take this rain-stone because we can't use it while your spell is on the sun.

Didiala got very angry.

You blame me; you think I am spoiling your magic.

He threatened to make *abutu* (competitive food exchange) to Yadivana and his brother. This frightened them and they returned home.)

The meeting agreed to collect *lokoloko* and Wakasilele stood again and admonished the people to follow Lulauvile's rules in planting and harvesting their yams. Tabwaika then came forward and said:

I am sorry for everyone. This sun was truly my fault because I quarrelled with these Lulauvile men and they made the big sun. You became thirsty for water and coconut milk and hungry for good food. I am to blame.

Everyone was angry with him, but they laughed and jeered and called him a joker and a liar. Someone said:

You apologise to Kimaola and Didiala and you say you are sorry we have suffered because of your pride and arrogance, but next year you are again going to make the spells on your yams yourself.

Tabwaika said:

No truly, I have learnt my lesson.

But he was indeed lying, for next year he ignored Lulauvile's rules as usual.

After the meeting everyone in the village contributed small sums of money, knives, plates, cups, pieces of calico or other *lokoloko* and they were given to Iyahalina, Wa'afui, Didiala and the Wailolo rainmakers. Didiala removed his spells from the sun and one week later rain fell. Everyone was happy and soon they were eating good food again.

This case raises a number of problems, not least of which is the fairy-tale-like sequence of magic-drought – magic-rain: that is to say, a sequence which the actors believe to be causal but which the anthropologist assumes to be coincidental. The empirical status of this case apart, what does it tell us about Kalauna leadership? Firstly, it is clear that Lulauvile *toitavealata* resent any threat to their privileged duty to 'look after' the yams, and that they are prepared to suffer unpopularity or worse to defend this privilege. Secondly, even if the sun-magic conspiracy of Kimaola and Didiala was an *ex post facto* fiction to 'explain' the drought in terms of strained social relationships, it was connived in by them and resulted ultimately, as they might have hoped, in a reinforcement of the fear and respect in which they are usually held. Thirdly, if we accept that by design or contingency the drought operated as a sanction for their authority, it was only partially successful in that the main offender, Tabwaika, proved unrepentant. Politically speaking, however, he was temporarily discredited and publicly shamed. Regarding other political aspects of the case, we may note that Kimaola's affinal relationship to Tabwaika obliged him to take an undemonstrative position, whereas a similar relationship enabled Iyahalina (whose father's brother's daughter Didiala married) to try to conciliate the old man on the community's behalf. Direct approaches to the suspected sorcerer or magician are generally avoided for fear of antagonizing him and increasing his determination to make the community suffer. The Wailolo rainmakers' deputation is an illustration of the futility of open negotiation in such cases; although having frightened them off, Didiala afterwards made his peace with them by getting Kalauna people to send them *lokoloko*. In doing so, he was probably also safeguarding himself by leaving open an avenue of blame should his own attempts to bring rain prove unsuccessful. It was the village meeting, not private diplomacy, which finally proved catalytic in getting Didiala to agree to end the drought and Tabwaika to admit that he was at fault. By having the authority to call public meetings, the councillor, though often seemingly politically ineffective is in a position to transform the nature of a social crisis by bringing it into the open air of a public forum.

ATTRIBUTES OF LEADERS

Having identified the leaders in Kalauna let us look more closely at their attributes as a class, at those things which differentiate them from non-leaders. The local stereotype stresses possessions: wealth, gardens and knowledge of magic and sorcery. These must be discussed before turning to other characteristic aspects of leadership which the stereotype tends to neglect: polygyny, following, achievement and mode of succession.

Wealth

Lokoloko (shell valuables and cooking pots, European trade goods), pigs, and gardens are all possessions which leaders are expected to have in greater quantities than other men. This is least true of trade goods and most true of native valuables and pigs. Of these categories of wealth only *lokoloko* are transmitted by inheritance. The wealth component of the Kalauna stereotype of their leaders is tested statistically in the following table, which compares ten leaders with twelve non-leaders. Both groups are stratified by (estimated) age between the limits shown, since age obviously has some bearing on these attributes. The control samples of non-leaders were chosen randomly from among married men in the estimated age categories, but close agnatic kinsmen of the leaders were excluded.

In Table 10, European tools refer to matchets, axes, adzes, picks, spades and other capital assets of this nature. I can offer no explanation, other than sampling bias, why the possession of tools does not show the expected correlation. Leaders did appear to own more trade 'luxuries', however, such as blankets, kerosene lamps, and items of clothing, although this is based on an incomplete quantitative assessment. My figures for cash in hand are also unreliable (even my closest informants would dissimulate about money), so I have not given them. It was apparent, however, that leaders of all ages had more ready cash than most non-leaders. Each time a youth returns to his hamlet following a spell of wage-labour, the hamlet 'bossman' can expect to be given a few dollars as an act of deference by whoever distributes the money. Token gratuities also find their way into the hands of the 'bossman' whenever cash for a bride or the occasional sale of copra comes into the hamlet. The Kalauna leader is hardly a 'banker', however, and much of the cash he receives thus is generally spent on his own behalf, though he may occasionally be approached for a 'loan' by a needy kinsman. He may be said to invest on behalf of his group sometimes, as when he buys piglets for future exchanges, or tinned meat and rice for various minor celebrations. Even though his group, as well as he, cannot consume these things, the prestige of giving belongs to both, and later there will be equivalent returns.

TABLE 10 *Wealth of Kalauna leaders and non-leaders: 1966*

Age group	Number of individuals bracketed		Native valuables	European tools	Pigs	Gardens
			Figures in these columns are averages			
35–40	Leader	(1)	6	6	5	6
	Non-leaders	(3)	1	7	1	7
40–45	Leaders	(5)	7	6	3	10
	Non-leaders	(5)	3	5	1	8
45–50	Leaders	(1)	?	5	3	8
	Non-leaders	(2)	0	6	0	5
50–55	Leaders	(2)	4	3	1·5	5
	Non-leaders	(2)	1	5	0·5	6
55–60	Leader	(1)	3	3	2	6
	(No non-leaders interviewed in this group)					
All age groups	Leaders	(10)	5	5	3	8
	Non-leaders	(12)	1·7	5·7	0·75	7

Leaders with special (usually magical) expertise are favourably placed to gain extra shell valuables, cash, piglets, food, seed yams and trade goods of various kinds, in payment for their services. Curers such as Kimaola, Nadeweya and Kaulubu, and protective magic experts such as Bwanakovi and Kafataudi, are in frequent demand by clientele from beyond as well as from within the village. Even those few leaders whose proficiency and enthusiasm for gardening amounts to an obsession find opportunities to capitalize materially from them; Yeneku makes regular sales of food at the patrol post, while Wakasilele has been known to sell his large yams to men

88 *Fighting with food*

in other villages wishing to best their rivals in competitive exchange. These and other methods of acquiring greater wealth in valuables, cash and pigs are open also to the non-leader with the appropriate qualifications. The fact that leaders appear to be the more wealthy is due both to the preponderance of such qualifications among them and to their being better placed to exploit them through their greater renown. In short, leaders in Kalauna tend to be wealthy because they are leaders; they are not leaders because they are wealthy.

Wealth in land and trees conferred by a favourable inheritance is subject to the same principle. There is no shortage of garden land in Kalauna and flexible rules of usufruct permit equitable distributions and minimize competition for land between groups. A man with plenty of surplus land cannot capitalize on it by exacting rent or favours for its use. If he tried to do so, those who had asked his permission to use it would immediately go elsewhere. Thus, land is not seen as a commodity to be manipulated in the interests of ambition. The same applies to the tree-borne products of the land. Coconuts, betel nut, breadfruit and other valuable trees are inherited in the same way as land, but I found no correlation between leadership and the number of such trees possessed. With increasing copra production, one might expect a person owning many coconut trees to be able to avail himself of some of the status attributes of leaders: a circle of helpers, an extra wife, more pigs, and even native valuables – which can be purchased, albeit with difficulty. Although there is some evidence of this happening elsewhere on the island, it has yet to occur in Kalauna where traditional leadership is still too firmly entrenched. One of my more enterprising informants regarded his copra-making activities as a disqualification for his otherwise valid candidature for the leadership of his hamlet. They brought him a measure of wealth but cast doubt on his potential interest and involvement in traditional spheres of activity. It may be that, as Kalauna people assert, 'money is boss' but the mere possession of money does not entitle one to boss others (cf. Oliver 1955, p. 203).

Gardens

Perhaps the most ambiguous column in Table 10 is the one which gives the average number of gardens worked by the individuals in each category, for although sizes were crudely standardized to balance the count, neither gross size nor number of gardens are ultimately diacritical in the indigenous definition of *tofaha* (lit. 'garden man'). This is one of the most central components of the leader stereotype, and one which is basic to native conceptions of achievement. I shall be concerned with this aspect of leadership in the following chapters and I defer a discussion of gardening

and its evaluation by Kalauna people until then; here I merely point out
that a leader's reputation as a *tofaha* may have more to do with quality
than quantity. This was brought home forcibly to me after measuring
some yam gardens and counting the mounds (i.e. yams) within them.
Men and their wives garden adjacent plots, which tend to be equal in size
and to have a similar number of tubers planted in them; but I was
intrigued by one or two cases of women who planted alone and far
surpassed the plot size worked, and the number of yams planted, of some
men who were accredited *tofaha*. I was dissuaded by my assistants from
pointing this out to such men, as any reflection on a man's gardening
prowess is a blow to his self-esteem, and to offer him statistical proof of a
woman's greater productive output would be to convince him that my
only object was to insult him. A partial answer was offered without
approaching these *tofaha* – it emerged that they were renowned for the
size of their individual yams. One of the women whose garden was larger
than theirs seemed flattered to have it mentioned to her, but admitted that
her yams could not compete with theirs in size. Similar criteria apply to
taro and banana gardening (see Chapter 7). For what it is worth, however,
Table 10 indicates that leaders in Kalauna tend to have more and bigger
gardens of all types than non-leaders.

Sorcery

It was stated earlier that a dozen or so Kalauna leaders had 'big names',
that is, renown well beyond the community. Wide renown is a corollary
of a leader's reputation in his own village, although certain aspects spread
with more facility than others. Prominent among these is fame gained
through participation in competitive exchanges and festivals, which is to be
discussed in later chapters. But no less common is fame based on a reputed
knowledge of sorcery. Along with other magical techniques sorcery is for
the most part inherited patrilineally, though it may also be purchased or
otherwise obtained from other categories of kin, through *solama* friendships
in other villages, or from 'foreign' working companions in other areas of
Papua. It proved difficult to investigate systematically the ownership of
sorcery techniques because few people willingly admit to knowing them.
Their possession is an open secret, however, and fairly general agreement
was reached between informants who were less reticent when discussing
the techniques belonging to others. The following table compares non-
leaders with the thirteen accredited leaders of 'big name'.

Only four of the acknowledged big-men are believed to lack any
knowledge of sorcery, and this factor was used by informants to explain
their retiring behaviour in some circumstances. Fear of sorcery dogs

almost everyone in Kalauna, and while it makes for superficially amicable, circumspect and polite social relations, it contributes greatly to, or may even create, the tenseness and oppression which a visitor can sense in the community. While it is an undoubted source of social control, fear of sorcery is also a significant limiting factor inhibiting leaders from exercising their full talents. I was told repeatedly by leaders that they had at various times cut back their garden production or killed off their pigs to avoid being objects of sorcery attack.

TABLE II *Distribution of sorcery techniques among Kalauna men*

(A)

	Leaders	Non-leaders	Total
Number of sorcery techniques attributed	56 (30%)	128 (70%)	184
Total leaders and non-leaders	13 (11%)	106 (89%)	119

(B)

Number of techniques attributed to individuals	0	1	2	3	4	5	6	7	8	9	10	11	12	13
Number of men to whom attributed	48	29	20	9	4	4	—	1	1	—	—	—	2	1

SUMMARY: Average number of techniques per leader: 4·3
Average number of techniques per non-leader: 1·2
40% of the men are believed to know none at all
Only 5 men are believed to know more than 5 techniques and 4 of these are leaders.

Fear of sorcery also appears to restrain most leaders from seeking pre-eminence in the community. If there was any exception in recent years it was Tobowa the first village constable (from *c.* 1945–61), who died of tuberculosis in 1963. Such was this man's reputation that I learnt more about him than about many Kalauna big-men still living. He was widely known as a man of prodigious strength and fierce temper. As a village constable his personal forcefulness was enhanced by government sanction, though it would have undoubtedly surprised the Administration to learn of his local infamy as a ruthless sorcerer and occasional necrophagist. It was Tobowa's sorcery (which is still thought to be wreaking havoc through his several heirs) for which people feared him rather than his physical strength or government office (see Chapter 6). Kimaola (the man who is credited with thirteen techniques in Table 11), is believed to have killed him finally, after Tobowa had been weakened by the tuberculosis inflicted years before by another rival.

The deaths of five Kalauna men (two of them leaders) within about five years were linked in the following manner. A number of reliable informants were in substantial agreement regarding this nightmarish sequence, but such is the secretive nature of the subject of sorcery that it is quite impossible to be certain how many other Kalauna people would interpret these deaths in the same way.

Trouble flared between two Kalauna leaders over an adultery case. Tobowa (of Anuana II, Lulauvile clan) beat the adulterous wife of a hamlet 'brother', but he was stopped by Towakaita (of Nouneya clan), a powerful sorcerer in his own right and one of the big-men of his day. Towakaita intervened to try to get Tobowa to take the adulterous pair to Esa'ala for a court hearing, reminding him that it was his duty as village constable to do so. Tobowa's response was to hit Towakaita too. Towakaita then resolved to sorcerize Tobowa. He conspired with Tomolele, a friend from Anuana I (Lulauvile clan), who was also an intimate of Tobowa. With instructions to hand it to Tobowa, Towakaita gave Tomolele tobacco bespelled with *yobiyobi* sorcery, which is believed to cause tuberculosis. 'Like Judas', as an informant said, Tomolele did so, and soon Tobowa was wracked by the disease. He is thought to have suspected Tomolele's betrayal, however, for within a year the latter and his brother, Kabudaiya, were dead – killed, people said, by Tobowa's vengeance sorcery. He had also attacked Inavelena, another man from Anuana I, but Kimaola (Heloava II) was able to cure him. Whether for this reason or because he was jealous of Kimaola's rising star as a leader of promise, Tobowa struck next at Kimaola with his sorcery. Kimaola was able to cure himself, however, and when he had recovered he planned his own revenge. First he afflicted Tobowa with *kasiwala*, a mild paralysis which kept him house-bound; then in his own good time he 'captured' Tobowa's voice in a bespelled tin. Kimaola is remembered as having predicted the precise moment of Tobowa's death, and when the moment came Tobowa did indeed die.

The only persons genuinely to mourn Tobowa were his own children. His albino son Siusiu, who had inherited most of his father's magic, was angered by the reactions of pleased relief which most people expressed. In order to 'frighten people and punish them for their disrespect', Siusiu sang a *valeimu'imu* spell to bring wind and the threat of spoiled gardens. He was particularly infuriated by the behaviour of Towakaita, moreover, who not only refused to disguise his joy at his enemy's death, but also encouraged Tobowa's young widow to ignore the customary mourning taboos. Towakaita personally sent her 'good food' to eat, and invited her (a classificatory sister) to live in his house. Siusiu did nothing about 'punishing' his father's widow (even though she was not his own mother), but he is thought to have sent a *yafuna*, an agent of mystical attack, to kill Towakaita, who died within the year.

An alternative reason for Towakaita's death was given by some informants. A fellow Nouneya clansman called Vaneveya had given money to his *venima'abi* Ilukwalukwa to help pay for a shot-gun the latter wanted to buy. Ilukwalukwa gave his first kill – a large wild pig – to Towakaita to distribute among his clansmen. Vaneveya, who felt that he deserved an extra-large share, was angered to receive a considerably smaller piece than Towakaita allocated for himself so he made sorcery against Towakaita and killed him. The latter's *unuma* retaliated, and it is suggested that Vaneveya, who died within a few months, was killed by Kafataudi's sorcery.

Evidence was accumulating by the time I left Kalauna that Kimaola was treading Tobowa's path to local despotism by the coercive use of sorcery, although his initial reputation was founded upon curing rather than killing. Kalauna leaders are not usually prepared to risk their lives, or those of their children by attempting to 'eliminate' their rivals, whether by sorcery or other means. And even Kimaola, if he proves to be an exception, still appeared to subscribe to general belief when he made frequent rhetorical references in public to the early death he anticipated for himself.

Wives

Although it was never suggested to me that polygyny is a characteristic attribute of leaders, there is a statistical correlation.

TABLE 12 *Polygyny of Kalauna leaders and non-leaders*

	Leaders	Non-leaders	Total
Polygynous marriages	5	7	12
Total leaders and non-leaders	13	106	119

The figures in Table 12 require some comment. Firstly, no man in Kalauna has more than two wives and I heard of only one case elsewhere on Goodenough of a man with three. Secondly, the figures for plural marriages in the table cover the entire period of my association with Kalauna. Some were contracted during these twenty-two months and others were dissolved through death or divorce. There were three polygynous leaders and only one polygynous non-leader when I arrived, but during the next twenty-two months two more leaders and six more non-leaders acquired extra wives, while one leader lost a wife through death and two non-leaders lost wives through divorce. Patterned differences are obvious between the two groups. All polygynous non-leaders are men under thirty years of age. Their secondary marriages are contracted typically with single girls a few years their junior and appear to be motivated by caprice rather than ambition or economic considerations. The second, younger wife is at a decided disadvantage to her senior co-wife. Bickering is common between them and the junior wife frequently dissolves the marriage by leaving her husband. On the other hand, all polygynous leaders are over forty. Here, economic interest rather than caprice appears to be the main motive for secondary unions, and such marriages tend to be highly stable – if only because the second wife is likely to be a widow or divorcée with diminishing marital opportunities.

Given the tendency of established hamlet leaders to seek an extra wife, it is perhaps curious that the advantages of polygyny should be so under-stated, for I was unable to satisfy myself that Kalauna men saw polygyny as a means of political advancement or as an appropriate index of status which big-men should seek to attain. While it was recognized, for instance, that a well-organized polygynous household is more productive than a monogamous one, no-one tried to explain a particular leader's success in exchange activities in these terms. A certain deceased Kalauna man is remembered for his five wives – but for nothing else. Far from making comment on his prestige or political status, informants were content to remark that his love-magic must have been very strong. These attitudes, however, are in line with the configuration of behavioural norms and values: the egalitarian ethic, the muted competition of politics played in low key, and the smiling dissimulation in the face of sorcery fears which tries to deny that there *is* competition. There is another good reason why the economic and political advantages conferred by polygyny are not extolled – they have their reciprocal disadvantages. Under the Goodenough marriage system the wife-taker is under permanent obligation to the wife-givers. It is thus the man with many sisters rather than the man with many wives who is better placed to benefit from affinal relationships. It is not the case in Kalauna, as it is in some other New Guinea societies, that polygynous unions are valued by leaders for the affinal linkages they create (cf. for example, Malinowski 1929, pp. 110 *et seq.*; Strathern 1966, p. 330).

Dependents and helpers

Leaders tend to have more children and other dependents than non-leaders. The average household size for our thirteen leaders is five; for married non-leaders of the same age range the figure is 4·2. Yet attitudes are not unequivocal on the value of young dependents and it is thought, for instance, that too many children are a handicap to would-be leaders since they consume food which might otherwise be used for political ends. One of the reasons offered for Bwanakovi's assumption of Ukevakeva's leadership in favour of his elder brother, was that the latter had too many dependent children 'eating up his gardens'. It was also said of Iyahalina that he could only become a leader once his six children became effective producers as well as consumers. Clearly, the particular stage of the domestic group cycle has considerable bearing on a leader's capabilities. If they are an obstacle to achievement when they are very young, children can be an obvious asset when mature. The continuing prominence of the older leaders in Kalauna may partly be explained by their broods of young workers. But here again, as in polygyny, the principle is not clear-cut. Women are not highly valued for their child-bearing capacity, and it is notable that of the ten wives of the five polygynous leaders, three appear to be sterile. Moreover, in the sexually inhibited culture of Kalauna, virility as evidenced by numerous progeny is something of which to be ashamed rather than proud, since it indicates an unseemly preoccupation with sexual intercourse. Finally, it is sometimes said that a man with many children is vulnerable; several fathers have tales to tell of how their sins of ambition were visited upon their children by sorcery.

TABLE 13   *Helpers of thirteen Kalauna leaders of renown: August 1967*

Leader	Clan agnates	Adult males over 16 Maternal kinsmen	Affines	Other	Adult females	Total
Yaneku	2	2	—	—	6	10
Didiala	7	—	—	—	11	18
Kimaola	5	—	1	—	7	13
Iyahalina	5	1	—	—	7	13
Malawidiya	10	—	—	—	10	20
Wakasilele	14	—	—	—	12	26
Tabwaika	3	—	—	—	2	5
Neailena	2	—	—	—	4	6
Bwanakovi	13	—	—	—	14	27
Ilukwalukwa	2	—	—	1	6	9
Nadeweya	3	1	—	1	9	14
Kafataudi	9	1	—	—	8	18
Kaulubu	9	1	—	—	9	19
Total	84	6	1	2	105	198

It is axiomatic that a leader must have followers, and it is logical to assume that in an acephalous society structured by localized, agnatic descent groups in which leadership is based on a hereditary principle, most of a leader's support will be derived from his co-resident agnatic kinsmen. As later chapters will show, the recruitment of 'followers' for specific purposes is rather more complex, but the general tenet that 'primary' allegiance is based on descent group membership and hamlet residence is not invalidated. Although it is in a sense a spurious demonstration of a known connection, Table 13 shows that the thirteen leaders of renown draw 90% of their basic support from clansmen.

There is no Kalauna word for 'follower'. A leader's supporters are his 'helpers' (*toleme*), which in English appropriately conveys the free and transactional quality of the relationship between a leader and those from whom he expects support in dealings with other groups. A leader's helpers, then, are composed of his own domestic group, his patrilineage and other members of his hamlet; and beyond that and in certain circumstances, his *venima'abi* and *fofofo*, his sisters' and daughters' husbands, his own mother's *unuma* and those men he calls *dala*, *weyo* etc. The extent of help he receives from those beyond his hamlet depends on their own primary allegiances. Helpers from this sphere are never a known quantity; they are obliged or constrained by factors I shall examine in later chapters.

In the fields of endeavour which matter most to Kalauna leaders – food exchanges and festivals – the working strength of dependents and hamlet helpers must be matched and supplemented by individual *venima'abi* partners and the wider *fofofo* group. Leaders are only as big as their *venima'abi* and *fofofo* allow. The mutual dependence of *fofofo* groups means that a leader with a weak *venima'abi* partner is considerably handicapped by his inability to initiate major food exchanges or festivals. 'He stays uselessly' as informants put it, being forced to let up the opportunities to 'make his name big', though the evidence suggests that there is incentive feedback; a potential big-man can inspire a weak *venima'abi* to become more worthy of him. It is true, however, that four of the five biggest men in Kalauna constitute two *venima'abi* pairs, and it is perhaps significant that the biggest man in Kalauna's traditional history – the despot Malaveyoyo – is said to have had two such partners.

Succession to leadership

In this section I introduce substantive case material on eight leaders (four *venima'abi* pairs), principally to illustrate modes of succession but also to exemplify some of the general points made about leadership and its status attributes in the discussion above. Some of the material presented here foreshadows later discussions on food exchanges and festivals, for it is

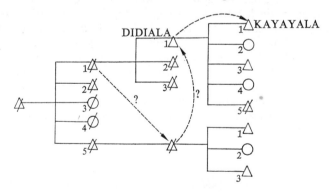

Genealogy 1. Skeleton genealogy of Didiala's *unuma*

through these agencies that ambitious young men draw attention to themselves and established leaders consolidate or extend their influence and renown. It will be seen that succession to the position of 'bossman' is usually a gradual process, and that it involves the 'grooming' of a pre-selected heir, whose assumption of the tasks of leadership is phased to coincide with the gradual retirement of his predecessor. This is particularly evident with regard to those Lulauvile leaders who are 'ritual guardians' (dealt with first below); for the amount of esoteric knowledge transmitted by a *toitavealata* to his heir is considerably greater than that possessed by leaders belonging to other clans.

Didiala of Anuana I

In his late sixties, Didiala is the most senior member of Anuana I and one of the oldest men in the village. Now quite frail and almost blind, he considers himself retired from the leadership of the hamlet. He see his present role as 'only to tell stories' (i.e. myths, tradition). Yet he remains, largely on account of his reputation for harmful magic and ability to influence the health of the gardens, one of the three most important men in the village. He bears himself with considerable dignity and is held in wide esteem and even awe by people within and beyond the village.

As a child Didiala had been reared in Anuana II, his mother's hamlet, and only returned to his own after he had married. It is not clear who was its leader at that time, but Didiala did not forfeit his own right to the leadership by his long residence elsewhere, and he took it over within a few years of his return. He was known then as a gardener of prodigious energy and claims to have sponsored a number of festivals and competitive exchanges.

Kayayala, Didiala's eldest son, is in his late thirties and he has long since inherited his father's shell valuables and control of the *unuma* land. He is also believed to have learnt his father's magic in preparation for his assumption of the role of *toitavealata*. Indeed, some informants – among them Didiala himself – were of the opinion that Kayayala had already 'taken his father's place' as *de facto* 'bossman' of the hamlet; and as proof of this it was pointed out to me that it is Kayayala's name, not his father's, which is called out to receive food and pig during distributions. Kayayala's reputation as a gardener of *tofaha* class is not well-established, however, and he is milder mannered and much less forceful than his father. Although he had inherited part of his father's renown through the latter's name, before it is forgotten Kayayala will need to build up a reputation for himself. At the present, despite the nominal transference of hamlet leadership to Kayayala, he remains very much in the old man's shadow in village affairs.

Iyahalina of Heloava I

Iyahalina is Didiala's *venima'abi* and wife's classificatory brother. Approaching sixty years of age, he is probably among the most intelligent men in the village;

a witty and forceful orator possessing a fund of traditional knowledge.[1] Like Didiala, he too sees his main role as guardian of the 'stories' (*nainiya*), although he would be the last to admit that he is ready for retirement from the active leadership of Heloava. It is not so long since he attained it in fact. After the tyrant Malaveyoyo's death (supposedly just before European contact), his youngest son Kaweya became Heloava's leader; he was succeeded by two of his sons, the second of whom taught all the magic of this important descent group to Kedeya and Iyahalina. Kedeya was 'bossman' until his death about 1962 when Iyahalina took his place. Iyahalina had never been regarded as a gardener of merit, and being a widower incapable of feeding even his own six children, it is highly improbable that he would have succeeded to the hamlet leadership in competitive circumstances. As it was, at Kedeya's death he was the oldest male member of this Lulauvile segment and the only person, moreover, to know its hereditary magic and lore. The opportunity also came late enough for him to have been released of the burden of trying to provide for his children; with one exception they were mature enough to feed themselves.

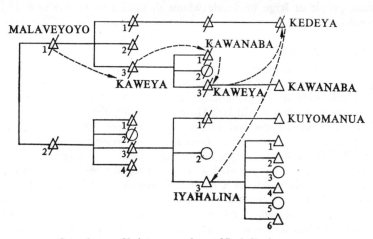

Genealogy 2. Skeleton genealogy of Iyahalina's *unuma*

Iyahalina is training for the succession his brother's son Kuyomanua and Kaweya's son Kawanaba. Kuyomanua is the elder and is considered the 'favourite', for Iyahalina publicly refers to him as the one who will take his place. Although Kawanaba's father and grandfather were 'bossmen' of Heloava in their time, Kawanaba himself has mixed feelings about the possibility of his failing to achieve it. On the one hand, he is anxious to learn all the magic that his father

---

[1] More than any other informant Iyahalina gave me the impression that he comprehended the whole of his culture. He was certainly capable of philosophizing about it and I owe many insights to him. Unfortunately he was rarely a forthcoming informant, being I imagine, deeply suspicious of my motives; and although he made a grand gesture of initiating me into his 'secrets' and intellectual lore just before I left the field, I am convinced that he told me only a fraction of what he knew. Certainly, he tantalized and manipulated me as no other informant did.

taught Iyahalina; he is also jealous and slighted when his name is not called at
food distributions as Kuyomanua's often is. On the other hand, Kawanaba is
admittedly afraid of becoming a Lulauvile *toitavealata* and lists the names of
his antecedents whose lives were 'cut in the middle' by exposure to sorcery
attack. It is for this reason, he maintains, that he has all but turned his back on
the village by spending many years working abroad and by turning his energies
to copra-making when he returned – conduct which he knew would weaken his
candidature for Iyahalina's position.

Should Iyahalina die soon, the question of succession will probably remain
open for a while, until either Kuyomanua or Kawanaba makes some definitive
public act to assert himself over the other; initiating a food exchange or performing one of the collective rites which are their prerogative would serve as acceptable
demonstrations of fitness. Alternatively, others in the community might take
the initiative by singling out one of them to receive pig or food at a major
distribution. This would be less conclusive but it would indicate public endorse-
ment of a successor, and Kawanaba has expressed his willingness to allow
Kalauna people at large to decide whom they wish to be the next Heloava
toitavealata.

Kimaola of Heloava II

Physically Kimaola is puny, resembling at first sight a rather stunted adolescent,
though he is approaching fifty years of age. His nickname, Kafama (Skinny),
refers particularly to his remarkably concave stomach, the legacy of some
affliction gained during World War II on the Kokoda Trail.[1] Despite his almost
child-like delicacy of frame and feature and his understandably weak gardening
capacity, Kimaola is probably the most feared and respected man in the community. This is due less to his ritual control of the yams and his other *toitavealata*
competences than to his personal armoury of formidable sorcery techniques.
He has island-wide repute as a curer and sorcerer and is believed to be as
invincible as he is fearless. At least three other Kalauna leaders are also greatly
feared for their knowledge of sorcery, but none of these possess Kimaola's
thick-skinned opportunism and sheer courage in publicly confessing to sorcery-
making when it seems to his political advantage to do so. Being endowed with
three sisters and no brothers to challenge him, Kimaola would be very favourably
placed by his forebears had they not also failed to provide him with any male
agnatic support at all. Kimaola's *unuma* genealogy can be given in full, so slender
is it.

Kimaola's main problem in replacing his father as 'bossman' of Heloava II
was to create a following in this generation and heirs for his hamlet's continuity
in the next. Having had four wives without producing any offspring by them,
the extinction of his line was clearly imminent.

---

[1] Kimaola shares with Bwanakovi the distinction of being the only Kalauna men to
have served as carriers during this epic chapter of Australian military history. There
could be few less appropriate descriptions of Kimaola, however, than 'fuzzy-wuzzy
angel', though it is perhaps ironic that in Kalauna the term *analosi*, derived from biblical
'angels', is thought to refer to *kwahala*, agents of mystical attack analogous to witches'
familiars, which are believed to be manipulated by Kimaola and other sorcerers.

Kimaola has solved the problem of a dearth of close agnatic supporters in the classical manner of Melanesian big-men: by attracting young men from elsewhere to settle his empty hamlet. This has been facilitated by overcrowding in the neighbouring hamlet of Anuana I. The five young men who joined him over the past several years are the remnants of a once numerically powerful *unuma* which has more recently been overshadowed by Didiala's burgeoning group. Since Kimaola's hamlet belongs to the same Lulauvile clan-section as Anuana I, these young men did not forfeit anything – save possibly their children's right to house sites in Anuana I – by joining him. They have ample land of their own and provided they stay with Kimaola they will probably inherit some of his too.

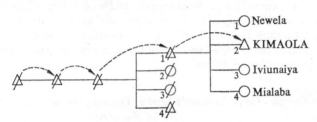

Genealogy 3. Kimaola's *unuma*

At least three of these young men were fed by Kimaola as children so they owe him the usual obligations due to a *faiyeya* or foster-father. His last marriage to a widow brought the opportunity to bind her two children to him in the same way. Not satisfied with these heirs and supporters, Kimaola approached his sister's husband Kafataudi a few years ago and asked to be given one of his three sons to rear. According to witnesses, when Kafataudi refused Kimaola took the child anyway and said it would die if Kafataudi should try to get it back. Now aged about eleven the child still lives with Kimaola.

In 1967 a further windfall brought more children into the hamlet. His elder sister Newela was widowed and brought her four children with her when she returned to live with her brother.[1] About a year later Kimaola married her off to Iyahalina in a well-timed political move. Her two male children remained with their mother's brother. Finally, just before I left Kalauna, a quarrel in Wailolo village resulted in a pair of brothers and their wives seeking refuge in Kimaola's hamlet, where their maternal kin from Anuana I were already living. To complete the list, Kimaola was sheltering a son of Tobowa (who died in 1963) until 1967, when he sent him back to his mother in Buveta after the lad had been seen stealing eggs ('in case you spoil my name with your thefts'). Table 14 summarizes the social composition of Heloava II at October 1966 and June 1968, the dates of my first and last Kalauna house census. Over the twenty months in between its membership increased by nine.

[1] Although it is usual for the dead husband's brothers to keep his children, in this case these men seemed quite happy to let them go, having several children of their own. The possibility of Kimaola having 'persuaded' the brothers to relinquish them cannot be entirely ruled out, however. Kimaola's only response to my queries was 'Herself', meaning that it was Newela's decision to bring her children with her.

A significant point about this extreme (and for Kalauna quite unique) example of the building of personal support by a big-man, is the way that it was accomplished without antagonizing – except for Kafataudi – the true agnates of the persons displaced. With one exception (and possibly also that of Newela's children) they were individuals, sibling sets or families already detached by natural processes from the wider descent groups to which they belonged. This applies even in the Wailolo case, for the two brothers were the only living male members of their *unuma*. With the exceptions mentioned, Kimaola did not need to prise them from other allegiances in order to attach them to himself. Most were, in a sense, social refugees in a society where descent group membership is of considerable importance for personal security and well-being. While equipping himself with a sizeable group of helpers and potential heirs, Kimaola reciprocally offered them through his firm leadership the benefits of social and economic security, as well as the reflected prestige of belonging to the group of one of the most powerful men in the district.

TABLE 14   *Composition of Kimaola's hamlet: October 1966 and June 1968*

Name	Sex	Hamlet of origin	Relationship to Kimaola
Residents at October 1966			
Kimaola	m.	Heloava II	—
Wa'aula	f.	Lalaveya	Wife
Tayaune	f.	Anuana II	Wife
Wadinavai	m.	Ukevakeva	Wife's son
Modinaiya	f.	Aluwaita	Wife's son's wife
Ivivi	f.	Ukevakeva	Wife's daughter
Matalokonina	m.	Valeutoli	Sister's son
Ewahaluna	m.	Anuana I	Classificatory son
Ubwana	m.	Anuana I	Classificatory son
Kiyodi	m.	Anuana I	Classificatory son
Kafama	f.	Mulina	Kiyodi's wife
Siyoka	m.	Anuana I	Classificatory son
Anavavine	f.	Ukevakeva	Siyoka's wife
Dimileleya	m.	Anuana I	Classificatory son
Awa'ebaiya	f.	Valeutoli	Dimeleleya's wife
Five children of the last three couples			Classificatory grandchildren
Additional persons present in June 1968			
Adienana	m.	Daulu'u	Sister's son
Kimaola	m.	Daulu'u	Sister's son
Kayaluwa	m.	Wailolo village	Siyoka's FZS
E'enaiya	f.	Wailolo village	Kayaluwa's wife
Vinedewa	f.	Ukevakeva	Kayaluwa's brother's wife
(Kayaluwa's brother was working abroad.)			
Three more children of original residents			Classificatory grandchildren

Summary:	Adults		Children		Total
	m.	f.	m.	f.	
Oct. 1966	7	6	3	4	20
June 1968	8	8	7	5	28

It is significant that with the consolidation of his group strength, Kimaola saw fit to sponsor a Fakili festival late in 1967, which was still flourishing when I left the field several months later. On a number of occasions during this period Kimaola made public references to his chosen heir, Kiyodi, and he let it be known that he was teaching him all his magic, including the yam lore and spells which are the prerogative of this segment of Lulauvile. Kiyodi is thus clearly marked as its next *toitavealata*, and has already performed a number of rites on Kimaola's behalf. It was interesting to observe the increased deference with which this rather shy young man was treated by members of the community at large; for the point was fully taken that if Kiyodi was to inherit Kimaola's ritual knowledge he would also thereby inherit his power for good or evil, and it was wise to be wary. The choice of Kiyodi rather than any of the other four men who joined Kimaola was neither random nor based entirely on personal preference. As the genealogy shows, Kiyodi is the most senior male of this *unuma* and his father, some say, was Anuana's 'bossman' before Didiala became leader some twenty-five years ago.

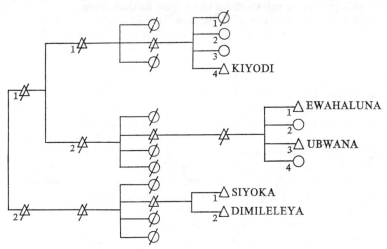

Genealogy 4. Skeleton genealogy of Kiyodi's *unuma*

Malawidiya of Anuana II

Although not an imposing or volatile man like Wakasilele, Kalauna's other young 'bossman' Malawidiya was an energetic gardener and a leader of quiet strength. Anuana II, Malawidiya's hamlet, is divided into two sections composed of two *unuma* each. The genealogically senior section holds the Lulauvile magic and lore brought from Yauyaba, but it defers to the other, junior section in the matter of hamlet leadership because it is the more recent arrival on the site. The senior section is *fofofo* to Aluwaita, and the junior section to Heloava II, Kimaola's hamlet.

When Enobwau the previous leader of Anuana II died, the only suitable candidate for his role was Malawidiya, even though he belonged to the junior *unuma* of the junior section. However, with Kimaola's help as *venima'abi*, he sponsored a successful Fakili festival in 1964 and thereby 'spread his name' and confirmed his position. Kimaola initiated his own festival a few years later and thus gave Malawidiya the opportunity to reciprocate his help.

Tragically and unexpectedly, however, Malawidiya died when the festival was scarcely six months old. In contravention of customary burial procedures, Kimaola and his group buried Malawidiya, ostensibly as a mark of their respect and mourning, though they refused to accept death payments from his kin. After the burial Kimaola spoke about stopping his Fakili festival but he was prevailed upon, by Iyahalina mainly, to let it continue as a form of memorial to Malawidiya. In fine political style Kimaola let himself be persuaded, though he assured the meeting that he was signing his own death warrant (i.e. inviting vindictive sorcery attacks) by allowing the Fakili to continue. Obviously, he had not wanted to squash prematurely the vehicle of his fame, and his undertaking of the burial duties and refusal of death payments can be interpreted as a move to secure public sympathy for himself, and to convey a sense of propriety to the dead man's kin before manoeuvring to keep his festival going.

If the Fakili festival was to continue, however, the problem immediately arose as to whom was to be Malawidiya's successor as leader of the *fofofo*. In ordinary circumstances a new leader would emerge in the course of time; in this instance one was required immediately.[1] There were only four possibilities: Enobwau's son Kwalaiwaka, Monaiya, Adikwaikwai, and Kabunuwa. (The remaining four men of Anuana II, who belonged to the senior *unuma*, were *fofofo* to Aluwaita. Kwalaiwaka was the most obvious choice since both his father and grandfather had been Anuana II 'bossmen' in their time, and although still a very young man he was known to be an industrious gardener. Iyahalina virtually nominated him as Malawidiya's successor in a speech at the burial. Monaiya, although a fully mature man, was considered to be a poor gardener and was publicly described as such by Kimaola while he was discussing the succession. Adikwaikwai was scarcely considered at all, for he was a timid bachelor, a gardener of no account and accordingly something of a figure of fun. Kabunuwa finally, had uncertain status as an *eda natuna*, 'a child of the road', or bastard. Neither his mother nor genitor were from Anuana II but he had been adopted and reared there by a childless Anuana man whose land he inherited when he died.

These were the candidates for the leadership of the Anuana II *fofofo* in the order of popular support. It was believed that Kimaola's decision would be crucial since the matter vitally concerned his festival. When the Fakili celebrations were resumed Kwalaiwaka did indeed take over some of the functions of the *fofofo* leader. But at the first major food distribution, held about a month after the burial, it was clear that Monaiya was the most prominent of the candidates, and Iyahalina was conspicuously 'training' him in the duties of a *fofofo* leader. Kwalaiwaka had been deprived of the leadership by his young wife, who had left him only the week before the distribution. Without a woman in the family he was unable to cook the enormous pots of food expected of him. When I left the field a month or so later, Monaiya appeared to be firmly in the saddle as

---

[1] The *fofofo*'s role in such festivals is detailed in Chapter 11.

Anuana II's new leader while Kwalaiwaka was still wifeless and 'staying use-lessly'. Obviously, permanent leaders are not made or unmade by such simple contingencies, and the question of the succession to Malawidiya will be reopened if Kwalaiwaka's wife comes back or when he remarries. Even if Monaiya retains the position of Kimaola's chief *fofofo* for the duration of the festival, once it is finished there will be fresh opportunities for Kwalaiwaka to assert himself, and in the last analysis it will be not Kimaola but the members of his own hamlet, Anuana II, who will decide who is to be their 'bossman'.

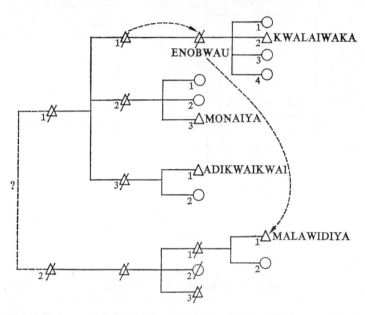

Genealogy 5. Skeleton genealogy of Kwalaiwaka's and Malawidiya's *unuma* in Anuana II

Bwanakovi of Ukevakeva

Bwanakovi is a man of impressive bearing with a deep, resonant voice. Aged about fifty-five, he is currently regarded as Ukevakeva's 'bossman' and rated as one of the biggest men in Kalauna. He is thought to know several lethal sorcery techniques and he has a considerable reputation as an industrious gardener. Until 1968 he was a polygynist, when one of his wives died of tuberculosis – supposedly inflicted upon her by sorcery many years ago to curb her own productive efforts. The succession to leadership in Ukevakeva passed from Bwanakovi's father to Vatako, his eldest son, in accordance with the rule of primogeniture. When Vatako died the second brother, Adianamatana, was passed over, and the third having already died, Bwanakovi succeeded. Although nearly ten years older than Bwanakovi, Adianamatana was deemed unsuitable for leadership, being frail, effete and soft-spoken with none of the determined and forceful bearing that distinguishes his brother. Adianamatana, moreover, had spent a considerable portion of his youth working away from the village, was an unambitious and indifferent gardener, and had six young children to feed compared to Bwanakovi's two.

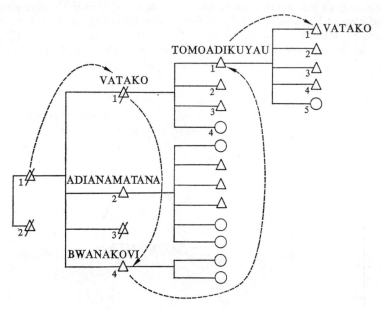

Genealogy 6. Skeleton genealogy of Bwanakovi's *unuma*

Bwanakovi assumed the leadership of Ukevakeva by sponsoring a Fakili festival shortly after the death of his eldest brother. Although he is still at the peak of maturity, he appears to be already edging aside to allow his own successor, Tomoadikuyau (Vatako's eldest son), to come into prominence. Nor does the process of 'grooming' end there. At the climax of a festival which Bwanakovi, Tomoadikuyau and a more distant agnate, Tomolaiyoko, sponsored in 1967 (see Chapter 11), there was discussion among these men as to who should act the role of *kaiwabu* at the final distribution. Bwanakovi declined on this occasion, saying that he had done it many times in the past, and he wanted Tomoadikuyau to be *kaiwabu* in his place. The latter wished to supervise the distribution of food to be carried out by the *fofofo*, however, so in turn he delegated his own adolescent son (named Vatako after his grandfather) to take his place on the *kaiwabu*'s platform. Despite Vatako's tender age and physical inability to consume the amount of betel nut normally expected of a *kaiwabu*, his father and Bwanakovi agreed it would be good training for him – for when he came to take on the leadership of Ukevakeva. Painted and bedecked with shell valuables, Vatako sat in the characteristic *kaiwabu* pose alongside his father's brothers throughout the climax of the festival. Although he remains the nominal leader of Ukevakeva, Bwanakovi was among the least conspicuous of the sponsors on this occasion. He was content to have his big-man's star eclipsed not only by his brother's son but also by his classificatory grandson. The process of 'grooming' for succession over two generations is probably unusual, but in this case it was illuminated sharply by the ceremonial roles associated with a large food distribution.

Kafataudi of Valeutoli

Leadership of Nouneya clan, which occupies the hamlet of Valeutoli, passed from Wa'afui to his brother's son Towakaita. In the decade before he died, Towakaita taught Kafataudi (his father's father's brother's son's son), all his magic and trained him for the leadership of the clan. Kafataudi was chosen because Towakaita's younger brother, Kumahelewa, had been brought up in Belebele, their mother's village, and returned only to quarrel with Towakaita and move once more to settle in Buveta. By so doing he renounced his right to the leadership of Valeutoli. The most senior man of all in this hamlet, Eda'ava, forfeited his right to lead by being a nonentity and a weak gardener. Kafataudi on the other hand, now aged about forty, showed early promise by his hard work,

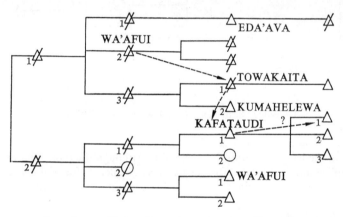

Genealogy 7. Skeleton genealogy of Kafataudi's *unuma*

ambition and active participation in Towakaita's exchange activities. By the time Towakaita died in 1965, Kafataudi was a thoroughly experienced 'bossman' and well on the way to earning a 'big name' for himself. Currently he is rated as one of the five biggest men in the village. In the event of Kafataudi's death, the leadership of the hamlet will probably pass to Wa'afui his father's brother's son, who, although older than Kafataudi, is his genealogical junior. According to rule, Towakaita's eldest son should succeed in the next generation, but Kafataudi is thought to be grooming his own eldest son, and providing he lives long enough he will probably be able to guide the boy into his own footsteps. This lad has already tasted the limelight. While his father was away in Port Moresby a few years ago, a Fakili food distribution was held at which Kafataudi's son was called to receive pig on behalf of his father. In some circumstances this is tantamount to the public recognition of a chosen heir.

Tabwaika of Lalaveya

The senior man of Foloyai clan is Tabwaika, first born of Tabueya, its previous leader. Despite the tiny size of this clan, with its adult male strength of only seven, it occupies two distinct hamlets. Tabwaika is the 'bossman' of Lalaveya; Neailena, the ex-local government councillor, is 'bossman' of Lakolakoya. Neailena is thought to be the most likely successor to Tabwaika as Foloyai's leader since Binamina, the latter's brother, spends so much time working abroad.

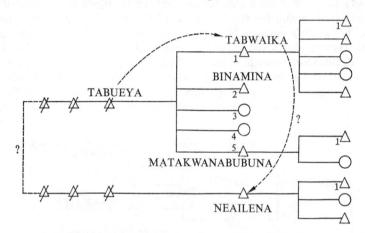

Genealogy 8. Skeleton genealogy of Tabwaika's clan

Although Tabwaika's eldest son is in his twenties it is unlikely that he will succeed to the leadership until Neailena dies. Although the possibility exists of a clear application of the rule of primogeniture, Neailena's forceful character and Tabwaika's son's youthfulness will probably cause it to be abrogated.

Wakasilele of Modimodia

Tabwaika's *venima'-abi* is Wakasilele who, still under forty, is the youngest 'bossman' in Kalauna. He is neither the eldest active male in his hamlet nor even a member of the senior line of descent. His pre-eminence in Modimodia and his clan of Malabuabua as a whole is to be attributed entirely to his domineering personality and ruthless drive. Despite his five young children he has made a name for himself as a *tofaha* – a man who can wield a food surplus to political advantage – and he is feared for this as much as for his uncertain temper and propensity to violence. Unlike Tabwaika and Neailena, Wakasilele is a *tonuakoyo* ('angry man') without the customary sanction of *dewa*. Wakasilele's achievements in the field of food production appear to rest to some extent on his strategy of tight co-ordination and control of the gardening activities of his three younger brothers, all of whom are energetic workers in their own right. While they were absent from the village for a period in 1967, earning money to buy him a shot-gun, Wakasilele pressed their wives into more vigorous service to make good the labour loss. One girl who refused to comply he sent back to her brothers.

Wakasilele has no sorcery and there is some evidence that the fact worries him. He was deeply perturbed, for instance, by the death of Malawidiya, and at the burial meeting he made a moving speech in which he likened Malawidiya to a sea-eagle (*manubutu*) 'stretching its wings and trying to stand, trying to hold together its brood, but falling down and dying'. He made it clear even by innuendo that he did not believe those who were blaming the spirits of the sea-shore for Malawidiya's untimely death.

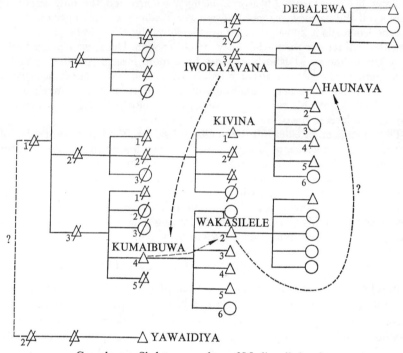

Genealogy 9. Skeleton genealogy of Modimodia hamlet

The question of who is to be Wakasilele's successor to the leadership of Modi-modia has not yet arisen, but providing Haunava outlives him, he will probably take his place. About the same age as Wakasilele and with the same number of brothers, Haunava also has the reputation of a *tofaha*. He is far less assertive, however, and although belonging to a senior line of descent, he is a generation junior to Wakasilele. Kivina, Haunava's father, had the opportunity to succeed to the leadership many years ago when Iwoka'avana died, but he never rose to it. As a young man he had shown himself to be a weak gardener, slow to pay back pig and food debts. Kumaibuwa, Wakasilele's father, emerged as the next 'bossman' until advancing age drove him into retirement and his eldest son into prominence.

Some residual authority – principally ritual – resides in these and other elders of this clan. Kivina and Kumaibuwa still hold some of the Modawa songs, while Alikaiyeya and Awatula, elders of the Malabuabua hamlets of Bulamameya

5

and Awakubawe, retain the spells and secret stories (*nainiya*) associated with the large and small Modawa drums. The possession of this ceremonial paraphernalia of the Modawa moiety by these elders means that they retain also the right to veto its use. They are said to 'boss' the songs, dances and drums, and without express permission to use them, vigorous young leaders like Wakasilele and Haunava cannot sponsor a Modawa festival. Kumaibuwa and Kivina are in process of passing on their special lore to their sons, while Awatula is likewise teaching his eldest son. Alikaiyeya, being a woman and the only surviving member of Bulamameya, cannot transmit her Modawa secrets to her own sons, but she has made it known that her grandchildren by Debalewa and her eldest daughter will receive them when they are old enough. Debalewa belongs to the most senior line of Malabuabua. Were he a more forceful personality and a better gardener he might have contested the succession to Modimodia leadership when his father's brother Iwoka'avana died. As it is he is very much under Wakasilele, despite his seniority in years. He is also pathologically afraid of sorcery and lives in his garden hut most of the time.

There is one other elder in Modimodia: Yawaidiya, the last male member of an almost extinct *unuma* of junior status. This man has no ritual control of the Modawa paraphernalia but he is respected for his pig magic, *vebawe*, which some of the other Malabuabua elders wield too, but none so successfully as he. In a prolonged quarrel with Wakasilele over the years he has, it is maintained, repeatedly driven away the latter's pigs into the bush with his magic or attracted wild ones to spoil his gardens. Flamboyant young leaders of Wakasilele's calibre are not without independent old wolves in their folds.

THE PRINCIPLES OF SUCCESSION

A number of points emerge from the examples of succession to leadership presented above. One is the extent to which the replacement of leaders is accomplished as smoothly as circumstances will allow. This is linked to another: the fact that there is a clear rule of succession which permits the early training of heirs by present leaders and their phased public acceptance by the community at large. Again, in the absence of a suitable candidate according to the rule of primogeniture, a current leader has some say in choosing his heir, though his choice will be subject to public approval expressed in such ways as 'calling out' his name to receive food for his group at distributions. Much depends upon the ambitions and abilities of the candidate himself; for a young man it is mandatory to have exceptional gardening ability, for it is this quality – summed up in the term *tofaha* – which equips a leader to participate fully in the political life of the community and pursue the goals of the culture.[1]

In Table 10 it was shown that seven of the sixteen Kalauna 'bossmen' were *not* the senior members of the genealogically senior *unuma* in their

[1] There are other aspects of the *tofaha* ideal which I discuss in detail in the following chapters.

hamlets. The general rule of primogeniture, then, expressed in the vernacular as *tomo'ainahona hi fatana* (lit. 'first-born takes his place'), proves to be only a proximate guide to the process of succession as it takes place in the context of hamlet life. Part of this context is shaped by biological factors largely beyond human control, such as differential fertility, mortality and sickness, which together operate to produce random effects of descent group growth and decline, and of individual eligibility (or otherwise) for leadership in terms of age or physical fitness. These factors, in short, produce the human material to which the rule of succession must be applied. Another part of the context is shaped by values or goal-orientations and the political process through which these are expressed and achieved. Here the rule plays a vital role in providing an explicit guide in cases when the biological or demographic circumstances are such that a number of physically eligible men are available to lead their hamlets.

GENERAL CONCLUSIONS

Having identified Kalauna leaders, discussed their status, role and substantive attributes, and having finally introduced several individual leaders in order to elucidate particular modes of achievement and succession, we are now in a position to characterize the pattern of leadership as a whole and the 'ideal type' of leader which the system appears to favour. In the main it will be obvious that these do not differ greatly from other patterns and types described in the Melanesian ethnography; though it will also be obvious that there are some differences of emphasis.

Kalauna leaders tend to belong to the senior generation. They are wealthier in pigs, gardens and shell valuables than the average non-leader and are more likely to have an extra wife. They also tend to have larger households and an average of seven adult male followers, of whom six are agnatic kinsmen. They are likely to be characterized by a 'big name' of renown, if not for gardening prowess and successful food distributions then for sorcery and other ritual powers. In personality, while being expected to demonstrate greater energy, self-discipline, oratorical skill, and somewhat more assertiveness than non-leaders, they generally try to adopt the cool and modest mien which the culture approves of in men and women, young and old alike. There is very little of the flamboyant self-aggrandizement which has been reported of big-men elsewhere in Melanesia (e.g. see Read 1959; Sahlins 1962), and even when such behaviour is ceremonially enjoined, it is usually performed self-consciously and with moderation.

Regarding their authority, there is no quality or attribute comparable to *mana* which is recognized by Goodenough peoples, and a clear distinction between a leader's personal power and his sanctioned authority is not easy to uphold. Nevertheless, I have heard the English word 'power' used in connection with Lulauvile's ritual control of the important staples, as when it was said that Kedeya brought 'power' from the ground because he carried 'a taro on his shoulder and a pig under his arm' when he emerged at Yauyaba. The appropriate term in the vernacular is *abaveimeya*: competence, ability to control, faculty. This, perhaps, may be seen as legitimate power, sanctioned by myth and tradition. It may be used of culture heroes and the modern *toitavealata* but it is not used of Malaveyoyo, the tyrant whose name is still anathema to so many, nor even of Tobowa, the despotic village constable. Although these and other men were greatly feared, however, I recorded few moral judgements regarding their arbitrary power (described in such contexts as 'strength', *toyoyi*) and no cases of such men being killed in popular revolt against their extreme conduct. Occasional despotism is probably not the worst thing the community can suffer. Droughts which threaten food shortages are the more common, while people are reminded every day of ubiquitous malignant magic and the existence in their midst of its practitioners.

The phenomenon of despots apart, there are what may be seen as structural restraints on bigmanship. There is firstly the fairly strong ideology of agnatic descent and patrilocal residence which generally ensures that a big-man's following is co-ordinate with his hamlet. A leader does not seek supporters from outside this range unless his own descent group is very small. Moreover, it is to be expected that leaders in an intermarrying community the size of Kalauna will be related to each other (frequently in more ways than one) as clan agnates, uterine kinsmen, and affines. In the language of conflict anthropology, the big-men of Kalauna are bound together by multiplex ties of customary co-operation which limit the extent of competition between them. This is also to say that although each leader represents a solidary descent group, his relationship to other leaders is not necessarily exclusively, nor even predominantly, political in nature.

It would therefore be inaccurate to say of Kalauna, as Sahlins generalizes for Melanesia (1962, p. 290), that 'leadership is a creation – a creation of followership'. Nor is it entirely true that 'personal power' is the 'indicative quality of big-man authority' (*ibid.* p. 289); nor yet again that

Big-men do not come to office; they do not succeed to, nor are they installed in, existing positions of leadership over political groups. The attainment of big-man status is rather the outcome of a series of acts which elevate a person above the common herd and attract about him a coterie of loyal, lesser men (*ibid.*).

While there is certainly an element of truth in these statements as applied to Kalauna, it is almost possible to state the opposite: that authority is socially ascribed, that leaders do assume a kind of office of hamlet headman-ship over political groups, while the attraction of followers from beyond these groups is the exception rather than the rule. It is Kimaola, a potential despot, who is the exception which proves this rule for Kalauna and also, perhaps, the general point that Sahlins appears to be making: that full-blown bigmanship is a correlate of 'loose' or 'flexible' social systems where the possibility exists for such leaders to detach allegiances and gain personal followings.[1] If the 'making of a faction . . . is the true making of the Melanesian big-man' (*ibid.* p. 291), then in Kalauna only Kimaola would begin to qualify. That he does so in other respects which exceed the norm – keen ability for political manipulation, shrewdness, opportu-nism, thickskinned courage – only goes to confirm the validity of the relationship. For the remainder of Kalauna, however, the 'tightness' of the social structure either inhibits the emergence of really big men or it obviates the need for them.

If leaders do not compete with each other for followers in Kalauna,[2] what restrains competition between the solidary groups they represent? We have noted the close-knit network of cross-cutting secondary allegiances formed by maternal kinship, marriage and fostering or 'feeding'. Further, marriage does not aggravate political conflict between groups by creating competitively useful alliances. Men, leaders included, are 'ashamed' to ask a wife's kinsmen for support and it cannot be expected as of a right. Finally, more glimpses into the operation of the *venima'abi* and *fofofo* partnership system have appeared in this chapter, and we have seen how it obliges pairs of leaders and their groups to co-operate in formal competitive circumstances. The larger clans and hamlets are cross-cut by the pattern of *fofofo* partnerships, which in some circumstances minimizes the possibility of competition and conflict within these units. The problema-tical succession to Malawidiya's place as chief *fofofo* to Kimaola, for in-stance, involved only half of Anuana II. In short, while there is some group aggrandizement in the competitive food exchanges which serve the community as its main political arena, the social structure provides its own checks and restraints on both individual and group competition.

A non-structural constraint of prime importance is fear of sorcery, and

[1] *Ibid.* p. 289 fn. '. . . the greater the self-regulation of the political process through a lineage system, the less the function that remains to big-men, and the less significant their political authority.'
[2] On the other hand it may be said that Kalauna leaders compete in a general sense to have their hamlet members acknowledge them as leaders, 'big-men', etc. That is, while they do not compete for followers, they do compete for reputation.

this has been alluded to throughout the chapter. Kalauna leaders are not notable risk-takers, and they do not appear to realize their full potential. Sorcery beliefs seem to be a potent factor in stifling ambition in the sphere of food production and pig rearing. Even Kimaola was 'normally' circumspect. I found him a comparatively poor man when I first made his acquaintance, which ill-fitted both his reputation and the indigenous dictum that a big-man is a wealthy man. It emerged that he had merely disposed of all his pigs and practised penury for awhile, as most other leaders find it advisable to do from time to time. Indeed, this differentiates the clever big-man from the upstart, the *tonualaka* (lit. 'man whose mind rises' – i.e. above itself) who is heading for trouble by his ostentation. The force of Oliver's observation on the apparent anonymity of the Siuai *mumi* (1955, p. xviii), is increased by the appreciation that Kalauna leaders deliberately disguise their status and tend wilfully to minimize those attributes which mark them out from their fellows. The difference remains, however, that a poor big-man is voluntarily so, and quite capable of being relatively wealthy when he deems it safe or advantageous.

The question arises, what of the stature of big-men in the past? Was it very much different in the pre-contact era? Without anticipating some of the conclusions of later chapters regarding factors crucial to this question, the answer must be a qualified negative. Writing of the end of the first decade of the century, only a dozen years after Bwaidoga received the Methodist Mission, Jenness and Ballantyne (1920, pp. 131–2) state:

Now his [i.e. the hamlet leader's] authority is slight, but formerly it appears to have been much greater . . . A few of the older head men still retain a considerable show of dignity and authority . . . But in most cases such authority as they may once have possessed has utterly disappeared.

But the authors offer no evidence to convince the reader that the leaders' authority was any greater in pre-contact times, and it is difficult to believe that a discernible loss could have occurred within a mere decade under the conditions of minimal contact that Goodenough had received. Admittedly, the existence of warfare provided opportunities unparalleled today for assertive men to command fear and respect as warriors, but the type – the *tonagona* – is not yet extinct and men still chew *cordyline* leaves to nerve and incense them for political confrontations.[1] Some of the qualities associated with leadership in the era of the *tonagona* are indeed still highly valued.

---

[1] Beer and other alcoholic drinks are valued primarily for the 'strength' and 'courage' they are thought to impart, though needless to say, they are not readily obtainable on Goodenough.

On the other hand, the emergence of an occasional despotic figure must be accepted as part of the pattern. Legends about the big-men of the past are as subject to nostalgic distortion as any other aspect of the traditional that small and parochial groups wish to identify with. But there is no mistaking the stature of the tyrant Malaveyoyo. Real big-men are those who, according to Burridge, 'transcend the system'.[1] One can perhaps recognize the mark of one in Tobowa, who defied convention by marrying a woman half his age; or in Kimaola in the case cited, when he buried a member of his *fofofo* and refused death payments. Of Malaveyoyo, however, it is said that he sponsored a Modawa festival although his birth into the opposite ceremonial moiety entitled him only to make Fakili; he ate his kinsmen's children and taught his warriors to eat their human captives raw. In short, these and other tales of Malaveyoyo's exploits present him as not merely 'transcending the system' but in a sense inverting it by reversing customary usages. Significantly too, this monster of antisocial crimes is also said to have innovated the competitive exchange system of *abutu*, which substitutes the gift and counter-gift of food and pigs for the vendetta of clubs and spears, thereby creating a new basis for political order and a new model for enterprising leadership.

[1] A point he made in a paper read to an Australian National University seminar in October 1967.

6

SOCIAL CONTROL

Some question of food or of women lies at the root of most of their troubles.

Jenness and Ballantyne, 1920, p. 202

It can be argued sensibly that it is precisely this, the manipulative, bargaining, transactional approach to life which *is* the system of their life. In other words that the 'endemic conflict' is not an upset or defect or an aberration or a friction of some idealized or perfect system, but that it is *itself* the system, together with the accompaniments and consequences which, logically, follow when most interests can only be attained through other people, i.e. on terms either of agreement or of force.

Stanner, 1959, p. 216

Given the large size of Kalauna, its segmental structure and its acephalous authority system, and given also a scheme of values which (as we shall see in the following chapter) appears to enjoin competition rather than co-operation, it is scarcely surprising that conflict is endemic and that the community as a whole suffers some acute problems of internal regulation. In previous chapters I have indicated how some of these problems are met through, in Nadel's (1953) term, the 'self-regulation' of institutions by which sanctions inhere in social relationships themselves. In the present chapter I examine other sources of social control: more or less formal coercive sanctions to which individuals in search of redress may appeal. We shall find the most important type of sanction to be what I call 'food-giving-to-shame', which is given elaborate institutionalized expression in competitive food exchanges (*abutu*) and festivals. Analysis of this mode of coercion, however, is deferred until later chapters by which time its relative significance will be more readily understood.

GENERAL ATTITUDES TO OFFENCES

There are no 'crimes' in Kalauna and therefore no 'criminals'. From the standpoint of the legal code of the Territory, of course, it is possible for a Kalauna person to commit many crimes for which he may be tried and imprisoned. But from their own point of view, there are only delicts; that is, offences against another person's rights as defined by 'custom'.

There has been no homicide by violence within the village for at least two generations; on the other hand homicide by sorcery is believed to occur several times a year. Despite this anomaly it is thought 'better' to die by a spear than by sorcery, for then one is sure to be avenged. I was unable to elicit a term for 'rape', and the idea of a woman being forced to submit to sexual intercourse against her will, while not entirely alien, is held suspect. If it could be proved that a man had committed such an act, he would be taken to the patrol office on an adultery charge or, if the woman was un-married, he would be ridiculed unmercifully and perhaps fined by her kinsmen.

Whatever a man does in Kalauna he will meet with no lasting stigma or permanent ostracism. The few outcasts from the community during my contact with it were such by choice and none was expected to remain so. But the fact that there were even a few individuals who preferred to live elsewhere for a time because they suffered 'shame' for an act or an accusa-tion, is indicative of the success of the socialization process. On the other hand, notions of 'sin' and 'guilt' are not conspicuous. It is not thought to be Christian piety which causes a man to refrain from avenging a wrong done him with the hope that 'God will punish' the offender, but an admission of weakness. While Christianity has provided a number of punitive concepts (for example, Hell is *yabamana ana delia* – 'Heaven's jail'), it has so far failed to convert Kalauna people to a radically new moral vision of their universe.

Delicts, then, rather than crimes and sins, are what concern Kalauna people. An important corollary of this is that interests rather than principles are at stake in the majority of disputes. Another is that 'it's not what one does but whom one does it to' which matters, for not all persons have equal access to the same sanctions in the defence of their rights. In view of these considerations, therefore, it is of little value to generalize that 'theft is punished by public shaming', 'adultery is punished by court action, often followed by *abutu*', or that 'failure to observe food-sharing obligations is punished by sorcery'. These statements, with their implicit norms, are made in similar form by Kalauna people themselves when appealed to for their 'custom' on the punishment of theft, adultery and greed. But since they apply to hypothetical delicts concerning unspecified parties, they convey only a most abstract sense of the appropriate sanction. Moreover, as substantive case material soon shows, it is, in Stanner's phrase, 'the manipulative, bargaining, transactional approach to life' (1959, p. 216) which characterizes the system of social control in Kalauna, rather than any structurally-determined set of jural rules with moral force. As a result of these factors the Kalauna person often experiences uncertainty as

5*

to the possible consequences of an act, while the ethnographer experiences frustration in seeking regularities in behaviour. Some regularities, of course, there are and must be. One can hardly conceive of a viable social system in which sanctions are arbitrary and *ad hoc* (Epstein 1968), for the mutual expectations which are the basis of any norm posit also standard expectations about the consequences which attend the breach of that norm. But in the virtual absence of superordinate justice, and in the presence of interests rather than principles, sanctions are flexible, multi-purpose, and eminently susceptible to manipulation. The 'operator' or potential wrong-doer in such a system must needs take into account numerous variables in his calculations of risk.

OFFENCES AND QUARRELS

For the ethnographer, too, faced with a multiplicity of variables, there is the problem of judgement; in this case as to which are significant and determinant. There are three important ones which invite consideration: nature of delict or offence, relationship of offender to offended, and type of sanction applied. But there is also a fourth which is crucial in this context: occurrence of disputation or some form of breach in the relationship between offender and offended. Without this the other three variables may have no social significance. The undetected thief, for example, has committed an offence, but no consequences flow from his act for he evades sanction and his relationship to the person from whom he stole is unaffected. Neither is the 'automatic' sanction of interest here. If the thief robs a tree which is protected by a spell and he subsequently falls sick, he is likely to admit that he deserved the punishment. He, or his kinsfolk, are obliged to ask the tree-owner to cure the thief, for which they give payment. The owner is likely to do so without taking further action against the thief other than mildly shaming him for his folly. Many sicknesses which occur in Kalauna are attributed to similar infringements of property rights, but since they do not usually affect the relationship between trespasser and owner, and since the sanction against trespass is in this instance seen as automatic and impartial, I do not classify such events as instances of either quarrels or sorcery.

Since our main interest is in the social consequences of delicts and sanctions (in 'endemic conflict', in short), it would seem a better procedure to classify and count quarrels rather than offences. A quarrel or a dispute is the observable symptom of a disturbance in the relationship between two or more persons, and it almost invariably signalizes the breach of a norm by at least one of the parties, though whether they are prepared to admit it openly is another matter. The range of offences about which people quarrel in Kalauna is extremely wide. 'He did wrong to me' (*hi koyona aiya'aikuya*), with the implicit corollary, 'for which I bear him a grievance', can apply to the whole gamut of offences against persons and property. Since the range of delicts is wider than the number of available sanctions, there is considerable overlap of sanctions for 'similar' offences.

'Trouble over food (and pigs)' and 'trouble over women' together account for about 90% of all quarrels. Analytically, it is possible to sub-classify these broad categories. Thus, I recorded cases which are illustrative of the following delicts concerning food and pigs: improper or unequal distribution, refusing a request for food, depriving a kinsman of food by hoarding, theft of food, damage to pigs and gardens, boasting about food, stealing from another's pot or plate, etc. There are other offences which Kalauna people regard as 'trouble over food' but which, more objectively, stem from infringement of rights of inheritance or of exclusive ownership of *dewa*, such as food magic. Disputes over food may also prove on closer examination to be the overt expression of competitive political manœuvres or wrangles over leadership. 'Trouble over women' includes adultery, marital quarrels, dissatisfaction over brideprice, seduction, and all infringements of a man's rights over his wife, sisters, daughters and brothers' widows.

There should be no illusion that a classification of quarrels in terms of precipitating offence or breach of norm can be rigorous. Any attempt to make it so would involve many arbitrary judgements, and the resulting correlations would be misleadingly firm and probably slanted. There is initially the problem of demarcating a quarrel, however, which must be faced if they are to be enumerated. What to the casual observer may appear to be a sequence of discrete quarrels may in fact be episodes in a single dispute rooted in the same set of grievances. The consequence of one quarrel may well be another, between the same or related parties. In the tables which I present below, a quarrel or dispute is treated as a countable unit only when it arises from a specific delict or breach of a norm, and when it is disconnected by a period of time from previous disputes between the same parties about other offences. A spasmodic, running quarrel between the same persons and over the same basic cause I regard as a single quarrel. For instance, a protracted quarrel between the members of two hamlets in Kalauna began about twenty years ago when two men disputed the ownership of a pig which one of them had speared in the bush. The situation was resolved by a competitive food exchange, *abutu*. A few years ago fresh quarrels, prompted by a widow re-marriage, occurred between the two hamlets. Insults were traded and *abutu* threatened.

When a sickness struck a man who had married the widow, the men of the other hamlet were suspected of sorcery, and there were renewed insults and *abutu* threats. Since the original quarrel over the pig caused the two hamlets to regard each other as 'food enemies', it influenced attitudes towards the widow's re-marriage, and although her dead spouse's brothers could not actually prevent it, they opposed it vociferously. Now, does this sequence constitute one, two or three quarrels? I regard it as two, for while they are clearly interconnected the first event concerns men who are now dead (and therefore would not figure in my tables at all) while the second and third events (the marriage and the sorcery accusation) involve the same disputants and the same immediate cause. In classifying this quarrel I place it in Table 17 ('Quarrels between men over women') in the cell defined by the variables of 'Non-related parties' and 'Sorcery', the latter being the sanction it was believed had been employed. A thoroughgoing classification would need to indicate as well that another sanction, the threat of *abutu*, was also used.

RELATIONSHIP OF DISPUTANTS

This variable is the most easily determined. For the purposes of this limited analysis it is sufficient to deal with only the broader categories of relationships. The most significant, as I have noted elsewhere, is that of patrilineal kinsmen.[1] This category is usefully subdivided into 'close' agnates (i.e. *unuma* brothers) and 'distant' agnates (i.e. clansmen). A preliminary analysis of my case material on disputes soon revealed the general truth of Kalauna people's contention that they do not quarrel with their affines nor with their mother's kin. Other than the threefold distinction between close and distant agnates, and a residual category of nominally unrelated men, the only further distinction of any significance for our purposes is that between unrelated men of one's own village and unrelated men of other villages.

SANCTIONS

An exhaustive study of sanctions would require some fine distinctions to be made between different kinds of food-giving-to-shame, between different forms of sorcery, and between various other types of rational and supernatural sanction. Such an unwieldy classification would be pointless here, and I have considered it necessary to lump formal sanctions under only six headings: food-giving, fighting, sorcery, fining, temporary exile and harangue. Some disputes are characterized by appeals to two or more of

[1] I do not concern myself here with disputes *between* the sexes.

these sanctions; in such cases I have classified them according to whichever was conspicuously the more definitive in settling the matter – according to the judgement of my informants.

Table 15 collates variables involved in discrete quarrels between men concerning food and pigs, all of which occurred during the period that I was in contact with Kalauna. This table indicates that food-giving-to-shame is the most appropriate sanction for this class of delicts occurring outside the category of agnates, but that sorcery, and perhaps also violence, are more likely to occur within this relationship category than outside it.

TABLE 15　*Quarrels over food and pigs:*[1] *Kalauna 1966–8*

Parties	Principal sanction applied						
	Food-giving	Fighting	Sorcery	Fine	Exile	Harangue	Total
Unuma agnate	—	1	1	—	1	1	4
Clan agnate[2]	1	—	2	—	—	3	6
Other (Kalauna)	3	—	1	—	—	—	4
Other village	4	—	—	—	—	—	4
Total	8	1	4	—	1	4	18

[1] Thirteen of these cases concerned food and five of them pigs. Cases of theft are excluded.

[2] In this and subsequent tables Lulauvile is counted as one clan; i.e. members of Lulauvile I and Lulauvile II are regarded as clan agnates.

Since the sample is too small for us to regard these distributions as significant, let us compare it with another set of cases which I recorded, but which belong to a period before 1966. As these reported cases are less detailed than the ones I was able to observe for myself, their classification is accordingly somewhat more dubious, which is why I present them separately. The cases in Table 16, in fact, come from a different 'universe', since tapping informants' memories for examples of quarrels tends to elicit only those well-remembered for their drama. Thus, perhaps, the predominance of fighting brothers, *abutu* exchanges within the village, and old sorcery suspicions which have hardened into certainties over the years. On the other hand, self-selective though this sample may be, it is a fairly useful one for the purpose of showing incidence of types of sanction. On the whole, too, it complements and confirms the distribution in Table 15 in several respects, showing that only in the matter of sorcery does Table 15 give the misleading impression of its being primarily a sanction used by agnates.

TABLE 16 *Quarrels over food and pigs between living Kalauna men: c. 1940–65*

Parties	Principal sanction applied						Total
	Food-giving	Fighting	Sorcery	Fine	Exile	Harangue	
Unuma agnate	—	4	1	—	2	?	7
Clan agnate	—	—	5	—	—	?	5
Other (Kalauna)	5	—	5	—	—	?	10
Other village	1	—	2	—	—	1	4
Total	6	4	13	—	2	1	26

Let us consider now the sanctions applied in quarrels between men over women. Table 17 shows the distribution of quarrels over women between different relationship categories of Kalauna men over a two-year period.

TABLE 17 *Quarrels between men over women: Kalauna 1966–8*

Parties	Principal sanction applied						Total
	Food-giving	Fighting	Sorcery	Fine	Exile	No apparent action	
Unuma agnate	—	1	—	—	—	—	1
Clan agnate	—	2	1	—	1	2	6
Affine	—	—	—	—	1	—	1
Other (Kalauna)	4	—	4	2	—	1	11
Other village	1	1	—	—	1	—	3
Total	5	4	5	2	3	3	22

In 11 cases out of 22 a man's rights over his wife were at issue in the quarrel. In half the cases also the disputes were between unrelated men of the same village. Table 18 gives a substantially similar picture, modified by a greater preponderance of food-giving-to-shame and correspondingly less appeal to other sanctions (except fighting). This is doubtless due to the bias of informants' memories (and probably my own selective interests during interviews) in recalling readily the dramatic and sensational cases at the expense of the mundane. Even so, on the basis of these two tables it can be said, for instance, that in one of three quarrels between clansmen over women violence resulted, or that between one-third and two-thirds of quarrels over women between unrelated men of the village involve food-giving-to-shame. Moreover, in these two tables there is the same tendency to use the food-giving sanction in quarrels between unrelated men as was

TABLE 18   *Quarrels between men over women: Kalauna c. 1940–65*

| | Principal sanction applied | | | | | | |
Parties	Food-giving	Fighting	Sorcery	Fine	Exile	No apparent action	Total
Unuma agnate	1	—	—	—	—	—	1
Clan agnate	1	1	—	—	—	1	3
Affine	—	1	1	—	—	—	2
Other (Kalauna)	9	3	2	—	—	1	15
Other village	2	1	—	—	—	—	3
Total	13	6	3	—	—	2	24

noted in the tables concerned with disputes over food. On the other hand, there is a contrast in the tendency to use violence: agnates resort to it quite frequently in their quarrels over food, less commonly in their quarrels over women. Agnates are also more likely to use sorcery against each other in disputes over food than they are in disputes over women.

In order to arrive at an estimate of the proportionate use of these forms of sanction, Table 19 combines the two main classes of quarrels. The relationship categories are telescoped to simplify the picture further: *unuma* and clan agnates having been merged, and affines subsumed under non-agnates of the same village.

Table 19 compares two sets of data of somewhat different orders, in the sense that 40 quarrels represent almost all the major disputes between men within a two-year period, whereas the 50 quarrels of the second set are a sample, and probably a numerically insignificant one, of all the quarrels occurring over food, pigs and women within some 25 years. The tables nevertheless reveal the two sets of data to be broadly comparable, and no striking contradiction is evident between them. They show agreement on the point of the respective importance of certain sanctions: food-giving is a good first, sorcery second, and resort to violence third. Other forms of sanction are less significant. General statements made elsewhere are amply confirmed: that food-giving-to-shame is only appropriate between non-agnates, while fighting is more frequent and sorcery at least as common among agnates as non-agnates.

Now that the incidence of implementation of the various forms of sanction has been considered it is necessary to examine them in more detail. *Abutu* and other forms of food-giving-to-shame are reserved for later chapters, but I discuss here the remaining types of sanction in order of increasing frequency of incidence.

TABLE 19 *All quarrels over food, pigs and women: Kalauna*

	Food-giving	Fighting	Sorcery	Fine	Exile	Harangue	No apparent action	Total
A. 1966–8								
Agnate	1	4	4	—	2	2	2	15
Non-agnate (Kalauna)	7	—	5	2	1	2	1	18
Other village	5	1	—	—	1	—	—	7
Sub-total	13	5	9	2	4	4	3	40
Percentage	(32·5)	(12·5)	(22·5)	(5·0)	(10·0)	(10·0)	(7·5)	(100·0)
B. c. 1940–65								
Agnate	2	5	5	—	2	—	1	15
Non-agnate (Kalauna)	14	4	9	—	—	—	1	28
Other village	3	1	2	—	—	1	—	7
Sub-total	19	10	16	—	2	1	2	50
Percentage	(38·0)	(20·0)	(32·0)		(4·0)	(2·0)	(4·0)	(100·0)
Grand total	32	15	25	2	6	5	5	90
Percentage	(35·5)	(16·6)	(27·7)	(2·2)	(6·6)	(5·5)	(5·5)	(100·0)

Fining

After citing examples of various delicts (theft, homicide, adultery, 'rape', sorcery) Jenness and Ballantyne conclude that 'the usual penalty for an offence is the payment of a heavy fine' (1920, p. 81), although they make it clear that demand for compensation was backed by the threat of violence. 'Club law is only resorted to when the evildoers refuse to compound and the aggrieved party considers itself the stronger' (*ibid.*). Compensation appears to have been in the form of shell-valuables, pots, food and pigs. Although this may well have been a common pattern of redressive action in the past, it is quite insignificant today – in Bwaidoga no less than in Kalauna. Several cases came to my notice in Kalauna, mostly in connection with theft. Thus, a man who stole another's fish poison (derris root) was requested (with the threat of *abutu*) to pay a few shillings compensation, which he did. Another man demanded two shillings compensation from a woman whom he accused of stealing beans from his garden. He threatened to take her to the patrol officer if she did not pay. Just before I arrived in Kalauna some schoolboys had speared a pig in the bush. It belonged to a Belebele man, and the councillor and village constable from this 'barrack' came up to Kalauna to demand compensation from the boys' kinsmen. The latter agreed to pay and collected the money (about £6) by cutting up the pig and selling pieces within the village. The two cases of fining which appear in Table 17 were exacted by the same man (Abela) for identical offences: courting his daughter without his permission. Although most people regarded this as a dubious delict, the offending youths paid up a few dollars in cash, afraid to protest because the man is a feared sorcerer of uncertain temper. I was unable to elicit any further examples of compensation being demanded from offenders who committed delicts concerned with women. It is considered proper for a man who steals another's wife to compensate her previous husband by the amount of brideprice he had paid her kinsmen, and also by an amount of food which is in explicit repayment of what the first husband 'fed' the woman during their marriage. But these payments, although compensation, should not be classed as fines. They are backed by threatened appeal to the patrol officer or by threats of sorcery; and *abutu* exchanges may take place independently of them. Some years ago a man whose wife was abducted by a villager from Wailolo sent the usual request for brideprice and 'wife-feeding' compensation. When the abductor brought them to Kalauna the offended husband presented him with five pigs and a mound of yams saying, 'I've tricked you into *abutu*. If you want to take my wife you have to take my pigs and food also.' The abductor was suitably contrite, and is still trying to pay back the unexpected *abutu* gifts. The sanction the offended husband appealed to in this case was thus food-giving-to-shame, not fining.

If we are to accept Jenness and Ballantyne's statements at face value, there has obviously been a great decline in the use of fining as a mode of restitution. This is probable to be associated with the abolition of fighting as the coercive threat behind this sanction, and with the correlative increase in resort to *abutu* and perhaps also to sorcery (see Chapter 10). Fining remains a significant sanction only in cases of theft, where the value of a stolen object is easily converted into cash. While the token value of shell-valuables has possibly not altered greatly, the social contexts in which they are transacted are becoming increasingly fewer as the number in circulation gradually diminishes. Other than in bridewealth repayments, I recorded no recent instance of shell-valuables being paid as compensation.

Temporary exile

Most instances of temporary exile occur following bitter quarrels during which the instigator or offender is made to feel the strong moral disapproval of the community. This may be brought about by harangue (as in the case presented on p. 45 above), by gossip or by the withdrawal of co-operation. Fear as well as shame may induce voluntary exile, as when an offender tries to evade other sanctions such as violence or sorcery. Four of the six cases tabulated above concerned men who thought it better to save their skins by leaving home for a spell of wage labour abroad. The remaining two cases were more akin to banishment: the offenders were made clearly to understand that their presence was, for the time being, not wanted. In one of these cases this moral pressure was reinforced by the supernatural sanction of the *talahaiyi* curse, which suspended social relations entirely between the offender and the person who pronounced it. Self-exile is perhaps the most comfortable course of action in these circumstances (see above pp. 44–5).

Harangue

What I call harangue is a component of many cases and is considered to be an effective sanction for many delicts (particularly when used by leaders), although it appears in my tables only when it is the sole sanction applied. The term, *laumamala*, is the same as the one used for rhetorical speech-making at meetings or festivals, and it would appear to imply a critical attack. Like the Trobriand practice of *yoba* which Malinowski makes central to his drama of the banishment of the Omarakana chief's son (1926, pp. 101 *et seq.*; 1929, pp. 10 *et seq.*), a harangue is preferably delivered from a house-step on a dark night, and, if the subject of it is a named individual, it may result in his temporary exile. Frequently, a man states his grievances against unknown offenders in this way with the intention of shaming them. Since the village is compact enough for most of it to be within earshot of a single shouting voice, it is an efficient and satisfying way of bringing delicts to public notice. The message is assimilated in absolute silence, and if a particular individual is being accused, he will be found sitting inside his house with head bowed under the imagined stare of the whole community. Informants declare, plausibly enough, that such harangues are less frequent now than they were in the past because the fortnightly village meeting, instituted by the local government councillor, serves a similar end in bringing grievances to public attention.

Fighting

Considering the somewhat violent existence of the pre-contact population, the positive values of warriorhood expressed in warfare, and the frequent need to resort to 'club law' as the only effective means of gaining restitution, violence is less common than one might expect in present-day Kalauna. There are those who continue to value it positively, since fighting is their 'custom', their *dewa*; and perhaps because it is expected of them, such people tend to live up to the reputation conferred through descent and inheritance by responding to offences with violent behaviour or the direct threat of it. Such people are in a small minority, however, and the rest seem to be thankful that coercion by violence is forbidden by administration law. The existence of 'fist-fighting' magic (which is probably a post-contact phenomenon), and of simulated aggression (*sefaiya*) in certain well-defined social contexts, is not evidence to the contrary. The former is generally associated with the wage-labour situation in which a man may find himself relatively defenceless among a group of hostile strangers. The latter is merely the ritualization of responses which characteristically provoke violence, and is to that extent indicative of the culture's success in taming it. There is evidence, too, that Kalauna people regard violence as an unsatisfactory, because ineffective, coercive sanction. The statement that 'before we used to spear someone who did wrong to us' is qualified by the rider: 'but that way was not good'. The value here expressed is of a pragmatic rather than moral kind, however, and 'the good' refers to social consequences. Child-beating and wife-beating, which together constitute by far the most common acts of violence in Kalauna, are seen in a somewhat different light, and no-one would gainsay the right of a man to chastise his wife or his own children (and only his).[1] But even here, most men

---

[1] It is untrue to say, as Jenness and Ballantyne do (1920, p. 202), that 'no man would dream of beating his own child'. I have witnessed it on several occasions, though it is a task often assumed by an elder sibling of the errant child.

do not beat them if other sanctions are immediately available (and providing, of course, they can control their tempers in time). On the whole, then, violence is seen as a less successful means of achieving ends than other sanctions, and when it occurs it is usually spontaneous – even among those who are pre-disposed to it by their *dewa*. Compared to sorcery it is a far from effective sanction. The following case material contrasts two Kalauna men of similar age and status, one an infamous sorcerer, the other a notorious fighter. While people are wary of offending either, the former emerges as the most 'successful' manipulator and the one most feared for his coercive powers.

Daudia of Mulina clan and Abela of Iwaoyana clan are similar in a number of respects: both are in their late thirties, both are second sons whose elder brothers are hamlet 'bossmen', and both are pleasant and amiable until roused – then they can be frightening in their fury. Daudia is *tonuakoyo*, an 'angry man', prone to sudden fits of violence. Abela is also *tonuakoyo*, but non-violent and remarkable, rather, for his ability to display cold and controlled anger, which he can turn on as easily as a smile. Despite these superficial similarities of personality and status, however, both men appear to possess widely divergent approaches to life. Daudia is an agnostic with a fatalistic streak, poor, unambitious and without pretentions. Abela is a church-going Methodist who likes to mention God in his orations at meetings; he is relatively wealthy and a potential entrepreneur, vain and somewhat pompous. Their different life-styles are reflected also in the means they take to assert themselves and manipulate others. Daudia relies upon his reputation for bad temper and fighting ability to get his own way in a dispute, while Abela relies upon his reputation as a sorcerer. There can be no doubt that Abela is the more 'successful' of the two men in his ability to gain deference from others. This can be shown by glancing at a number of incidents in which they have been independently involved.

Daudia has been in the patrol officer's court no less than eight times, although he has so far managed to avoid being sent to jail. (This he attributes to his 'court-case' magic, *vilaiya*, which 'makes your face strong, your lips straight and your tongue slow to answer questions'.) All except one case was brought about through his penchant for violence. Two were for fighting on plantations abroad, two were for fighting his wife's brothers (who belong to a different village), one was for fighting with his own brother, one for beating his wife, and one for leading a punitive raid down to Belebele village. 'Fighting is my custom', Daudia says, and he is prepared to admit that he gains little by it; for although it is a *dewa* which belongs to his clan as a whole, he is the only Mulina man who others avoid co-operating with.

Abela, as far as I know, has never been the defendant in a 'court-case'. Like Daudia, however, he has quarrelled bitterly with his elder brother several times, though blows were not exchanged. Abela expresses his independence by living with his household in relative isolation from the village (see p. 28). He lived for a time in his wife's village, Eweli, in order to be able to learn some of his father-in-law's sorcery, and he rarely misses an opportunity to assert to Kalauna people (in public meetings), that Eweli sorcery is more swift and deadly than Kalauna sorcery. It is a matter of opinion, however, whether Abela or his elder brother Yaudili (who inherited their father's considerable magic lore) is the more feared. Like all master-sorcerers, they also possess fame as curers, though Abela appears to be the more energetic and to have the bigger 'practice'. Another source of Abela's wealth is the fines he righteously demands from those who wrong him or his kinsmen – though a more uncharitable view would perhaps regard this as extortion. I mentioned above (p. 123) how he exacted cash fines from youths who courted his daughter without permission. On the occasion of Tomokova's adultery with Kwayaya's wife (see pp. 214–5), Abela (Kwayaya's FFFBSS) threatened Tomokova with sorcery unless he paid over a compensatory pig to Iwaoyana. This demand was successful, as was his similar threat to Neailena in 1965 to get the latter to pay back brideprice to the wronged husband of an Iwaoyana woman. Abela received a cut of the return, and also some of the additional brideprice which Neailena paid to the woman's Iwaoyana agnates. Neailena was councillor at the time, and was thus ironically the first Kalauna man to pay the £20 brideprice set by the new council rule (see p. 52). Backed by his brother, in 1966 Abela also tried to demand compensation from Akumaiya of Malabuabua, following the latter's adultery with Taula's wife (Taula is Abela's MZS). This attempt failed, however, because Akumaiya's eldest brother Wakasilele is also a *tonuakoyo* not to be trifled with. He met Abela's sorcery threat with a sanction of his own speciality. Brandishing a bush-knife at the two brothers, Wakasilele warned them: 'If anyone dies, I'll cut your necks off.' Violent, 'fighting' men can thus occasionally put sorcerers in their place.

SORCERY[1]

The notion that sorcery may have a quasi-legal role in inducing conformity to norms and punishing infractions is a familiar one; indeed, it was initially formulated with respect to data gathered less than a hundred miles from Goodenough (Malinowski 1926, pp. 85 *et seq.*). Even closer than this, the general complex of sorcery beliefs on Goodenough is almost identical to that of Dobu, and in stating concisely the uses to which it is put I can add little to Fortune's characterization:

To sum up, the black art is used not only for collecting bad debts and enforcing economic obligation, in vendetta to avenge one's own sickness or one's kinsman's death, to wipe out any serious insult offered to one, and for the sake of 'trying it out' to see how it works. It is also used generally to 'cast down the mighty from their seat' (1932, pp. 175–6).

---

[1] This section contains a highly condensed discussion of the social role and consequences of sorcery beliefs in Kalauna. The content of these beliefs is not discussed, and many other important aspects are omitted through lack of space; indeed, sorcery might have formed a principal topic of a somewhat differently constructed book. As it is, I hope to explore Kalauna sorcery more thoroughly in subsequent publications. Jenness and Ballantyne discuss several of the innumerable sorcery techniques (1920, pp. 141–4).

The coercive potential over groups as well as individuals of personal sorcery and the class of food sorcery called *valeimu'imu* is quite considerable when, as in Kalauna, all subscribe to the belief that misfortunes, individual or collective, can and usually do have human magic as their cause (see Chapter 8). While the logic of the belief system may well be self-contained, however, analysis has to take account of the 'reality' that most beliefs in sorcery are empirically false. It is at this point that investigation becomes difficult. Sorcerers admit to a knowledge of techniques only a little more often than they admit to causing particular instances of sickness or misfortune. To a probing European they tend to admit even less.[1] One is also dealing with compounded ambiguities: the victim believes he has been sorcerized by X who may or may not believe that he has done so, and only if it is to his advantage will he 'admit' it. Others may believe Y is responsible, who may or may not privately agree. Direct action (other than delayed vengeance sorcery) is rarely taken unless X or Y admits or claims responsibility, in which case he is likely to be inviting compensation for a delict. Whether this is given or not will depend largely upon the 'justice' of the believed attack or the fear in which the suspected sorcerer is held. Alternatively, modes of divination may point to X or Y, but these men do not thereby automatically agree that the divination is correct, and they may continue to deny the accusation. All one can hope to do in analysing involved sorcery cases is to consider the contextual relationships between individuals and groups concerned, and assess the degree of 'disturbance' in them. Rarely, perhaps, is there a neat answer since the belief system provides alternative explanations. Culture change has also had something to do with this in Kalauna, and not merely in the introduction of the idea of God as a causal factor. The following abbreviated text will serve to illustrate this:

Before we had only our own kind of sorcery, so when someone got sick or died, his brothers could look at him and tell what had caused it: whether it was for pig or gardens or women or whatever. Then they would remember who was angry with him for that thing and go to him and ask him to make their brother better. If he was dead they would wait and wait maybe a year then pay him back.

---

[1] See Jenness and Ballantyne 1920, p. 133. Fortune's comments (1932, pp. 166, 288–94) on the difficulty of obtaining data on a practice which is forbidden by colonial law still apply, although the impediments are perhaps fewer now than they were in 1929. Goodenough Islanders, for instance, for fear of later reprisal from those they wish to accuse, simply do not risk taking their complaints of sorcery attack to the patrol officer, who for his part is largely unaware of and therefore unconcerned with the problem. Attitudes of sorcerers with respect to the government are proportionately more relaxed. It remains a covert and secretive topic within the village, however, and one rich in euphemism, allusion and metaphor. These reasons alone make the investigation of sorcery the most trying of any subject.

But today many men go to other places like Samarai or Moresby and they learn other kinds of sorcery. They come home and they do them and now we don't know who it is.

Possibly because it is depriving the elders of what they regard as a legitimate sanction, a bone of contention between the generations in Kalauna is that the young are bringing back to the village too much foreign sorcery from their working trips abroad. Some blame this development on literacy, which enables young men to write down the formulae of spells in strange languages, which they would otherwise be unable to memorize. Other complain also that the young hastily purchase *kwauna* (the harmful form of a spell) without bothering to acquire its *manawana* (the antidote form), so that although they are able to afflict their victims they are unable to cure them.

If uncertainty exists as part of the current belief system concerning sorcery, it is at the expense of weakening the restitutive or regulative aspects of sorcery beliefs in particular cases. Furthermore, if we are to regard a specific sorcery accusation as a conscious or unconscious recognition, not merely of strain in the relationship between victim or accuser and the person accused or suspected, but also of the existence of a grievance which requires settlement or a wrong which requires redress, then we must be able to show that the victim or accuser takes steps to remedy them in the hope of countering the misfortune. Only then would we be justified in regarding sorcery beliefs as a contribution to the maintenance of social norms, or more generally as being a positive instrument of social control.

The twenty-five instances that appear in Tables 15 to 19, of sorcery wielded as a sanction during or following a quarrel, can be regarded in this light. In each case the sorcerer was held to have a more or less valid grievance against his victim (or against a close relative of the victim), and in each case the victim or kinsmen of the victim revealed by their conciliatory behaviour some appreciation of this fact. If they possessed the concept, Kalauna people might be prepared to concede that these were instances of 'legitimate' sorcery, or at least that the victims had brought the attacks on their own heads by infractions of the sorcerers' rights.

However, these twenty-five cases represent less than one-quarter of the total number of suspected sorcery attacks which I recorded as occurring within Kalauna. In other words, in the majority of cases there was an apparent absence of previous quarrelling. But, in acknowledging that (in Fortune's words) 'where there is the fire of sorcery . . . there has been very often the smoke of a quarrel' (*ibid.* p. 166), Kalauna people also well know that grievances may be nursed in secret, so that when they are struck down a part of their fear at least stems from ignorance of the agent and his motives. In the absence of infallible divination techniques, imputations of sorcery attack tend to spring from a victim's dialogue with his social conscience. He reviews his relations with everyone in the community (or his kinsmen do so on his behalf), and it is not difficult to find a number of people whom he feels he may have offended. On the other hand, his choice may be narrowed by the nature of his affliction, for only certain men know certain sorcery techniques. Then the victim is driven to wracking his memory for possible ways in which he might have wronged such individuals. At all events, accusations are never made randomly, and it is this fact which gives their distribution intrinsic interest. Frequencies of accusation provide what Marwick calls a 'social strain-gauge', an indicator of the 'tension-points of a social structure' (1964, p. 263).[1] The following table, which collates broad categories of relationship between sorcerer and victim with believed reasons for attack, classifies ninety-one instances of

TABLE 20   *Association between reason given for sorcery attack and relationship categories involved*

Attack believed to be linked with	Relationship between sorcerer and victim			
	Clan agnates	Affines	Other	Total
A. Quarrel over delict concerning				
Food	15	2	13	30
Women	2	4	11	17
Insult	4	1	3	8
Theft	—	—	6	6
B. Other				
Competition between leaders	5	—	1	6
Vengeance	4	—	5	9
Envy of youth and beauty	1	—	3	4
Don't know	4	3	4	11
Total	35	10	46	91
Percentage	38.4	11.0	50.6	100

suspected sorcery, most of which occurred either a few years before or during my stay in Kalauna. It includes only those cases in which the victim and the accused belong to Kalauna, and only those cases in which individual sorcery was thought to have been used; cases characterized by the use of

[1] The next attempt to utilize this concept for Melanesian societies (Lawrence and Meggitt 1965, pp. 17–18) did considerable violence to it. These authors use it in the sense of 'safety-valve' i.e. as something which 'operates' as a 'tension-release' in society, whereas Marwick clearly intended the concept to be an instrument in the tool-kit of the anthropologist, without making any assumptions about the 'functions' of sorcery.

valeimu'imu, the sorcery of collective misfortune, are excluded (see Chapter 8).

Three further distributions should be recorded in order to complete the picture: sex of victim and accused, the number of fatal as against non-fatal attacks, and the number of particular individuals thought responsible for the ninety-one cases of attack.

TABLE 21 *Association between sex of victim and sex of sorcerer*
(Fatal attacks in brackets)

| Sorcerers | Victims | | |
	Males	Females	Total
Males	55 (22)	28 (19)	83 (41)
Females	5 (1)	3 (0)	8 (1)
Total	60 (23)	31 (19)	91 (42)

TABLE 22 *Distribution of accusations among sorcerers*

Number of accusations per sorcerer	1	2	3	4	5	6	7	8 ... 13
Number of sorcerers accused	29	7	2	1	1	2	—	1 ... 1

Taking the tables in reverse order of presentation, we note that 44 individuals (40 men and 4 women) were believed responsible for the sample of 91 attacks. Most of these sorcerers (66%) were accused only once, but one man (Tobowa), was suspected of as many as 13 (14%) of the attacks.[1] Table 21 confirms the local assumption that the majority of sorcerers are men, and the generalization that most of their victims are also men. Of the eight attacks attributed to women, only one was fatal, and since this victim was an infant, supposedly killed as a substitute for an elder sibling, the general belief that women do not know lethal sorcery is not seriously invalidated. The higher proportion of females killed when attacked by men justifies the belief that women are 'easier' to kill than men. This notion may be invoked by informants to explain why a sorcerer attacks a female when his grievance is with her husband, father or brother. At least eight females in the sample were in this way suspected of being substitutes for males.

[1] As a microcosm of the total sample, these 13 attacks attributed to Tobowa are instructive since they illustrate fundamentally the same patterns of distribution. Thus, nine of Tobowa's victims were men, and four were women; eight were agnates, one was an affine (his wife), and four were unrelated; six of the attacks were attributed to his grievances over food, three were thought to be motivated by vengeance, two by his competition with other leaders, one by the adultery of his wife, and the motive for one was not known.

Turning now to Table 20, it will readily be seen that as many as one-third of all attacks are attributed to disputes or offences concerning food, and that over one-third of the victims of all attacks are members of the same clan as their suspected sorcerers. Just how significant this association is can be demonstrated by the calculation that the average person's clan agnates constitute between 12·5% and 14·3% of the community's population, depending upon whether one counts Lulauvile as two clans or as one. Now if sorcery accusations were to be random within the village, between 12·5% and 14·3% of suspected sorcerers would be members of the same clans as their victims. The figure from my sample, however, is 38·4%.[1]

It would be difficult to prove or disprove statistically the hypothesis that such incidence of sorcery accusations between agnates reflects tensions arising through co-residence rather than patrilineal relationship *per se*, although it is clear from the content of the cases that most accusations can be attributed to stresses and strains arising from the system of relationships itself. To take an extreme example:

When Madiaiwao died in 1967 after a harrowing sickness, his clansman (FFFBSS) Abela was widely suspected of killing him (though not of making him sick initially). Abela, among others, had been called in by Madiaiwao's father to try to cure him. After weeks of fruitless attempts by the curers, his father had killed a pig for them to spur them to greater efforts. Abela and his brother Yaudili had demanded that the pig be given only to them, the two curers who belonged to the donor's clan. But the sick youth's father had insisted on sharing it also with those – such as Kimaola – belonging to other clans, whom he could not risk offending. Madiaiwao died shortly afterwards; 'for pig', it was whispered. Within weeks a young woman also died – as it happened whilst Yaudili was in her presence ostensibly trying to cure her of a post-parturition sickness. She was a clanswoman of the two brothers (FFBSD), and the reason for her death was generally thought to be that she had eaten of the pig which Abela and Yaudili had wanted for themselves.

Co-residence was not a factor in either of these linked cases of sorcery accusation of an agnate, for Abela dwells with his family in isolation at Edu'edu while Yaudili lives in the recently colonized hamlet of Wakulava. Other examples would show that stresses arising from close co-residence are a negligible factor, except, of course, in so far as overcrowding within the

---

[1] It can be argued that the incidence of sorcery accusations between adult males is the most important measure, since we are interested primarily in conflict between men. If Lulauvile is treated as a single clan, 26 out of 61 sorcery attacks involved male agnates, or 42·6%, whereas the null-hypothesis 'expected' value is 14·3%. If Lulauvile is regarded as two clans, the figure for intra-clan sorcery is 32·8%. (The count of 61 sorcery cases involving adult men includes 15 in which the victim was a child or a woman. These were regarded as substitutes for fathers or husbands as the real objects of attack.)

community as a whole breeds and exacerbates disputes on a gross level by creating and sustaining high frequencies of social interaction.[1]

One further point about Table 20 deserves comment. It will have been noted that there is no column specifying uterine kin under the heading 'relationship between sorcerer and victim'. Of all the cases of sorcery I investigated only one could be genealogically interpreted as an instance of disaffection between a man and a maternal kinsman. Kalauna people do not deny the possibility of sorcerizing a member of one's *susu*, but they are discomforted by the idea (though no more so than by that of sorcerizing a *fofofo* member, of which I have five cases), and could offer me no examples. The 'exception' which proves the rule that this is a characteristically warm and tension-free relationship concerns Tobowa the master-sorcerer.

Tobowa's mother's brother's son regularly went fishing and just as regularly supplied Tobowa with a portion of his catch. On one occasion he failed to do so, and his wife (who belonged to Lulauvile clan, as did Tobowa) fell sick, grew thin and almost died. Her husband interpreted her illness as punishment directed against himself for failing to give Tobowa his accustomed gift. The latter was called in to cure the woman, which he did and for which he was suitably paid. Although he never admitted to causing the sickness, it was tacitly assumed that he had, and his effective cure was regarded as sufficient proof. It was not considered remarkable that a clanswoman should be made to suffer for the displeasure Tobowa felt towards his maternal kinsman.

THE SOCIAL COST OF SORCERY

Although Kalauna people, like the Dobuans (Fortune 1932), sometimes regard sorcery as a legitimate mode of redress, and are themselves aware of its regulative role in safeguarding norms by the threat of its use, and while they might also be prepared to agree with Malinowski that 'it is a way of emphasizing the status quo' (1926, p. 93), few would go so far as to pretend that it was a 'beneficent agency' (*ibid.* p. 94). It need hardly be said that more suffering is attributed to sorcery than to any other cause. Moreover, the psychological strain of living in such a sorcery-ridden community is considerable, especially when there are so few degrees of kinship within which the occurrence of sorcery is unthinkable. Indeed, informants admitted the possibility of sorcery even within the nuclear family, although I recorded no instances of accusation between parents and children, only one between siblings and three between husband and wife. The Dobuan can feel comparatively secure in the bosom of his *susu*, which forms his residential base. The Kalauna individual is denied even

---

[1] As a possible index of stresses caused by overcrowding, sorcery accusations in Kalauna would need to be compared with similarly intensive data from other villages, which unfortunately I lack.

this. It will be a problem for later chapters to pursue as to why sorcery should be found so close to home; for the moment I am concerned only to indicate some of the consequences.

There is evidence that madness, amuck behaviour, mass hysteria and comparable pathological states may be linked with, if not triggered by, chronic or acute fears of sorcery. Certainly, Kalauna people themselves posit an explicit connection. There is a class of behaviour familiar to them, the cause of which they usually attribute to sorcery attack. This is *kwava*, madness or amuck. It is a temporary and spontaneous state. In an extreme manifestation, the victim is thrown into a fit of frenzied violence during which he brandishes weapons, chants war spells, chews *cordyline*, and whoops through the village, hacking at houses and lunging at the cowering occupants. The fit usually ends within the hour and the victim falls weeping into unconsciousness, to awake with no memory of the terror he caused. There is no recollection in Kalauna of anyone being killed by an amuck individual, though two or three of the dozen or so men in the village who seem temperamentally predisposed to it are liable to run amuck in any one year. It happened four times during my stay, but only once was there any apparent danger to life.[1] The villagers take no chances, however, and when the cry of '*kwava!*' echoes through the evening (when amuck attacks almost invariably take place), they scramble into their houses, draw up the log steps, and hunch silently, well away from the thin walls which can be penetrated by a spear.

Individuals who run amuck usually blame their attacks on sorcerers whom they accuse of 'spoiling their minds' or of sending spirits to possess them. One such man, unusually articulate whilst in this state, loudly declared his intention of spearing the sorcerer and, significantly, repeated several times that it was *yavia ana tova*, war-time, i.e. when killing a sorcerer could be done with impunity.

Further evidence of the preoccupation of such minds is derived from an event in which Aiwao, a mild and unviolent case of *kwava*, attended Kimaola's festival celebrations one evening. Normally a quiet and retiring man, he burst into a sustained babble, part gibberish and part pointed good sense. In oracular tones he declared that God (*Yaubada*) was talking to him and telling him people's minds. Prefacing each outburst with the words 'I know you', he addressed in turn several of the people present, accusing a hamlet brother of making sorcery against him, telling a woman that she gossipped too much, and another that her pig magic was good. After embarrassing more people in a similar way he turned to Abela, one of the more notorious sorcerers, and said: 'In your mind it is still dark, like war-time. The dirt of our ancestors still clings to you, and you have

[1] The life was not necessarily my own, although I was twice confronted by individuals in this state, one of them my own interpreter (cf. Fortune 1932, pp. 54–5).

charcoal in your basket.'[1] Abela's eyes bulged, but he said nothing. Most people were silent; Aiwao was speaking for them all, but the experience of hearing in public what people hardly dared say in private was acutely embarrassing. Aiwao then declared that he would tell who was sorcerizing whom, and the reason why little children died, but before he could do so he broke down and wept. The following day Wakasilele warned him never to come to the festival again: 'You make people ashamed.'

I recorded only one instance of a woman running amuck, although she was said to have been 'struck' by the hostile ghost of a man eaten by a crocodile. There was one harmless madwoman in the village, said to have been afflicted by the sorcery of a co-wife many year before, and there was a young married woman who suffered chronically from Ophelia-like fits of singing and weeping. She was thought to have been sorcerized by a former suitor who was jealous of her marriage to another man. Women, on the whole, seemed to manifest fewer symptoms of pathological fear of sorcery than men, and the fact that they are thought not to be able to kill by sorcery is, perhaps, an expression of their weaker paranoiac tendencies. Their general social role does not bring them into such keen competition as do men's, and they are proportionately free of some of the emotional strains that burden their menfolk, though not necessarily exempted thereby – as we saw in Table 21 – from sorcery attack.

The relatively high incidence of amuck behaviour among men, however, seems clearly related to the psychological syndrome of a superficial cordiality masking private fears and hatreds, and an almost unrelieved state of subconscious stress. Most men cope, helped perhaps by seeking release in the practise of sorcery themselves, or in *veyaina*, malicious gossip, which is thought to be almost as damaging. Fortune makes a relevant phenomenological observation for the Dobu when he is reminded of the man amuck by the emotional state of a sorcerer recounting details of a 'kill'. 'I would be inclined to connect the running amuck . . . with the state of mind engendered by witchcraft and sorcery' (1932, p. 163).

It would appear significant not only that most of the men I recorded as being subject to amuck believed themselves to have been sorcerized, but

---

[1] This statement has a metaphorical density of meaning. *Yuyuvana*, darkness (also ignorance), is synonymous with 'war-time', the pre-contact era. It contrasts with *imalina*, light (also knowledge), which is a colloquialism for the mission era. *Bwanene*, personal dirt, is used particularly of dirty skin, which is a supposed characteristic of the ancestors. They are conceived of as having washed but rarely, and as having painted themselves with layer after layer of charcoal in permanent readiness for war. Terms for the ascending series of ancestors are words which mean differing degrees of dirtiness; the men who came out of the earth at Yauyaba are thought of as the dirtiest of all. Charcoal, besides alluding to this penchant of foregone generations to darken themselves for war, is also a metaphor for the stuff of sorcery, which Aiwao is accusing Abela of keeping in his basket – along with the betel nut and tobacco that he will give to unsuspecting friends.

also that they all claimed to possess no sorcery of their own. This suggests that for certain personality types amuck may be a patterned alternative to making their own sorcery or resorting to other magical evasive action when they feel threatened by the nefarious activities of others.[1] At all events, they appear to experience a kind of catharsis, although the belief system denies them more than temporary relief by setting them firmly in a vicious circle: for they regard their affliction as proof of that which they had hitherto only suspected. That this vicious circle can be broken without the overthrow of the entire belief system is demonstrated by the Bwaidogans, who, while continuing to believe in the possibility of sorcery, are almost entirely emancipated from fears of it. Without fear and the hatred engendered by fear, the projective mechanisms which aggravate a sorcery-conscious community are idle, and accusations cease. The way is open to alternative theories of causality. Deaths in Bwaidoga are attributed to non-human spirits, God and even disease, for the nearby Mission hospital has done much to demonstrate the value of European theories of sickness. A relevant factor also is the substantially lower crude death rate in Bwaidoga: 1·4 per 100 as against 3·2 per 100 for Kalauna. Whatever the reasons, the fact remains that I heard not a whisper of sorcery in Bwaidoga in five probing months. Nor did I learn of a single case of amuck.

If amuck and similarly pathological behaviour afford certain individuals release from intolerable anxieties generated by suspicions of sorcery, what of the community as a whole? The culture appears to provide no institutionalized cathartic outlets, but permits rather the accumulation of quite tangible tensions, particularly after a death has occurred. The post-burial gathering of the kindred of the deceased discusses the cause of death, but there is no public divination and speeches are invariably circumspect and seemingly designed to suppress rather than to release tensions. However, these can explode spontaneously in a form of mass hysteria, such as I witnessed several days after Malawidiya's burial in April 1968.

The nerves of everyone in the community were raw following the death of this hitherto healthy young leader. Although the funeral orators had been virtually unanimous in casting the blame on a sea spirit, there was a quiet but widespread

[1] Reay (1959, p. 190) observed that neither leaders nor sorcerers ('who find constant expression for aggressiveness') were among those affected by 'mushroom madness', a form of amuck found among the Kuma.
I am aware that there is a growing body of literature on the subject of amuck or 'possession' in New Guinea, especially the Highlands (see Koch 1968 for bibliography), and that the bulk of this is suitably cautious about the 'causes' of such behaviour. Most writers see the need to take into account social, cultural, and psychopathological data. Here, I am merely pointing to the local parameters of a general phenomenon. I do not want to suggest that amuck behaviour is everywhere associated with sorcery fears, even in the D'Entrecasteaux (cf. Chowning 1961).

conviction that he had been the victim of sorcery. His ghost was reportedly seen several times, both in his gardens and in the village, ostensibly trying to inform his kinsmen of the cause of his death. The atmosphere of foreboding thickened. Other deaths were expected, for omens were seen and dogs howled at night. My neighbour and his family apologetically moved into my house, perturbed by the stones he said were thrown onto his roof every evening.

The tension reached a pitch when the tell-tale flicker of a *kwahala*[1] was seen one dark night. A cry went up and men surged excitedly out of their houses and chased wildly through the village, hurling stones and abuse at the thing. I joined the mob and felt some of their fear and witch-hunting fervour, though I couldn't see what we were supposed to be chasing. On questioning the others later, it appeared that few of them had seen anything either, although they did not doubt those who claimed that they had.

The following night the *kwahala* was seen again, and there was another wild eruption of screaming, as the men of the village scrabbled through the dark hamlets after their phantom. Two men claimed to have slashed it with their bush-knives, and when it had disappeared there was laughter and the elation of victory. It was fully expected that the morning would reveal a man – the sorcerer who sent the *kwahala* – dying of wounds in his hut. When there was none (at least in Kalauna) the importance of the incident receded; the tensions of the previous week had been dissipated. My neighbour moved back into his own house, and Malawidiya's ghost was not seen again.

There was an interesting sequel to this event. Kimaola had been absent from the village during the days of mounting tension and the nights of its release in hullabaloo, but when he returned and learnt of the visitations he characteristically made capital from them by claiming responsibility. He said that he had sent the *kwahala*; not to attack anyone, but to guard and protect the community during his absence from further evil attacks by *yafuna*, the type of spirit which he maintained had killed Malawidiya.

NON-INDIGENOUS INSTITUTIONS

To a large extent, the mechanisms of social control which are the subject of much of this book were shaped by forces and constraints alien to the indigenous society. In a later chapter I shall argue, for instance, that

[1] *Kwahala* may be described as 'familiars' belonging to certain sorcerers. A *kwahala* lives in a stone kept by the sorcerer, and is thought to emerge in the shape of a birdlike creature on the instruction of its master, who directs it to a chosen victim. A *kwahala* may also be sent to kill indiscriminately. It is thought to tear the spirit out of a person with its long talons and vampire-like teeth, without, however, leaving a mark on the body. The victim languishes and dies within days of the attack. A *kwahala* is detectable by the flickering glow caused by the flapping of its wings over the lights situated in its axillae. There are some correspondences between the *kwahala* lore of Goodenough and the flying witch lore of other areas of the Massim, although it should be stressed that in contrast to the witches of Dobu, the Trobriands and Molima, for example, *kwahala* are not thought to be women, nor even autonomous agents (cf. Fortune 1932, pp. 150–3; Malinowski 1929, pp. 39–40; Chowning 1959).

'fighting with food' was an adaptive response to the social consequences of a peace which was enjoined by the colonial government. Something needs to be said, therefore, about those non-indigenous institutions which have a direct impact on the current configuration of social controls, and some of which, indeed, were introduced for the specific purpose of altering indigenous regulative processes. A survey of techniques of social control and the types of sanction they utilize would not be complete without some evaluative comments on the roles of court, constable and councillor in Kalauna.

TABLE 23   *Convictions and gaol sentences at Bolubolu: 1966–7*

(Goodenough Islanders only)

Offence	Average length of sentence (in weeks)	Number of individuals convicted
Adultery	6	24
Tax defaulting	5	62
Lighting fires	11	24
Theft	5	6
Damage to property	8	2
Assault	7	5
Threatening behaviour	6	2
Riotous behaviour	5	16
'In possession of knuckle-duster'	3	3
Total		144

During the time that I lived there, more than a dozen Kalauna people were imprisoned for the following offences: adultery, tax defaulting, lighting grass fires without permission, threatening behaviour, and theft of government property (nails and the rubber sealing rings of fuel drums). Of these cases only those concerning adultery were brought before the patrol officer by Kalauna plaintiffs. In the absence of court records at Bolubolu, it is not known how many cases are heard each year, or the proportion of them that are prosecuted by indigenous plaintiffs. I would not expect this proportion to be very large, however. Table 23 gives some idea of types of cases which are most commonly heard by the patrol officer, based on a file of Warrants of Commitment. It gives for a period of two years the number of convictions for particular illegal acts.

A few comments are necessary to interpret these figures. First, although tax defaulting accounts for more convictions (43%) than any other offence, it is of no direct relevance to this discussion, and it is sufficient to note that the figure is an indication of the economic problems of the island in general and of the local government council in particular.[1] Second, the high average sentence imposed on persons convicted of lighting grass fires is to be viewed in the context of the severe locust plagues of 1966–7, and the Administration's resolve to impress upon the islanders the grave consequences of providing favourable breeding grounds by their practice of casual burning-off. Third, it will be noted that the last four categories of offences are concerned with the control of violence, and that together these account for 17·4% of all convictions. The main point to be stressed, however, is that few of these crimes of violence are likely to have been brought to the notice of the patrol officer by villagers themselves. The last two sets of convictions were in fact the outcome of intervillage brawls which took place within a few miles of the patrol office. At a very generous estimate, those convictions which resulted from appeal to the patrol officer by plaintiffs would account for no more than 27·1% of the total (i.e. those concerned with adultery, theft, damage to property, assault and threatening behaviour), a total of 39 convictions over a period of two years for a population of some 10,000. This low figure would appear to confirm my general impression – and that of my informants – that appeals to the patrol officer to arbitrate in disputes, to seek restitution for wrongs or to compel recognition of rights, are extremely rare given the amount of conflict found in village life.[2]

Apart from those cases of adultery, theft or assault (the last two likely to be intervillage affairs) which the village constable feels it his duty to report, few people seriously consider taking their grievances to the patrol officer. There are several reasons for this, most of them hinging on general attitudes to the Administration. It is not the place here to tease out the historical factors which gave Goodenough Islanders their peculiar view of Europeans and their culture, and it need only be said that they find face-to-face relationships with them disturbing and even frightening. Their experience of white men in general is that they like to intimidate and browbeat, and the patrol officer is not expected to be any different in this respect. In their faulty understanding of the Administration hierarchy, they attribute the patrol officer with almost boundless powers and frankly admit to being afraid of him: an attitude which a few officers find it hard

---

[1] During this period the council's annual tax-rate on Goodenough was from $2 to $6 for men and a fixed 20 cents for women. Kalauna men, having few exploitable resources, were assessed at $2. (Decimalization took place in Australia and its dependencies in February 1966, although throughout the period of my fieldwork Goodenough Islanders continued to 'think' in terms of shillings and pounds. £A1 = $A2.)

[2] An officer commented with regard to the entire D'Entrecasteaux: 'As always with this Sub-district the level of petty offences was low. Whether this connotes a virtuous ?oc'ety or the local settlement of offences against individuals is unknown, but the latter appears to be more believable' (*Patrol Report* 1958).

6

to resist exploiting. Some men possess magic spells designed to make them cool and unafraid (and able to get away with lying) while standing in front of the patrol officer's desk during a 'court-case'. Women particularly are likely to become almost petrified with fear in such a situation, and will agree to any suggestion that is put to them in order to escape it. I have heard men complain bitterly of their wives' failure to support them when the patrol officer turns to them for their statements; and one woman, no mean harridan in the village, is remembered as having defecated in fright when she was addressed sharply.

It is perhaps not surprising, then, that the patrol officer's court is appealed to but infrequently. In addition to inhibitory fear, there are rational doubts about the value of such appeals. While the officer's impartiality may not be in question, there is felt to be an arbitrary element in his judgement, so that the outcome of a case cannot be predicted. It is realized also that he is likely to be unaware of the intricacies of their problems and ignorant of the less conspicuous aspects of their customs. Moreover, even those Kalauna men who are regarded by their fellows as 'experts' in the matter of handling the court-case situation, and who have derived some confidence from their 'success' in the past, often reveal a profound ignorance of European attitudes in general and a miscalculation of the patrol officer's anticipated responses in particular.

Neailena, for instance, prides himself on his ability to 'handle' Europeans, though an unkind judgement would pronounce him unctuous and sly. As Kalauna's councillor for a number of years, and as the veteran of several court-cases before that, he is regarded as one who 'knows'; for him not even a magical aid is necessary to stop his knees from trembling when faced by a stern patrol officer. Despite his supposed expertise, he took the unprecedented step of taking his two wives to court for fighting each other, requesting the patrol officer to give them a severe warning. The latter, of course, inquired into why they had been fighting, and their husband's favouritism towards one and unkind behaviour towards the other came to light. Neailena was dismayed and thoroughly shamed to receive the severe warning himself.

A corollary of the fact that most Kalauna people (plaintiffs no less than defendants) find the patrol officer's court a disagreeable experience, is that threats to appeal to this source of arbitration are fairly common. But the threat itself is a sanction which is weakened both by the infrequency with which it is carried out and by the general attitude that it is 'wrong' to do so unless other means of coercion or persuasion – except possibly sorcery – are found to be ineffective. In other words, people with grievances are encouraged to resort to less drastic modes of redress; they are under a moral obligation to keep their quarrels within the community.[1] Few sanctions can be more drastic for mutually-sustaining *venima'abi* partners than a formal breaking of their relationship; yet this is what occurred when a man reported his *venima'abi*'s son-in-law to the patrol officer for an ulterior vengeance motive. In his indignation at the act, the man's *venima'abi* declared the relationship at an end.

If for the majority of Kalauna people the patrol officer's court stands for punishment rather than for litigation or arbitration, the village constable who is in theory an appointee of the government and is thus answerable to the patrol officer, might be expected to be a powerful figure in local affairs. As one whose official role it is to maintain law and order within the community, which in effect means taking troublemakers and law-breakers to the patrol officer, the village constable is a man of some authority. Whether or not he exploits it to the full would depend, one might suppose, upon the extent to which he is prepared to risk his popularity – or as he would see it, his life. When the office-holder is himself a fearless and unscrupulous sorcerer as was Tobowa, the first of Kalauna's constables, his power might be expected to be absolute. Yet there is something wrong with this picture. Feared and eventually hated though he was, there is no evidence to suggest that Tobowa abused the sanctions inherent in his office. In the twenty years of his reign as the biggest man in Kalauna, Tobowa failed to innovate new social expressions of leadership; and unlike Bumbu of Busama, he did not create a vast household of henchmen, nor exact tribute from his subject villagers (Hogbin 1951, pp. 154–60). Furthermore, the prerogatives Tobowa did gain for himself – willing assistance in his gardens, the best cuts of pork, a permanent supply of betel nut and tobacco – were in essence no different from those accorded other big-men. He was merely able to insist upon them more forcefully. Kalauna people recall Tobowa as a sorcerer first and a 'policeman' second; which is to suggest that he would have been the kind of leader he was whatever his official role. He remained the fearsome big-man until his death, which was some years after he had been obliged to resign his office owing to the ravages of tuberculosis. There is little doubt that he was held in fear because of his sorcery, his physical strength and his violent temper, rather than because of his influential position with respect to the government. It is unlikely that he could have remained constable as long as he did

[1] It is also 'wrong' to involve members of other villages in confrontations with the patrol officer. Although it may be the only hope for a man to gain restitution *vis-à-vis* another village (particularly in the cases of theft, damage to property or assault) the appeal to 'Government' may be regarded by the offender's village as an offence in itself. Note the case of Kalumana, who gave a shaming gift of pig at a Sagali festival to a man who reported him to the patrol officer for a relatively trivial delict (see Appendix).

without at least the passive support of his villagers, and it is doubtful if he would have been able to hold onto this support if he had needed to make frequent use of the sanctions available to him through his appointed office. In short, Tobowa's despotic tendencies seem to have been 'normal' phenomena, 'permitted' by the indigenous political system, and not 'extraordinary' or 'pathological' developments fostered by government interference in establishing an official authority (see Salisbury 1964, p. 237). This conclusion is supported by the tales of Malaveyoyo, who died before Europeans came to the island, and by the recent emergence of Kimaola as a pre-eminent figure in the village. Despotic individuals may be rare, but they are not new to Kalauna.

Lauya'ava, the man who replaced Tobowa as village constable, was the latter's own nominee. He is a pleasant-faced young man with some command of English, which recommended him to the Administration officer who confirmed the appointment. Lauya'ava was conscientious in his duties and this made him enemies. Knowing no sorcery himself, he felt vulnerable even while his protector Tobowa still lived.[1] As soon as the latter died, however, Lauya'ava was displaced by Ilukwalukwa, an older and more ambitious man, who saw the job as a short-cut to renown. He is said to have threatened Lauya'ava with sorcery unless he nominated him as his successor. As the current village constable, however, Ilukwalukwa is not a notable leader. People are wary of his temper, and generally obey his decisions when it comes to interpreting government orders, but the leaders of the village brook no nonsense from him and women giggle behind his back at his officiousness. His earlier ambitions have been thwarted to a great extent, and the office itself is being eclipsed – phased out according to Administration policy – by the relatively new role of local government councillor.

Since the council was proclaimed in 1964, Kalauna adults have elected two men to represent them, each for a period of two terms. The councillor's role is vaguely conceived as a paternal one. At village meetings speakers sometimes refer to him as *tamada*, 'our father', and on one such occasion I heard him liken himself to God looking after His flock. While he is said to 'look after' the village, however, it is principally in its relation to the outside world that his role is seen to be important. Here he is at best a village representative, at worst a mere messenger. Thus, in the matter of voting in the Territory-wide elections for new House of Assembly representatives, Kalauna people were content to let the councillor do their thinking for them, if only because he was in a better position to meet and assess the various candidates (see Gostin *et al.* 1971). On matters of more vital moment to them, such as a threatened increase in council taxation, the

[1] Lauya'ava was one of the four men who ran amuck during my association with the village (see above p. 134).

men of the village dictate the councillor's stand, and even accompany him to the council's general meeting to ensure that he does not betray their interests.

Within the village, there is an appreciation in theory of the powers of the councillor as an agent of law and order; more powers are attributed to him, in fact, than he possesses by ordinance. But in practice, his authority is effectively small. Villagers know that they should 'register' births and marriages with him, report to him all sickness, obey his directives (based on council rules) to pay £20 brideprice, fence (or kill off) all their pigs, dig pit latrines, keep the tracks to the village clear of undergrowth, and do any other community tasks that he assigns to them. They believe that the councillor can report them to the patrol officer for failing to perform these tasks, but with a few exceptions they perform them laxly or not at all. Nor does the councillor take any action save to exhort them anew. For their own part, people realize that they are intractable, and lament their failure to plant more coconuts or do other things that the councillor advises for their own good. 'We are bad people', they sigh, 'we should do what *tamada* tells us. It's our own fault that the village is spoilt by pig droppings and that we have no money to pay our tax.' Similar refrains are voiced by a series of orators at every village meeting. Verbally the councillor receives fullest support; but it is as if the utterances themselves were enough, giving exemption from action. This, too, is recognized as when people say, 'we only talk', adding, 'that is why we need a man who can get angry and shout at us like children to make us do things'.

Neailena, councillor from 1964 to 1967, was relatively successful in stirring people and directing them towards what he saw as the public good. He got the men to level a road part of the way up the mountain to the village, and it was serviceable for a vehicle for as long as a year. By allotting a portion of it to every man, whose responsibility it was to keep it clear of scrub, he overcame the problem of convening work-gangs. But the road fell into disrepair once the novelty of its existence had faded, and a similar fate befell Neailena's 'general garden' project (which was to be used to feed official visitors to the village), not to mention his initially successful attempts to get people to fence their pigs and dig latrines.

When Neailena stood down, wearied of the job, he was replaced by a younger man, Adikimone, a morose but idealistic ex-schoolteacher with a fair knowledge of English. His plans to galvanize the villagers into constructive action came to nought, and at the end of his first year in office he appeared to have been less conspicuously effective than his predecessor, whose quick temper and fighting spirit he lacked. People felt safe in ignoring him. It is unlikely that he will be prevailed upon to stand for re-election when his second term is up.

Comparative material on the councillors of other Goodenough villages is fairly consistent with this picture of relatively ineffective leadership, and each election results in a high turn-over of councillors with inevitably damaging effects on the continuity of the council's policies and projects. The problems faced by most councillors appear to be the same: they complain that their villagers do not listen to them, that although they possess sanctions they are afraid to use them, and that they are ready scapegoats for everything from failed marriages to tax increases. The job is poorly paid and it is for many a burden of unaccustomed responsibility which their culture ill-equips them to carry. It also involves a baffling contact with alien etiquette and institutions. Exhorted by the European Advisor, bullied by a dynamic President, threatened by their villagers (the possibility of being sorcerized is very real for most of them), worried by the need to get 'results' in the face of indifference and apathy in their villages, they receive as reward only a portion of the respect and prestige accorded to traditional leaders. The ambiguities of the councillor's position can be summarized, perhaps, by saying that while he has authority, it is legitimized from beyond rather than from within the village.

If the local government council was established too recently to have greatly affected Kalauna community life, the fairly new institution of the regular village meeting convened by the councillor is having some discernible effects on regulative processes. Tobowa was said to have called general meetings occasionally at which community issues were discussed, grievances aired and troubles brought to light.[1] But there seems to have been no traditional precedent for this, and it is only since the councillor has been required to report to his people on the proceedings of each fortnightly general council meeting that village meetings have become institutionalized. Since they often last for several hours, such meetings justify a holiday from the gardens and are enjoyed as social events with sometimes unexpected excitements. Meetings invariably take the same form. The councillor reports at length on council business and news that he has heard from other villages. He invites discussion on these topics and when this peters out he declares the meeting closed. Everyone claps and there is a lengthy pause (during which it is hoped that the anthropologist will leave!); but even more people drift along and it is clear that the 'real' meeting is about to begin. The councillor announces that people may now talk about anything they wish, which is the signal for the commencement of a true forum. A speaker will raise an issue, perhaps a specific one like the incursion of pigs into his gardens, or a general one like the rising incidence of sorcery, and other speakers – mainly the leaders of the

[1] I hesitate to call these meetings 'informal courts', though they have some characteristics in common with the informal courts which Berndt describes for the eastern Highlands (1962, pp. 318–80). I hope to examine 'judicial procedure' in such meetings and evaluate their contribution to social control in Kalauna in a future publication.

community – will follow him. They relish the opportunity to practise their wit at the expense of personal targets, and display their wisdom and moral rectitude at the expense of more general ones: the people of other villages, the younger generation and the opposite sex. For their part, women speak but rarely. Disputes are in this way brought into community focus. Delinquencies and delicts are brought to light. Offenders are given a public shaming and innocent plaintiffs gain public sympathy. Occasionally feelings run high enough for blows to be exchanged, and the closest thing to a brawl that I saw in Kalauna developed during a public meeting.

It would be misleading to characterize this crude form of litigation as a significant contribution to social control in Kalauna, just as it would be erroneous to maintain that the councillor or the village constable were true guardians of law and order. Most of the disputes that I saw handled through the forum remained effectively unresolved, and some might even have been exacerbated. The meeting does appear to have an important 'safety-valve' function, however, which is probably more than ever necessary in this growing village. As such it tends to speed up, as it were, those processes which do make for settlement (or at least accommodation) of conflicting interests. The diffuse sanctions of public opinion are more potent now than hitherto, thanks to this means, and the village leaders seem to be conscious of this when they use the arena of the public meeting to deliver homilies on moral conduct. The councillor's role in social control is a complementary one to that of the forum he instituted. He investigates disputes in an official capacity and often serves as a mediator. But while he tries to appear to be laying down the law (or his version of it) on particular issues, he is in fact merely applying pressure on parties to reach settlements in their own way, and he seems quite powerless to change the usual processes of social re-adjustment following the breach of norms.

Having examined several sources of social control in present-day Kalauna and put into empirical perspective various types of sanction, it is necessary to begin the study of food-giving-to-shame which emerged (see Table 19) as the sanction appealed to most readily. It is one which will be shown to serve the political order of the community no less than the individual in search of redress for a wrong, and it is one which, more than any other, is given complex institutional elaboration. It is buttressed, moreover, by an intricate configuration of values relating to food, which must be analysed in some detail before the full significance of food-giving-to-shame can be understood.

7

THE SOCIAL VALUE OF FOOD:
FULL GARDENS AND SMALL BELLIES

It is a truism that Melanesian peoples in general value food in ways which transcend its intrinsic value for them as a necessity of life. Its valuation is such that it appears to be used everywhere to create, maintain and manipulate social relationships. Food has the lowest common denominator and the greatest ease of convertibility of any valuable, and as a species of wealth it is crucial to the working of most indigenous political systems. One does not need to read deeply in the ethnography to appreciate that pig festivals and food exchanges signalize a fundamental cultural interest of Melanesian peoples.

My intention in this chapter and the next is to explore some aspects of Kalauna attitudes towards food, for the institutions which this book is concerned to examine are incomprehensible without an understanding of its socio-political value. Indeed, from this source springs the organizing ethic of the social system. Other values such as those vitalizing prestige, individualism, egalitarianism, kinship and community, are made commensurate through and by reference to food. For a Goodenough Islander food is the measure of all things. This is not merely to say, as Marie Reay does of the Kuma, that food '. . . stands for or signifies people's interests' (1959, p. 89), or that it is the idiom through which other values are expressed, though as we saw in the chapter on kinship, food *does* signify interests and *is* a convenient idiom for many social relationships. More importantly, however, food is exalted, to some extent valued 'abstractly and idealistically', and in many circumstances appears to the outsider to be given 'factitious' and 'inordinate' value.[1] These 'excessive' features of the value scheme are associated particularly with the 'political domain' of Kalauna society, thereby meriting close examination.

Kalauna people distinguish between vegetable or subsistence food

---

[1] The terms are Stanner's (1958, p. 2). Although I do not mean to draw a parallel between Goodenough Islanders' valuation of food and cargo cultists' valuation of cargo, I have found aspects of Stanner's interpretation of the latter illuminating for the former. I am also indebted to him for re-vitalizing the concept of social value, which makes sense of institutionalized conduct more readily analysed in terms of 'purpose' than in terms of 'function' or 'structure'.

(*au'a*) and flesh or meat (*kevakeva*). All edible animals, fish and birds are *kevakeva*, just as almost everything else that is eaten is *au'a*, though when unqualified the latter usually refers to those vegetable foods – yams, bananas, taro – which are the main staples. I shall follow this usage here, using the shorthand 'food' to denote collectively these important crops. In this account little mention will be made of pigs. This is not to under-estimate their importance in the total value system, but they are peripheral rather than central to it, and Goodenough Islanders regard them as expendable in a way which is unthinkable for vegetable food. Indeed, some villages have responded to a local government council rule to the effect that pigs must either be penned or killed by choosing the latter alternative. Like Kalauna, however, most villages simply ignore the rule.

YAM GARDENING

For a number of reasons it will be useful to introduce this account of Kalauna food values with a brief description of the yam gardening cycle. It is an action sequence of definable duration and empirically, as well as in the minds of the actors, it is the most important single, regulated activity in community life. In addition to providing a background against which the high value set on yams can be appreciated, this account will illuminate further the role of the *toitavealata* of the yams and make more explicit the extent of his ritual authority (cf. Jenness and Ballantyne 1920, pp. 123–32).

It should be noted at the outset that the 'yams' I shall be concerned with here are *Dioscorea alata*, of which Goodenough Islanders distinguish some twenty types. The 'lesser yam' or '*taitu*' (*D. esculenta*), which appears to be the main staple in the Trobriands, is regarded with comparative indifference by Goodenough Islanders. In direct contrast to the Trobriands, moreover, it is *kuvi* ('large yam') and not '*taitu*' which is on Goodenough 'the principal object of magical endeavour' (Malinowski 1935, p. 137).

The pattern of land utilization follows a six- or seven-year cycle. For at least two generations the entire community has, in any one year, made its yam gardens in the same area. 'We plant together', one is told, 'so that we are not jealous of each other's yams.' The final decision as to where to make the gardens is said to reside with Kimaola and Didiala, the Lulauvile *toitavealata* who share the hereditary secrets of yam cultivation. However, the site of new gardens is largely determined by the six- or seven-year fallow cycle and the pattern generally is to work in a clockwise direction around all the available land on the slopes below Kalauna. Each *unuma* works its own patrimonial land within the general area chosen. If it possesses no land in that area it borrows some from *unuma* which are better endowed.

148 *Fighting with food*

Figures for land use for yam gardens in 1967–8 suggest that as many as 50% of Kalauna men were gardening on land to which they did not possess primary rights. Land is borrowed on an individual rather than *unuma* basis. Even brothers may have secured usufruct from different kin or affinal sources, and their gardens may be some distance apart. This influences the composition of the co-operative group, for while the social basis of co-operation in the clearing phase is generally agnatic kinship or common clanship it is not so in all cases; proximity of garden plots counts for as much. Borrowing is free, and if a man gives money or yams to the owner this is explicitly in return for magical services the owner may have performed, rather than 'rent' for his land. Informants maintain that until quite recently the members of *unuma* or clans tended to keep together as far as the land holdings would allow, but that nowadays there is far more 'mixing'. As we shall see below, there is a large element of individual opportunism in the reasons for 'mixing'.

The yam gardening cycle dominates the Kalauna calendar, which is divided firstly into two unequal seasons, the southeast and northwest monsoons, and secondly into about a dozen periods, based not on the waxing and waning of the moon but on the position of the sun as it rises above the mountain ridges of Fergusson Island. Some of these periods are named after the appropriate yam gardening activities which should take place during them, though most are named after the personified behaviour of the sun itself.[1] In June, when all the yams of the previous year's crop have been harvested and stored, and sweet potatoes have been planted in the same ground, the new yam gardening cycle can begin. The activities of the cycle fall into five well-defined phases: the preparation of the plots, the planting of the seed yams, the 'killing' of the yams, the 'stealing' of the yams, and the harvest.

Preparation

The first operation of all is performed in secret by a member of Anuana II. At least five persons in this Lulauvile hamlet know the spells and rites which according to the mythical charter, were acquired by their ancestor Uyavaiyava from a bird culture-hero. One of these persons visits the ground where he is to plant his own yams, and begins to cut the grass with an edged stick of black palm, simultaneously singing the spells which it is believed will make a soft and fertile bed for the seed yams. This magic is intended to work for the whole community. The singer (*tokweli*) returns to the

[1] In Dobu gardening activities are 'regulated by the position of Pleiades in the sky' (Fortune 1932, p. 127); in the Trobriands they are 'correlated with the sequence of moons' (Malinowski 1935, p. 53).

village and the message is disseminated that next day all may now begin the task of clearing their own plots.

Groups of men who are to plant adjacent gardens work together in cutting down the waist-high kunai grass and small shrubs. This operation is performed without further magic, though each man may sing to himself his *yaleyale* spell to give him more fortitude for the task. A score of men will generally manage to clear six or seven plots in a day. The work is done with concentrated effort over as many days as it takes to clear all the plots of the members of the co-operative group and those of their wives. Husband and wife have adjacent but separate plots, for their seed yams are inherited individually and must be kept apart (cf. Fortune 1932, p. 69). When the cut grass has dried, the plots are fired to rid them of the rubbish and, it is said, to soften the ground. A few days after the burning, women sweep the plots with short brooms in order to scatter the ash and clear up the remaining rubbish. Rain is hoped for at this stage and some generally falls within the following weeks.

When new grass begins to sprout it is the time for the same group of men who co-operated in the clearing stage to unite for the arduous work of prising up and turning over the top-soil in huge sods. Women and children sometimes assist by turning over the sods when they have been lifted by the men using lengths of metal piping or shafts of mangrove wood. The sods are then left for the rain to disintegrate; if there should be no rain within a month they are broken up with digging sticks or mattocks.

Planting

The planting phase is initiated by one of the Lulauvile I *toitavealata*. For the last several years Kimaola alone has performed the rites, Didiala being aged and somewhat infirm. Kimaola, moreover, has relished the prestige and authority rewarded by the task. It was said that formerly these two men (and sometimes Siboboya also) took turns to perform the rites since the singer is obliged to observe certain taboos; notably to abstain from sexual intercourse all the time that the yams are in the ground, and from eating any of the yams from the crop which his magic nurtured. The prohibition on sexual intercourse while the yams are growing, however, extends to all men who aspire to be *tofaha*, while no-one should have intercourse while the yams are being planted. Sex is held to be inimical to all crops in the early stages of their growth, for it is believed to contaminate the hands and through them the crops, which then exude a scent attractive to wild pigs, white ants or crop-mould.

By August the southeast season is approaching an end. The sun rises at a point mid-way along the profile of Fergusson and the ground should be fully prepared to receive the seed yams. Kimaola goes alone to his own garden and performs the first part of a great cycle of spells based on the myth of Kikifolu (another bird culture-hero) who brought Goodenough soil from Muyuwa (i.e. the Northern Massim) and the secrets of the cultivation of large yams. Kimaola plants a single seed yam in a small raised mound into which he also inserts a twig to act as a prop for the shoots which will appear. A week later he returns to inspect the shoots which should be growing out straight from the seed. He ties the shoots to the forked prop with a 'tying' spell and plants another seed yam – not a whole one this time but a slice of the sprouting end. He beds this in the same manner as the first and sings another spell. A week later he returns to inspect the shoots, and if both are growing straight he cuts the leaves off the first yam's shoots, sings a spell and throws them in the nearest river to be carried downstream, symbolically to Muyuwa, from whence Kikifolu fetched the secrets of yam growing. Kimaola then returns to the village and announces that general planting can begin.

Planting is done individually or with the help of a spouse, and apart from a spell that is sung over the first seed yam to be planted in the plot, no further garden magic is used at this stage. During the planting period, however, which may take anything from two to four weeks, *yaleyale* spells are sung by the gardener to increase his working strength, and *sisikwana* spells to suppress his hunger; for while he is planting he may eat no food from the time he rises at dawn until he finishes his day's work in the late afternoon.

When all the seed yams have been planted and the first shoots have appeared, Kimaola visits each garden in turn where he repeats the same 'growing' spell. On his return to the village he 'closes the road' by placing a small branch across the main pathway to the garden area. This is said to make the yams grow big and fast; if it were not done the shoots would curl and grow slowly. No-one may use the road for a few days or until Kimaola removes the taboo; anyone caught doing so would be expected to pay Kimaola a shell-valuable as compensation for, it is said, 'spoiling' his magic. About a month later Kimaola visits each garden once again and sings a series of spells to 'call' the big yams from other villages and other islands. These spells appeal to the ancestors (*toveyaveya* or *inainala*) to bring the 'spirits' (*maiyau*) of big yams from wherever they may find them. The ancestors thus exhorted are not necessarily in the direct line of ascendancy of the singer; the names of any dead men remembered for their ability to grow large yams are recited in the spells.

Following this operation, Kimaola again 'closes the road', ostensibly to allow the ancestors to work without interference from the gardeners. At this time, however, there is little work to be done in the yam gardens save weeding, and during the months of December, January and February, men plant bananas, attend to their taro gardens, go fishing or just 'walkabout for nothing'. It is the lean period, the height of the northwest season when heavy rain may fall for days on end. During February, Kimaola visits his own yam garden at intervals of a few days and sings a sequence of spells which are nevertheless believed to act for all the gardens.

It should be added that in mid-February a 'catch-crop' of small yams (*haliali*) is harvested by some, mostly widows and men with many children. These yams are planted in the previous season's gardens alongside the sweet potato crop. Men deign to have little to do with them, and little magic is associated with their planting, growth or harvesting. Lulauvile men are said to be unable to touch or even look upon *haliali* until their main yam crop is harvested, lest the latter be small specimens like the former. (One of my cooks was a Lulauvile man and he refused to prepare *haliali* for this reason.) Other villages are thought to grow more *haliali* than Kalauna because (it is explained with a tinge of contempt), lacking a *tokweli* of Kimaola's knowledge and stature, they tend to plant and harvest their yams 'anyhow'.

'Killing' the yams

The next major phase begins in March when Kimaola has 'made the sun right', that is, chosen the auspicious time. He takes a 'yam stone' from its special bag kept in a recess of his house, and places it with a spell on top of three special leaves on one of the yam mounds in his own plot. He then fetches a container of water from a nearby river which is mentioned in the Kikifolu myth, and sprinkles its contents over his plot with an incantation to produce rain. (Kimaola did not perform these rites for the community in 1968, as a plague of scarab beetle larvae had attacked the yam crop in February. He abdicated responsibility for the condition of the crop at this point by instructing the villagers to harvest when and how they wished.)

The stone that Kimaola uses in these rites has been handed down his father's line. Other men inherit similar stones which, however, they will have already placed in their plots when the foliage was beginning to thicken, about the time when heavy rains were expected. The stone is partially buried to prevent anyone from seeing it. Its purpose is said to be twofold: to prevent the rain from washing away the mounds and the yams within them, and to forestall later attempts by others to spirit away the biggest yams in the plot. Such stones are removed at harvest time, washed, and put away carefully in the owner's house. They have a potency which makes any but the true owners reluctant to touch them, and on many occasions growths on the limbs and bodies of Kalauna people were pointed out to me as being caused by careless handling of yam stones.

The rite involving the stone which Kimaola performs is said to 'kill' (*luvealika*) the yams, and their leaves are expected to begin to wither from this time. The day after Kimaola has 'killed' his own yams, the rest of the community goes to the gardens and virtually the same rite is performed by a number of other individuals. An important factor in a person's original choice of garden site now becomes apparent. Many but not all men know some version of the magic with which to 'kill' their yams, but certain men and women (of Lulauvile in particular) are reputed to possess stronger magic than others. These persons (*tokweli*) are at this time in demand by all the people who have plots on the same parcel of land to perform the spells on their behalf. A man may request a particular plot of land because it is in a parcel which he knows is going to be ritually 'looked after' by a certain *tokweli*. On the other hand, a kin group intending to cultivate its own land may invite a *tokweli* belonging to another group to join it and 'look after' their yams. These *tokweli* are not necessarily big-men and some of them are women, but they would all at some time or another have proved the efficacy of their magic by producing yams large enough to have been remarked upon and remembered by the community.

The *tokweli* visits in turn each plot in the group he is looking after and selects a yam-mound with luxuriant foliage. On this he places the three special leaves as Kimaola did in his own plot, and weighs them down with an ordinary stone – unlike Kimaola who used a potent inherited one. The *tokweli* then sings his version of the spell designed to bring the yam 'spirits' from afar. Having done this for all the gardens in the group, which may number up to a score, he stands by the last one and appears to address the yams: 'This is your true home. Other men may call you but you must not go.' A portent in the form of a thunderstorm is expected to follow this sequence, to signify that the ancestral spirits are coming from Muyuwa in response to the spells.

The following week, each individual visits his garden bursting with impatience for a peep at his yams. On the way he will select from the bush a stick from a special tree and shape it into a crude digging-stick (*aba'-aiyala*). Each *unuma* has its own species of tree from which sticks are made, and its own secret spells for their use. In his plot, the individual carefully digs into the mounds of two or three yams, singing his spell as he does so. Satisfied as to their size, he carefully replaces the soil, hides his digging stick in the garden and returns home. The period from the time of the 'killing' of the yams to the time when they are harvested a month or so later is thought to be the crucial one for the size of the tubers.

'Stealing' the yams

All garden ritual up to 'killing' stage is concerned to encourage the natural growth of the yams; all ritual beyond this point is directed to the magical 'theft' or 'alienation' (Fortune's term) of the yams of others. It is significant, therefore, that following the 'killing' of the yams no more collective magic is performed; Kimaola's job and those of the lesser *tokweli* are finished. For the remaining weeks until the harvest it is, ritually speaking, every man for himself (cf. Fortune 1932, p. 128).

While the *aba'aiyala* spell associated with the digging stick is intended to keep the yams safely theft-resistant in their mounds, there is an element of risk attached to exposing the yams at this stage. Great secrecy surrounds the coming and going of people to their yam plots. Some men sleep in their garden huts (which they are beginning to build in preparation for the harvest) in order to inspect their yams late at night or early in the morning before anyone else is in sight. For the other side of the *aba'aiyala* coin is the *aifoleya* spells, which are intended to entice into the singer's garden the yam spirits of the man who is spied digging with his *aba'aiyala*.

It is not essential for a person to expose his yams and be seen doing so in order for them to be magically stolen, for a few men are thought to possess *aifoleya* spells of exceptional potency. Tabwaika, for instance, is reputed to be the worst (or best, depending on point of view) yam thief in the village, and few people are willing to make their plots near his for this reason. It is a tribute to his *aifoleya* magic that he is believed able to steal his neighbours' yams without catching them being exposed. There are few rules to this battle of spells; a man may 'call' his own brother's yams to his plot if he thinks they are bigger than his own. It is pointless for a man to 'steal' his wife's yams because he has the right to dispose of them anyway, but most other relationships may be subject to the strain of mutual suspicion. In contrast to the Dobuan pattern, however, sorcery is not made against persons suspected of 'stealing' yams, and this is not the reason why 'over successful gardeners' are in danger of sorcery attack (Fortune 1932, p. 176).

One of my younger informants had made a garden for the first time in 1967 with seed yams given him by his *faiyeya* or adopter, from whom he was also due to learn gardening spells. They had planted adjacent gardens and the youth had entrusted the whole ritual sequence to be done by his *faiyeya* on his behalf. During the harvest he complained to me that his *faiyeya* had magically stolen all the biggest yams from his garden, and he would not accept my explanation that the seed yams he had been given by the same man were inferior. He consoled himself with the prospect that the following year he would have acquired the very spells which deprived him of his best yams this year.

The mechanism by which the yam's spirit or *maiyau* is thought to be transferred from one yam to another is obscure. There was some disagreement between informants as to whether the spells act directly on the *maiyau*, enticing it to leave its present abode for one in the spell-singer's yam, or whether the ancestral spirits are agents which perform the task on the singer's chanted instructions. Some spells appear to address the yams themselves (or their *maiyau*), while others address the ancestors, so the root of the inconsistency probably lies here.[1]

One indigenous interpretation of the role of ancestral spirits in magical yam 'stealing' verges on the sociological. According to this, the ancestral spirits are summoned by Kimaola from their home in Muyuwa to live in the gardens while the yams are growing. When he and the other *tokweli* ceremonially 'kill' the yams the ancestors return to Muyuwa. The subsequent phase of yam 'stealing' from one's neighbour is thus accomplished without the help of the ancestors. This interpretation accords with the common understanding that what distinguishes the magic of the *toitavea-lata* and *tokweli* who sing spells on behalf of collectivities, and the magic of the individual who sings spells on behalf of himself only, is that the former 'call' big yams from other islands and other villages, whereas the latter 'calls' big yams from neighbouring gardens within the community. A progressive segmentary reduction is implicit. The complex magical accompaniment to the yam gardening cycle takes on an increasingly individualistic and competitive character as the end of the cycle approaches; conversely it becomes decreasingly communal and co-operative. At the the one extreme is Kimaola's appeal to the ancestors to come from Muyuwa, Duduwe, Yaluwata and Yauyaba (all places associated with the Kikifolu myth) and to bring big yams for the community he is 'looking after'. At the other extreme is a post-'killing' spell which involves taking a yam shoot sprouting from a pregnant mound in a neighbour's plot, stretching it across the path between the gardens, and making it touch a shoot from a mound of one's own while singing a spell which instructs the yam to 'change' mounds, plots and owners by flowing through the bridging vines.

[1] Jenness and Ballantyne imply that a yam's *maiyau* is itself 'called', and state that it 'travels backward and forward as the singers call it from this place and that' (1920, p. 124). Elsewhere, however, they give an incantation together with a native's explanatory comments, which clearly say that it is the ancestral spirits which bring the yam's *maiyau* to the garden of the singer (1928, p. 170). Points of contrast with Dobuan belief, therefore, are significant: Goodenough Islanders do not attribute individual volition to their yams, and do not speak of them as persons (cf. Fortune 1932, pp. 107–9). There is much less identification between Goodenough 'family lines' and 'lines' of seed yams (*ibid.* p. 108), and the efficacy of a descent group's yam magic is not restricted to its 'own' strain of yams (*ibid.* pp. 118–19). Presumably, the idea of a communal *tokweli* like Kimaola would seem absurd to a Dobuan.

Harvesting: the value of secrecy

The harvesting phase begins in April when the sun is descending the profile of the mountain on the neighbouring island. The decision to commence is a prerogative of the *toitavealata*. The dead foliage has already been removed from the mounds during the previous days in preparation for the expected announcement.

In 1967 it was Didiala who gave the word. At a village meeting called by the councillor in mid-April, the old man stood up when the other business had been cleared and declared: 'I am tired and hungry. I have waited long and we must now dig up our yams together. You must look in your gardens and see if you have large yams or small.' He went on to discuss the crop situation in general, giving his opinion on the adequacy of the taro gardens and the quality of the banana plantings, almost as if he were a visiting agricultural officer. As I was planning to visit Bwaidoga for a period, he concluded his speech with an exhortation to his listeners to bring me large new yams 'so that other villages will talk about us and say that we treat our white man well'.

The harvesting phase takes to their logical conclusion the increasing individualism and secrecy of the preceding phases of the yam gardening cycle. Some gardening groups, particularly if they form a kinship unit, may hold an informal 'harvest feast' (*kaudobo*) on the day they begin to dig up their first yams. During the day's work they roast small tubers over fires, exchange them with each other and eat them there in the garden before returning to the village. They do it 'because they are happy', and no other significance attaches to it. There are no harvest feasts, gifts, exchanges or distributions on any scale larger than this, and even *kaudobo* is felt to be appropriate only when kinsmen are gardening a single parcel of land together. Only one group did it in 1968 though this was partly because the yam crop, owing to the ravages caused by scarab grubs, was not felt to be a matter for rejoicing.

Malinowski writes of the Trobrianders:

... what is socially enjoyed is the common admiration of fine and plentiful food, and the knowledge of its abundance ... It is this indirect sentiment ... which makes for the value of food in the eyes of the natives. This value again makes accumulated food a symbol, and a vehicle of power. Hence the need for storing and displaying it (1922, pp. 171–2).

In Kalauna, abundance excites envy rather than admiration, and if accumulated food is also a 'symbol and a vehicle of power' for Goodenough Islanders, this is in itself excellent reason for not displaying it, except at the major exchanges where status relations are being wrought and challenged. In day-to-day community life, food should not be displayed. It is not only bad manners to walk through the village on the way home from the gardens with food on one's head or shoulder, it is also dangerous, since it is an invitation to sorcery attack from observers who might regard the display as an implicit insult or intent to shame them. ('Does he think we don't know how to plant food?') Paths which skirt the village are used by returning gardeners to reach their own hamlets.

Similarly, there is no communal harvest inspection as there is in the Trobriands.[1] While yams are dug 'respectfully', as one informant put it, and handled with keen pleasure and even affection, these sentiments are as private to the Kalauna gardener as they are public to the Kiriwinan. In the Trobriands, harvest displays are among other things a form of public demonstration that the individual is capable of meeting his *urigubu* obligations. With no such obligations in Goodenough, on the other hand, it is politically expedient to be secretive about the size of one's harvest. This applies also to the size and state of one's taro and banana gardens. While such things are a matter of considerable interest to other members of the community there are few open or direct means of finding them out. As in Dobu, 'all such curiosity is vented by stealth' (Fortune 1932, p. 129). People do not visit each other's gardens unless invited to work there or on some legitimate errand giving them good excuse.[2] Casual calls are regarded with suspicion. An informant said:

If a man [non-kinsman] came to my garden to talk and chew betel nut, I would sit with him, but I would think: Why has he come? Maybe he wants to spoil my yams with magic, or maybe he is thinking of making *abutu* to me and has come to see how much food I have. I must watch this man, and perhaps I should go and spoil *his* garden to be safe . . .

Direct questioning on the state of another's gardens is ill-mannered. I blush at recalling the innocent way I initially made a conversational gambit of genially enquiring of a person how his crop was faring. The puzzling reticence of the responses I received confounded my expectation that any subsistence gardener would be willing, if not positively eager, to discuss his principal interest in life. Later I learnt that between Goodenough

---

[1] Malinowski mentions, however, that there are undercurrents of jealousy on the occasions of harvest displays and public inspections. Cf. '. . . many a man is believed to have died because of his good gardens' (1935, p. 175). In Dobu, where there is also 'no competitive display of the harvests of different gardens', sorcery may be provoked by the conviction that one's best yams have been magically stolen (Fortune 1932, p. 128).

[2] Compare Dobu (Fortune 1932, pp. 75, 106), where gardens are the 'private resort' of the family, though here a principal reason is that they are the place for 'conjugal intimacy'. Goodenough Islanders, like Trobrianders in this respect (Malinowski 1935, p. 119), prohibit intercourse in the gardens, believing that sex is harmful to the crops.

Islanders who are not close relatives general conversation tends to avoid such topics. When they are raised, people mention their own gardens only with guarded reticence or casual dissimulation – the behavioural manifestations of profound mistrust in others. Being an outsider I was able to get men to talk freely about their gardens, but only when they were alone or in the presence of close kin or sworn friends. As with so many other aspects of Kalauna life, group discussion inhibited rather than encouraged the flow of information. This syndrome of caution and mistrust will become explicable as we examine related attitudes and, in particular, those concerning the uses to which food is put. Here it may help to anticipate, by saying that yams and other prestige foods are used to shame and to inflict injury to pride and reputation as well as to nurture and nourish family and self. The contradictory values which food embodies makes it as facetious and offensive to ask a Goodenough Islander how his yams are doing as it is to ask an arms manufacturer how his business is faring during a civil war.

As he harvests his yams, a man sorts his crop into three piles: one for seeds to be replanted, one for yams to be consumed by himself and his dependents, and one for preservation in readiness for exchanges. The last are the biggest of the crop, *amoena* (lit. 'real food'), and will neither be replanted (unless a famine threatens) nor eaten by himself nor his kin. He ties the *amoena* into bundles and lays them carefully in his garden house, covering them with smaller yams from the other piles so as to hide them from prying eyes. It is risky as well as ill-mannered to peer into a man's garden-house when he is absent, however, and people say they do not do it for fear of the consequences of being seen. At best they would be shamed by being 'talked about' (*veyaina*); at worst the owner of the garden-house would present them with one of his biggest yams and a scathing comment to the effect that this was what they were looking for. But genuine visitors might peep also and it is from friends and close neighbours, too, that an owner conceals his yams. One of the secret *dewa* of Enowei's *unuma* in Mulina is the technique of building a false roof where the *amoena* can be stored safely and secretly.

A man is delighted when he comes to harvest his yams and finds a few big ones among them.[1] Informants agree there is no joy like that of excavating a large yam; but it is a joy they cannot communicate. Even to their wives and kinsmen they will mask their elation with glum faces and mutter their yams are 'small, too small'. Since, with a few exceptions,

---

[1] It might be noted at this point that Goodenough Islanders do not 'artificially' increase yam size by intensive care methods, such as those practised by the Abelam (Lea 1966). Nor are yams the focus of a 'phallic cult' as they are in Abelam (Kaberry 1965–6, p. 340).

everyone else behaves the same way the deception is less a strategy than a convention. Even the 'few exceptions' are also pandering to a convention. These are men, Kafataudi and Tabwaika among them, whose 'grandfathers' were known for their big yams and were obliged (or permitted) to publicize the fact. Their descendants are likewise obliged or permitted to mention – but not to boast of – their prize yams. The possibility of their deception remains too, however, so the strategic use of the lie is limited. The dissimulating yam-gardener may well be motivated by the desire to astonish others at a later time, when he produces his prize specimens in an exchange. But his principal motive appears to be one of self-preservation, for the convention of lying about the size of one's yam points up the dangers of boasting.

To boast is to display 'hubris' (*yakaikai*),[1] and it is probably no coincidence that 'to dig up yams' is *yakaina* and 'to deceive' (though more commonly expressed by *vefwaiya*) is *yakayakaina*. Being one of the cardinal sins in Goodenough morality, 'hubris' – particularly in relation to one's gardening ability – offends the egalitarian ethic and invites the retribution of sorcerers. *Yakaikai* behaviour is appropriate only for *kaiwabu*, those persons who are elevated above the crowd during the ceremonial climax of the Fakili or Modawa festival. By the same token, boasting in a highly dramatized form is appropriate only in the most vicious quarrels when other norms are also being threatened, or when food is being given aggressively to an enemy in *abutu* exchanges.

Even a *kaiwabu* or an *abutu* sponsor can be too overweening, however. A Mataita man who strutted in self-display at an inter-village *abutu* he organized in 1967 wore several five-dollar notes pinned to his shirt. This was going too far, informants agreed, and their disgust was mingled with pity in anticipation of the fate they assumed would befall him. 'Maybe he wants to die', said one observer laconically. This man's attitudes were as atypical as his conduct. He was a fairly young man who for many years had served a European trade-store owner as storeman and labour recruiter. He was known, and generally disliked, over the whole island as a clever, grasping man who got on well with Europeans but did nothing to 'help' his fellows. He wore the money on his chest, he told me, to show lazy people how he could have a bank account as well as make big gardens;

---

[1] English-speaking Goodenough Islanders translate *yakaikai* by 'pride', but while this term might be appropriate according to a rigorous Christian morality, it no longer conveys in general usage the opprobrium and derogation of *yakaikai*. The insolence, arrogance and 'sinfulness' of the Greek 'hubris' make it a more fitting translation. (Cf. Peristiany 1965, p. 16: '*Hubris* . . . is a negation of one's social condition. "Over-reaching" shames one's fellows and sets standards which cannot be maintained without disputing the social order.')

how he could earn money as well as plant food for his children. Fear of sorcery did not worry him; he would fight anyone who tried to harm him thus.

In summary, the 'admiration of fine and plentiful food, and the knowledge of its abundance', to use Malinowski's words, are rarely given public expression on Goodenough. There are no yam houses in the villages, and contrary to the Trobriand convention of displaying the best yams on the outside of the storehouse, Goodenough Islanders keep their largest yams in secret recesses of their houses whence they have been transferred from the gardens on a dark night. It says much for the principle of rank in Kiriwina and its absence in Goodenough, that 'in villages where a chief of high rank resides, the commoners' storehouses have to be closed up with coconut leaves, so as not to compete with his' (Malinowski 1922, p. 169). Without chiefs, Goodenough Islanders totally inhibit display in accordance with the values of their more egalitarian political system.

'SISIKWANA': THE MAGIC OF HUNGER-SUPPRESSION

As in the Trobriands, it is shameful in Goodenough to admit to hunger,[1] for it carries the implication not only that one is a poor gardener, a man of no worth in oneself, but also that one's kin are neglecting their obligations to feed, and one's fathers their obligations to teach. The word for hunger is *yahala*, but this is only used within the family circle. The commonest euphemism in use between adults is *mafa hi launa* (lit. 'drum-it-sounds') which refers to the grumbling of an empty stomach. Other euphemisms are even more colourful and circumlocutory, such as *ma'abuabua ai hi luvemwaha danidanina* ('white ants are nibbling (?) inside the tree'). A small stomach is a notable feature of native ideals of beauty, while old people are envied their small appetites and Europeans admired for what are believed to be restrained eating habits. Consistent with the shame associated with hunger on the one hand and eating on the other, filling foods such as taro and plantain are often given personal preference over yam, sweet potato, ripe banana and other fruits. It is claimed that a breakfast of taro or plantain will last the eater until nightfall without his feeling hunger, whereas the other foods are said to satisfy for only a few hours. The general proscription against eating anything at all before working in the gardens, however, means that many adults eat nothing during the day for many weeks of the year. Some refuse to eat before and during work of any kind in the gardens; others defend their laxity by saying the proscription applies only to days of planting. The sanction for this practice is the risk

---

[1] 'Abstention from food is to them a virtue and to be hungry, or even to have a sound appetite, is shameful' (Malinowski 1935, p. 227).

of spoilt crops. The *inainala* or ancestral spirits, who are appealed to in the spells of garden magic, are believed to know whether or not a person has eaten when he is working in their vicinity. It is said to be their 'rule' that a person should not plant (or tend, according to some) his gardens when he has food in his stomach, and they are thought to send white ants to consume the crops of an offender.

Hunger suppression and abstention from eating have a more profound rationale than these, however, and once more it is magic which gives the clue to it. The most highly valued form of magic in Kalauna is the class called *sisikwana*, which may be rendered as 'anti-hunger magic'. Without *sisikwana*, it is said, crop magic (*afo'a*) is almost worthless, for there is no point in growing big food unless the grower can restrain himself from eating it. Without *sisikwana*, I was told, a man cannot 'respect' his gardens; instead he is 'ashamed' of them because he 'eats and finishes them'.

Sisikwana is a slippery concept because it has other uses than what appears to be the primary one of hunger-depressing spell. Asked for his *sisikwana* a man will probably give the name of a bird, and may repeat a few lines of a spell which feature in a particular story or myth (*nainiya*) owned by his *unuma*. The whole spell is valuable and secret *dewa*, and persons belonging to other descent groups should not even speak those few lines which are generally known and associated with particular birds, myths and *unuma* (see Chapter 4).

In addition to these special *sisikwana* which are integral to the myths and *dewa* of an *unuma*'s heritage, there are numerous spells which, because they are not the property of particular descent groups, may be regarded as unexclusive or undifferentiated. In native theory, every *afo'a* or garden spell has its complementary *sisikwana*, though it sometimes happens that one is transmitted from person to person without the other. This body of spells, like the *sisikwana* associated with the exclusive myths and stories of the descent groups, is generally inherited from father to son in each generation, though as with other forms of property there are other modes of transmission. A son might be taught a *sisikwana* by his mother on the understanding that he does not pass it on to his own sons; an adopted son may inherit his *faiyeya*'s *sisikwana*; a young man may set out to acquire one by performing services for a senior kinsman of a more distant line; and finally a man may purchase one from another with money or shell valuables. While the special *sisikwana* of the *unuma* may be known only by the eldest brothers of the sibling sets comprising the *unuma*, their juniors are likely to know a number of *sisikwana* of the undifferentiated type. In short, most adult males and many adult women in Kalauna know at least one *sisikwana* spell of one kind or another.

Women's *sisikwana* call for special comment since their pragmatic function underscores the high valuation set on food conservation. A 'good' wife is often defined in terms of her ability to economize on food consumption, and *sisikwana* are, some would say, indispensable aids to this end. A woman may learn such spells from her own mother or her mother-in-law. They affect every phase of a housewife's food-preparing role in the domestic unit. Thus, when she goes to fetch food from the gardens she should sing a *sisikwana* 'to make her eye non-desiring' so that she is not tempted to gather the best food first. When she peels her vegetables at the stream she should sing a *sisikwana* 'to make a sharp knife blunt' so that she is discouraged from peeling too much. (Old men still deplore the universal use of knives by women today. Traditionally, they maintain, knives made of bivalve shells were restraining factors in that they were blunt and uncomfortable to wield.) Finally, the good housewife should sing a *sisikwana* over the food as it is being cooked. All these spells are thought to contribute to the effect of making the eaters' stomachs well satisfied with the amount of food in the pot, and replete for hours to come. A husband fortunate enough to have such a thrifty wife might congratulate himself: 'My belly is full, yet my gardens remain. I found a good woman.'

The *sisikwana* which men use have two everyday uses: to suppress hunger while working in the gardens and to depress the appetite while lazing at home in the village. In contrast to the special *sisikwana* associated with the *dewa* of a descent group which may not be sung in the presence of children lest it inhibit their growth, some of the general *sisikwana* may be sung over children to make their stomachs shrink. One such formula runs:

> *Kama kasekasenaya*
> *Kasekasekuyo*
> (*Kama* its desiring
> My desiring)

Kama is the phasmid, *Eurycantha latro*, which is remarkable for its immobility and, according to native observation, its tiny liver (*asease*), which is thought to be the seat of desiring. The spell makes an implicit comparison between the calm, contented stillness and the small non-desiring *asease* of the *kama* and those of the singer, and it is sung while he plucks and chews a short length of creeper called *yalaluana* (*Piper* sp. ?). Its taste is extremely bitter and it is said to prevent the desire for food from early morning until night. Given to a child who is eating too much it is said to make his 'belly small'.[1]

---

[1] Roheim (1945–6, p. 332) records a spell connected with 'the peculiar Normanby Island magic of spoiling children's appetites', though he implies that adults do not magically suppress their hunger by means of similar spells.

Simple *sisikwana* spells such as the above abound in Kalauna. Like women's *sisikwana*, they are regarded as essential items in an individual's equipment for survival.

'LOKONA': FOOD CONSERVATION BY ABSTENTION

Abstention from eating, to which end *sisikwana* is a magical aid, is desirable principally because it is a mode of food conservation and an aid to the creation of a surplus. The deliberate setting aside of food for this purpose is called *lokona*, and the most drastic use of certain *sisikwana* is to render this surplus inedible. In the lore surrounding *lokona* one again perceives a theme characteristic of Trobriand attitudes to food, but in Kalauna the logic is once again pushed to extreme lengths. Thus, according to Malinowski:

> In years of plenty it sometimes happens that the best tubers . . . are never eaten. Exposed to sun and rain, they sprout and send out long shoots, and become less palatable for eating. Because this is a sign of *malia* [i.e. prosperity], it is not a matter for regret but for congratulation (1935, p. 231).

In Kalauna, on the other hand, *tolokona* (men who do *lokona*) deliberately deny their appetites in order to produce hard, rotten or otherwise inedible foodstuffs which are sources of considerable prestige in themselves. Again too, the contrast between Trobriand collectivity and Goodenough individuality is apparent. The storehouses of rotting yams are a symbol of sub-clan wealth in Kiriwina; the yams which rot secretly in a Goodenough Islander's house are an expression of personal wealth and strength.

Let us consider the conduct of an individual *tolokona*. We have seen how a man attempts to produce magically large yams at the expense of his neighbour, and we have noted how he dissimulates about his biggest yams and carries them home under cover of darkness to place them in a secret recess in his house. In addition to himself, only his wife has access to this chamber, for she keeps some of the large yams from her own garden there too. Here, the husband either bespells the yams he has selected for *lokona* or verbally 'forbids' them to his wife by marking them in some way. If there is no danger of his children inadvertently eating them he is likely to choose the former alternative. The type of *sisikwana* used is generally the one associated with his *unuma*'s secret *dewa*. It is thought to act directly on the yams and 'spoil' them, making them unpalatable and even dangerous to eat. Many of the large yams given in *abutu* and other exchanges are for this reason thrown away by the recipients. If children were to eat such yams growth would be inhibited. If women were to eat them their breasts would shrivel and be incapable of lactation. (These effects are also attributed to the inadvertent use by women and children of certain forms of *sisikwana* used exclusively by men on themselves, such as the chewing of betel nut with lime from a bespelled container.) The 'spoilt' yams, however, affect men who eat them by reversing the beneficial effect of the *sisikwana*: their appetites are increased and their stomachs distended. Such are the supposed effects of the most potent *sisikwana*, though few descent groups in Kalauna are attributed with *sisikwana* of such spoiling power. Even so, as a general rule, the larger the yam the more likely the person who receives it in an exchange is to be 'afraid' of it and to throw it away, no matter who grew it and practised *lokona* with respect to it.

A man with children under the age of discretion will not usually risk doing *lokona* by direct spoiling. Indeed, there is somewhat more prestige attached to the alternative method of self-restraint, and a man might justly feel more proud of himself for resisting the temptation to eat fine, healthy yams. Such a man is said to have a 'heart of strong resolve'. Although it is conceded that the longer a yam is kept the less palatable it is, any kind of yam is better than none in the period of general food scarcity between early January and late February. This is *hihu ana tova*, when 'everyone wants to eat'. The self-restraint a man exercises is, of course, aided by his general *sisikwana* spells and by other ritual means, such as putting aside on a shelf a piece of cooked food which dries and hardens as the householder's stomach is supposed to do. Other spells may appeal to the *inainala* spirits to 'look after' the yams in the house and help prevent their owner from eating them.[1]

I was unable to determine by observation exactly how long the *tolokona* kept those yams selected for the purpose before throwing them away. It was claimed that yams could be kept for as long as twenty months,[2] that is, until shortly before the second harvest after the *lokona* yams were dug up. But it was said to be an effective demonstration of a *tolokona*'s 'strength' for him to be eating the hard yams of even the previous harvest when most other men are eating the fruits of the new crop. I met no instance of this, however, and I suspect that few men ever did it, and that few yams

[1] It is in connection with the ancestral spirits that Jenness and Ballantyne make their only reference to the custom of *lokona*, though they do not name it and obviously did not pursue the matter: 'Each man places one of his largest yams in the back of his hut to rot. This is to pay the spirits, though what they do with it the natives were unable to say' (1920, p. 126).

[2] According to Massal and Barrau (1956, p. 13), yams harvested at full maturity may be kept for 'several months' if 'stored in a dry, dark, cool and well-ventilated place'. Kalauna people do appear to preserve their yams under optimal conditions. These authors, however, presumably refer to the edibility of the tubers when they say 'several months'. But this is a culturally variable factor, and is scarcely considered relevant by Kalauna people when doing *lokona*.

would be in fit condition to eat almost a year after harvesting them. More commonly, the practice is to put the mouldering yams in a coconut leaf basket and toss them unostentatiously behind the house – but not so secretly that no-one will notice them. Alternatively, a big-man may leave the basket on his sitting circle. This act may be interpreted almost as a challenge, and few men would be sufficiently confident of their powers to resist sorcery attack to risk such a display of 'hubris'. I never saw this done during my stay in Kalauna.

I was also unable to determine how many men practised *lokona* in the modes described above. As with many other traditionally secret aspects of their lives, direct questioning rarely elicited straight answers, so hearsay had to be relied upon. Most men were thought to practise some form of *lokona*. This includes the youngest and still unmarried, for they were learning the art and were encouraged by their elders to 'spoil' their yams with *sisikwana*. Indifferent gardeners or those with many children were said not to practise it, while some of my informants declared themselves too afraid of sorcery to do so. Without exception all the leaders, whether just 'bossmen' or big-men of extra-village fame, were said to be *tolokona*. However, there are differences in quantity and type of food conserved by *lokona*; while yams are the principal crop to be subject to *lokona*, bananas and taro are allowed to rot too. Evidence of *lokona* is more obvious in the last two cases for these crops are left in the gardens. I vividly recall my companion's clucks of admiration and envy as we skirted Wakasilele's taro and banana gardens one day. The banana plants nearest the path and for a dozen yards distant from it were heavy with rotting fruits which had burst their skins and were swarming with insects. An enormous taro garden, planted at least a couple of years before, seemed untouched. Its uncontrolled growth gave it a lush and exuberant appearance, clearly suggesting a studied neglect by the gardener. My companion, Kawanaba of Heloava, remarked: 'See! He's truly *tolokona*. If I were his enemy I would be afraid of him.' But he added as an afterthought: '. . . wasting God's food.'

Kalauna people are fully aware that their *lokona* practices are disapproved of by native missionaries. I say 'native' because so far as I am aware no European missionary has appreciated the extent, nor even the existence, of the custom. Returning to Kalauna on one occasion after a spell of work in my Bwaidogan field base, I was assailed with the usual questions as to the state of the gardens there and the relative abundance of food. Answering in the expected vein, I replied that while there was plenty of fish to eat, the yams were small and the manioc plentiful. (Manioc is the least valued of all available staples.) My listeners nodded sympathetically and with smug complacency. I announced to them my discovery that Bwaidoga people no longer sang *sisikwana* or practised *lokona*. 'Mission spoilt them', said one old man in explanation. A younger man grinned at me slyly, 'We're bad, eh?', he said.

Although *lokona* is liable to be confused with wasting by persons unfamiliar with the values involved, Kalauna people make a clear distinction between them. *Au'a hi venuiheyaheya* is wasting food (lit. 'food he discards') and a person who does this is *yakaikai*, 'hubristic'. It is said reprovingly, not of the *tolokona*, but of the person – sometimes a child inadequately socialized – who 'eats anyhow', biting promiscuously of several pieces of cooked food or ripe fruit without finishing any. The concept of waste is here clearly opposed to *lokona*, for while the one rejects in the interests of a pandered appetite, the other rejects in the interests of other values and in despite of appetite. Waste is the useless squandering of food when it could be converted by *lokona* or restraint into political capital and personal prestige. No less important is the factor, to be discussed in more detail later, of food conservation. The English folk dictum 'waste not want not' goes a long way towards explaining Kalauna's perception of the difference between what is seen as capricious food wasting on the one hand and calculated food conservation on the other. That *lokona* foods are expected ultimately to rot or be eaten by insects does not invalidate the distinction any more than the expenditure of capital on a short-term prestige project invalidates the distinction between spendthrift squandering and calculated investment.

Less obvious, perhaps, is the concept of wasting buried in the phrase *au'a hi aluyena*, which refers to food peelings carried downstream from the place of vegetable preparation, and also to the lazy woman's practice of peeling off too much food with the skin. The notion of the peelings being carried down to the next village (or worse, out to sea) is anathema to the leaders of Lulauvile, those ritual guardians of the community's food.[1] Any form of food-wasting is supposed to anger them. 'Do you think you know how to grow big food?' they can charge the offender, 'later you will find none and be hungry.' Iyahalina, who is better qualified to speak on *lokona* than anyone since it is said to be one of Heloava's '*dewa* from the ground', believes food-wasting is on the increase. Men today are gardening more but practising *lokona* less. His grandfathers, he maintains, made small gardens: one for yams, one for taro and one for bananas. His grandmothers made fewer trips to them for food because in the old days people ate less. He concurs, therefore, with the Bwaidogan missionary who taught

[1] The principal themes of two of the most important Lulauvile myths, Oyatabu and Hudiboyaboyaleta (owned by Kimaola and Iyahalina respectively), concern the re-securing of food for Goodenough by bird culture-heroes after its loss by being carried down a stream and across the sea to Muyuwa.

a generation of Kalauna children that they must not waste food 'because it is God's present and it is sinful to reject it'. However, Iyahalina strongly disagrees that *lokona* is wasting. Unlike those men today who 'eat anyhow' and are therefore 'hubristic', the *tolokona* is dignified by his restraint and his motive: 'he does *lokona* because he wants to be strong and for people to respect him'.

'TOLOKONA' AND 'TOFAHA'

Just as a big-man is assumed to be or to have been a *tofaha* so he is also assumed to be a *tolokona*. They are complementary aspects of the same social value. Big-men are those whose gardens are full and whose bellies are small. It is said of *tolokona* that as a mark of respect 'we cannot walk in front of them when they are eating', and it is indeed better for their reputations if they are never seen to be eating at all by other than close kin. This applies most forcefully to the Lulauvile *toitavealata*, who would not think of eating in public. When they visit the beach with a party they retire to the bush to eat; when they visit another village they are given the privacy of a house to eat in – if not they refrain from eating altogether.[1] This is said to be because they are 'boss of food'. 'They advise us about the gardens and show us how to keep our food by not eating it too quickly ... How can we listen to them and respect their words if we see them eating?' In short, these men are expected to set examples of restraint to their fellows.

A *tofaha* may be defined as a man who is known to work strenuously in his gardens, usually but not necessarily planting more seeds than the normal gardener, and harvesting crops of better size and quality than average. A *tofaha* must also be a *tolokona* to make his efforts to produce a sizeable surplus worthwhile. Although crop magic (*afo'a*) is considered essential to a *tofaha*'s success, it is in no sense a substitute for rational horticultural knowledge and skills. Ritual techniques are seen as complementary; and just as good soil is given its due in Kalauna people's explanation for the reputation they have for producing the largest yams on Goodenough, it is believed that without potent *afo'a* the soil's potentialities could not be realized. The *tofaha*, then, is not merely one possessing powerful crop magic; he is skilful, conscientious and very hard-working. He is said to 'respect' his gardens, and their emergent neatness from what

---

[1] Jenness and Ballantyne (1920, p. 131) appear to regard such 'restrictions' as evidence of the 'headman's authority', and comment that in Bwaidoga, Ukuna and Kabuna 'he must still eat his food apart, though other restrictions with which he was once surrounded have now been dropped'. The restrictions they mention, however, all relate to the social value of food, rather than to the status of a headman as *expressed* by taboos.

to an outsider seemed a hopeless chaos of scrub and bush is testimony to this sentiment. With his stomach contracted by *sisikwana* and his muscles fortified by *yaleyale* (the magical technique to produce physical energy), the *tofaha* is indeed an impressive worker.

Once planted, the *tofaha*'s yams require little personal attention save from his wife who weeds them. To produce good taro the ground has to be thoroughly softened before planting. The plants must be weeded at intervals and a mound raised around each one as it grows in order to produce a big tuber. Plantain, the other staple prestige food, requires considerable attention to produce fruits of the desired type. These are so-called 'red' bananas, which are made by tightly covering the growing bunch three or more times with bundles of dry leaves. The skin of the bananas treated in this manner turns a mottled rusty colour, presumably from lack of sunlight. 'Red' bananas are considered more tasty than uncovered 'white' ones, although it would appear that the hard work involved in making them red is the main factor in their high valuation.[1] Redness rather than the size of a bunch is the criterion used in estimating the value of a man's plantain contribution to an exchange, since bananas grow and even reproduce without attention, and while magic may be used to encourage their growth, none is available to the lazy gardener to make them red. There is no magical substitute for the skill, energy and strength of the man-who-covers, *toaikeva*. Furthermore, a gardener cannot demonstrate his virtues by allowing uncovered 'white' bananas to rot, unless there is ample evidence in the remainder of the garden of his industry and *lokona* in the form of covered 'red' bananas which are also rotting. A garden-full of rotting 'white' plantains alone would testify to casual neglect rather than to purposeful abstention. *Lokona* is meaningful only when practised in relation to the most valued fruits of one's labour.

The *tofaha*, then, with evidence in his gardens of his application and self-discipline, is said to be 'happy' (*vemwamwala*).[2] He is happy, too, if he has a number of large yams hidden in his house, even happier if he knows he will never need or want to eat them, and happiest of all if, prior to the next harvest, he is able to toss the hard and mouldy tubers behind his house for the pigs to snuffle and the neighbours to see. For a Kalauna man, happiness is not only a rotting yam, it is also a garden of overgrown taro and insect-ridden bananas. Once again, it is not public sentiment that relishes the sight of unused and unusable food, as it is in the Trobriands, but the private joy of an individual in the strength of his body and the

---

[1] Covering also protects them from flying foxes and causes them to ripen faster.

[2] Perhaps 'exultation' would better convey the meaning of *vemwamwala* in this context. It is, however, the same word used by missionaries to denote the 'joy in finding Jesus Christ', etc.

efficacy of his magic, the restraint of his appetite and the murmured tributes to his achievement.

Full gardens plus *lokona* equals more than prestige, however. They represent a defence against both other men and nature. Backed by his gardens, the *tofaha*'s reputation gives him a political standing which is all but impervious to challenge. His hard yams and his over-ripe gardens are like cocked guns: deterrents composed of the most formidable weapons the culture knows. In the last analysis, too, they are a defence against famine, a topic which will concern us in the next chapter.

For the sake of his prestige (and as he sees it, his life), the *tofaha* must manipulate the ethic of egalitarianism. For *lokona*, like good gardening, must not only be done but must be seen to be done – though not to excess. *Lokona* yams are disposed of unobtrusively, but not as unobtrusively as they were brought into the house after the harvest. Taro and banana gardens are passed by others on their way to their own plots, or while in search of game or pepper leaf, so the *tolokona* energetically tends and then neglects those plants which can be seen from the path. It is a form of display, but it is unostentatious and restrained. No-one says what he has seen in the *tolokona*'s garden to his face, for one does not admit to envy even jokingly.

Tofaha, as we have seen, believe themselves to be highly susceptible to sorcery attack, and since their *lokona* practices as well as their visible productive efforts make them clear targets, they periodically lose nerve and retreat from the dangerous arena of competitive production. Yaneku of Ainaona clan is such a man. Powerful, well-built and with modest manners, he is said to possess extraordinarily effective *yaleyale* spells. It is true that he exhibits what amounts almost to a compulsion to work. As soon as he finishes one garden, people say, he plants another. In 1967 he had planted no fewer than three yam gardens and nine mixed taro and banana gardens – more than twice as many as the average for each category. But Yaneku is afraid of sorcery so he does not do *lokona*. With his considerable surplus of food he feeds his wife, five children and himself more than usually well and frequently gives food to his brother's children and his wife's kin. His wife also makes a weekly trip to the patrol post with a large basket of food to sell to the station staff. Much still remains for use in contingent exchanges, but Yaneku is careful not to let it seem as if he is conserving it by *lokona* methods. His caution may only be temporary, however, for it was not long since he did practise *lokona* with a more or less conspicuous rotting surplus of food each year. Then he fell sick with an injured back which he attributed to sorcery. He recovered but interpreted the affliction as a warning and began to fear for his children. Seemingly unable to resist the compulsion to plant, he cut back on *lokona* instead.

Iyahalina, with his tradition-conscious attitudes, disapproves of Yaneku's excessive gardening. It is part of the 'new custom' which he deplores. He enumerates the Kalauna men who have adopted this 'new custom' and died, the latest of whom was Malawidiya. The 'old custom', he maintains, was for one man in each *unuma* (by which he may have meant 'hamlet') to be its sole *tofaha* in order to avoid jealousies within the group. Indeed, he warned the five young men of Heloava, his 'sons', not to compete against each other for reputation, but to agree to allow just one 'to go ahead' and excel in gardening and *lokona*, lest they be tempted to sorcerize one another and lest they also attract sorcery from outsiders dismayed by their collective strength.

The possibility of acute conflict between close kinsmen is thus clearly recognized. We are at the heart of a dilemma, at the intersection of two conflicting sets of values having, as it were, different loci. The scheme of values which motivate enterprise and stimulate productive effort in this society properly belong to the 'political domain' of group survival and group competition. Iyahalina rightly implies, however, that in modern Kalauna these values have somehow intruded into the domain of kinship, bringing with them the odour of sorcery fears. Discussion concerning how and why this might have occurred I reserve until a later chapter, when all the necessary evidence and the remaining parts of the pattern have been presented. For the moment let us merely recapitulate.

I devoted this chapter to an examination of some of the more positive aspects of a scheme of values which partly transcends and partly inter-penetrates the scheme of values proper to the kinship domain. In order to highlight the former I have virtually ignored the latter, since to reach an understanding of the conduct involved in coercive food-giving, the focus of interest must be on food as a source of conflict and an idiom of competition, rather than on food as a source of sustenance and an idiom of co-operation. We have by this route been led to Iyahalina's pessimistic view of Kalauna descent groups as riven and fractured by the internal rivalry and mutual suspicion of 'brothers'. If the value system examined here were the only one with vitality, then we would be justified in supposing that corporate groups could not long survive the dissensions created by such competitive specifications of life. We have seen, for example, that although yam gardening enjoins co-operation on a large scale at the beginning of the cycle (though nowadays not necessarily the co-operation of kinsmen), individual interests increasingly assert themselves until by harvest-time it is a free-for-all, with every man pitted against his neighbour. The magical theft of yams, the secrecy of suspicion during the harvest, the jealous inhibition of display, the cruel strategies of hunger-suppression and conservation – all express and reinforce an ideology of extreme individualism. They are practices which run counter to those integrative values of kinship which provide the moral basis of corporate grouping in Kalauna. Yet it is this crucial dimension of regular, mundane and simple co-operation between kinsmen, evidenced daily in such activities as house-building, plot-clearing, hunting or fishing, that we need to be reminded of in order to balance Iyahalina's pessimistic picture. The values of kinship – amity, willing co-operation, honest reciprocity, warm generosity – still persist. They may be threatened, weakened and sometimes negated by the intrusive values from the political domain, but they have not been overthrown. They are asserted with each gesture of voluntary assistance between kinsmen. A man does not need to rationalize his conduct when he helps a kinsman to perform a necessary task, nor does the latter need explicitly to thank him. Such values are still self-evident and axiomatic.

Change has occurred nevertheless. Iyahalina's model of the past connotes a more viable and harmonious group integration. Indeed, it is easy to suppose that the co-operation of kinsmen was then a more vital condition of survival; mutual trust and amity more at a premium than today when steel tools, a wider variety of crops and universal peace have permitted if not encouraged greater individual self-sufficiency (cf. Scheffler 1964, pp. 401–2). Whether or not individualism is actually on the increase, as Iyahalina believes, it is a reasonable postulate that the values geared to food production divide rather than unite, and that were it not for the countervailing set of values which underpin the customary rules of food distribution, the society would probably be atomized into dispersed homesteads. Indeed, as I pointed out earlier, the model of a dispersed society is one which appeals to Kalauna people when the tensions of community living seem unsupportable. It is, moreover, the empirical pattern to emerge in the foodless times of *loka*, which provides the main theme of the following chapter.

1   Mud Bay from inland Mataita. Inside the bay, centre of picture, is Bwaidoga. Wagifa Is. to the left

2   Mulina girls try a new hair style

3   Kimaola (left) and Didiala (right)

4 Housemoving. Men leading are (l. to r.): Dimeleleya, Siusiu (an albino), Manawadi, Daudia
5 Iyahalina orates at a post-burial meeting in Heloava

8

THE SOCIAL VALUE OF FOOD:
EMPTY GARDENS AND BIG BELLIES

An amusing comment on such periods of distress was afforded by an incident which occurred at the mission station . . . The students requested Ballantyne to reduce their daily rations of food, for 'if we eat a great deal now', they said, 'our stomachs will become distended; then when a famine comes how shall we fill them?'
                                                           Jenness and Ballantyne 1920, p. 33

Drought, crop failure, food shortage, hunger and starvation – in short, *loka* – are experiences with which Goodenough Islanders are quite familiar. General droughts and attendant food shortages of varying degrees of severity have been recorded several times since European contact (see p. 3–4 above). In addition there have undoubtedly been many local droughts of serious proportions which the Administration was unaware of and thus failed to document. In the memories of local European inhabitants there were, for instance, droughts in the years 1949–50 and 1960 of which I could find no official record. My own arrival on the island in August 1966 coincided with the tail-end of a long dry spell which had begun to cause concern in some parts of the island. 'Doctor's wife' Margaret Spencer describes the 1957–8 famine on Goodenough as a 'very quiet and slow affair, a genteel and calm starvation' (1964, p. 141); yet initially, she points out, 'routine patrols to the island found nothing unusual, heard nothing unusual'. This almost certainly has been the case for many of the less severe and more highly localized droughts and human privations. Moreover, with their shame of admitting to hunger and their tendency to attribute the causes of natural misfortune to human agencies within their own society, Goodenough Islanders are unlikely to admit 'hardship' to visiting officials or appeal to them for food relief. It is highly probable that in the absence of immediately visible evidence, such officials have frequently been deluded into believing that all was well in the communities they patrolled.

The three most serious famines to occur since European contact are scantily documented. In December of 1898 a hurricane devastated much of southeast Papua.

It seriously diminished the food supply, added to which there was a bad drought in many parts of the coast. The islands of the D'Entrecasteaux seem to have suffered the worst and many of the natives who were starving were only too glad to be signed on as carriers for the goldfields (*British New Guinea: Annual Reports*, 1899–1900).[1]

In the same report the resident magistrate at Samarai wrote:

The food supply all over the district has been very scanty for the greater part of the last twelve months, and until April 1900, no yams or native food were obtainable. The D'Entrecasteaux group seems to have suffered most from this scarcity: in fact in some parts of these islands the natives were mere skeletons . . . In some parts of Goodenough Island it was reported that the natives of that island sometimes eat human flesh for want of other food.

A narrower perspective of the same period is given by Jenness and Ballantyne (1920, p. 32):

So terrible was the distress at this time that [Bwaidogan] children were exchanged for food with Belebele and Kwaiaudili, where they were killed and eaten. Friends even exchanged children with one another, and in at least one instance a father murdered his own child, and all his relatives joined in the feast. It was dangerous for a child to leave his parent's side for a single moment lest he should be carried off to swell the cannibal pots.

Little more than a decade later, when Diamond Jenness joined his missionary brother-in-law in Bwaidoga, famine had struck Goodenough Island again. By their account 'the one in 1912 was comparatively mild, yet even that caused great dislocations in the ordinary modes of life'.[2]

On both these occasions the government did nothing to ameliorate conditions. When the creeping starvation of 1957–8 was discovered, however, seed yams were widely distributed and labour recruitment on the island was closed. The latter measure appears to have been a wise and necessary one, since the rehabilitation of the post-drought period was delayed by the absence of an excessive number of able-bodied men. There were some officials who saw in this the cause of the famine, and blamed the poor state of the gardens and the deficient diet on over-recruitment. A thorough patrol in 1958 estimated that up to 42% of the adult male population was absent, and that over 70% of the diet of the resident

[1] According to Mair (1948, pp. 122–3) as many as 1,000 Goodenough men signed on in 1900.

[2] *Ibid*. See pp. 32–3 for a brief account of these 'dislocations'. There is some irony in the authors' failure to have grasped the significance of the *sisikwana* value complex; the incident quoted at the beginning of this chapter would have seemed less amusing to them if they had.

population consisted of 'green cooking bananas', i.e. plantains (Cole 1958). This state of affairs, however, appears to have been a spiraling one which began when more and more men left their villages during the drought of the previous year. As a response to food shortage caused by adverse climatic conditions, the initial exodus of a proportion of the men is not necessarily a bad thing since it reduces demands on existing food supplies. Only if they remain away for as long as their contracts stipulate is the effect of over-recruitment deleterious. The cause of the 1957–8 famine in Goodenough was as usual drought, but its effects were prolonged by over-recruitment, or rather, by the failure of sufficient men to return once conditions for full-scale gardening were favourable again.

'LOKA': THE CONCEPT OF DOOM

For the Goodenough Islander, *loka* is the state of being without food on a communal scale. It is a chilling word and is not spoken lightly. Some say that *loka* is a spirit that dwells near the village, ready to be called upon by the spells of sorcerers who wish to banish food from the community. Old men say that '*loka* lives near us all the time'. Indeed, if they are very old it is a spectre that they will have seen several times. They all agree, however, that the *loka* of their forefathers' day were worse than the *loka* of their own lifetime. Some attribute this reduced threat to the knowledge of more food magic by recent generations, others to a wider variety of food plants and bigger gardens. The spread of steel tools about the turn of the century would certainly account for a measure of increased security gained through more productive cultivation, while the relatively recent introduction of manioc, maize, pumpkin, pineapple and especially sweet potato, has greatly broadened the subsistence base (cf. Jenness and Ballantyne, 1920, p. 34).

The *loka* of the distant past are described by informants with awe and relish in stylized verbal formulae which betray frequent repetition. Omens are heard: ancestral spirits disguised as birds sing in the village. Portents are seen: the sky darkens and 'ash' falls to smother the land.[1] Coastal villages are swamped by tidal waves. The 'big wind' comes, toppling houses and stripping trees of their fruit. Next the 'big sun' scorches the grass and bakes the ground 'like stone'. Feasting stops and fasting begins. Taro is moved to the creeks, but these soon dry up and the plants wither. Already

[1] Cf. Brookfield (1961, p. 44); Watson (1963, pp. 152–5); and Glasse (1963, pp. 270–1), each of whom reports the existence of legendary accounts of 'ash falls' in the New Guinea Highlands. It is impossible on present evidence to say whether such legends commemorate a single volcanic event (e.g. Krakatoa) or a sequence of roughly contemporary localized ones.

the old people's eyes are 'turning around in their heads with hunger'. Families repair to the bush every day to search for food: roots, nuts, berries, wild yam and the despised famine foods *laiwai* and *baima*, which resemble bitter crab apples.[1] Soon only those with *lokona* yams and strong *sisikwana* remain in the village; others live in the bush sleeping in caves or between the roots of trees. Armed sorties are made to the coast to steal fish and sago, and even the precious betel nut palm is cut down for its succulent heart. Seed yams have been eaten, the bush has been scoured and the gardens are still empty. The old people then die in the village while the young are dying from sickness in the bush. The strong of one village have been killing and eating the weak of another for some time; now they turn to their fellow villagers. Parents begin to exchange their children to eat – the ultimate transaction of a disintegrated society.

Such are said to have been the phases of severe famine and traditional responses to them. Under modern conditions *loka* assumes somewhat different forms, though the tendency is to conceive of it in the same relent-less manner – as a shedding of sociality and culture. The factual aspects, taking the *loka* of 1957–8 as our model, are that wind and sun destroyed a season's crop of fruit trees, yams and taro. After replanting as much as they could, men left for work abroad. Feasting and exchanging had already stopped. Insect pests flourished in the dry heat and attacked sweet potato, banana and coconut leaves, reducing the possibility of a good crop the following year. Extraordinarily heavy monsoon rains washed away many of the new yam gardens. Some men returned and replanted again, but since there was so little to eat they went away once more. Women were forced to pick bananas before they were fully ripe, thereby reducing returns as time went on. Children showed the signs of malnutrition and old people died more frequently. Skin diseases became more prevalent and infant and maternity mortality rates rose. Men who returned found unwelcome burdens and another prolonged dry season. In impotence and despair they left the village yet again . . .

'MANUMANUA': THE RITUAL OF IMMOBILITY

It would be mistaken to assume that Goodenough Islanders accept *loka* fatalistically, although the tales they tell of it tend to convey this attitude. Indeed there are a number of important ritual countermeasures designed to drive away *loka* and bring back *malia*, prosperity. These appear to vary from village to village. Jenness and Ballantyne (1920, p. 151), for instance,

---

[1] It is significant that these two wild fruits are taboo to members of Lulauvile. Their mandate as 'food providers' makes famine foods anathema to them.

describe an interesting Bwaidogan rite concerned with frightening away *Aiyogona* (which they translate as 'bad food'), for its spirit 'attends at every feast and must be driven away at its close'. Modern informants do not recall ever having seen the rite performed and could add nothing to Jenness and Ballantyne's account, except to state that the purpose of the rite was to prevent *loka*. *Aiyogona*, in fact, is more accurately translated as 'rubbish food', i.e. peelings and other waste. The rite makes more sense in the light of the sentiment regarding 'waste not, want not'; the banishment of the spirit of waste food, conspicuous at any feast, is also the banishment of the spectre of famine.

One of the most elaborate of these rituals is, appropriately, the property of Lulauvile in Kalauna and of those related segments of Lulauvile found in neighbouring villages. This *'dewa* from the ground' is called *manumanua*. Traditionally, it was said to be performed every year during *Uwaboda*, when the sun is said to be 'waiting' at its most southerly point, corresponding to our December. This is the beginning of the 'time of hunger', when *tolokona* come into their own and others are obliged to eat despised foods. For the past generation at least, *manumanua* has only been performed contingently when *loka* threatened. The last occasion of the full-scale rites was apparently in 1957 or 1958.

The Lulauvile leaders announce the day of the rites beforehand, as it is mandatory for everyone to stay at home observing silence and complete inactivity.[1] Two of the leaders (*venima'abi* pairs) cook several pots of food and exchange them. They are eaten by both hamlets represented, but not by the two *toitavealata* themselves. These men are engaged in singing their different but complementary *sisikwana* spells, initially shut up in their own houses then together, seated on a leaf mat in the centre of the village. The rites and spells are designed to depress the appetite of the whole community, and to make food generally unpalatable. To this end, the Lulauvile people who eat from the pots on this day consume only sparing mouthfuls, and when the rites are complete other members of the community come and take pinches of the bespelled, bitter food.

As a form of mass anti-hunger magic, *manumanua* would appear to invite comparison with the *vilamalia* magic of the Trobriands, which is 'intended to make the food last long' by 'acting on the inhabitants of the village' (Malinowski 1922, p. 169).[2] *Vilamalia*, however, is performed over the harvested yams in the storehouse to divert appetites from them,

---

[1] See Roheim (1945–6, p. 333) re Normanby Island notions: 'Immobility is connected with hunger. When hunger time begins, they just stop moving. They spread their mats out and sleep as much as possible'.

[2] See Malinowski (1935, pp. 219–28) for a more detailed account of *vilamalia*. Cf. also Roheim (1946, p. 762) for a Normanby Island parallel.

to make the villagers 'inclined to eat the wild fruits of the bush . . . and to refuse to eat yams, or at least be satisfied with very little' (*ibid.*). The true analogue, perhaps, of *vilamalia* in Goodenough is the individual *sisikwana* which men perform for themselves as an aid to their practice of *lokona*. In contrast, although *manumanua* involves the use of appetite-depressing magic on a communal scale, it is a contingency rite performed not to aid preservation of a state of prosperity but to ward off famine and to ease the community through a period of food shortage. It is significant, therefore, that *vilamalia* means 'village prosperity' whereas *manumanua* means 'staying in the house', i.e. having no need to glean the gardens or scour the bush for food.

Tambiah (1968, pp. 201–2) has recently argued that Trobrianders 'have postulated a homology between the yam house and the human belly', and that the *vilamalia* rite '. . . is really a metaphorical analogy urging the human belly to restrain its hunger and greed for food. It is the belly that "hears" and "understands" the rite which is performed on an inanimate object . . .' (i.e. the storehouse), since in Trobriand belief the belly is not only the 'receptacle of food', the 'seat of emotions and understanding', but also the 'storehouse of magical formulae'. Attractive and elegant though this interpretation may be, it does not hold for Goodenough (though Tambiah's theory is not thereby invalidated, of course). As far as I could determine, the *manumanua* rites are addressed to *loka* (to banish it), to food (to make it bitter), and to the human belly (to restrain it). Further, the house (*manua*) is not 'equated' with the belly, even though it is here rather than in a separate storehouse that a man keeps his yams. Finally, Goodenough Islanders regard the mind (*nua*) as the seat of magical knowledge, and this is located in the head and not in the belly.

Derivative and simpler forms of *manumanua* are owned by Lulauvile I and are today in the hands of Didiala and Kimaola. The 'true' *manumanua*, however, is rightfully claimed today only by Iyahalina. This claim is associated with duties and prerogatives which devolve on the Heloava leader, whoever he may be. Thus, Iyahalina regards it as his duty to make frequent tours throughout the year of all the garden areas in use, singing *sisikwana* spells as he goes. These spells, like the ones used in the *manumanua* rites, are intended to work on a communal scale and are therefore called *sisikwana lakaina* (i.e. 'big' *sisikwana*) to distinguish them from the individual type. Iyahalina performs another communal service which is seen as complementary to Kimaola's annual prospering of the yam crop. As ritual guardian of the taro, Iyahalina initiates taro planting and prospers its growth, but since taro gardens are widely dispersed and tend to be planted and harvested more irregularly, his role in performing communal food-magic is less conspicuous than Kimaola's. In addition, just as Kimaola might be approached by the leader of a group of yam-gardeners with a request to perform intensive magic over their yams, so might Iyahalina be requested specifically to prosper the gardens of a taro-gardening group. For these extra services they are paid in shell valuables. In Iyahalina's case the taro prospering also involves a miniature *manumanua* ceremony in which pots of food over which *sisikwana lakaina* has been sung are exchanged. The rite is designed to act on the individuals constituting the gardening group to assist them in refraining from gathering the crop too soon. Their appetite for taro is said to be 'spoiled'.

'VALEIMU'IMU': THE SORCERY OF SCOURGE

Although *loka* is vaguely personified and is colloquially blamed for 'chasing the food away', people believe that a human agency is ultimately responsible for invoking *loka* by magically summoning the things which ruin their gardens: crop pests, excessive rain, wind or sun. This class of anti-social magic is called *valeimu'imu* in Kalauna, and it is much feared. There are more than a score of *valeimu'imu* techniques distributed unevenly among about a dozen men. Needless to say, the Lulauvile leaders have the monopoly, and as I illustrated in a previous chapter with reference to the case of Didiala's sun magic, these scourges provide a potent sanction for their ritual authority. Further case material involving the same individuals is presented below. Besides documenting the development of a quarrel between leaders, it points up the importance in the belief system of crop-prospering and crop-spoiling magic; ideology is again shown to be manipulated for political purposes.

Iyahalina's ancestors carved wooden food bowls (*nau'a*) which are used in the 'true' *manumanua* ceremonies and form one of Heloava's more important *dewa*. Spells sung over them are said to 'bring back the food' when *loka* has 'chased it away'. When Nimayasi, a Heloava man, deliberately broke one in grief at the death of his sister, Iyahalina and Didiala berated him soundly in a public meeting, calling him 'empty' (*kakawana*) because he knows no food magic, a 'lazy gardener' (*tonima'avilana*) because he barely produces enough food even for his children, and 'hubristic' (*yakaikai*) because he is careless with food and does not do *lokona*. These are among the most shaming epithets in the culture.

> How are you going to find food when we die? [Didiala asked him.] There is no *loka* now because we look after Kalauna; but when we die, my brother-in-law and I, perhaps you are going to die too. Are you going to steal Belebele's food to live? This *nau'a* that you break thoughtlessly; it was here for our food, our big food. But you don't know these things, you are 'empty'. Kawanaba,

Kayayala and Kuyomanua, they are all small boys, they don't know these secrets yet. Only we old men know, so who will protect you when we die?

Predictably, Tabwaika of Foloyai defended Nimayasi

You mustn't be angry with him. His father gave him that *nau'a*. It is not his fault if you didn't teach him your secrets. Maybe you big men are afraid because your secrets for making big food are not good enough, and you get angry with him because you are frightened of *loka*.

Tabwaika's defence of Nimayasi against the anger of Didiala and Iyahalina was at least partly motivated by his previous conflicts with these two older men. His clash with Didiala and Kimaola over their right to 'boss' the yams was described above pp. 82–6. His quarrel with Iyahalina came about as follows.

Tobowa, the much-feared sorcerer of Anuana II, had rightful claim to the same *manumanua* and *sisikwana lakaina* magic that Iyahalina now holds, for just as the latter is a direct descendant of the culture-hero Kedeya, so could Tobowa claim descent from Kedeya's 'brother', Uyavaiyava. It is said that when Tobowa first fell sick with tuberculosis, he decided that only his sons should possess the powerful *manumanua* and *sisikwana lakaina* techniques. In Heloava, both Iyahalina and Kedeya had learnt them from Kaweya before the latter died (see Genealogy 2, p. 97 above). Kedeya was 'bossman' of Heloava I and although Tobowa did not regard Iyahalina as an immediate threat to his plan, he is believed to have tried to kill them both by sorcery. Kedeya died but Iyahalina did not. Shortly after Kedeya's death Tobowa met his own end (see p. 91). Iyahalina, having succeeded to Heloava's leadership, now believed himself to be the sole leader in possession of *sisikwana lakaina* and *manumanua*. Tobowa's sons had learnt them, he knew, but they were both young unmarried men – one a professed Christian who eschewed magical knowledge and lived for long periods abroad, the other an albino who was unlikely ever to become 'bossman' of his hamlet. To Iyahalina's fury and indignation, however, he discovered that just before he died, Tobowa had taught these exclusive and prestigious forms of magic to Tabwaika. This was presumably motivated by spite, though perhaps also by some gratitude (as is the custom) towards Tabwaika, who had done some calculated ministering to Tobowa during his sinking physical condition. Iyahalina's quarrel with Tabwaika thus dates from his discovery that the latter had usurped a vital Lulauvile II prerogative. Subsequently, both men took every public opportunity to needle each other.

In October 1967, three days of torrential rain (amounting to eleven inches) washed away some of the newly planted yam gardens. The rumour was abroad, supported by Tabwaika, that Didiala had performed his *kwei ana valeimu'imu*, rain sorcery, because he was angry with someone. He was known to be harbouring a grudge against those involved in a quarrel with him over the break-up of his second son's marriage, and the failure of the divorced wife's kin to return the brideprice. Following a few weeks of dry weather, however, the climate of opinion in the village also changed regarding the harmful effects of the rain, which was seen retrospectively as largely beneficial. Didiala himself, of course, had said as much all along.

In mid-November 1967, a hurricane struck southeastern Papua.[1] Ferocious winds were experienced on Goodenough, though there was little damage. Tabwaika capitalized on this event by half-jokingly suggesting that Iyahalina had brought the wind to follow up Didiala's rain. Iyahalina is one of the few men in Kalauna attributed with the magical control of the winds, just as Didiala is the only one known to possess rain-magic. Iyahalina was righteously angry at the suggestion of this conspiracy to bring *loka* – for it is thought that one man's *valeimu'imu* is insufficient to 'chase away' all the food. Concerted ritual action is believed necessary, and this was precisely the significance of Tabwaika's innuendo. Iyahalina confronted Tabwaika, accusing him of malicious gossip, and the two men quarrelled openly. Tabwaika's response was to declare that at the end of his festival (which had begun in November) he would present Iyahalina with his biggest pig (see Chapter 11). When the finale of Tabwaika's abortive festival was imminent, Iyahalina became unnerved and began diplomatic negotiations to get Tabwaika to change his mind. As I had to leave the field before this festival ended, I do not know if Iyahalina was successful, or whether he was obliged to accept the pig.

In February 1968, a small plague of scarab beetle larvae (*obala*) attacked the yam tubers, causing concern to many Kalauna people. Everyone's garden suffered the ravages to some extent, but worst afflicted were those on a tract of land on which some Iwaoyana and Mulina people had made gardens. Iyahalina was at once suspected of bringing the pest, since he is one of the few men in Kalauna known to possess the *valeimu'imu* technique of *veobala*. He was thought to have good reason, too, for a few months earlier an Iwaoyana man had struck Adiyaleyale, Iyahalina's son, during a public meeting at which Adiyaleyale's adultery with an Iwaoyana man's wife was being discussed. This was merely the latest in a series of quarrels which represent the 'normal' state of traditional enemy relations between Heloava I and Ukevakeva hamlets, or more generally, between Lulauvile and Iwaoyana clans (see Chapter 4). Some people suspected that Adiyaleyale himself was responsible for the plague of *obala*. His flight from the village, so the interpretation went, was consistent with the behaviour of others in the past who had made retaliatory or vengeance sorcery to 'chase away the food'. Kimoala, however, whose hereditary right and duty it was to perform the annual yam magic, privately suspected Iyahalina, and he made nightly appeals from his house-step (in the direction of Iyahalina's house!) to whoever had brought the plague to send it away again. He declared his own magic powerless against the threat, and about a month later, when it was quite obvious that the insects were not going to go away – at least until they became beetles – Kimaola announced that he would not be responsible for the timing of the subsequent phases of the yam gardening cycle. In view of the plague, which was not of his own causing, he would step aside and allow each gardening group to decide for itself when to harvest its yams, since those worst affected by the pest would need to begin the task of 'killing' their yams immediately, in order to salvage as many as they could. Kimaola added that he would forbid anyone in Kalauna to make *abutu* with yams that year.

---

[1] 'Cyclone Annie' caused loss of life and considerable material damage in the Louisiades (*South Pacific Post*, 17 November 1967).

7*

These events, all of which occurred within six months, serve to illustrate my general point that the possession of crop-scourging magic of the *valeimu'imu* class is a potent sanction; but they also illustrate the fact that the leaders who hold these sanctions can be embarrassed by natural misfortunes with which they do not necessarily wish to be associated. It is a point of some importance, too, that public credence is given to such men's involvement only if they are known to be nursing grievances. Thus, while Iyahalina was not, as far as I know, seriously held to be responsible for causing the 'big wind' in November, he was indeed held to blame for causing the beetle plague in February. The difference was one of credible motivation, and on the second occasion Tabwaika had no need to begin rumour-mongering.

The ideology which finds its most powerful expression in the forms of magic under discussion rests on the critical relationship between ecological conditions and a precarious subsistence base. It is not unusual to find in non-literate, small-scale societies of simple technology that worldviews are 'socio-centric',[1] such that 'disturbances' in the natural order are causally attributed to 'disturbances' in the social order. *Valeimu'imu* accusations in Kalauna, whether overtly or covertly made, well illustrate this principle. Deep grievances resulting from quarrels are more frequent than the minor ecological disturbances which they can be adduced to 'explain', and as the cases presented above indicate, the community is never at a loss to do so, although there may be some disagreement as to who is venting his anger and for what precise reason.

Considering the remarkable damage that *valeimu'imu* is thought capable of, it is rather astonishing that the community should appear to be so passively tolerant of the sorcerer's malice. That *valeimu'imu* is vicious and indiscriminate, affecting the agent's gardens no less than those of whom he is thought to be seeking to punish, is seen as a measure of the depth of his resentment, the size of his grievance or the fierceness of his anger (cf. Oliver 1949b, p. 15). It is regarded as quite fitting that the sorcerer should himself suffer whilst inflicting suffering on others; indeed, it provides the main hope of inducing the sorcerer to revoke his destructive magic. The anomaly remains, however, that there are no institutionalized means by which the community may 'control' the *valeimu'imu* sorcerer,

[1] Firth's term (1959, p. 80), used of the Tikopia: 'For them, natural order and prosperity were related to social harmony. Disorder in nature, untoward events, lack of prosperity, were to be related to social defects such as the religious division of the society or the feebleness of its premier chief.' But note that for the Tikopia: '. . . the association of natural event and social circumstance was one of indirect rather than direct causation – or perhaps hardly one of "causation" at all. It was rather that the "unnatural" condition of society was manifest in the abnormal conditions of nature.' For Kalauna the causality *is* direct in most instances: particular men are thought responsible for creating particular natural crises. 'Social defects' are relevant only in that they are thought to motivate individuals who are personally offended by them.

nor even formal channels through which he can be approached for negotiation. The dogma (which has the effect of heightening the fantasy for the outside observer) is simply that any direct approach to the sorcerer, with its implication of a public awareness of his culpability, would merely serve to 'strengthen his resolve', or more literally 'make his head hard', and thus cause him to prolong the communal affliction.

These considerations apply to sorcerers who are leaders and thus non-subordinate to the dictates of others; in the case which follows, an attempt to make *valeimu'imu* was thwarted by a leader with some authority over the sorcerer. In the conventional view the motivation of the attempt was classic: anger and grief over a death. One of the most drastic disturbances that can occur in a small community is the death of a member, and fear of *loka* is perhaps greatest at this time. The public washing ceremony which follows the burial is less a rite of purification than an explicit ritual counter-measure against the *valeimu'imu* which might have been performed by a grief-stricken, avenging kinsman of the deceased. The post-burial ceremonies are thus concerned not with the future state of the dead but entirely with the future prosperity of the living.

On the death of Malawidiya in 1968 his *venima'abi* (food exchange partner) Kiyodi was particularly grieved and angry. Kimaola, closely watching his heir Kiyodi, caught him singing a *valeimu'imu* spell over Malawidiya's grave. Kimaola had already invited Kiyodi to perform the principal role of *tomonaya* in the washing ceremony, so he alerted a number of men, who also knew the appropriate incantations, to listen carefully to Kiyodi to ensure that he sang them correctly. Kiyodi was still unaware that Kimaola suspected his intention, and although he ostensibly performed the *tomonaya* role correctly, the old men were later able to confirm that he had jumbled the prophylactic incantations incoherently. Learning this, Kimaola confronted his heir and remonstrated with him. He was particularly concerned because the *valeimu'imu* that Kiyodi had sung was *welavi*, a type which is intended to make the yams tiny.[1] As ritual guardian of the yams, Kimaola accused Kiyodi of 'trying to spoil his name', and demanded that on the following day he should perform the antidotal rites (*manawana*) to 'take off' his *valeimu'imu*. Accordingly, most of those who had participated in the bogus post-burial ceremony underwent the *manawana* rite the following day. Since this involved bathing in water into which various leaves with irritant juices had been squeezed, the participants were acutely annoyed with Kiyodi. Kimaola saw to it that he received a painful ducking as punishment.

A further word on the circumstances of this event might be helpful. The yams that year had already been spoiled for many people by, it was widely believed, the *valeimu'imu* of Iyahalina. Kimaola might well have acquiesced in Kiyodi's plan to avenge Malawidiya's death but for his Fakili festival, which in

---

[1] Jenness and Ballantyne (1928, pp. 174–5) give an example of a Bwaidogan *welavi* incantation to destroy 'taitu' yams.

this and the following year would require large and dependable food resources. However, he is most unlikely to have agreed to the use of a *valeimu'imu* technique which attacked the crop of which he is the ritual guardian; and it is strange that even Kiyodi should risk damaging the reputation of the 'office' that he was himself heir to. Unfortunately, I did not investigate the possibility that Kiyodi was indirectly attacking Kimaola by trying to discredit him or spoil his festival. On the other hand, it is possible that *welavi* was the only kind of *valeimu'imu* known by Kiyodi, though he was in process of being taught Kimaola's repertoire of spells. It may be significant, too, that Kiyodi's own father is remembered as having spoilt the yams with *welavi* following the death of a young wife.

If death provokes a social crisis which is seen as a possible threat to the community's well-being, it is because men affected by particular deaths are thought capable of inflicting general suffering by magically attacking the community where it hurts most: its gardens and its belly. Again we have seen how sequences of action and patterns of behaviour can be dominated and sometimes determined by the high valuation placed on food. Vicious circuits are created in the belief system by these values: the strong gardener is threatened by the sorcery of his competitors, not simply because they envy his industry but principally because they are afraid of the power resources he possesses in his surplus food; deaths are attributed to competition and quarrels over food and are avenged by assaults on the community's food supply; the elaboration of magical techniques for the production of food is complemented by the elaboration of sorcery techniques for its destruction. There is a cruel symmetry in this logical system which culminates in *tufo'a*.

'TUFO'A': THE SORCERY OF GLUTTONY

It is almost predictable that the most unmitigated evil of which Good-enough Islanders can conceive is a voracious and insatiable hunger. Kalauna people can cope with Iyahalina's plague of yam-pests, with Didiala's scorching sun and with any other kind of *valeimu'imu* which, after all, invoke non-human agents to destroy the crops. What they believe themselves incapable of coping with, however, and what inspires them with an almost mystical dread, is *tufo'a*: hunger magic which causes men themselves to deplete their gardens and food stores. *Tufo'a* forms a unique class of anti-social magic in itself, being complementary and opposite to the beneficial class of *sisikwana*. Thus, in native categories of thought, most magic has two 'sides' or aspects: *manawana* (front) and *kwauna* (back). Generally speaking, the former is positive and beneficial, the latter negative and harmful.[1] In the wider conceptual scheme *sisikwana* is regarded as the *manawana* of *tufo'a*, which is seen as the *kwauna*. There are two types of *tufo'a* as there are of *sisikwana*: *kabisona* and *lakaina*, small and big. The former is to afflict an individual, the latter a whole community. Like *sisikwana*, *tufo'a* acts on the belly, either directly or through the spiritual agency of *inainala*. In the one case *inainala* may be summoned to reside in the stomach to fill it up, in the other they may be summoned to reside in the stomach to eat all the food the victim swallows, thereby denying him its satisfaction. The main symptom of *tufo'a*'s affliction, therefore, is a constant hunger which eating fails to appease. The victim eats ravenously all day long to no benefit; he devours the produce of his gardens then begs from his brothers; he turns to theft and scavenging in the bush. Finally reduced to feeble emaciation, he sits in his house 'plucking at the strands of his mat' in the apathy which precedes death by starvation. On the collective scale this magic raises the spectre of *loka*.

Only two men in Kalauna are believed to know the collective version of *tufo'a*: Iyahalina and Siusiu, Tobowa's albino son. Tobowa's eldest son refused to be taught this and other evil magic as he professes strong Christian beliefs. Iyahalina, too, a nominal Methodist, is carefully considering whether or not to teach it to his heirs. Ownership of *tufo'a lakaina*, like *sisikwana lakaina*, is the prerogative of leaders of Lulauvile II, and an awareness of their possession of these supreme magical techniques underlies their legendary claim to have been the 'real bossmen' of Nibita peoples when they dwelt at Kwabua.

In the villages of Awaiya, Mataita, Eweli and Belebele, where branches of Lulauvile are living, *tufo'a lakaina* was known by certain leaders but is now said to be forgotten. Indeed, I could find no instances anywhere of the suspected use of *tufo'a lakaina*. Iyahalina thinks that his ancestor Malaveyoyo was the last to use it. As a form of 'ultimate deterrent' *tufo'a lakaina* will eventually become obsolete in the changing social and moral conditions of modern Goodenough. At present, however, it is still a potent threat and Iyahalina was not above invoking it as such when he and other Lulauvile members visited Mataita in 1968 to mourn the death of a Heloava woman who had married there. After the customary speeches of the widower's kin apologizing for their poverty and inability to give a pig to Heloava as death-payment, Iyahalina spoke to them sharply about their

[1] These categories do not always coincide with our ideas of what are beneficial or harmful. A love-magic spell, for instance, is seen as *kwauna*, while the spell used to take it off is *manawana*. Love-magic is thus seen as a form of benign sorcery. There is a form of sorcery which is believed to excite sexual desire; this too is *kwauna* and its antidote *manawana*.

being the cause of his 'sister's' death by working her too hard and making her bear too many children; for she had died during her eighth confinement. He wanted only one pig, he said, and closed his speech with the question: 'Do you think I have forgotten how to make *tufo'a*?' A large pig was brought for him immediately.

Tufo'a kabisona, the 'small' hunger sorcery for afflicting individuals, is still more than just a threat and I recorded a number of cases of its suspected use in Kalauna. This also is confined to men of Lulauvile II, though others besides Iyahalina and Siusiu are thought to know it. It is plainly of lesser social moment than the communal version.

A summary

The scheme of values I have been examining may be expressed concisely by a number of paired oppositions which can be set in the general formula A : B :: C : D, as in, for instance:

Sisikwana : Tufo'a :: Malia : Loka

where *sisikwana* is the magic of food abstention, *tufo'a* the magic of compulsive food consumption, *malia* the abundance and *loka* the dearth of food. The left-hand column is 'good' and 'desirable', the right-hand column 'bad' and 'undesirable'.

Manawana ('front')	*Kwauna* ('back')
Sisikwana	*Tufo'a*[1]
Afo'a[1]	*Valeimu'imu*
Lokona	Wasting
Full gardens	Empty gardens
Satiety (small belly)	Hunger (big belly)
Tofaha	*Tonima' avilana* ('lazy gardener')
Malia	*Loka*

Two other important oppositions which have been implicit in the analysis may be added:

Village (sociality)	Bush (isolation)
Life	Death

CULTURAL ADAPTATION

It will have become evident by now that there is some sort of dialectical relationship between the environmental conditions of Goodenough, the

[1] *Tufo'a* was thought by informants not to have any etymological connection with *afo'a*. The latter was construed as *a* (root of 'food') *fo'a* (to sprout or bud). *Afo'a* is the class of magic concerned with making food grow well. *Tufo'a* was construed as *tufo* (part or remainder), *a* (food).
Since *tufo'a* is believed to work on the belly and *afo'a* on the crops, the following formula holds

Afo'a : Tufo'a :: Full Gardens : Empty Belly

experiences its people have enjoyed or endured with respect to those conditions, and their cultural attitudes towards food. It would be difficult to propose a rigorous ecological determinism to account for this value system, since neither cultures nor ecologies are uniform in the D'Entre- casteaux, but the fact that Goodenough is subject to periodic droughts and consequent food shortages has clearly had profound effects upon the worldview and value system of its inhabitants. We have seen that they have suffered at least three serious droughts and famines in as many generations. What amounts almost to a collective obsession with the bases of subsistence is evidence of a deep collective anxiety about the possibility of their disappearance; for *loka* as these people perceive it predicates the demise of society as they know it. The ambivalent set of attitudes towards the size and state of bellies and gardens seems inextricably bound up with attitudes towards a fickle environment. The potential survival value of the practice of *lokona*, for instance, needs no stressing. It is fully recognized by the natives as a food-conserving device which can mean the difference between life and death. It is possible, too, that the individualism and egalitarianism of Goodenough culture are in part dictated by ecological adaptation, not merely from the point of view of subsistence techniques but also from that of survival techniques. At the very least it can be said that Goodenough Islanders have built into their culture, and made a prominent part of their value system, an institutionalized preparedness for drought and famine. That they have, as it were, over-elaborated this theme and that it is magically- based does not make it any the less psychologically effective, nor, in the case of the food-conserving devices, any the less selectively advantageous.

These adaptive considerations aside, we have noted at several points in this chapter what is more germane to the general thesis: the consequences for political behaviour of the valuation set upon food and the acute aware- ness of the possibility of its disappearance. We saw, for instance, that natural misfortunes, or the threat of them, can be put to political advantage by leaders who lack other than ritual bases for their authority. Conversely, leaders can be embarrassed by natural misfortunes with which they do not wish to be associated but which others attribute to them – a fact which political opponents may capitalize upon. Perhaps the most interesting aspect of the culture's preoccupation with food, however, is the manner in which food-getting, food-keeping and food-giving serve political ends. For while the attitudes, beliefs and values which motivate these activities may well have developed as adaptive ecological responses ensuring maximal security in an unreliable environment, both they and the activities them- selves have also been developed as political resources in the adjustive process of one group's accommodation to another.

FOOD IN KALAUNA FOLK-HISTORY

To pull together the themes of this and the previous chapter and to pave the way for the following one, let us consider briefly Kalauna folk-history. What follows is essentially an abstract of some of the most important myths and legends as these relate to the community as a whole. It is a synthesis which does not do justice to the richness and complexity of Kalauna myths and oral history, but it is one which received the solemn approval of Iyahalina who, in the weeks before I left Kalauna, had rewarded me like a patient neophyte with some of the final pieces of the pattern.

In the beginning, people lived under the ground. They did not plant and they did not eat food, neither did they copulate nor die. After finding the hole at Yauyaba, some of them came out to live on the earth and others (*tubuvagata*) stayed behind and are still there, neither eating nor dying. Although the Lulauvile ancestors brought food with them as their *dewa* they did not plant at first as they had neither crop magic nor *sisikwana*. These were given to them later by Niania-lawata 'the mother of all Nibita'.[1] According to one myth, after the ancestors had settled the earth the leader of the *tubuvagata* sent a woman to instruct them to live as they had done whilst under the ground: neither to plant food nor eat it; neither to copulate, fight nor die. The woman inverted the message, however, turning it into a positive injunction. Men planted, grew food, ate, seduced their brothers' wives, fought and killed. Traditional enemies were established and Modawa and Fakili festival cycles were begun. Food was plentiful, but fighting was with coconut husks, clubs and spears, for competitive exchange (*abutu*) had not yet been invented. Some three or four generations ago Malaveyoyo was Nibita's 'bossman'. Everyone was afraid of him because he was very strong and knew how to kill by sorcery. Tomonauyama, Ukevakeva's 'bossman', was jealous and resentful of Malaveyoyo's authority and tried unsuccessfully to spear him. Malaveyoyo was about to retaliate when Tomonauyama challenged him: 'Wait! If I finish all my taro, yams and bananas first then you can kill me.' The two big-men sang their *sisikwana* and did *lokona*; they spoilt each other's crops with their *valeimu'imu* and finally Malaveyoyo invoked his *tufo'a lakaina* magic. The whole island suffered famine and the people began killing each other for food. Malaveyoyo himself led raiding expeditions to Eweli and overcoming his followers' disgust, taught them to eat their captives raw. Soon only Malaveyoyo and Tomonauyama with their respective *unuma* remained in Nibita village; everyone else had fled to the bush in vain search for food. There they exchanged their children to eat. Meanwhile Tomonauyama had squandered much of his *lokona* food by giving it to people who brought him firewood, betel nut and pepper

[1] She and her rather shadowy husband, Yaloyaloaiwao, reappear as the progenitors of the heroes and heroines of many of the myths I collected on Goodenough (cf. also Jenness and Ballantyne 1928). They appear to be regarded as 'Olympians' rather than as ancestors, however, and it is never made explicit whether they dwelt under the ground with humans.

leaf, until he had only one huge yam left. He used this yam as a pillow, but one day his own kinsmen stole and ate it while he slept. When he awoke and found it gone he wept and fled the village, leaving Malaveyoyo supreme. The latter tracked his victim down and killed him by a blow across the throat with his club.[1] After he and his brothers had eaten Tomonauyama, Malaveyoyo took his bones and buried them with *sisikwana* and *manumanua* rites to end the famine, and he made new *nau'a* (wooden bowls) to bring back prosperity and plenty. He promoted a Modawa festival to attract the people out of the bush and back into the village, and when it was concluded after a year he distributed food and pigs among the whole of Nibita. He told the people that fighting and cannibalism must finish; that henceforth they must fight only with food. But Tomonauyama's sister wanted revenge. She cooked pots of food with shell valuables hidden inside and took them to a Kwaiaudili village. After eating her food and finding the valuables, the Kwaiaudili men asked her what she wanted. She told them. They set up an ambush and invited Malaveyoyo and his kinsmen to come for pigs. They came and only Malaveyoyo's son escaped alive. Before being speared to death Malaveyoyo doctored his own body with sorcery, and the whole village, save one girl, died from eating his poisoned flesh. Soon after this event, the Mission and the Government came to Goodenough. Men still sometimes want to 'chase away' the food with their sorcery, but Christianity is 'changing their minds'. Men still sometimes want to fight with spears, too, but the Government stops them so now they fight with food instead.

This condensed but fairly representative view of Kalauna folk-history offers several themes which have relevance for this study, but here I mention only those concerned with the relation between food values, leadership and social control. The main dialectic of the story is apparent. There are four temporal sequences characterized by the absence or presence of food and the absence or presence of society. Whereas the absence of food in the primeval state of underground non-social existence was associated with a moral purity, the inverted injunctions created a state of social existence which bred conflict and thus the need for social controls. The result of overt competition between leaders for supremacy was an utterly uncompromising struggle which edged the society into famine and towards virtual disintegration. Although they adopted a mode of non-violent contest it proved catastrophic for community and contenders alike. It is perhaps puzzling, therefore, that informants should see in this contest a prototypic form of *abutu* or competitive food exchange, for this is today one of the most highly valued and politically significant institutions in the society. The paradox might be resolved by conceiving of the contest as a

---

[1] In another version of the story Tomonauyama *won* the contest with his yam and Malaveyoyo killed him out of anger and jealousy. Significantly, this is Ukevakeva's version and is scorned by Iyahalina, Malaveyoyo's 'grandson'. Both versions agree, however, that Tomonauyama fled the village while Malaveyoyo remained.

mythical inversion; a statement of how *not* to conduct *abutu*. Instead of doing their best to out-give each other as contenders in *abutu* must do, they did their worst to out-deprive each other; instead of obeying the code of rules which ensure that *abutu* is a controlled, integrative surrogate for fighting, the rivals in the mythical contest used destructive magic indiscriminately with a disintegrative effect more calamitous than their fighting could ever have been; while as to their conduct, Tomonauyama was too generous and too careless to win the contest, and Malaveyoyo too ruthless and vindictive to escape ultimate retribution.

The most general lesson of the tale, however, concerns the absolute dependence of community and culture upon food resources, and this is dramatically underlined by telescoping into a single episode what, historically, must have been several periods of famine. Famine means not only individual suffering but the attrition of kinship values and ultimately the total negation of social life. This is expressed by the abandonment of the village for the bush, the fragmentation of kin groups, the eating of uncooked human flesh, the theft by Tomonauyama's brothers of his last yam, and that terrible symbol of cultural suicide, the eating of children.

9

COMPETITIVE FOOD EXCHANGES: THE ETHNOGRAPHY OF *ABUTU*

My informants frequently said: 'Now we no longer fight our enemies with spears; it is taboo; now we only fight with yams.'   Kaberry, 1941, p. 344

Like the Abelam of north-east New Guinea, Kalauna people assert: 'Before we fought with spears, but today we fight with food.' My main intention in this and the following chapter is to examine in the light of this statement the contemporary form of *abutu*, a species of competitive food exchange.[1] The implication that aggressive food-giving with intent to shame an opponent is a surrogate for feud or warfare emerges quite clearly from the data. What is less compelling, however, is the suggestion that such food-giving is also a peacekeeping device and a mode of dispute-resolution. Thus, while it is not difficult to show that men provoked to anger reach for their yams rather than their spears, it is less easy to demonstrate that by so doing they are guaranteed restitution or settlement of their differences. Like fighting, *abutu* can compound problems of social control rather than solve them. On the whole, however, the observer must agree with the participants: 'abutu is less disruptive than fighting and therefore preferable to it as an institutionalized response to certain delicts.

Abutu is a regulative, organizational institution rather than a structural one. Empirically, it is a complex set of operations involving the exchange of food by persons exercising choice in the pursuit of specific goals which may loosely be defined as political. However, it crosscuts the conventional analytical categories of 'economic', 'political', 'religious', etc., and for this reason I have found it more useful to consider it in terms of 'transective' concepts such as 'operation', 'transaction' and 'value' (see Stanner 1963, p. viii). These concepts also facilitate assessment of the relationship between *abutu* and other exchange systems in the society, particularly the Modawa–Fakili festival cycle to be described in the last chapter.

[1] The etymology of the word would appear to be *a* – root of 'food', *butu* – 'loud noise'. *Butu* is occasionally used metaphorically to mean 'fame'.

SOME PARAMETERS

Abutu between 'hostile' factions of the village take place about once a year in Kalauna. They are only occasionally planned in advance, most being contingent and 'declared' spontaneously. They are nevertheless virtually an annual event, and at least ten took place during the decade 1958–67. *Abutu* between villages, while similar in form and scale, tend to be slightly less frequent and to take place for somewhat different reasons. Kalauna had engaged in eight intervillage *abutu* over the same decade. The significance of the distinction between inter- and intravillage *abutu* will emerge below.

During my stay in Kalauna I witnessed two *abutu*: one between contestants within the village in October 1966, and one between Kalauna and Eweli, its neighbour to the north, in January 1968. At least a dozen more were threatened between October 1966 and June 1968, but they did not eventuate. Both *abutu* which did take place during this period were full-scale affairs, which is to say that the whole village participated in them. This nowadays tends to be the rule rather than the exception, unless the two parties to the *abutu* belong to the same clan. The relation between size, scale and frequency of *abutu* is determined largely by food resources; if more than one are held in a gardening year those subsequent to the first would tend to be smaller in terms of quantities of food exchanged, and more limited in terms of the number of participant individuals and groups.

STATUS SETS

The principal transaction of *abutu* is the competitive exchange of vegetable food and usually but not invariably pigs, by two parties who regard each other, temporarily if not permanently, as enemies (*nibai*). Each party to the *abutu* is made up of four categories of actors which together form what Barth (1966, p. 5) would presumably call a status set. Concisely, *inuba* (lit. 'initiator(s)') are the principal combatants, *fofofo* their unconditional supporters, *veo'owana* specific supporters linked matrilineally to *inuba*, and *tabotabo* residual helpers who stand in a variety of relationships to *inuba*, and are likely to be committed to supporting the opposing *inuba* also.

The term *inuba* applies to the individual challenger and the person he challenges, and to their respective agnatic kin groups up to the segmentary level at which *fofofo* are formed (see Chapter 4). As sponsors or initiators of the *abutu* and those who are being tried by the contest, they are expected to provide the greatest amount of food in proportion to their numbers.

Only the leading principals, however, the individuals who initiate the *abutu*, are expected to exhaust their food resources completely. Beyond this, the *inuba*'s role is conspicuously and deliberately non-participant. All organizing and speech-making, all pooling, exchanging and redistributing of food is performed by the *fofofo*. The *inuba* are obliged to look on without interference, even if fighting should occur. For the duration of the *abutu* they are *kaiwabu* and should behave as such, affecting utter disdain for the proceedings.[1] Finally, as *inuba* they may not eat any of the food or pork which is involved in the *abutu*, particularly that given to them by opponents. This food is their *niune* or prohibited food.

Fofofo are frequently described as 'those who eat our *niune*'. They are also said to be the 'children' (*kwamana*) of the *inuba* they serve, who in the same context can be called 'parents' (*ainana*).[2] *Fofofo* should serve their *inuba* as grown children serve their parents: unconditionally, unstintingly, and up to a point, unquestioningly. The *fofofo* make (and on the opposing side, should receive) the challenge on their *inuba*'s behalf, and they should perform all the operational and organizational tasks associated with the *abutu*. Finally, they eat their *inuba*'s *niune*; and so that the *inuba* shall not go hungry, *fofofo* give them food from their own gardens (*kamoabi*) and perhaps one of their own pigs.

Veo'owana are self-selected supporters of *inuba*, usually their *tubuya* (sisters' sons, fathers' sisters' sons etc.), who share the *inuba*'s prohibitions and like the *fofofo* commit themselves to giving *inuba* their undivided assistance. Not everyone whose mother came from the *inuba* group chooses to be *veo'owana*, though generally at least one of a set of siblings will do so. It is yet another tacit acknowledgement of the permanent obligation that wife-receivers owe to wife-givers (mother's kin in the following generation). Since they are identifying with the *inuba*, food that *veo'owana* receive in the exchange is their own *niune* and must be given to their own *fofofo*, who give them *kamoabi* in return.

The residual category of persons involved in an *abutu*, the *tabotabo*,[3] are defined simply by belonging to none of the other categories. *Tabotabo* may include such friends, more distant kinsmen (*dala*, *weyo*, etc.), and affines as wish or are obliged to give their support to one or both sides. The food they receive in return for helping an *inuba* is exchanged with their own

[1] See Chapter 11 for a full analysis of *kaiwabu* behaviour.

[2] It should be noted that 'true' kinship terms take possessive suffixes. Pronominal forms (*yaku kwamana*, my child; *yaku ainana*, my parent) put these in a separable or detachable semantic category of persons. Their 'detachability' arises from the need to reverse the terms with the roles, i.e. in contexts where the *fofofo* becomes *inuba* (and thus 'parent') and the *inuba* becomes *fofofo* (and thus 'child').

[3] Etymologically, *tabotabo* is probably a reduplication of the root of *tabona* 'above' or 'on top', a word which is also used of food added to a pile.

fofofo so that *tabotabo*, too, do not eat food that is directly received in *abutu*. If the side that a group of *tabotabo* are supporting should win heavily, and the 'enemy' be unable to reciprocate the quantity of food given them, these *tabotabo* must, like the *fofofo*, be prepared to await their repayment. It is the 'burden' of the winning side to be deprived of food and to have less to eat than the losers.

Within the ranks of the *tabotabo*, the affines of the *inuba* deserve special comment. Men who are married to women of the *inuba* group are expected to give generous help to their affines. Men whose sisters are married to *inuba* are less obligated, but providing they owe no special allegiance to the other side they would also be expected to help. *Tabotabo* caught in the middle by a primary relationship to both sides must weight their obligations carefully to avoid offending one or the other. The same stricture, of course, applies also to those men who are *inuba* or *fofofo* on one side and related affinally to the 'enemy'.

Wasimala's sister was married to Adiyaleyale, Iyahalina's son, whose *abutu* with Ukevakeva took place in October 1966. Wasimala belonged to Adiyaleyale's wider *fofofo* group of Lulauvile I, but his wife was a member of Adiyaleyale's *abutu* 'enemy', Ukevakeva. Wasimala tried to help both sides equally by giving several large yams to both – to his *fofofo* openly but to his wife's kin secretly, as is the custom in such circumstances. Even so, his sister found cause to criticize him bitterly, for she discovered that one of the yams he had given to help his affines in Ukevakeva, Adiyaleyale was unable to match in size and thus pay back. In the same *abutu* Kimaola, one of the 'wider' Lulauvile *fofofo*, gave most aid to his *inuba*, but he also sent a few yams to Ukevakeva under cover of darkness because two of his sisters had married there, and more importantly, one of them had a personal grievance against Adiyaleyale which Kimaola wished to support.

Since it is possible for *tabotabo* to be more numerous than the other three categories put together – and this would be the case in a full-scale village *abutu* – their total contribution can be at least equal to that of the others. An *abutu*, therefore, can be lost or won depending upon the strength of an *inuba*'s support from this quarter. There is a rider, however, for *tabotabo* are unlikely to commit their biggest yams or any pigs to an *abutu* which only marginally involves them, and for this reason their contributions are ultimately rated lower than those of the other three categories. Further, whereas the *inuba*, *veo'owana* and *fofofo* should be virtually undivided in their support of the main protagonist (the *fofofo*, at least, subject to the kind of considerations mentioned in the examples above), the *tabotabo* as a whole may be expected to split their allegiance and help both parties to the contest in varying degrees and according to personal weighing of obligations and individual calculations of advantage.

Since the obligations tend to run along kinship lines, the distribution of allegiances of any set of *tabotabo* for any given *abutu* situation is fairly predictable.

As an illustration of the cross-cutting pattern which can result from differential *tabotabo* obligations, let us consider a hypothetical *abutu* between two big-men, Kimaola (Lulauvile clan) and Kafataudi (Nouneya clan). The following distribution of allegiances of the members of Mulina (a small clan which would be regarded as nominally and collectively *tabotabo* in this case), is based on their own assessment of whom they would help and why.

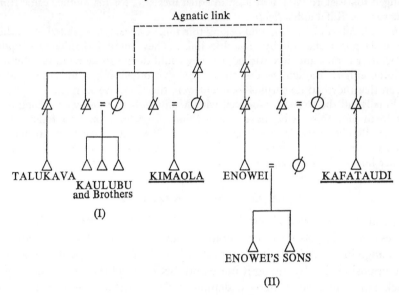

Genealogy 10. Skeleton genealogy of two Mulina *unuma* showing relationships to Kimaola and Kafataudi

1. Kaulubu and his two brothers would help Kimaola, since their mother was his father's sister. They are his *tubuya* and therefore potential *veo'owana*.
2. Belonging to the same *unuma* as Kaulubu, Talukava would also help Kimaola, though he would have less obligation to do so and if for personal reasons he chose to support Kafataudi too, Kimaola would have no grounds for complaint.
3. Enowei would support Kimaola, his classificatory *tubuya*, because Kimaola's mother belonged to Enowei's *unuma*. If Enowei's wife were still alive, however, he would be obliged to give Kafataudi token assistance since her mother was Kafataudi's father's sister and Enowei called him 'brother-in-law'. Since she is dead and Enowei had remarried, only his sons by this woman remain in any sense obligated to help Kafataudi.
4. Enowei's two grown sons, however, would be equally obliged to help

Kimaola since their mother belonged to the same clan-section (Lulauvile I) although they do not call him 'mother's brother' as the relationship cannot be traced. In other *abutu* circumstances one of these brothers could choose to be *veo'owana* to Kimaola, but because Kafataudi is the 'enemy' *inuba* in this hypothetical instance, he would be offended if Enowei's sons identified themselves with Kimaola to this extent. *Veo'owana* implies a partisan pledge to support one side to the exclusion of the other. In this case Enowei's sons would demonstrate their support of both as *tabotabo*.

5. Kwalauya is the only adult male member of Mulina's third *unuma*. Although a good personal friend and *aveyau* (eating companion) of Kimaola, he would feel obliged to assist Kafataudi at least in equal measure, for his mother came from Ukevakeva, Kafataudi's *fofofo*.

6. Gidagida and Leoleo, who belong to a fourth *unuma*, are related to neither Kimaola nor Kafataudi by traceable links. They could individually support whichever contestant they wished, or they could demonstrate neutrality by not helping either – though there is the danger that others might interpret this to mean that they had no surplus food and were therefore 'weak' men.

Finally, all the women associated with Mulina – both those who belong to it by birth and those who have married into it – would tend to follow their husband's obligations and wishes, including those they may have created by their own marriages. *Abutu* is a man's game and most of a woman's produce is at her husband's disposal.

OBJECTS OF TRANSACTION

A great deal was said about food in the previous chapters, but here it is necessary to discuss it from the point of view of its use as the commodity of exchange in *abutu*. The dominant intention of a party to *abutu* is to shame the opposing side by giving it more and 'better' food than it is able to pay back simultaneously, thereby demonstrating – within the terms of the culture – greater power, worthiness, and even virtue. A considerable body of lore exists, therefore, concerning the definitions applicable to quantity and quality of food and the comparative merits of different types of produce. Interesting though this lore may be, there is no space to treat it in any depth here. It is well to bear in mind, however, that as the repository of most social values, food has multiple referents; in giving certain types, quantities or qualities of food in *abutu* the donors are 'saying' certain things about their relationship to the recipients. At a gross level this means, for instance, that food which it is appropriate to give to an enemy in *abutu* is highly inappropriate for giving to affines in a marriage exchange. In the former case a certain type of yam, painted and with a pandanus streamer attached, connotes hostility and intent to wound – it wears the dress of warriorhood. The same yam given to an affine would be something of an atrocity and few men would have the nerve to commit it, whatever their personal feelings towards a wife's kinsman. Stated crudely, there are distinctions to be made between food given and received in a kinship context, in an affinal context and in a context external to these, which may be labelled 'political'. The last is the realm of 'enemies'. Food is welcomed as nurturing in the first context, accepted as satisfying in the second, and feared as shaming in the last. The first is given informally and received willingly, the second is given modestly and received diffidently, and the last is given aggressively and received with a reluctance which is dissimulated by a show of indifference. Somewhere in the middle of this range of attitudes, mediating between welcome and unwelcome food and between the kinship and the political domain, stand *fofofo*, who accept the shaming and potentially dangerous *niune* given by the enemy. (It is dangerous in a more than political and symbolic sense, because the possibility exists that the enemy has spoilt it by sorcery or by *lokona* techniques. Some of the most magnificent food given in *abutu* is actually thrown away by the *fofofo*, who are as susceptible to 'poisoning' as their *inuba*.)

Yams are the food concerning which there is most lore and to which the culture has ascribed the most versatile social uses; they are also the crop for which there is most identification between the grower and his produce. 'If we did not grow yams we would be like dogs', people say. It is not surprising, then, that yams are the supreme *abutu* food. There are seasons when few, if any, yams are available, however, and at these times *abutu* can be made with taro or bananas as the principal exchange food. An *abutu* challenger has the prerogative of choosing his weapon, and there is an obvious strategic advantage in this, for he will be aware of his own strength and his opponent's weakness. But the structure of *abutu* enables the other side to deploy its own particular strength in turn, so that the challenger who eschews yams in favour of another crop when yams are in fact available is courting defeat.

Yams given in *abutu* are displayed and measured in a variety of ways, depending upon their size and type. Concisely, those of relatively uniform medium size are laid side by side along a platform (*deudeu*) which may be anything up to a few hundred feet long. A vine measure (*liva*) is placed along the length of the *deudeu* on top of the yams. These are paid back by the opposite side in the same manner, using the identical *liva* to demonstrate equivalence. The largest yams are displayed separately, and are measured individually by means of pandanus 'string' tacked with thorns along their greatest length and width. Such yams are usually decorated with streamers and sometimes painted with ochre. They must be paid back according to variety and size as measured by the *liva*. The smallest yams and *taitu* are set in small piles on the ground or, if sufficient utensils are available, stacked into large wooden platters around a single long yam which acts as a centre-pole. Such piles may also be measured by a *liva* pinned from one side to the other over the greatest height, and must be paid back in the same manner, using the same utensil and the same *liva*; on the other hand, they may be measured by the basket-full when they are carried away. It is the big yams, however, which are the donor's pride and glory, and in which can reside the recipient's shame and defeat. *Liva* of such yams are kept in the house of the *abutu* protagonist, perhaps for years, until he can pay them back. If he dies without having done so, his heir inherits them and refers to them as his *hiyo* (spear). Like thorns in his conscience, the *liva* are sharp reminders that he has unpaid debts. Shame is the spur to repayment, as we shall see below.

Taro are laid on small platforms and measured in the same way as *deudeu* for yams. Good *abutu* taro should be round rather than long, and the leaves are generally left attached for preservation and decoration. They are not otherwise decorated and few, if any, are measured individually with *liva*. Individual banana bunches, too, are rarely measured. They are tied to large upright structures (*aiyala*) and counted by the bunch – by means of notches on a coconut leaf stem – as they are cut down and carried away by the recipient's *fofofo*. 'Red' plantains should predominate on the stand as evidence of the donors' gardening industry, and 'red' ones should be paid back in similar proportion or the return will be scorned as unequal and beggarly. Other foods may be given in *abutu*, but in generally insignificant proportions in relation to the three main crops. Whatever is given in addition to these must be large enough to test the opponent: exceptional specimens of sweet potato, *waboya* (*Amorphophallus*), and even giant pumpkins. Manioc, in fact, is the only common crop which it is unthinkable to give in *abutu*, for like the edible fruits of trees, it has minimal social value. 'People do not fight over manioc' it is said.

Pigs are important objects of transaction in most *abutu*, and an *abutu* without at least one pig given on either side is felt to be as incomplete and unsatisfactory as one without yams. About three-quarters of the total number of *abutu* for which data were recorded involved pigs. Only domestic pigs may be given, however, and the prohibition on the use of fish, wallaby and other game applies also to wild pig. The principle is the same as that behind the fitness of the main food crops for *abutu*; because they are not nurtured by the donor's resources, wild pigs are no more evidence of gardening industry than manioc or breadfruit. Individual or collective wealth in pigs is thus conceptually reduced to a denominator of wealth in food. (The conversion is only made in practice when piglets are purchased with food – usually baskets of yams.) In *abutu* pigs are measured with *liva*, and the return animals should be equivalent in size or preferably (from the donor's point of view) slightly larger. Pigs are said to be 'dead' when they are given but they are in fact carried away alive by the recipients. They must be eaten, however, and not kept for further rearing.

OUTLINE OF 'ABUTU' OPERATIONS

The ceremonial quality of much *abutu* conduct permits fairly general description. In the outline that follows, the basic operations performed by the actors are mentioned without too much qualification, though an exhaustive treatment would require digression into the great variety of contingencies and conditions which affect the form of any particular *abutu*. Thus, all *abutu* consist of a number of relatively discrete phases: (1) the challenge, (2) the first prestation, (3) the return prestation, (4) the second prestation, and (5) the final redistribution. These phases, with the occasional exception of (4) constitute the invariant structural form of *abutu*. However, particular circumstances such as prior relationship between contenders, season of the year, scale of community involvement, and not least, reason for *abutu* may add certain behavioural elements to, or subtract them from the internal organization of the phases, as, for example, when a food type which was absent in the first exchange is introduced in the second exchange, or when an *inuba* 'buys' the help of unrelated *tabotabo* in an attempt to avert defeat.

(1) *The Challenge*

The person wishing to initiate *abutu* consults his *fofofo* to determine their willingness to help. An accepted mode of doing this is to cook a large pot of food and invite the *fofofo* to share it. When they have eaten, the *inuba* springs his request upon them. (It was apparently the old practice to solicit the help of non-kinsmen in making a raid upon an enemy by giving them *giya*, a pot of food with shell valuables hidden inside, before requesting their assistance. In the conversion of this custom for *abutu*, the food the *inuba* cooks is supposed to be the one he intends to use in his main challenge, and providing the *abutu* goes well it will be the last time he eats that type of food until his gardens are replenished.) Since '*inuba* is boss' and *fofofo* have just eaten his food, the latter are unlikely to refuse his proposal. Preliminary strategies are laid, foods to be used in the *abutu* decided upon, and the number of probable supporters assessed.

Before dawn next day the *fofofo* leader (ideally the *venima'abi* of the challenger), with painted face and a hornbill feather in his hair, leads the way to the enemy hamlet, to the house of the man to whom *abutu* is to be made. If it is to be an intervillage contest the journey takes on some importance. The *fofofo* lead their *inuba* to 'clear the dew', a service which status inferiors (e.g. wives, younger brothers) perform for their 'betters' under normal conditions too. Besides chilling the legs, dew is supernaturally dangerous (mildly so), being thought of as urine of the ancestral spirits. While entering the enemy hamlet the *fofofo* ululate loudly in the standardized cry of the *abutu* challenge: 'waaaaa-eeeeee'. The sleeping hamlet is awakened abruptly and is alerted for what is to follow. The leader of the *fofofo* goes to the house-step of the man to be challenged and calls his name, asking if he has run away and if he has not, to give him (the *fofofo*) some food, as he is cold from walking through the dew. He holds out a single yam (or taro etc. if the *abutu* is to be transacted mainly in other foods). This gift is the 'clincher' (*veabi*) and requires the return gift of the same kind to signalize that the *abutu* challenge has been accepted.

If the *fofofo* of the challenged man fail to come forward with the return *veabi*, or if the challenged himself refuses to accept it, there can be no *abutu*, and the visiting challengers must return home masking their disappointment by a show of righteous anger and contempt. They win by default, of course, and before they leave the enemy hamlet they will jeer abusively at the challenged party for their weakness and timidity.

If the *veabi* is accepted, the *fofofo* 'bossman' of the challenged will commence the stylized war-prance called *sefaiya*. He hops stiffly, lunging and feinting slightly, holding his right arm slightly bent as if he were clutching a throwing-spear. He whoops and works himself into a simulated rage, crying insults at the challengers. He may be joined by other members of his clan, one of whom by this time will have placed the *veabi* return gift into his crooked 'spear hand'. The visiting *inuba* and *fofofo* sit or stand by with studied unconcern. It is not their role to behave threateningly in a hostile hamlet or village, and they appear to close their ears to the insults, looking anywhere but at the prancing furies in front of them. They may even break into song to suppress or disguise their own swelling anger. The challenged *fofofo* leader harangues them:

You think we can't pay back your yams? You think we have no pigs? You think we don't know how to garden? You think we are birds or dogs and can't plant food? You think we remain idle all our lives? Well, we'll show you! You'll see who can plant better! We don't spend all our time copulating with our wives like you!

Such harangues may be loaded with subtle innuendo or crude obscenity, depending on the depth of enmity between challengers and challenged, and upon the personalities of those doing the *sefaiya*. These staccato declamations vary little in theme, however, and almost invariably stress the incompatibility between gardening prowess and sexual indulgence. Later, when the enemy come to the challengers' hamlet, the latter's *fofofo* will have their turn, and the *sefaiya* harangues will reverse the imputations.

(2) *The first prestation*

The visitors return home to organize their initial prestation. As they reach their own hamlets they ululate loudly to inform those remaining that their challenge was accepted and that the *abutu* is on. The rest of the day is spent building the food platforms in the *inuba*'s hamlet. Women, children, and all superfluous males from the hamlets of the *inuba* and *fofofo* are dispatched to the gardens to fetch food. Several trips might be made during the day, and it is a testing occasion particularly for the growing young men, who make a four mile trip to the reserve banana gardens near the coast, climb the thousand feet back to the village with 100 lb bunches on their shoulders, then ascend the mountains behind the village in order to fetch as much taro as they can carry. When a Kalauna youth can do this his father will be proud to tell him that 'soon you can take my place'. Throughout the day other helpers from the *tabotabo* category bring food for the *inuba*. The *fofofo* are busy laying out the food and searching for the pigs which have been earmarked for the *abutu*.

If the preparations are almost ready by nightfall, the *fofofo* leader will make another journey to the enemy at dawn next day to tell them – without ceremony – to come for their food. The enemy *inuba*, however, remain at home and it is their *fofofo* and their womenfolk who arrive unobtrusively and sit quietly in the *abutu*-maker's hamlet. The latter's *fofofo* leader harangues and insults them with histrionic gestures, challenging them to pay back quickly if they can, which he pretends to doubt. Tardy helpers of the *inuba*, mainly *tabotabo*, come forward with additional food and may do *sefaiya* too – less to insult the visitors than to draw attention to themselves and make public the nature and amount of their contribution. The *inuba* are sitting nearby 'making' *kaiwabu* and feigning lofty unconcern for the proceedings. In fact, they are likely to be observing carefully the *tabotabo* contributions, not only to note mentally who is supporting their cause and who is not, but also to note the type and quantity of each individual contribution. For at a later date, when their roles are reversed, each helper will expect to be assisted by the current *inuba* in similar proportions. The proportionate contributions of the status categories as wholes are seen at a glance, however, for the yams and taro platforms are subdivided into marked sections as shown in Fig. 5. Likewise there may be a number of separate banana stands for the respective contributions of *inuba* (including *veo'owana*), *fofofo* and *tabotabo*. If pigs are being given they are tied under

banana stands (*aiyala*)
(one for each category of donor)

large
yams
(*kuvi*)

kaiwabu and
other *inuba* sit
on sitting circle

piles and platters
of small yams etc.
(*ikuku*)

CHALLENGERS' HAMLET

yam platform (*deudeu*)

taro
platform
(*deudeu*)

pigs

000... *Inubane*	000... *Hinafane*	000... *Tabone*
(*Inuba's* yams)	(*Fofofo's* yams)	(*Tabotabo's* yams)

enemy *fofofo* and visitors

Fig. 5. Layout of the first stage of *abutu*

the appropriate donors' section of the yam platform. Only *inuba* and
fofofo are likely to give pigs.

The credit-displaying phase (*ivemataiya*) is now complete and the
enemy's womenfolk begin to gather up the food, stuff it into their baskets
and carry it away. The enemy's *fofofo* apportion the loads and themselves
carry away bunches of bananas, the larger yams and the pigs. They might
need to make several trips and the hamlet will probably not be emptied
of food until nightfall. Despite the careful layout of food, demarcated
according to donor categories, the enemy are not concerned to preserve
these when they carry it home. As far as they are concerned, all the food and
pigs they have taken was given by the challenging *inuba* to their own *inuba*.

That evening the challenging *inuba*'s *fofofo* cook for them using food
from their own larders, as it is supposed that the *inuba*'s stocks will have

been depleted. Large pots are cooked by each individual *inuba*'s *venima'abi*, a service which will be reciprocated when their roles are reversed in some future *abutu*.

Following the enemy visitors back to their homes, we find them dumping all the food around the edge of the *inuba*'s hamlet in piles segregated according to food type, and the yams into further groupings of size. The *fofofo* report to their *inuba* the day's events and discuss with them the logistics and strategies of paying back. If pigs have been received they will be killed and distributed by the *fofofo* the same evening, but no food will be shared out at this point. The whole village is likely to feast on pork. As the *fofofo* cut up the pigs, one of them calls out the names of 'bossmen' of the *tabotabo* category. The respective *venima'abi* of the latter come forward to take away the pieces for redistribution among their own kin groups. The *inuba*'s own *fofofo* are likely to have a whole pig to themselves if there are more than two. This is *aiyebulubuluya bawena*, the compensatory pig for 'wetting the legs with dew', a metaphorical reference to the total service which the *fofofo* are performing for their *inuba* in managing the operations of the *abutu*. Because the *fofofo* would be 'ashamed' to eat pork when their *inuba* have none, they give them a compensatory pig of their own to eat with the pots of food which the individual *venima'abi* cook for their partners.

(3) *The return prestation*

Next morning the *lufata* phase begins – the matching and paying back of the food received by the enemy the day before. Similar structures are built in the *inuba*'s hamlet and food is fetched and displayed in the same fashion as in the opponent's hamlet, with the difference that as it is brought from the gardens, food is matched with that which had been received the previous day. While this is going on the scene is one of confusion as piles of matched ('paid'), unmatched ('unpaid'), and unmatchable yams, taro and bananas proliferate. By the end of the day, however, a pattern will have emerged resembling that of the first, credit-displaying phase. But now, there will be yet more food structures, some called *fatana* ('paid'), and others *matagina* ('credit' lit. green). The former represent the measured return of the food the challenged *inuba* had been given the previous day; the latter represent the extra food which they are forcing on the challenging enemy and which they in turn must pay back. An unequal *abutu*, of course, may result in no *matagina* being given, and may be lost by the challenged being unable to pay back all they had received. In any case, there are likely to be a fair number of yams which cannot be matched in size and variety and the *fatana* platform for yams will thus be correspondingly shorter.

At dawn next day, the leader of the *fofofo* goes to tell his opposite number to come for his *inuba*'s food. Only when the enemy party have arrived and seated themselves unobtrusively, are the pigs to be paid back brought out and tied under a platform. The *sefaiya* dramatics commence and the visitors chew betel nut and ignore their prancing hosts. The latter may have hoped to spring a surprise on the visitors by keeping hidden until an appropriate moment a *matagina* pig or two, and a few awe-inspiring yams which the donors are confident will never be paid back in a life-time. If the visiting *fofofo* are ruffled they must not show it, and their leader may get to his feet and quietly thank the enemy for paying back their food quickly and topping it off with a 'small' extra gift. Now they will take it away, he says, and try to find a small return present. Even if they had been presented with a pig the size of a cow to give to their *inuba* (and thus be obliged to eat themselves), the *fofofo* would call it a 'chicken'.

The disparagement of the enemy's efforts to shame them (which can be compared to the refusal to be provoked into anger by ceremonial abuse), is a quite standardized reaction to a highly charged and hostile political situation. If restraint breaks down and an *abutu* is marred by physical violence, it is most likely to happen at this point. The challengers, who have set their strategies and gambled confidently on a win, are in the enemy hamlet and find, perhaps, that their plans have come unstuck: that their opponents had more food reserves or had been given more assistance than the challengers had bargained for. While Kalauna (who have a reputation among Goodenough Islanders for being thin-skinned and itching to fight) had never caused or suffered a death during an *abutu*, tales of minor brawls were fairly common. Invariably they involved the *fofofo* of both sides and were settled by members of the neutral *tabotabo*. Invariably too, they took place in this phase of the *abutu* when provocation by the hosts became too great for the visitors to swallow. In an incident I witnessed, however, tempers were ignited among the hosts by a quiet hint of the visiting *fofofo* leader that he would like to eat some pig with his food. This was an insulting reference to the fact that although the hosts had paid back the pigs received the previous day, they had not added a *matagina* pig. A small scuffle broke out but imminent violence was redirected into an uproar of *sefaiya*-prancing and thereby harmlessly ritualized. Even while this was happening some supporters of the hosts had rushed to their own hamlet, grabbed an unsuspecting pig, and laid it squealing at the feet of the visiting *fofofo*.

A common cause of altercation is for the host *inuba* to introduce a different food crop into the contest than those initially specified by the challenger. If it was to be a yam and banana *abutu*, and on trying to pay

6 Third stage of *abutu*: Lulauvile men place a pig under the yam *deudeu*
7 Fourth stage of *abutu*: Iwaoyana match Lulauvile's yams in Ukevakeva

8 Kiyodi, Kimaola's heir
10 *Lauhiwaiya*. Kimaola's *fofofo* inspect the line

9 Aiyabu mourns her brother Malawidiya
11 Men dance on the Mataita Sagali platform

back in the same coin the enemy find themselves at a disadvantage, they will probably decide to 'escalate' the contest by making a platform of taro, which they trust will be their opponents' Achilles' heel. On coming for their pay-back the challengers will thus find themselves challenged, and may protest vociferously that they have been the victims of trickery. In their turn, the host *fofofo* answer to the effect that their enemy appears to plant only yams and bananas, so it was thought good to teach them what taro is. The visitors have little option but to accept the gift and return home to amass their own taro for the *matagina* pay-back.

(4) *The second prestation*

The third phase of confrontation (*matagina ana lufata*) occurs on the following day, during which the original challengers pay back the *matagina* given them by the enemy and try to top it with *matagina* of their own. Resources are stretched at this point and only the most committed *tabotabo* are likely to add to what they gave in the initial contribution. The *inuba* and *fofofo* up to clan level, however, will reach deeper into their food stores and make further forages into their gardens. If they can give in excess of the enemy's *matagina* they will have won the contest, for this is the third and final round.

There is no finale, no ceremonial declaration of the winners, and as the enemy *fofofo* and their womenfolk come for the last time to take away their matched *matagina* and whatever else the hosts could top it with, the feeling (in an observer at least) is one of anti-climax. The main parties to the *abutu* look worn and defeated, even if they have sustained a technical victory. No-one shouts abuse at the disappearing, food-laden figures of the enemy, and the time for histrionic *sefaiya* is past. The principal *inuba* counts his *liva* measures and finds, perhaps, that he has a platform of taro ten feet long and a dozen yams of various types and sizes still to pay back. His enemy, he notes, owes him eighteen bunches of bananas, a couple of wooden platters of 'taitu', and six yams of an impossible size. Their pigs were equal. He may conclude that he has won because of the bananas, while his opposite number, making similar calculations in his own house, may conclude that the victory is his because of the taro. A few months later they will tend to agree with everyone else that it was 'fair', a drawn contest. Only unmatched pigs and a wide discrepancy in the amount of unpaid vegetable food (particularly yams) can add up to victory or loss. Moreover, one *inuba* might win in yams and his opponent in pigs – an ultimately satisfactory state of affairs because it enables the descendants of each to claim partial victory and obliges neither to admit to total defeat. This is conditional, however, on whether outstanding debts are paid.

8

(5) *The final redistribution*

As soon as the enemy have carried off the last of their booty, the *fofofo* begin the immense task of distributing their own food given by the enemy. Whereas it had been laid in piles handy for measuring, now it has to be put in mixed piles representing the component *unuma* of the *fofofo* and the *tabotabo*. The piles of food are made commensurate in size with the size of the recipient *fofofo* group, so that a numerically large *unuma* with a numerically insignificant *fofofo* is allotted a small pile. Leaders' names are called and the wives of their *venima'abi* come forward to take away the food in baskets. The principle of *niune* is applied even in the redistribution. Only the piles laid out by the *inuba*'s *fofofo* for themselves are taken by the latter's own wives and, of the whole community, only the *inuba* have no piles allotted to them. No attempt is made to issue larger amounts of food to those *tabotabo* who were most generous with their support, for balanced reciprocity is not important at this point. But if the *abutu* was a fairly even contest, all contributors (except the *inuba*) will receive more food than they gave, for there is the enemy *inuba*'s contribution to be spread among them. Those who do receive more than they contributed may give *kamoabi* food from their own stocks to the *inuba* of their side. It is primarily the *fofofo*'s task to give *kamoabi*, however, and to support over a period those of the *inuba* who stripped their gardens. Finally, in *abutu* held within the village in which certain *tabotabo* help both sides, it may happen that some of the yams (say) which were given to help one side come back to the donor via his *fofofo* group in the final redistribution of the other side. This will be avoided if possible, though it is not a matter of shame or undue concern. What is not possible is for the recipient then to pass this food on to the *inuba* as *kamoabi*, for it had entered the exchange and been thereby converted into the *inuba*'s *niune*.

Any remaining pigs will have been cut up and distributed at the same time as the vegetable food, and the principles of redistribution by *fofofo* are the same. *Venima'abi* of the *inuba* will cook the latter's pots of food for the last time, and with it *inuba* will eat *kamoabi* pork. While the *fofofo* are butchering their own pig, the carvers put aside the guts, internal organs and the flesh over the belly to be cooked separately. When this has been done some of the 'big-men' of the community are invited to share it. This is an exclusive feast for the elders and hamlet leaders of the *tabotabo* category. If it had been an intravillage *abutu*, these men will sit at such a feast in the other *fofofo*'s hamlet too. It is the only feasting as such which occurs during *abutu*, and is one of the rare occasions when Kalauna men can be seen eating out of doors in relatively public circumstances. The *fofofo* feast them, it is said, because they were burned by the sun and chilled by the rain while watching and advising on the redistribution. The poetry of this rationale attempts to disguise the main reason; for it is covertly admitted that where pig is being shared there is envy, and where there is envy there is sorcery. The custom of 'feasting the elders' is the *fofofo*'s defence against potentially envious *tabotabo*.

DEBTS AND DEBTORS

For everyone save the *inuba* of both sides the *abutu* is over. An *inuba* protagonist who was defeated heavily might begin already to dream of revenge, though return contests between the same individual opponents seem to be very rare. Before another *abutu* can take place, the loser has to make good his debts and this can take him several years. Even then the winner, when challenged a second time, would be able to rest secure on his previous victory and refuse engagement without loss of prestige. The stigma of an outright *abutu* loss can therefore last a lifetime, though few people – not least the victorious enemy – would provoke the loser by casually reminding him of the fact. It would require a provocative circumstance, a situation in which the loser had committed some new delict against the winner, or in some way annoyed him. Then the inequality in the relationship would be revealed. The winner would need only to remind his enemy of their past *abutu* encounter ('do you remember how you couldn't pay back my food?') for the latter to be shamed into making amends.

Essentially the same principle applies to those linked by old *abutu* debts. The creditors possess the ascendancy and the coercive potential. Since *abutu* is a group event built around the opposition of two individual competitors, and since the latter are representative members of corporate descent groups, the debt relationships between them take on a corporate aspect, so that clan *A* can rebuke clan *B* for owing them several yams or a pig. The group strength of clan *B* will to a large extent determine its collective reaction to the reminder: whether it eats humble pie or takes it as an insult and demands another *abutu*. The device can also misfire, for young hotheads, thinking to exploit what they believe is a relationship of ascendancy over another descent group, may provoke an incident which brings to light, in the memories of wiser men, older debts (perhaps of a kind incurred in non-*abutu* contexts) which are owed by those making the provocative reminder.

Abutu debts are paid back piecemeal and without ceremony, whenever the debtor has the good fortune to dig a yam of the right size and type, or manages to grow a pig to the correct girth. His *venima'abi* takes the item to the creditor and demonstrates equivalence with the string *liva*, which he then throws away, while the creditor passes the item on to his own *fofofo* for their consumption. For the conscientious man, each item that is paid back reduces the threat that one day the enemy *fofofo* leader is going to say to him: 'I'm still waiting for my yams.' The main sanction to enforce payment of such debts, therefore, is the diffuse one of shaming. Destruction of *liva* does not exempt the debtor from repayment; it merely leaves him open to the scorn and contempt of his creditor if he should discover the fact, or his children to the shock and shame of discovering unpaid debts they knew nothing about. Although the creditor does not have a 'copy' of the string *liva*, he keeps a mental record (or sometimes nowadays a written one), which he transmits to his heirs. A generation after the original *abutu*, then, when *liva* have been lost or hopefully destroyed, the debtor's son may run foul of the creditor's son and be told: 'Why do you make this trouble with me? Your father didn't pay back our yams after our fathers made *abutu*. Maybe you aren't going to either.' Informants suggest that the shame generated by such an encounter would send the debtor's son in search of several of the largest yams he could find to give them to the creditor's son, even though proof of the debt in the 'invoice' form of *liva* no longer existed. To exorcise his shame, in fact, he would deliberately 'over-give' by doing *veumaiyiyi*, the practice of casting the shame back onto the one who shamed by giving far more than was due. This escalation of resentment and shame can theoretically result in a food-giving feud reminiscent of 'potlach', in which each party makes periodic inflationary gifts to the other. A sustained hostility expressed in this manner is apparently rare, and I could obtain few examples.

Men sometimes discuss *abutu* as if the sole reason for the contest was to give the enemy *liva* which they cannot pay back quickly. The implication here is that the *abutu*-maker is hoping for a long-term political ascendancy. The importance of paying back as quickly as possible is underlined by the fact that fellow clansmen and *fofofo* will assist the individual debtor when their corporate self-respect is threatened by the existence of large *abutu* debts. It is, moreover, an acknowledged trap for the potential leader to be tardy about paying his food and pig debts, however he incurred them, and perhaps particularly dangerous for him to neglect his *abutu* debts. While there are few ways in which a big-man can suffer loss of prestige, nothing is more damaging to reputation than long-standing food debts. Iyahalina is sometimes privately denigrated for this reason, though he is quite unconcerned since he claims to base his reputation on his wisdom and ritual inheritance rather than on any youthful glory as a dynamic *tofaha*. But Iyahalina and the other *toitavealata* are exceptional in having potent power resources elsewhere than in their gardens.

10

COMPETITIVE FOOD EXCHANGES
AND SOCIAL CONTROL

Since all wrongs in Tangu may be seen as, or may be reduced to, a hampering or reduction of food-producing potential, such breaches of equivalence are restored by food exchanges . . .   Burridge, 1965–6, p. 400

When Kalauna people say 'we fight with food' they have in mind a class of activities of which *abutu* is but one (albeit the principal) institutionalized form. For want of a better term the essential element in *abutu* conduct – its common behavioural denominator – is 'food-giving-to-shame'. This is a syndrome of psychological, sociological and cultural components which occurs frequently in Kalauna, in situations which are not necessarily resolved by formal *abutu* contests such as I described in the previous chapter. Thus, when Mata'au speared Uyavaiyava's pig by mistake, thinking it to be a wild one, Uyavaiyava insisted that Mata'au take the pig: 'You wanted to eat it, you killed it, so I give it to you.' *Hi abutuna*, it was said; he *abutu*-ed him. There was no question of formal *abutu*, however, mainly because Uyavaiyava's mother was a member of Mata'au's clan. Nevertheless, Mata'au gave the pig to his *fofofo* to eat, and some time afterwards they repaid Uyavaiyava's pig at a festival distribution. Again, when a large group of uninvited guests from another village attended a mortuary distribution, they were given the lion's share of the food, simply to shame them for a breach of etiquette. There was no real rancour and no formal *abutu*, but this was tacitly and mutually recognized as *abutu* conduct. These examples demonstrate that the 'food-giving-to-shame' response is not unique to the elaborate form of *abutu* we have been discussing, although this is its major expression, or as Goodenough Islanders would say, its 'big name'. After *abutu*, the most conspicuous and systematized expression of the syndrome is found in the Modawa–Fakili festivals which are to be examined in the next chapter.

These examples also point up the fact that 'food-giving-to-shame' is patterned, purposive behaviour, triggered by a delict and pursued as a course of redress. In this chapter I shall examine formal *abutu* contests from this standpoint, with a view to assessing their significance as instruments

208 *Fighting with food*

of social control in Kalauna. We have seen that the general motivation of participants in *abutu* is the desire of each party to shame the other by giving more food than can be simultaneously paid back. The superiority of the creditors over the debtors amounts to a political and moral ascendancy which enables the former to insult the latter with relative impunity. From the point of view of those who are challenged, it is thought preferable to refuse an *abutu* challenge and swallow the inevitable jibes about being 'afraid', than to accept, lose heavily and become deeply indebted and thus vulnerable to periodic shaming. However, it is not always possible to avert *abutu* by refusing a challenge. This is especially true of 'trouble' *abutu* – those which are initiated as a response to some delict. *Abutu* are not usually undertaken lightly; like warfare they need to be provoked by specific incidents.

TABLE 24 *Reasons for* abutu *in Kalauna*

Cause	Intravillage	Intervillage	Total
Adultery	4	0	4
Divorce	10	4	14
Traditional enemy	0	11	11
Insult	5	1	6
Property offence	3	0	3
Total	22	16	38

I gathered data on thirty-eight cases of *abutu* in which Kalauna people have been directly involved since about 1920. There have probably been at least as many again which informants had forgotten. Information on the first dozen or so to be remembered is sketchy, and much of the circumstantial detail has an unmistakable legendary flavour. For the period up to the Second World War only six *abutu* were remembered. The remaining 32 occurred during the last twenty years. About 18 of these took place before 1960 and the remaining 14 belong to the period 1960–7. Table 24 breaks down the 38 recorded cases into intervillage and intravillage *abutu*, and classifies them according to the principal reasons for which they were said to have been held.

INTERVILLAGE 'ABUTU'

One of the most striking features of this distribution is that the majority of intervillage *abutu* were said to have been instigated because the parties were traditional enemies (*nibai*), whereas this rationale was given for none of the contests held within Kalauna. This point needs some comment.

Firstly, it is possible that a fair proportion of the eleven intervillage *abutu* were precipitated by causes such as those given for the other categories, but that these have been forgotten or minimized and the main cause rationalized in terms of *nibai* ideology. Typical explanations as to the reason for these eleven *abutu* were: 'We had plenty of food that year so we went to our enemy and asked them for *abutu*'; 'we always make *abutu* to those people – they are our enemies from the time of war'; 'we weren't

TABLE 25   *Frequency of* abutu *between Kalauna hamlets and clans*

	Kwakwaiboka	Aluwaita	Anuana I	Heloava II	Anuana II	Heloava I	Modimodia	Awakubawe	Bulamameya	Lalaveya	Lakolakoya	Ukevakeva	Buveta	Ilobelobe	Valeutoli	Mulina
Kwakwaiboka																
Aluwaita																
Anuana I																
Heloava II																
Anuana II																
Heloava I																
Modimodia		1														
Awakubawe		1														
Bulamameya																
Lalaveya		1			1		1	1								
Lakolakoya																
Ukevakeva	1		1*		1*		2	1								
Buveta		1*														
Ilobelobe										1*	1					
Valeutoli					1		1*				1					
Mulina							2					1	1			

* *Abutu* occurring between traditional enemies.

angry with them, but they killed our grandfather, so we wanted to "show" them'; 'they came to us and asked for food and pigs because they remembered that we ate their ancestor'. Yet these 'excuses' were rarely offered when intravillage *abutu* was being discussed, and were never given as the principal reason, merely as partial justification for a contest which was precipitated by another cause. Indeed, only five of the twenty-two *abutu* recorded in the intravillage category were between *inuba* who were traditional enemies at the *unuma* or hamlet level (see Table 25).

There is clearly a principle involved here of some sociological importance. This is that relations between *nibai* belonging to different villages are more formal, being structured perhaps entirely by reference to this inherited relationship of enjoined hostility. Within the village, on the other hand, *nibai* relationships are modified by other ties and other bases for inter-action. The community, moreover, probably cannot afford the unmodified expressions of enmity which are appropriate to *nibai* belonging to different villages. Even so, *nibai* relationships within the village are at least as acrimonious in content and perhaps even more embittered than those beyond the village. Kalauna men gave me without embarrassment the names of their extra-village *nibai*, but they hesitated, dissimulated and only finally identified (but not by name) their traditional enemies within the village. (Iyahalina was particularly touchy on this subject, and refused to discuss it if any other than Lulauvile clansmen were present. He was evidently distressed by what he believed to be the continuing enmity of the descendants of the victims of Malaveyoyo.) Granted the need for more circumspect conduct between intravillage *nibai* among whom there is a delicate *modus vivendi*, it is to be expected that intravillage *abutu* should have different rationales and serve somewhat different sociological ends from intervillage *abutu*. The latter might appear to be expressions of on-going feuds, though it is perhaps more accurate to represent them as events which reinforce *nibai* relationships; for it is as if *abutu* contests between villages were held in order to perpetuate these relationships and prevent them from lapsing. Indeed, if they sometimes do lapse, new 'food enemies' can be created (see Chapter 4). In general, then, whereas enemies within the village appear to pose a basic threat to its integrity, traditionally hostile groups beyond it offer a means of affirming that integrity, since an *abutu* between a Kalauna descent group and one belonging to another village invariably causes the communities to unite against each other. The need to emphasize the existence of enemies without and underplay the existence of enemies within is one of the fundamentals of political sociology.

These political factors are linked to the role of leaders in intervillage *abutu*. Their more prominent role in this context than in intravillage contests points to the former as being more suitable than the latter for status display and prestige acquisition. Intervillage *abutu* are easier to plan without the enemy's becoming wise to the threat of a challenge; strategies and skills are thus at a greater premium than they are in intravillage *abutu*. With the former, too, go somewhat greater ceremony: *sefaiya*-dramatics are more elaborate, food displays more artistic, and *kaiwabu*-acting more conspicuous. As far as I could determine, all the intervillage *abutu* I recorded as being between *nibai* were instigated by leaders, whereas the principals in at least fifteen of the intravillage *abutu* were non-leaders at the time of the contests. It is of some significance also that the seven intravillage *abutu* which were in fact initiated by leaders, were for reasons (mainly 'insult') which might be interpreted as reflections on their prestige or threats to their status. There is little doubt that whatever their other sociological functions, intervillage *abutu* serve leaders as public arenas for prestige-seeking competition. They provide paths to renown, and through feedback, enhancement of status within the leaders' own communities. While this element is not lacking in *abutu* contests within the village it is far less conspicuous for many reasons, principal among which is that in this context *abutu* is less a war of declared enemies than a battle of temporary rivals.

INTRAVILLAGE 'ABUTU'

There are different types of *nibai* which enable Goodenough Islanders to claim with some justification that all *abutu* are between enemies. In the 'true' *nibai* class are those 'from the ground', those created during 'wartime' by killing and cannibalism, and those 'food enemies' made in post-contact times. These are the enemies involved in intervillage *abutu*. But there is a very important category, *vavine adi nibaidi* ('woman's enemy' or 'enemy over woman'), created within and for a single generation by adultery or divorce. Since village endogamy prevails, so too do 'women' enemies' occur most frequently within the community. Again, since there is a tendency for persons to be referred to as 'enemies' for the duration of some temporary quarrel, it is not difficult for any *abutu* to be underwritten by an appeal to the 'enemy' status of the opponents. Even so, there is usually a distinction made between *abutu* declared between traditional enemies, of which it is said *luluna ya kudana* ('his bone I suck'), and *abutu* declared between temporary enemies, of which it is said *vavine wowone dakedake* ('women scandalize'). The former, as we have seen, tends to be an affair between villages, the latter mainly an internal community matter.

Since over a quarter of all recorded cases of *abutu*, and nearly three-quarters of those within the village were precipitated by adultery or divorce (which is often preceded by adultery), the relationship between 'marital offences' and *abutu* must be explained. Indeed, whereas challenges provoked by other causes are frequently averted, refused or delayed long enough to allow tempers to cool, this appear rarely to be the case where such marital offences are concerned. During my association with Kalauna I observed twelve incidents which threatened at the time of their occurrence to be resolved by *abutu*, though for one reason or another such contests did not eventuate. Of these twelve quarrels two concerned divorce and

8*

adultery, but there were very sound circumstances preventing either from resulting in *abutu*, and the grievances were taken care of in the alternative food-giving contexts of a festival.

The relationship between food and sex is a profound theme of Goodenough culture, although there is no space here to pursue it in depth. Food and sex are intimately associated with concepts of shame and self-respect, infamy and renown. Previous chapters have indicated, for example, that sexual intercourse and crop planting are held to be incompatible; that an active sex life is believed to be at variance with an active gardening life, so that the charge of being a 'womanizer' (*tokelelefailina*: lit. 'man-who-copulates-excessively') carries the implication of being an ineffectual gardener or *tonima'avilana*. A philanderer is thus doubly despised and doubly shamed. The general relation of *abutu* to sex offences becomes apparent in that the self-respect and virtue of the man accused of philandering are being tested by public appraisal of his gardening capacity.[1]

The relation between *abutu* and adultery is even more specific. Adultery is believed to afflict the cuckolded husband with *doke* (skirt), the symptoms of which are a swollen stomach (where the wife's skirt is thought to materialize), weakness and a general malaise. *Doke* is transmitted by the 'spoiled' hands of the adulterous woman when she cooks the food which her husband later ingests. It has serious implications for the gardening ability of the victim. (Note again the implicit equation: big belly equals empty garden.) Indeed, an acknowledged technique of revenge for an *abutu* loss or of forestalling an *abutu* challenge is to seduce one's enemy's wife in the hope that she will transmit *doke* to him and thereby incapacitate him for gardening. Adultery, therefore, is seen not simply as a property offence, a theft of the sexual services to which a husband has exclusive rights by virtue of marriage, but principally as a threat to the husband's health and integrity as a man and a gardener. Symbolically, the cuckolded husband is feminized by the growth of a 'skirt' within him.

Popular belief assumes that a woman who leaves her husband to marry another has acted under the irresistible influence of her paramour's love-magic (see Chapter 3). The latter will be assumed to be responsible for enticing her away and no-one will be more convinced of this than the abandoned husband. His wife has been 'stolen' and he now has a 'woman's enemy'. The offence against him is called *hoyalana* and it is a point of personal honour and group propriety to challenge the offender to an *abutu* contest: *hoyalana ana abutu*. Ten of the twenty-two intravillage *abutu* recorded were of this category. It matters only that the woman

[1] Cf. the analogous case among the Abelam of New Guinea (Kaberry 1941, p. 215; 1965-6, p. 349).

divorced the man, not that adultery was committed prior to her doing so, though it will tend to be assumed that adultery, carrying the threat of *doke*, had been committed prior to the divorce. If the man divorces the woman himself for reasons other than adultery, there is usually no *abutu*, though the man she subsequently marries is still regarded as in some sense a personal enemy, and he is scrupulously avoided thereafter.

The fact that wife-stealing is much more common than *hoyalana ana abutu*, however, means that not all offended husbands are able to gain retribution in the ideal manner. Many factors may discourage or prevent them: personal inadequacy, weak agnatic or *fofofo* support, depleted food resources, prior relationship to offenders, some degree of satisfaction gained by alternative means (including other modes of food-giving-to-shame), and of course, sheer procrastination.

INTRAVILLAGE 'ABUTU' AND SOCIAL CONTROL

Ideally, *abutu* should transform conflicts into contests by placing disputes in a public arena, allowing people to take sides to arbitrate the issues by appeal to common moral attitudes and cultural values. The extent to which *abutu* in practice, however, may be considered a 'redressive device', or a 'technique of social control' which is 'integrative', is quite problematical; for it is not enough merely to assert that it is a 'mechanism for displacing conflict' or a 'surrogate for fighting'. A mode of 'social control' which can conceivably aggravate rather than dampen enmity may be more disruptive than integrative. A 'redressive device' which allows the offender to come off best is hardly that at all; for despite popular expectations there is no guarantee that an adulterer who is challenged to *abutu* will lose the contest. Moreover, grievances might not be dissipated by *abutu*; they may well be reinforced.

Even as regards 'enforcing conformity to norms', about which informants are most explicit, the empirical evidence points both ways. It is said that *abutu* can be invoked 'to teach people good manners', 'to teach them a lesson', or 'to punish them'. The hint of coercion is typical, for Kalauna people regard all agencies of social control as dependent upon sanctions which bite. The threat of *abutu* is seen as one such sanction: to induce good, norm-oriented behaviour. An *abutu* threat, or in the next stage a challenge, is thought to be an appropriate response for an injured party to make – whether the nature of the offence against him is a slur on his gardening ability or the theft of his wife. But the offender will not necessarily be cowed or coerced into making amends if he is confident of numerical support at least equal to that of the person he offended. When Wakasilele 'stole' Buyoya's wife, Buyoya remarked mildly: 'I cannot be angry. There are only myself and my young brother.' In other words, the injured party must be in a position of some strength before he can afford the attempt to wield the coercive sanction of *abutu* threat or challenge.[1] Moreover, *abutu* may conspicuously fail to enforce conformity to norms, as when the adulterer Makiyuwe was 'punished' in an *abutu* contest, but was found to be sleeping with the same woman less than a year later. In this case other sanctions were brought into play – namely, the threat of violence and sorcery – and the offender felt compelled to flee to Port Moresby for safety.

The range of sanctions available to Kalauna people was dealt with in Chapter Six, where it was seen that 'food-giving-to-shame' constituted the principal category of sanctions appealed to in 35.5% of all recorded disputes (see Table 19). Since it proved to be the commonest, in discussing its shortcomings as a technique of social control it must be remembered that Kalauna people themselves display confidence and even faith in its ability to achieve their ends. Before attempting to reach any final conclusion as to the sociological significance of *abutu*, therefore, it will be helpful to examine and assess individually a number of substantive cases.

The six examples summarized below have been selected from among those *abutu* occurring in Kalauna in recent years. They are presented to highlight some of the more significant points mentioned in this chapter and the previous one: precipitating causes, political alignment of clans, social relationship between antagonists, variable scale of *abutu* and its sanctioning effects, if any. Five of the cases involve opponents from within the village, and one concerns an intervillage *abutu*.

1. *Kwayaya* v. *Tomokova c. 1962. Cause: Divorce*

Kwayaya of Ukevakeva hamlet, Iwaoyana clan, was married to Vilawabu of Belebele village, and his sister Neola was married to Tomokova of Modimodia hamlet, Malabuabua clan. Kwayaya left the village to work in Port Moresby for 18 months, leaving his sister with instructions to keep an eye on his wife and three children. After he had been away for about a year, however, his brother-in-law Tomokova made love-magic over Vilawabu and seduced her in Kwayaya's own house. The adulterers were caught by Kwayaya's father's brother's sons who reported the offence to the village constable. An informal court was convened in Ukevakeva, at which Vilawabu declared her intention of divorcing

---

[1] Buyoya's attitude was characteristically defeatist. A 'position of strength' might also refer to a moral one. The practice of helping secretly, under cover of darkness, the side opposite to the one which a person is committed by virtue of primary allegiances, gives some scope for the expression of private sympathy. With 'right' on its side, an ostensibly weak party might thus manage to win a contest. The extent of private sympathy is very difficult to gauge in advance, however, as impulsive *abutu* challengers may learn to their cost. It can also be neutralized by the existence of other, 'political' considerations which are irrelevant to the main moral issue – as can be seen in Case 1 below.

Kwayaya and marrying her new lover. She took her knife, skirts and pots and went to live with Tomokova, taking only her youngest child with her. Neola likewise took her possessions and the youngest of her three children, and told Vilawabu that she could take her place because she was going back to Ukevakeva to wait for her brother. The village constable took Tomokova to the patrol officer and he was sentenced to three months' imprisonment for adultery.

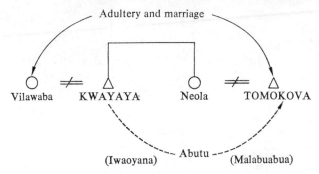

Genealogy 11. Tomokova's adultery

Shortly after Tomokova was let out of jail, Kwayaya also returned to the village and immediately challenged Tomokova to *abutu*. It was a full-scale one and involved the whole village. Most people were disgusted with Tomokova's conduct and sympathized with Kwayaya and his sister. Even so, Tomokova won the *abutu* by a margin of food which Kwayaya had still not paid back by 1967. Tomokova remains far too ashamed to remind Kwayaya of the debt, however, and continues to avoid him where possible. Tomokova's win can be attributed to his clansmen's determination to trounce their *nibai*, Valeutoli, which is Ukevakeva's *fofofo* and therefore responsible for taking, eating and paying back most of Malabuabua's food. They had made *abutu* a year or two previously and the outcome had been unsatisfactory for Malabuabua. Other Kalauna groups were now also taking the opportunity to fight Ukevakeva and Valeutoli. Lulauvile was split, for one of its sections committed itself to supporting Tomokova, while members of the other revealed their private sympathies for Kwayaya by supporting both sides. Subsequently both Kwayaya and his sister married members of their *fofofo* in Valeutoli.

2. *Siboboya* v. *Debatalo. c. 1963. Cause: Insult*

Siboboya, leader of Aluwaita hamlet of Lulauvile I, was a widower whose dead wife belonged to Awakubawe hamlet of Malabuabua clan. His only son Wasimala married an Iwaoyana girl in 1963. While the girl was living in her father-in-law's house during her trial marriage, she was accosted one day by Amauli, a shrewish woman from Awakubawe who was married to Debatalo of Buveta hamlet, Iwaoyana clan.[1] Amauli warned the girl against marrying Wasimala, saying that

---

[1] Debatalo had had to meet an *abutu* challenge as the cost of marrying her for she had been married to another man first.

his father Siboboya had killed his wife by immoderate sexual demands and excessive childbearing, and that Wasimala had probably inherited his father's ways: 'So you too will die young if you marry him.' The girl was distressed but defended her intention of marrying Wasimala. 'Already I've eaten their food.

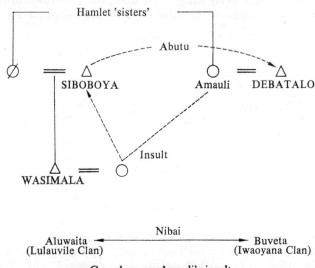

Genealogy 12. Amauli's insult

I cannot waste it. I can bear many children. Never mind if I die like my mother-in-law.' She informed Wasimala of the incident and he told his father. They consulted their *fofofo* and decided to challenge Amauli via her husband. They could not make *abutu* against her natal group, since this was the same one that Siboboya's wife and Wasimala's mother had belonged to. On the other hand – and this was the deciding factor – Amauli's husband's clan is Lulauvile's traditional enemy in general, and his *unuma* Siboboya's *unuma*'s *nibai* in particular. Debatalo's grandfather was said to have killed Siboboya's grandfather in the gardens one day and then eaten him. In the *abutu* the whole of Iwaoyana was aligned against the whole of Lulauvile. Malabuabua helped both sides since Amauli was a clanswoman and Wasimala was a clanswoman's son. Siboboya won the contest in terms of yams, Debatalo in terms of pigs, creating debts which they (or more properly their *fofofo*) can remind each other of in the event of further dispute.

3. *Talukava* v. *Wakasilele. c. 1964. Cause: Property offence*
Talukava of Mulina clan had made banana and taro gardens close to one of the several large streams which gush through Kalauna territory. Wakasilele of Malabuabua and Silowai of Iwaoyana were engaged one day in damming portions of the stream to fish for eels and prawns. Wakasilele unwittingly closed off a small branch which irrigated Talukava's gardens. Daudia, Talukava's father's brother's son, chanced to be passing and noticing this, immediately began to berate

Wakasilele and Silowai for trying to spoil his 'brother's' gardens. Wakasilele protested that he was unaware of the gardens since Talukava had neglected to *tabu* the streamlet or mark nearby trees to advertise the presence of cultivation. Both Daudia and Wakasilele are infamous for their quick tempers, and the argument soon developed into *abutu* challenge and counter-challenge. *Abutu* was made the same day with vegetable food only, and because of its hurried execution, not all Kalauna men were able to participate or even learn of it until it was over. Mulina lost fairly heavily since it is a small clan which contains its own *fofofo*, and it had Malabuabua and Iwaoyana plus their respective *fofofo* ranged against it. Several Lulauvile *unuma* which had taken Mulina women in marriage supported Mulina. Talukava's own mother, however, was a Malabuabua woman and he was considerably embarrassed by the *abutu*, which put him in the position of having to 'fight' his mother's clansmen. It is most unlikely that he would have challenged Wakasilele to *abutu* himself. Yawaidiya, one of his mother's closer agnates, actually helped Talukava with food for the *abutu* instead of his own clansman Wakasilele, but he told Talukava the quarrel was his own fault for not having clearly marked his property.

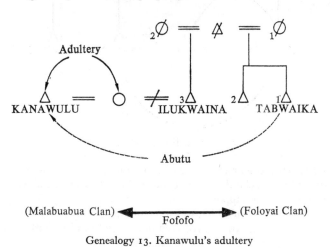

Genealogy 13. Kanawulu's adultery

4. *Tabwaika* v. *Kanawulu*. *c. 1962*. *Cause*: *Adultery and Divorce*

While Ilukwaina of Foloyai clan was working abroad, Kanawulu of Malabuabua stole his wife with love magic. She abandoned her two adolescent children and went to live with her lover. Tabwaika, Foloyai's leader and Ilukwaina's half-brother by the same father, challenged Kanawulu to *abutu* on Ilukwaina's behalf. Malabuabua is Foloyai's *fofofo* so the contest was very limited in scale. Only Kanawulu's brothers helped him with food, while the rest of Malabuabua supported their *fofofo*, such was their anger and disgust. Few other groups took part, and Tabwaika won heavily. Kanawulu and his brothers were greatly shamed by having no *fofofo* to eat their *niune*. They disposed of it by giving some to their affines and throwing the rest away.

5. *Binamina* v. *Ilukwaina. c. 1962. Cause: Adultery*

A few months later Ilukwaina returned and learnt of his divorce. Within weeks he was in trouble himself. Tabwaika's full brother, Binamina, caught Ilukwaina in adultery with his wife Wayaha, a Malabuabua woman. Binamina first demolished his own house in a rage then attacked Ilukwaina with a stone. Anuana men (Ilukwaina's mother's kin) intervened and carried the injured man to their hamlet. Binamina's response was to beat his wife, tell her she was divorced, and rush off to his gardens to get food for the *abutu* he was going to make to Ilukwaina.

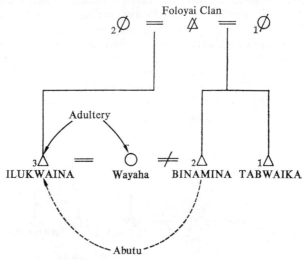

Genealogy 14. Ilukwaina's adultery

This contest also was brief and of limited scale since it was that almost unheard of thing, *abutu* within the clan.[1] Worse, it was within the *unuma*. Tabwaika and the remaining Foloyai men supported Binamina, as did their *fofofo* Malabuabua – except for Wayaha's *unuma* which was too embarrassed by her adultery to want to support either side. Ilukwaina received help only from his mother's kinsmen, and he lost the contest by a considerable margin. His own *fofofo* could not accept his food as *niune* since they were opposing him and actually supplying some of it, so he was obliged to give it to the Anuana men who had supported him. The breach between these two half-brothers was such that the same community could no longer hold them both. First Ilukwaina moved across the village with Wayaha (now his wife) and his children by his first wife, and settled in Lakolakoya, Foloyai's second hamlet. Then Binamina left the village to dwell in Awaiya, a small village on the coast, and in 1964 went to Port Moresby where he still remained in 1968 where I met him for the first time as I was about to leave Papua. Binamina's response to his wife's adultery with his half-brother was

[1] One other case of intra-clan *abutu* was remembered by informants. This was also provoked by the theft of a man's wife by a fellow clansman. Two separate *unuma* of Iwaoyana were involved, however, and the opponents were not able to trace relationship. Their respective *fofofo* were also different *unuma*.

seen as typically violent and excessive by most commentators. It is his *dewa* to be violent but the resort to *abutu* was felt to be highly improper since it split the clan and embarrassed the divided *fofofo*. It was thought that most men in his position would have appealed instead to the sanction of 'cursing' by invoking a clan *talahaiyi*.

6. *Kwalauya v. Adoka; Kaniyowana v. Yaneku. c. 1964. Causes: Divorce and inter-village* Nibai

Kwalauya's first wife, an Ukevakeva woman, had divorced him a few years previously and married Adoka of Budibudi clan, Belebele village. Kwalauya had planned to make *abutu* to Adoka for some time, and in this year had planted extra taro gardens in readiness. A Budibudi woman had died a few months before and Adoka, as hamlet leader, had sponsored a mortuary exchange for her (see Chapter 11). After this exchange had taken place, Budibudi men were considering making *abutu* to a traditional enemy as another form of 'memorial' to the dead woman. Although Kwalauya is not Adoka's true *nibai*, nor Mulina Budibudi's, Kwalauya saw his chance and sent his *fofofo* to challenge Adoka to *abutu*. Adoka accepted. When Mulina and other Kalauna groups went down to Belebele to fetch their repayment of the food given in the first stage, they were angered to find that Budibudi had 'escalated' the *abutu* by introducing bananas as an additional crop to the yams and taro specified by Kwalauya. A fight between the respective *fofofo* was narrowly averted.

The *abutu* was 'escalated' in another sense, too, by Kaniyowana, a man belonging to a different Belebele clan. He had set out platforms of yams and a large pig in his own hamlet and then called Yaneku and Awakili, of the Kalauna clan of Ainaona, to come and get them. He was declaring a sub-*abutu*, as it were, and by having everything prepared was giving Yaneku and Awakili no opportunity to refuse. Kaniyowana's and Awakili's grandfathers apparently became 'food enemies' in the past by mutual agreement, though there had been no further contests between them after the first. Kaniyowana was apparently using the *abutu* between Adoka and Kwalauya to launch his own in a bid for the leadership of his own hamlet. Yaneku and Awakili were infuriated by the peremptory nature of the challenge. (They had already, as *tabotabo*, supported Mulina with some food the previous day.) Whereas Mulina took another day in which to accumulate food for the final round of their *abutu*, the Ainaona men and their supporters rushed off to their gardens the very same day and presented Kaniyowana with his pay-back. The incident was recalled by informants with particular clarity because Neailena of Foloyai ran amuck in his fury at being given food 'for nothing'. Foloyai is not Ainaona's *fofofo* nor are they fictionally related, but being the two smallest clans in Kalauna and, moreover, physically adjacent, they usually 'join together' and identify with each other to match the strength of their single *fofofo* Malabuabua. On this occasion Neailena identified with Yaneku and Awakili to the extent that he not only tried to attack Kaniyowana physically while doing *sefaiya*, but he also had to be prevented from stripping his gardens bare for the cause of his friends. Kaniyowana was roundly defeated by several pigs. In the main contest Kwalauya won in taro but lost in bananas.

THE SOCIOLOGICAL SIGNIFICANCE OF 'ABUTU'

The above cases illustrate most of the empirical possibilities of *abutu*. It might be asked, therefore, how far each served the ends of social control; that is, to what extent they redressed the wrongs done to individuals, averted fighting by channelling conflicts into a less disruptive form of expression, induced conformity to accepted norms of behaviour by 'punishing' the wrongdoers, and finally, to what extent they were socially integrative modes of collective action.

Except in the sense of gaining satisfaction by out-giving their opponents and thereby causing indebtedness, none of the injured parties in the strict sense 'redressed' the wrong done to him. While the sense of 'honour satisfied' hardly constitutes redress it is, however, a not inconsiderable factor in a society where there are so few other forms of restitution. Moreover, it is highly improbable that a patrol officer's court could have awarded similar satisfactions to the injured parties as did these *abutu* (see Chapter 6). To Binamina, for instance (case 5), the satisfaction of shaming his half-brother, not only by giving him far more food than he could repay but also by depriving him of the help of his *fofofo*, must have been considerable. But the nature of the offence (or rather the status of the person who committed it) precluded any form of healing redress, and the grievance it engendered is probably permanent. This case is especially interesting because it is so extreme, and on theoretical grounds Goodenough Islanders would probably protest that it could not happen, for as incest negates a system of kinship and marriage, so *abutu* between brothers negates the sub-political system of *fofofo* and *nibai*. But happen it did, and the instance reveals how ingrained the '*abutu* response' is in Goodenough Islanders. Binamina first wrecked his house in a fury of displaced destructiveness, then turned upon the object of his anger, and when prevented from physically wounding Ilukwaina further, set about psychically wounding him by trouncing him in *abutu*. While this *abutu* probably averted further violence and punished the offender by shaming him deeply, it failed conspicuously to re-integrate their relationship.

It is possible that in each case *abutu* averted fighting between the antagonists, although in the intervillage double confrontation (case 6), where fighting threatened in the *abutu* situation itself, it is likely that had there been no contest there would have been no cause for conflict. To take another case (No. 2), it is difficult to imagine Amauli's insult to Siboboya resulting in violence. She was well-known for her troublesome shrewish tongue, and it is likely that her husband's kinsmen would have disassociated themselves from the issue by ignoring any direct physical attack on her should one have been made. This personal insult was not redressed by wringing an apology from her, but some satisfaction was doubtless achieved from the attempt to belittle her affinal group which was, after all, a traditional enemy.

Were any of the offenders 'taught a lesson', as Goodenough Islanders fondly believe that they should have been? Tomokova, who stole his brother-in-law's wife (case 1), was far from being the 'good man' who is the ideal *abutu*-winner, but win he did. However, the nature of his offence keeps him deeply ashamed towards Kwayaya and this prevents him from capitalizing on his victory. He dare not remind Kwayaya of the food still owed him. It is possible, of course, that Tomokova would have been justly punished by an *abutu* loss, had the event not been turned to political advantage by his own clan, which was in effect fighting other issues. At the very least, however, the *abutu* publicized Tomokova's offence. Amauli (case 2) was scarcely in a position to be punished for her insult by the *abutu* itself, except in so far as attention was drawn to it. But her husband was said to have berated her soundly for causing the quarrel. The *abutu*, then, may have had the effect of bringing sanctions to bear on her through others who were inconvenienced by it. The impetuous contest sparked by Daudia and Wakasilele over Talukava's stream (case 3) probably averted a pitched fight, considering the reputations for violence of the first two men, but neither party could have been 'taught a lesson' by the event. As it was, the challengers were ultimately more ashamed than the challenged; Wakasilele stood his ground that the trespass had been an unwitting one, while Talukava was considerably embarrassed by an *abutu* contest with his mother's clan. Both Kanawulu and Ilukwaina were successfully shamed by the *abutu* action taken against them (case 4), but it is doubtful whether it caused them to regret their offences altogether. Both were still married to the same women in 1968. Finally, 'punishment' was not a factor in the intervillage contests (case 5), though the heat generated by the sub-*abutu* drew such a fierce response from the challenged party that Kaniyowana, the instigator, might be expected to have 'learnt his lesson' with regard to peremptory *abutu* challenges. Adoka's theft of Kwalauya's wife was sufficiently long ago for wounded pride to have healed, and the contest was merely (from Kwalauya's point of view) the proper mode of vindicating his honour.

The extent to which these *abutu* also brought about settlement of differences, so that the parties in conflict could continue their relationships purged of grievances, varies according to whether the offence concerned women, and whether they were traditional enemies. Thus, between at least four pairs of opponents there is still a breach, expressed by shamed avoidance or cool hostility. But this is the expected form between 'enemies over women' and it is the usual price of divorce in this culture. Ostensible reconciliations have been made following the three other *abutu* which were provoked by reasons other than divorce, but the breaches were less profound in all cases. Whether grievances have been entirely dissolved is impossible to say, though it is unlikely in the two cases in which the antagonists were traditional *nibai*.

What then is the significance of *abutu* for Kalauna as a regulative, integrative institution? We have seen that it is redressive in only a limited sense and only on some occasions. It offers little in the way of compensation or reparation, perhaps more in the way of setting straight a felt imbalance. But since it is resorted to by people with grievances as a mode of remedying the wrongs done them, they must be the judges of whether or not they gain satisfaction – and on the whole they appear to do so. From the point of view of the community as an entity, its functions are perhaps more unequivocal. *Abutu* is socially regulative to the extent that it publicizes offences, and thus shames offenders regardless of the actual outcome of the contest. In most cases, perhaps, it also shows an offender to what extent the community disapproved of his behaviour, and so would seem to discourage conduct which is not generally acceptable. Moreover, it acts to redress the balance of political sections within the village, when this is disturbed or threatened by conflict between individual members of these groups. Generally speaking, the more serious the conflict in terms of a threat to the status quo, the more concerned will parties to the *abutu* be to avoid defeat. The harder they try to out-give each other, the more balanced will be the outcome, and the status quo will be preserved. An even contest brings about a form of *détente*. It is significant, therefore, as a peace-keeping institution, even though much of its ceremonial expression is couched in the language of warfare. *Abutu* does not necessarily resolve conflicts arising from the clash of interests, but it at least projects them into a moral dimension where appeal can be made to the most basic, pervasive and unquestioned values. By the nature of its concern with food-production and food-giving, *abutu* forces resort to some first principles of the culture. In this respect it might serve a similar integrative function to contingent communal rituals in other societies.

THE DEVELOPMENT OF 'ABUTU'

It remains to consider the historical significance of *abutu*, and to offer some speculative theories on the course of its development. All the available evidence points to the conclusion that *abutu* exchanges were quite insignificant in the pre-contact past. Indeed, some indigenous opinion stoutly maintains that 'before there was no *abutu*, only fighting'. Kalauna people on the whole, however, appear to accept the legend or myth that Malaveyoyo invented it and that it is fully indigenous. None would accept my suggestion, for instance, that *abutu* was imported from Fergusson in post-contact times along with a number of other forms of food exchanges and distributions, though it was conceded that it might be paralleled by similar institutions in western Fergusson.[1] The non-indigenous sources of information are negligible. In patrol reports covering more than sixty years, I found only one reference to *abutu* – made by a Papuan agricultural officer who described it as a 'yam war' *Patrol Report* 1966). The fact that Jenness and Ballantyne do not mention *abutu* in their monograph would be inexplicable unless it is assumed that *abutu* were irregular and fairly inconspicuous events in the immediate post-contact period. Some form of *abutu* appears to have existed at the time, however, for the authors list it in their dictionary, where they define it as 'a feast of uncooked food' (1928, p. 222). It is unlikely that they ever witnessed one, for none of the 'feasts' that they describe remotely resemble present-day *abutu*.[2]

My contention is that although some form of *abutu* existed prior to contact, it developed and flourished only after the suppression of fighting, for which it served as an effective surrogate. The highly systematized institution of *nibai* is clearly modelled on a situation of blood-feuding. In its intervillage form, *abutu* is a kind of ceremonial feud in which food and pigs are the weapons of challenge, duel and restitution. While a good case cannot be made for the symbolic equation of pigs and men in indigenous Goodenough thought,[3] it is true that one's biggest pigs are

[1] Yamelele, for instance, appear to have a form of competitive food exchange between villages and a system of *fofofo* partnerships.

[2] It is reasonable to suppose that the severe drought which the island was suffering at the time of Jenness's visit prevented large-scale food exchanges of any kind, though some feasts are mentioned as having occurred (1920, pp. 169–70). However, it is inconceivable that Ballantyne (who dwelt on the island for at least a decade) could have failed to learn something about *abutu* if it had been as conspicuous an event then as it is today.

Although not an anthropologist, Ballantyne was paid warm tribute by Jenness for his collaboration in the research (*ibid.* pp. 11–12). The ethnography of the Massim owes much to early missionaries such as Abel, Ballantyne, Bromilow, Chignell, Copland King, Giblin, Gilmour and Newton.

[3] The origin myth of the western Fergusson *sagali* festival (which is being adopted on Goodenough) stresses the substitution of pigs for human victims in the distributions which climax it, while Molima refer to an enemy corpse as 'pig' (personal communication, Dr A. Chowning). It should perhaps be noted that informants denied that *fofofo* partnerships were utilized in the distribution of human meat. The only taboo on eating a corpse was observed by the actual killer. Jenness and Ballantyne (1920, pp. 87–8) state that cannibal victims were usually exchanged between villages; but this notion seemed alien to Kalauna people, who insist that they kept their kills not only within the community but generally within the clan.

appropriately ear-marked for giving to one's *nibai* – the descendants of the persons who killed and ate one's ancestor.

It is pertinent to consider informants' opinions on the subject of the growth and changed emphases of *abutu* over the generations, for they help to suggest a rational and sociological hypothesis of development. In doing so it is useful to distinguish between enemy-oriented, intervillage *abutu* and delict-oriented, intravillage *abutu*. The restrictions (not fully binding, as we have seen) on *abutu* between kinsmen, affines and *fofofo*, define it as basically a political institution which regulates relations between nominally autonomous clan groups. The role of leaders in *abutu* also points to its essentially political nature.

According to Iyahalina:

Before, our fathers made *abutu* only to their *nibai*, because they wanted to 'try' each other to find out who was the biggest man. They made *abutu* 'for *kaiwabu*' [i.e. to gain prestige, demonstrate status, strength etc.].

The legendary invention of Malaveyoyo notwithstanding, it is highly credible that *abutu* has been enlarged and reshaped by successive big-men in the past, as they sought to exploit it to further their personal interests in gaining renown, prestige and thereby a measure of power at the expense of their *nibai*. Although perhaps not as useful a vehicle for fame as Modawa or Fakili festivals, *abutu* offers many of the advantages of a short-term festival, as their respective descriptive terms suggest: *abutu* is *etomadu* ('to put on quickly'), Modawa and Fakili festivals are *lumiami(a)* ('to remain indefinitely'). The latter are long-term projects suitable for crowning a leader's career, the former a brief skirmish suitable for establishing a name.

The suppression of warfare by the colonial government closed what was probably the main avenue to leadership fame, but it also made gardening safer and permitted steel tools to become generally available. These were the factors involved in the post-contact boom in gardening activities, and the creation of larger surpluses of food than could ever have been achieved hitherto. But, complains Iyahalina:

Now *abutu* is too big. Today many people have big gardens. Before, our fathers had big yams but small gardens. They didn't work every day because they did *lokona* properly. They looked after their food. They had one garden for *lokona* and one for eating, that's all. Now people are planting and planting, and eating and eating all the time. And they are always thinking about making *abutu*.

It is a point of some importance that December in the Goodenough calendar is sometimes called '*abutu*-time'. Nowadays it is regarded as the most inappropriate season for *abutu* because it is the beginning of the hungry period. Indigenously, however, as Iyahalina confirms, it was the season in which *tolokona* came into their own. Large-scale *abutu* at this time would have been (as they still are) impossible. But small-scale *abutu* between competing big-men using scarce resources would be highly efficacious in the prestige-stakes. (Note also that under such circumstances of general hardship, even the smallest *abutu* would be socially beneficial. The food that is pooled in these exchanges is always redistributed among a larger number of people than that which contributed. Inequalities of production result in equable distribution; thus does the industrious gardener indirectly subsidize the less able in return for the latter's esteem. From the point of view of cultural ecology, competitive food exchange is clearly a useful adaptive mechanism.)

We have seen that within the community *abutu* serves other purposes than that of allowing aspiring leaders to demonstrate their gardening industry and capacity for *lokona*. It is now, and has been for at least a generation, a mode of redress available not merely to leaders but to every man capable of making large gardens. (Of the six *abutu* I recorded which can be dated as occurring prior to the Second World War, only one appears to have been between men who were not hamlet leaders.) Its development as a redressive device may be speculatively correlated with social changes undergone during the era of *Pax Australiana*: the growth and nucleation of communities and the probable increased frequency of disputes associated with more intensive social interaction; the changes in marriage patterns and the postulated increase in divorce rates; the emancipation of young men from some of the authority of their elders; the suppression of violence as a mode of settlement in favour of shaming; and the role-shift of leaders from aggressive warriors to calculating food-managers.

Perhaps none of these changes has been radical (even the role of war-leader was revived a few years ago when Kalauna made a foray down to Belebele), and perhaps none has been disruptive enough to alter beyond recognition Kalauna society as it was three generations ago, though some traits seem to have disappeared and new ones taken their place, some values have been modified and some attitudes re-defined. Consider, for example, the following statement by Kaulubu, a middle-aged leader of some discernment, whose father was born about the turn of the century:

When our fathers made *abutu* they made it one man against one man, or one *unuma* against one *unuma*. Today we make it one *yabu* against one *yabu* or one 'barrack' against one 'barrack'. People see. They watch each other and get angry. They get jealous of their brothers' [i.e. kinsmen's] food, and make sorcery against them.

He is speaking of shifts in values and attitudes as well as of changes in the scale of *abutu*. He deplores its growth because he believes it promotes competitiveness, to which he attributes an increase in sorcery attacks. According to his received model (one which is confirmed by other informants of the same age group), the *abutu* of his father's generation involved only four parties: two *inuba* and their respective *fofofo*, or alternatively, two pairs of enemies linked as *fofofo* thus:

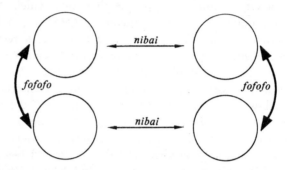

There were no *veo'owana* and no *tabotabo* (role categories 'carried over' from festivals), for the contest was contained by the enemy sets. According to this view *abutu* has escalated from a duel of big-men pitting their resources against each other, to something of a free-for-all in which everyone may become involved, and in which almost any man may challenge or be challenged. In doing so, Kaulubu argues, men risk the disapproval of their kinsmen, who are jealous of each other's food output and bids for leadership and prestige.[1] It is perhaps a way of saying that the growth of *abutu* to present-day proportions is undermining the solidarity of the descent groups which it earlier tended to aggrandize.

This is more explicit in the way another informant pinpoints a source of conflict in currently construed *abutu* obligations:

Today we use *veo'owana* when we make *abutu*. It is bad because those men who are *veo'owana* and help their mothers' group make their own group angry with them. They can die from sorcery. Before, our fathers only helped their own *unuma*; their mothers' not at all.

Other informants made frequent comment on the juggling of obligations that *tabotabo* have to accomplish to avoid giving offence when they are related to both parties to an *abutu*.

It is likely that the conditions which followed the abolition of warfare

[1] See Iyahalina's comments in Chapter 7 (p. 169) on the same problem of in-group competition.

permitted a relaxation of clan solidarity. Indeed, for the growth of communities composed of autonomous patrilineal clans, it is a virtual prerequisite for village integrity that other, non-agnatic links be created or strengthened.[1] If, as my informants indicate, the solidarity of agnatic descent groups has been weakened by *abutu* and the intrusion of competitive values from the political domain, then it has been the price to pay for the reinforcement of other consanguineal ties. Those links with mother's kin, with *tubuya* etc. and with affines which *inuba* exploit today, are also those links which make for firmer community solidarity. It is conceivable, therefore, that in addition to providing leaders with a useful avenue to local fame, and men generally with a non-violent form of social control, the inflationary growth of *abutu* was one of the processes by which the post-contact expansion of communities could be accommodated. Although informants deplored the escalation of *abutu* to the point where allegiances have to be divided, it is possible that without it Kalauna, and other villages of its size, would have segmented and dispersed long ago.

[1] See Hogbin and Wedgwood (1953, p. 259) on the cohesion of discrete multi-carpellary parishes.

11

FESTIVALS

To give is to show one's superiority, to show that one is something more and higher, that one is *magister*. To accept without returning or repaying more is to face subordination, to become a client and subservient, to become *minister*.

Mauss, 1966, p. 72

In Chapter 4 the ceremonial moiety division was discussed from the point of view of *dewa* and social identification. It was noted that while the moieties serve no structural end such as the regulation of marriage, they provide the organizational basis for ceremonial exchange cycles. The main purpose of the present chapter is to describe and assess the cultural and social significance of festivals – the constituent unitary events of the moiety-based cycles. Empirically, the individual festival (a 'Modawa' or a 'Fakili') is characterized by regular food exchanges and nightly entertainments over a period of many months. It is climaxed by a large pig and food distribution at which debts are paid and other created, thereby linking it to other festivals of the same and other cycles. The Modawa/Fakili festival cycle is the most spectacular institutional complex that Goodenough Islanders possess; perhaps as important to them as the *kula* is to some other Massim societies. This appears to have been so for the fairly recent past, but the status of such festival cycles in the more distant past is problematical.

While it is generally asserted by Goodenough Islanders that *abutu* – in its present form at least – is a recent 'custom', there is consensus on the antiquity of Modawa and Fakili. They were *dewa* 'brought out of the ground' by the ancestors. This dogma is not contradicted by the fact that some clans, as I noted in Chapter 4, acquired their moiety affiliation more recently, nor by the fact that many of the songs and dances associated with Fakili and Modawa are acknowledged to have been learnt within the last few generations. However, the point made earlier should not be forgotten: that the original moieties might well have been Hiyo and Modawa, the 'fighters' and the 'peacekeepers', and that Fakili has been assimilated to Hiyo over the course of time.[1] Notwithstanding the tendency of modern

[1] Possibly as an indirect effect of the prohibition of warfare, since the comb (*fakili*), which is used as a musical instrument, forms a more appropriate symbol of complementary opposition to the drum (*modawa*) than does the spear (*hiyo*) in an era of peace.

Goodenough Islanders to classify themselves as *either* Fakili *or* Modawa, as either 'singers' or 'dancers', and to project, in short, a quasi-moiety scheme, the possibility remains that there were originally three customary categories, perhaps differentially grouped in different parts of the island.

The problem cannot be solved by recourse to documentary sources, since not even Jenness and Ballantyne mention the existence of a moiety system. This omission seems even more curious than their failure to discuss *abutu*, which is explicable in terms of its probable insignificance in the immediate post-pacification period. Indeed, the same explanation might well apply to their having overlooked festival cycles, and thereby the ceremonial moiety system which is ideologically tied to them. There are what might be interpreted as oblique references to Modawa and Fakili in the 1920 monograph, but they are not conclusive.[1] It is possible that the authors' then-fashionable concern with totemism and their pre-conceptions regarding its systematization led them to misinterpret their data (see *ibid.* pp. 66–9). As to why they failed to stumble across prolonged festivals climaxed by spectacular food distributions, it is not enough to argue that such events were precluded by the famine conditions which prevailed at the time of Jenness's visit, for Ballantyne had long experience of the area.[2] Clearly, whilst superficial ethnography is doubtless partly to blame, it is likely that such festivals as occurred in this period were relatively inconspicuous events to an outsider. Just as *abutu* appears to have flourished since contact, so too, it might be expected, did festival cycles. Like *abutu*, festivals would probably have been smaller in terms of both lavishness and number of persons involved. Speculatively, then, European contact provided the enabling conditions of peaceful intercourse and relative ease of communication, while the boost to the subsistence economy given by steel tools, and the search by aspiring leaders for new modes of prestige-acquisition provided the stimuli.

SOME PARAMETERS

Festival cycles are based on single village communities. Depending upon the number of sponsoring groups (nominally clans) within the village, a

---

[1] See *ibid.* p. 68, where 'drum' is given as a Bwaidoga hamlet's totem, a hamlet which today does indeed affiliate to Modawa; p. 165, where the characteristic percussive instrument of Fakili is mentioned as 'taking the place of the drum in one dance'; p. 169, where feasting and dancing are described in a way which could refer to the middle phase of a Modawa festival.

[2] Large-scale festivals were observed during the same period by missionaries at Bartle Bay, on the mainland adjacent to the D'Entrecasteaux (see Seligman 1910, pp. 589–606). Despite the many interesting parallels between festivals and feasts described in the Massim ethnography and those found on Goodenough Island today, I refrain from documenting and discussing them in this work.

full cycle may take anything from four to a dozen years to complete. This assumes that there is a minimal period of 'resting' between the end of one festival and the commencement of the next. The duration of each festival within the cycle can vary from a few months to as long as three years. The principal factors which determine the length of a festival are availability of resources and political considerations of various kinds. Economic resources are fundamental. Surpluses must be deliberately created by the sponsoring group and its *fofofo*, both by planting extra gardens before and during the festival, and by acquiring and setting aside a number of pigs for the final distribution. Nominally, the length of these festivals is geared to pig growth, and eighteen months to two years is sufficient time for the piglets obtained at the commencement of a festival to reach fat maturity. However, gardening plans can go awry with unfavourable climatic conditions, and pigs can be lost, inadvertently injured or killed. A festival might be brought to a precipitate conclusion by factors such as these.

TABLE 26   *Festivals in five villages: 1966–8*[1]

Village	Type of festival	Length of festival				
		Aug. 1966	Jan. 1967	Aug. 1967	Jan. 1968	July 1968
Belebele	Modawa			├──────	──────────	──────────┤
Eweli	Modawa	├─────┤				
	Fakili				├─────	──────────┤
Kalauna	Fakili		├────────	───┤		
	Fakili				├───	──────────┤
	Seli				├──┤	──────────┤
Mataita	Sagali	├───────────	──────────	──────────	───┤	
Wailolo	Sagali	├───────────	──────────┤			

[1] Seli and Sagali festivals are discussed below. It should be noted that I capitalize these words to indicate that they are names analogous to Modawa and Fakili. When festival names are used as common nouns they are italicized (*seli* – a song; *modawa* – a drum, etc.).

Political considerations influence the decision of the sponsoring *inuba* to terminate or prolong their festival. Apart from the fact that pigs may need to be grown to a certain size to match those owed by the *inuba*, the leaders might see no advantage in holding a long festival. They may also be discouraged from doing so by their *fofofo*, who are wearied of the onerous tasks they must perform, or by other prospective *inuba* who are awaiting their turn to promote a festival. At least one year is thought necessary for the 'news' or 'fame' of the event to reach its maximum extent; more than two years is thought to be excessively demanding upon *inuba* and *fofofo*, and is probably the point at which returns, in the form of prestige and fame, begin to diminish relative to the expenditure of resources. The majority of festivals for which I gathered data lasted from one to two years. Table 26 shows, for the two-year period of my association with Kalauna, the various festivals which were begun, continuing, or completed in Kalauna and neighbouring communities. Eight distinct festivals belonging to five different cycles are represented in this arbitrary two-year slice of time.

TABLE 27 *The festival cycle in Kalauna*

Chief sponsor hamlet and clan	Chief *fofofo* hamlet and clan	Festival	Date
TOMOLAULAWA Modimodia, Malabuabua	TABWAIKA Lalaveya, Foloyai	Modawa	*c.* 1960
AWAKILI Kwakwaiboka, Ainaona	TOBOWA Anuana II, Lulauvile	Modawa	*c.* 1962
TOWAKAITA Valeutoli, Nouneya	ILUKWALUKWA Buveta, Iwaoyana	Modawa	*c.* 1963
MALAWIDIYA Anuana II, Lulauvile	KIMAOLA Heloava II, Lulauvile	Fakili	1964–6
BWANAKOVI Ukevakeva, Iwaoyana	KAFATAUDI Valeutoli, Nouneya	Fakili	1967
KIMAOLA Heloava II, Lulauvile	MALAWIDIYA Anuana II, Lulauvile	Fakili	1967–9?
TABWAIKA Lalaveya, Foloyai	WAKASILELE Modimodia, Malabuabua	Seli	1967–8

The general pattern of Kalauna's festival cycle since 1960 is shown in Table 27. It will be noted that types of festival do not necessarily alternate, and whether they do or not is thought to be immaterial. Far more important is the reciprocation between *fofofo* pairs, and six of the seven festivals can be linked in this way. For instance, Tabwaika and Kimaola, who undertook the burdensome role of *fofofo* leadership to their respective sponsors, were 'paid back' subsequently by sponsoring festivals of their own and having their *fofofo* (erstwhile *inuba*) serve them in turn. The only Kalauna clan not represented in this list is Mulina, which is numerically insignificant when it is remembered that one half is *fofofo* to the other. The last Mulina-sponsored Fakili festival was some twenty years ago.

When I left Kalauna, Kimaola's festival was expected to last another year. The completion of Tabwaika's, on the other hand, was imminent.[1] It had been a half-hearted affair from the beginning, partly because it lay

---

[1] This festival was called a Seli. Tabwaika's clan, Foloyai, is Hiyo and has no right to use Fakili customary entertainments (see Chapter 4, pp. 64–5).

in the shadow of Kimaola's far more vigorous festival, and partly because Tabwaika's brother, Binamina, had tried to direct events by letter from Port Moresby. Despite his repeatedly stated intention of returning to the village, he had failed to appear. Tabwaika and his chief *fofofo* and *venima'abi*, Wakasilele, were weary of waiting and the week that I left Kalauna they had begun to discuss the proposed pig and food distribution which would mark the end of the abortive festival. Both Wakasilele and Kafataudi (of Nouneya) were proposing to sponsor Modawa festivals in the near future, though they had not agreed on which of them was to do it first. Although two festivals of different kinds may run concurrently in the same cycle (as indeed Tabwaika's Seli and Kimaola's Fakili were doing), it is inappropriate for two of the same kind to run parallel and competing courses. 'Other villages would laugh at us if we had two Fakili or two Modawa going', said one informant. As far as the nightly entertainments are concerned, such a situation would involve an absurd duplication of program. For the five years up to 1973, then, the schedule of festivals in Kalauna had been approximately fixed, although it is by no means immune to contingencies such as death, drought, or a significant shift in the political balance of the community.[1]

Festivals are 'entertainments' which redound to the political credit of their sponsors; a more leisurely way than *abutu* of accumulating a fund of power and prestige. In this respect they serve similar ends to mortuary or memorial feasts and exchanges in other D'Entrecasteaux societies (see Chowning 1960; Guy 1937; Roheim 1946). The post-contact era on Goodenough, however, has seen the importation from Fergusson Island of many observances and practices associated with death, among which is the concept of the memorial celebration sponsored by a kinsman of a dead man. Today, just as a quarrel may precipitate *abutu*, so might an unexpected death occasion the sponsoring of a festival. Moreover, festivals may be combined in a number of complicated ways with the imported elements from Fergusson mortuary customs. Although this is not the place to document or discuss these with the thoroughness they deserve, it is necessary to mention Sagali, which is by far the most spectacular cultural import.

Despite its primary significance as a memorial feast and distribution in western Fergusson, Sagali[2] is to Goodenough Islanders merely an alternative form to their own Fakili and Modawa festivals. In the cases that I investigated there was no explicit connection between a death and the sponsoring of a Sagali festival. To date, few villages have ever held a

---

[1] A year after leaving the field I learned that Kimaola's Fakili had been recently concluded, and that Kafataudi had promoted a Modawa.

[2] Cf. also Fortune 1932, pp. 199–200. In the Trobriands *sagali* is a 'ceremonial distribution of food' (Malinowski 1922, p. 148).

Sagali and many Goodenough Islanders have never seen one, although Bwaidogan elders recall one as early as the 1920s. In the last decade or so about five have been held in eastern Goodenough, and I witnessed two during 1967–8 (see Table 26). Sagali is seen as a fashion, a 'new thing', which still requires men from Fergusson to advise and assist Goodenough sponsors in its planning and execution, particularly in the culminating phase when a platform forty feet high is erected to support a group of dancers and butchered pigs for distribution.

My general point is that not only have the indigenous forms of festival on Goodenough been stimulated into a vigorous florescence since pacification, but that they have also been supplemented and diversified by the adoption from Fergusson Island of memorial feasts, mortuary exchanges and other practices associated with death. Occasions for sponsoring festivals have thus been multiplied, and there are many modes available today for the leader wishing to 'make big his name'. By combining numerous different elements, some imported, some indigenous, he can create 'new' and hitherto untried sequences of feasts, exchanges and festivals (see Roheim 1946 for a Normanby Island parallel). It is a point of equal importance, however, that the majority of festivals which occur on Goodenough are unconnected with death, and cannot be described as 'memorials'. Of the seven festivals held in Kalauna since 1960, only Bwanakovi's was specifically prompted by a death (that of Madiaiwao, a classificatory son of Bwanakovi). It is interesting, too, that when Kimaola's chief *fofofo* died during the former's Fakili, it was felt by many that the festival should be terminated. It continued with the understanding that henceforth it was to be 'for Malawidiya's memory'. Festivals can easily become 'converted' to memorial events while they are in process, though they appear to be infrequently promoted as such at their inception.

THE STRUCTURE AND ORGANIZATION OF A FESTIVAL

Three main phases of any festival are customarily distinguished: *aihina kulina*, 'lighting the fire', which is the initial phase of ceremonial inauguration; *seliseli* or *dayadaya*, 'singing' or 'dancing', the prolonged middle period of regular entertainments and feasting; and lastly *aidaba*, the 'cutting' of the festival, the grand finale which is characterized by a large-scale distribution of pigs and vegetable food.

The status set involved in a festival is identical to that found in *abutu*, but whereas the latter consists of two opposed 'sides' which are mirror images of each other, a festival involves only one set of *inuba*, *fofofo*, *veo'owana* and *tabotabo*. Briefly, the role of *inuba* as sponsors is to provide the bulk of the resources and direct the course of the festival, but remaining the while conspicuously aloof from the mechanics of the event. *Fofofo*'s role is to perform all the executive tasks as well as to supplement resources. As in *abutu*, *veo'owana* are self-selected from among the sponsors' 'sisters' sons', and their function is to support the former by virtual assimilation to the role of *inuba*. *Tabotabo* are 'the public', the residual category of persons and groups on whom depends the ultimate success of the festival.

The opening phase: 'Lighting the fire'

While their forthcoming festival is in the planning stage, *inuba* and *fofofo* will generally attempt to keep it a secret from the rest of the community, though it is a simple matter for the curious, by checking whether extra gardens have been made, to satisfy themselves that the rumours which are abroad have substance. Finally, perhaps at a village meeting called for other purposes, or more conventionally from a house-step one quiet evening, the chief *fofofo* will make an official announcement to the effect that his *inuba* wishes to pay back all his pig and food debts, so he is going to promote a 'small' *laubihala*, a celebration or entertainment. The *fofofo* leader adds on his own account that he will now repay the effort and deprivation which his *inuba* endured when their statuses and roles were reversed. Nothing is said in reply, and the village still waits for substantive confirmation of the announcement, though to back down at this stage would cost the *inuba* and their *fofofo* loss of respect.

A few nights later the festival is inaugurated. The leading *fofofo* lights a fire on the stone sitting circle belonging to the *unuma* of the chief sponsor, which is likely to be within a few yards of his house. This is done with a small ceremony. The fire will be relit here in much the same manner every night that there is to be entertainment for as long as the festival lasts, and it is a symbol of hospitality, warm relationships and shared pleasures. For the first week or two while the festival is being launched, only the *inuba* and *fofofo* gather around the fire. If it is a Modawa (or that rarer event, a Sagali) dancing to drums takes place. If it is a Fakili, singing to the beat of combs on lime gourds is the main form of entertainment. *Seli*, a song form which is currently by far the most popular on Goodenough, may be interspersed with Fakili songs or, in the case of those Hiyo sponsors who do not possess the inherited right to use Fakili or Modawa customs, *seli* itself may be the principal entertainment.

Until the leading *fofofo* makes a shouted invitation from his *inuba*'s sitting circle, the community at large, the *tabotabo*, may not attend the nightly entertainments. As with most breaches of etiquette the sanction is shaming, and appropriately in these circumstances, this is accomplished by food-giving.

Thus, when young Adiwai of Iwaoyana, blissfully ignorant of the rule, joined the *inuba* and *fofofo* at the opening of Malawidiya's festival, he was treated with lavish hospitality and mock solicitude. But to 'teach him good manners', he was called upon to receive a whole pig at the climax of the festival over a year later. The magnitude of this gift suggests that there was a political aspect to the incident, however, and that the Lulauvile donors were using Adiwai's offence as an excuse to give their Iwaoyana enemies a large pig. Certainly, the latter were inconvenienced, and Tomoadikuyau (Adiwai's father's brother's son) was infuriated enough to hit the youth for his foolish offence – an act which caused Adiwai to leave his own hamlet and take up residence in Mulina.

When the open invitation is made to the *tabotabo* to join the festival – to come and sing or dance and eat the *inuba*'s food – the orator adds a plea for visitors to leave their enmities and their 'bad things' (sorcery) behind, and to come in a spirit of joy. He says of the festival: 'It's name is play-thing; it's name is happiness', and tells the *tabotabo*: 'It is your thing, so you must make it good.'

The middle phase: 'Lauhiwaiya'

To celebrate the public opening of the festival it is usual to hold a large cooked food exchange called *lauhiwaiya*. This is a significant event, not only because it initiates the longest phase of the festival, but also because it gives the community at large clues to what might be called the political intentions of the *inuba*. For in offering an opportunity for food-giving, *lauhiwaiya* is a vehicle for *abutu* behaviour. (Indeed, the first *lauhiwaiya* I witnessed was colloquially introduced to me as an *abutu* by one informant.) Although there is no space to describe this exchange in detail, its organiza-tion must be outlined.

The entire community contributes to the *lauhiwaiya* with pots of cooked food (prestige dishes only, saturated in coconut oil) and wooden platters piled with uncooked tubers. *Venima'abi* partners cook for each other and contribute on each other's behalf; some element of competition is thus ensured at even the most basic level. The actual exchange takes place during the late afternoon, the whole of the earlier part of the day having been spent preparing the food. The pots are laid in a single line on the ground in the *inuba*'s hamlet, and parallel to them the donors place their platters of uncooked food. One end of the double line is composed of the food contributed by the sponsors of the festival, the middle section is that contributed by the *fofofo*, and the other end is formed by the pots of the *tabotabo*. The *fofofo* busily arrange the pots and platters to their satisfaction while *tabotabo* and *inuba* sit looking on and singing *seli* or other songs.

The chief *fofofo*, who has been briefed beforehand by the leading *inuba*, then commences the distribution. Beginning first with the *inuba*'s contribution, he walks down the lines of pots and platters calling the names of the designated recipients. There is an expectant silence while this is done, for although the *fofofo* says no more than 'so-and-so, his food', much significance is attached to the name called and the number of pots assigned to its owner. The *inuba*'s pots are generally given to 'enemies', but while traditional enemies within the village are not surprised to receive a number of large pots, there are likely to be other members of the community who, while recalling some half-forgotten quarrel or supposedly secret delict against the *inuba*, are stunned by the public gift of shaming proportions. They may affect indignation and protest at being given so much; but the *fofofo* ignores them and the *inuba* are unapproachable. They are obliged to accept their gifts with as good a grace as they can muster, while a rash of whispered speculation breaks out among the rest of the *tabotabo*. The *fofofo*'s pots may be given likewise to *inuba*'s enemies, for the *inuba* control the apportionment of all the food. But the *fofofo*'s enemies are likely to be given some of the *fofofo*'s pots too. *Tabotabo*'s pots are given to other *tabotabo* in approximately the same proportions as the recipients contributed.

When all the pots and their accompanying platters have been apportioned, *tabotabo* leaders make short, almost stereotyped, speeches of thanks for the munificence of the gifts they received and of apology for their own inadequate contributions. Women then come forward to carry away pots that have been assigned to their husbands' *fofofo*. Families feast on the cooked food in the privacy of their homes, then later in the evening, dressed in their best, all return to the *inuba*'s hamlet for a whole night's entertainment. Next morning they are fed from several large communal pots provided by the *inuba*. Since the latter may eat none of the food prepared for the *lauhiwaiya* (it being their *niune*), their individual *venima'abi* cook them food separately as in *abutu*. It is brought to them after the *lauhiwaiya* exchange is complete.

To dwell for a moment on the political significance of the inaugural *lauhiwaiya*, it should be clear that given the possibilities for *abutu* behaviour, it is the first opportunity of the *inuba* – and of their leader especially – to show their hands in a demonstration of intent. Idiomatically, the festival is a 'plaything', a 'happiness', but no Goodenough Islander has any illusions about its also being an instrument for the public infliction of shame and therefore a means by which to assert dominance. Men called to receive the *inuba*'s and *fofofo*'s food at the *lauhiwaiya* are thereby forewarned that they will be singled out to receive 'big food' and pigs at the climax of the festival many months later.

At an Ukevakeva *lauhiwaiya* in 1967, Wakasilele was given several more pots than he had anticipated, and he was sufficiently rattled to write to his three brothers in Samarai, urging them to return home and prepare more gardens to meet the threat of subsequent *lauhiwaiya*. As Kafataudi's *nibai*, Wakasilele expected an enemy's share, but Kafataudi (Ukevakeva's chief *fofofo*) was also exercising his right to throw a personal punch: Wakasilele had all but forgotten that many years before, one of his brothers had seduced Kafataudi's wife. Thus, it was said, the extra pots.

Tabotabo caught off-guard by a large gift must be prepared for the next *lauhiwaiya*, and contribute to it at least as many pots as they expect to be given. Only in this way can they avoid being shamed. (No-one is shamed if *tabotabo* 'over-give', however, since they are merely contributing to a pool, the redistribution of which is not their prerogative. It is regarded as ill-mannered and boastful to contribute more pots than one might reasonably expect to receive in return.) Since expectations tend to be better matched in subsequent *lauhiwaiya*, they are less dramatic events than the first of any festival.

There are more subtle ways of stating the ill-health of a relationship between *inuba* and *tabotabo* than by simply giving extra pots of food. We saw in an earlier chapter how promising young leaders can be 'nominated' by groups other than their own by being called upon to receive food at distributions. This is but one aspect of the significance of 'calling out' recipients in *lauhiwaiya*. In the very selection of names the *inuba* may be displaying by nuance derision and malice as well as political calculation. By omitting to call out the 'bossman' of a group, the latter is understandably slighted – the implication being that he is undeserving of his apparent status. An underling, perhaps a younger brother, who is called in his stead is understandably embarrassed – the implication being that he should take his brother's place as leader of his hamlet. To call a child's name is not always just an indulgent anticipation of his adulthood – it wounds the father by anticipating his death and replacement. Sometimes an old man's name is called, that of a retired leader or a senile stay-at-home. The bitter joke may be a reminder of his bygone days of glory and his present inability to meet debts. The first question anyone not an acknowledged leader asks on being called to take his *unuma*'s or his hamlet's pots is: 'What was my wrong?' There may be no satisfactory answer or one found only in the conscience of the person thus called. Clearly, however, there has to be a norm for these pointed name-callings to depart from if they are to be effective. The norm is that the 'bossman' of each hamlet or food-receiving unit shall be called; where he is not, in perhaps four cases out of every ten, it is possible to detect the presence of either spite or a sanction. Both are rationalized innocently by the *fofofo* if pressed to explain why *this* young man or *that* old man was called. In the one case he is being given 'practice' for adulthood, in the other he is being shown respect for his seniority. But these are explanations which only the more naive accept.

Even more subtle was Kimaola's belittling of his sister's husband, Kafataudi, at his *lauhiwaiya*. Kimaola arranged that the pot of food cooked by his sister on behalf of her child (who was Kimaola's *tubuya* and thus a potential *veo'owana* helper), be given to Kafataudi's *venima'abi*, so that Kafataudi was obliged to receive it in exchange and eat it. Kafataudi protested in vain that he had been given his own pot, that it was his wife's (and child's) *niune*, since one had cooked it and the other donated it. Iyahalina, Kimaola's chief *fofofo* on this occasion, assured Kafataudi that it was a coincidence and advised him to eat it, it being 'only food'. If Kafataudi was prepared to overlook this calculated attempt to embarrass him as an unfortunate mistake, he was left in no doubt when, some months later at the next *lauhiwaiya*, Kimaola employed the same tactic again. Kafataudi once more received his own pot containing food from his own garden, cooked by his own wife, and given through his own child. Again he protested and again he was told it was 'only food'. There was much speculation on Kimaola's motive for this devious shaming ploy and, before I left the field, no final consensus. However, the most satisfactory explanation hinted at was that Kimaola was driving deeper the wedge he had himself placed between Kafataudi and his son, whom he was in process of adopting (see above, p. 99). By this clever manipulation of pots, the boy's *veo'owana* link to Kimaola was being stressed at the expense of his filial tie to Kafataudi. In effect, Kimaola was saying to Kafataudi: 'See! This boy is my sister's son more than he is your own.'

The middle phase: 'Vebiala'

During the long months of the festival's middle phase, the *inuba* try to keep alive public interest. Regular attendance of a fair number of people is essential for the 'fame' of the festival to spread and redound to the credit and prestige of the sponsors and their *fofofo*. The Fakili or Modawa must not be allowed to grow 'cold'. After the first month or so there is an inevitable waning of interest on the part of the *tabotabo*; later still, on the part of the *fofofo*; and finally, even on the part of the *inuba* themselves.

These are phases which I was able to document for Kimaola's Fakili in 1967. Kimaola was more fortunate than most *inuba*, perhaps, in having money enough to entice and sorcery enough to intimidate potential visitors. Thus, he frequently supplied tobacco and rice in addition to the usual betel nut and cooked staples, while evening attendances rose sharply following an incident which he exploited to his advantage. Wasimala of Aluwaita (technically one of the *inuba* since Aluwaita is part of Lulauvile I), fell sick and suffered hallucinations in which he experienced attacks by spirits. He was cured after a few weeks by Enowei's exorcism magic, but some days later, Kimaola made it known that he had himself sorcerized Wasimala as punishment for not attending his Fakili celebrations more regularly. Wasimala and his father Siboboya had stayed away, they protested, because they were ashamed at having no pigs – an excuse which Kimaola would not accept. He hinted broadly that others, too, might find themselves possessed by spirits if they did not come to his nightly entertainments more often.

More conventional methods of keeping alive public interest in a festival are to hold periodic *lauhiwaiya* exchanges, special guest nights (*vebiala*), at which particular individuals are honoured, or simply to invite parties of guests from other villages. *Inuba* with well-stocked gardens should manage to promote a *lauhiwaiya* every three months or so. In the intervening months a *vebiala* may be sponsored by arrangement with the individual to be honoured. The latter may take the initiative himself and send a message to the effect that he is intending to make his *début* at the festival on a certain date; alternatively the *inuba* may invite someone from within or beyond the village, who has not been seen at the festival for some time, to come for *vebiala*. Either way, the visitor makes his appearance wearing some new item of clothing, an exquisite new feather or a new basket, and he is given as much betel, tobacco and food as he can consume. Next morning he is presented with many pots of food by the *inuba* and *fofofo*. Some of the pots are redistributed by the guest's *fofofo* among the other visitors, and others are taken home by the same *fofofo* for their own consumption. A man who is honoured thus reciprocates when he is an *inuba* of his own or an agnate's festival. In this way serial festivals within the community are linked by chains of reciprocal feasting, while parallel festival cycles proceeding in different villages are interlinked by *vebiala* exchanges. While the *vebiala* subject is usually a big-man, it is not essential to be one in order to be honoured in this manner; unless he selects himself (and he probably would not do so if he were not a leader for fear of being thought presumptuous), the only criterion the festival sponsors consider is whether or not he will be capable of paying back the food given to him.

In addition to being a device for reviving interest in a festival, *vebiala* is also used as a means of circumventing the dampening effects of a death among *tabotabo* of the village. Normally, out of respect for the bereaved kinsmen, the festival is suspended for a number of weeks. At the end of that time, the *inuba* invite the deceased's kinsmen (who will be observing mourning taboos) to come for *vebiala*. The agnate closest to the dead person will be the one who is honoured; he will shave, wash, dress in finery and go prepared to break his taboo on eating 'good' food. In addition to pots of food he is given several shell valuables as compensation for his loss, but this is equally to be interpreted as inducement for his tacit approval of the resumption of the festival. General mourning thus ceases, for it is incompatible with the celebrations and good food which are the essentials of any festival. Only widows and widowers are unable to circumvent their onerous and prolonged mourning in this fashion, and they are expected to stay away from the festival altogether.

Criteria of success

By devious or conventional means, then, the *inuba* strive to keep their festival 'warm', and keep its 'name' spreading outwards across the island like ripples on a pond. It requires, as we have seen, some ingenuity and a steady supply of food resources. In addition to the periodic *lauhiwaiya* and *vebiala* events, the *inuba* are expected to provide a pot or two of cooked food for visitors every night that they attend to sing or dance. (They are usually fed in the early morning before they go home to sleep.) Without these nightly displays of hospitality, attendance would dwindle; at all costs the *inuba* must create and sustain a reputation for generosity. The *inuba*'s dependence upon *tabotabo* visitors for the success of their festival is made explicit in the thanks which the chief *fofofo* utters as he gives the weary singers or dancers their breakfast: 'We are ashamed because your eyes ache and you are chilled by the dew.' The *inuba* can share none of the food (nor betel nor even tobacco) that they give to their guests, for it is their *niune*. Every night that the *inuba* supply food for their guests (and *fofofo*), their *venima'abi* cook them pots of food in return, which the *inuba* may eat only in the privacy of their houses after the guests have gone. Nor are eating restrictions the only ones to irk the *inuba*. For the duration of their festival, they must avoid any kind of conduct which would reflect unfavourably upon them and thus discourage people from attending their entertainments. Although under constraint to avoid quarrels at this time, *inuba* are not prevented from taking action against offenders, for they have the instrument at their disposal for inflicting shame. The sanction is double-edged, for *tabotabo* also are wary of crossing the *inuba* (or *fofofo*) of an on-going festival.

There is one major exception to these statements: an adultery offence committed against the *inuba* or *fofofo* must be tacitly overlooked by them while the festival is in progress. This is not a mandate for licence, though some *tabotabo* men and *inuba* or *fofofo* women appear willing to exploit the

circumstances. It is a fact that *inuba* and *fofofo* womenfolk suffer considerable demands upon their labour during a festival; they are not only under
pressure to assist their husbands in maintaining an abnormally high
garden output, but on them fall the chores of carrying, preparing and
cooking great quantities of food for the unrelenting celebrations. At the
periodic *lauhiwaiya* they are each obliged to cook several pots of food within
about twenty-four hours, some of which will be distributed among the
visitors the evening before and the evening after the actual *lauhiwaiya*
exchange. For the *lauhiwaiya* only *kumakava* is good enough, and this is
the most demanding of all dishes to prepare.[1]

For these and other duties, *inuba* and *fofofo* womenfolk gain scant
reward. The social benefits of a successful festival are reaped mainly by
their husbands; the glory the women receive is only a dim reflection, the
entertainments they join are dulled by repetition and inadequate sleep,
and they are even denied a taste of the banquets of food they have cooked.
It is perhaps not surprising that they sometimes rebel, either by divorcing
or by committing adultery at the first opportunity, knowing that their
husbands will be restrained in their reactions, if not totally acquiescent.
Of course, once the festival is over the offended husband may retaliate in
the manner he thinks appropriate; by *abutu* (though he will doubtless
already have given the adulterer a shaming pig at the festival's conclusion),
or by resort to court action. If his wife did not divorce him he may then
beat her, but this prospect is unlikely to deter her at the time, after she
has been beaten already perhaps for sleeping when she should be cooking
for visitors, or for refusing to work harder in the gardens. Wise men,
therefore, do not drive their wives too hard, knowing that if they do, in the
last analysis they themselves will be the losers.[2]

The success of a festival is not readily measurable, although *inuba* will
be satisfied if they have managed to attract regularly fairly large numbers
of people who have ostensibly enjoyed themselves and gone away well fed.
They will be assured then that the 'name' of their Fakili or their Modawa
will have reached distant corners of the island, that their leader's name and
that of his chief *fofofo* – he who 'supported the burden' – will be on
strangers' lips, and that in the future these men will be shown deference in

---

[1] *Kumakava* is made from taro and certain types of plantain, which are cooked together
in coconut oil over a slow fire in a large Amphlett pot. The woman sings spells to prevent
the food from burning and the pot from cracking, but arduous labour is necessitated by
continual stirring with a paddle. It is a task which men frequently undertake in other
Massim cultures (cf. Malinowski 1929, p. 16; Fortune 1932, p. 190).

[2] Although the principal rationale supporting the prohibition against an *inuba* or *fofofo*
taking offence at adultery is couched in terms of preventing scandal and preserving the
'good name' of the festival, it is a point of some significance that *inuba* at least are theoretically *kaiwabu* during their festival, and that the role demands detachment and aloofness.

foreign villages, and their kinsmen able to air their connections proudly. But the months of disciplined work and restraint during which a local fame has been nurtured and spread is merely stage-setting, advertisement and dress-rehearsal for the drama of the festival's climax.

The concluding phase: 'Aidabana'

The decision to end the festival is taken by the *inuba*. If they are dissatisfied with the number of pigs they have reared for the event, they make excursions to neighbouring villages with their *fofofo* to purchase a few more with shell valuables or cash. Word is spread as widely as possible of the day of the finale. Special invitations are rarely sent, it being rightly assumed that everyone living within a radius of several miles will come if he possibly can. As the geographical and social distance increases from Kalauna, so are visiting parties smaller. But nowadays, at least, representative leaders from every village within a day's journey (and even some from Fergusson Island) can be expected to appear. The more visitors that come and the more villages represented, the more the *inuba* will be elated by the confirmation that the fame of their festival is universal. This elation may be tempered by worry about whether they have sufficient pigs to ensure that every visiting leader is given pork, and a last-minute effort to buy or borrow more pigs might be necessary. Since it would defeat the aim of the festival to allow anyone to leave at the end bearing a grudge against the *inuba* for neglect at the distribution, it is in the corporate interest of the whole village to prevent this, lest at some future date a Kalauna man visiting some distant village has it cast in his teeth that his compatriots denied pork to visitors at a festival. Indeed, it becomes evident that the festival's climax is a matter of pride and concern to the whole community, and that while sectional rivalries within it are undiminished, these are of secondary importance to the cleavage between the host village and outside visitors. The image of the traditional political unit is at stake. Intervillage rivalry is indicated by the willingness of *tabotabo* from the host community to give as much food as they can to swell the amount for distribution; in this sense they are 'helping' the *inuba* to make their festival a success for the sake of the village's fame. Yet intravillage rivalry is also expressed in the way sub-groups vie with each other to supply the most; in this sense they are competing for their own local fame.

The layout of food and pigs in the *inuba*'s hamlet takes as long as two days to complete, for platforms and stands must be built and the food displayed to maximum advantage. As in *abutu*, massive stands of bananas are constructed (generally one by each clan), as well as platforms to support the large frameworks in which taro and yams are displayed. In contrast to *abutu*, however, the unit of exchange is not the individual yam or taro but a framework of fairly standard size. It is therefore inappropriate to contribute the large yams which are the principal *abutu* weapon; quantity rather than size or quality is needed, and the same applies to taro. Pride of place in the food display is given to the platform on which lie crudely butchered pigs, though these are covered by coconut leaves to protect them from sun and flies, as well as to disguise from visitors the amount of pork to be distributed. A few live pigs are hung underneath the platform, as these are to be given whole.

The distribution is scheduled to begin about mid-day. By then most visitors will have arrived and settled themselves into village contingents. *Tabotabo* from within the village will have been present for some time, helping the *fofofo* to put the finishing touches to the food stands, greeting friends among the visitors, or simply striding up and down with that self-importance and assurance which distinguishes the residents from the visitors. The latter tend to be quiet, well-behaved and even timid – tentative responses to the uncertain temper of a strange political community. Everyone is brightly attired, wearing flowers, scented leaves, ornaments and their newest clothes. Faces are painted, bodies oiled, and mouths bright red with betel juice. There are two focal points in the animated scene: the platform on which the pigs are laid, and the platform on which the *kaiwabu*, 'the chiefs of the feast', are seated. The *kaiwabu*, who represent the *inuba*, number from one to half-a-dozen men and women. Their conduct and its implications will be discussed in some detail below.

The leading *fofofo* now ascends the platform of pigs and begins his welcome speech to the expectant crowd. He enumerates all the villages represented in the audience, greets them and thanks them for suffering the discomfort of sun and rain to attend his *inuba*'s 'small party'. 'We didn't tell you to come, the festival itself called you', he says. He regrets that there are but a few small pigs to be shared, but hopes that those visitors who receive nothing will not go away angry. His *inuba* are poor men, he says, and there will be barely enough pork to pay back their debts. He hopes that people have left their sorcery at home with their spears, for this is a joyous thing, a happiness that should not be spoilt with malice. He can see his own enemies and those of his *inuba* in the crowd, and although he would like to give to these enemies all the pigs, he cannot, he says, for then those not already his enemies would want to become so. Perhaps his enemies would like to fight him, but now there is 'Government', so if they came for war and not for food they should go home . . .

The orator pauses for a while, betel nuts are distributed, and seated groups break into song again or, if it is a Modawa festival, dancing recommences. Finally, the chief *fofofo* begins the distribution. First he calls names of leaders from other villages who have come to receive repayment of pork and food given to *inuba* or *fofofo* at earlier festivals. These return gifts (*tutula*) account for up to a third of the total number of pigs (but considerably less of the total amount of food) given at a distribution. Often the debts paid thus have stood for years and occasionally even for decades. When the recipient's name is called, his *fofofo* come forward to carry away the pork and food indicated by the orator. It is the recipient's *niune*, and after they have carried it home the *fofofo* distribute it among themselves and their kinsmen.

When the back-log of debts has been cleared, the orating *fofofo* announces that he will now commence to give 'presents'. This introduces the most dramatic part of the entire festival, and the mood of the gathering is keyed up in anticipation. The 'presents' of pork, whole pigs and food-frames are, of course, designed to create new debts among friends and enemies. The understated reference to 'presents' (*nuakabubu*) covers two distinct categories of prestation, however: *taladidika*, which are token gifts to friends and visitors, and *ketowai*, which are shaming gifts to enemies. Although the amounts of food and pork given in each category are about equal, *taladidika* gifts are spread over many recipients whereas comparatively few *ketowai* gifts are made. The size of an individual *taladidika* gift depends principally upon the size of the recipient's *fofofo*'s hamlet if he is from within the village, or the size of his contingent of fellow-visitors if he is from another community. The size of an individual *ketowai* gift depends upon the size of the recipient's offence in the eyes of the *inuba* or the degree of enmity between the groups giver and taker represent.

The chief *fofofo* of the festival calls out the category of gift together with the name of its intended recipient, alternating '*taladidika* pig' with '*ketowai* pig' or randomly juxtaposing them to maintain a state of tension in the audience. *Taladidika* gifts elicit no response beyond an informal 'thanks', but *ketowai* recipients frequently respond with a challenging query. This enables the *fofofo* orator to present a pithy statement of the wrongs to which the gift is supposedly a response. Indeed, whether the recipient protests or not, the *fofofo* leader is unlikely to forgo the opportunity of making public the specific details of the offence. The *ketowai* gifts are in fact the high point of the whole festival, which the earlier series of *lauhiwaiya* exchanges merely foreshadowed. The visitors delight in unexpected scandals or delicts suddenly brought to light in this fashion, and they enjoy, too, the discomfiture of the exposed offenders. Even for long-suspected offences there is the keen pleasure of anticipation and a readiness to be surprised at the amount of pork and food given to *ketowai* victims. The offence may have been an utterly trivial one in the eyes of the offender, and perhaps a fairly unimportant one in the eyes of the offended, but the public nature of its disclosure – plus the additional barbed witticisms which the orator sometimes cannot resist – inflicts shame and may even provoke fury in the recipient. Anger may indeed be close to the surface on such occasions, and at least one scuffle might be expected to break out during a distribution, when the *fofofo*'s insulting remarks which accompany a *ketowai* gift trigger violent responses in the recipient and his supporters. Far too many of the people present have an interest in the peace of the festival to allow such incidents to escalate, however, and they usually end in harmless displays of *sefaiya* by those who have been antagonized. The ritualized aggression of the *sefaiya* is accompanied by counter-insults and boasts that the recipients are not 'afraid' of being given food and pig. Needless to say, a *ketowai* gift cannot be refused without loss of dignity and reputation.

Having chewed his clan's potent *cordyline* (see above, pp. 68–9), Manawadi was in a boisterous mood at Nibogana's Sagali festival climax in Wailolo. Stimulated by betel nut and the presence of many pretty girls from other villages, excited by the drums and the festival atmosphere, he was *kasisi* (swanking), however, rather than *vetayakulo* (hooligan-like). But when Nibogana's chief *fofofo* called Manawadi's name to receive *ketowai* pig his mood changed abruptly. Enowei, his father, asked: 'Do you mean my son or Manawadi from Wakonai?' Nibogana's orator pointed to the thunderstruck Manawadi. 'Why do you give pig to him – he's only a small boy?' asked Enowei indignantly. The man on the platform said: 'It's for Kaniyowana [a Belebele man who was in the relationship of *veo'owana* to Nibogana and thus able to use the latter's festival as a vehicle for his own gifts of pork]. He says that Manawadi stole his canoe bailer.' Manawadi almost exploded with indignation as he tried to explain that he had merely borrowed it and returned it to Kaniyowana's canoe after a few minutes. The orator ignored him and addressed Enowei again: 'Do you want us to give you a whole pig?' Before he could reply, Kaulubu (a member of Enowei's *fofofo*) mounted the platform, humped the proffered half-carcase onto his back and carried it to the ground. Nibogana's womenfolk brought several yams and a bunch of bananas to go with the gift of pig. The man on the platform turned his attention to the next name on his list. Manawadi had not recovered from the shock of being given *ketowai*. He was trembling with anger and his eyes were staring. He grabbed a knife and made towards where Kaniyowana was sitting, but before he had moved a few paces, his father and Malawidiya had grasped him by the arms and wrenched the knife from him. They tried to soothe him by saying that they would be able to pay back the pig quickly, but it was some time before, as Manawadi himself put it, his 'head stopped going round'. Later in the afternoon, he chewed betel nut which was afterwards diagnosed as some of that thrown around by the sponsors 'to send away the spirits' which are thought to attend all Sagali festivals. After chewing, Manawadi broke into a sweat and

fell down in a faint. Enowei guarded him and told Wailolo men to stand away:
'otherwise you might kill him'. Kaulubu and Kimaola sang spells over him and
he soon revived. His mother's brother's widow, a Wailolo woman, invited him
to her house to eat some yams: 'to make you strong again'. He did so, but said he
was 'ashamed' because it is 'bad' to eat food in the festival host's village.

Manawadi derived some consolation from the fact that he was by no means the
only one to receive *ketowai* pig for a trivial offence on that occasion (see Appendix).
Indeed, he remains convinced that he committed no offence at all – that if
Kaniyowana's bailer was lost, it was not he who lost it. He deeply relished the
prospect, however, of paying back the pig to Kaniyowana, which he would do
at the end of Kimaola's Fakili festival. 'When the *fofofo* call his name', he said,
'I can ask them to say 'Kanitowana' [i.e. a small species of fish], so that when he
hears it he will get very angry!'

In addition to *inuba*, both *fofofo* and *veo'owana* have the right to give
ketowai to personal enemies at the distribution. Likewise they may repay
their debts received at other festivals or in *abutu*. There is a feeling that
abutu debts should not be paid through a festival distribution, that this is
to 'mix the customs', but it is sometimes done without comment. However,
a man can refuse to accept the payment of an *abutu* debt at a festival, and
the *inuba* or *fofofo* would not press him to take it. Debt payments and
ketowai can be refused also if other than the acceptable categories of persons
try to give them, such as sisters' sons of the *inuba* who are not acknowledged
veo'owana. On the other hand, there is no restriction on the category of
persons within the *tabotabo* to whom *ketowai* may be given. An unusual
instance was recorded of an *inuba* giving *ketowai* pork to his own wife,
to shame her for her refusal to cook for him on one occasion.

Nor is there any restriction on the type of offence for which *ketowai* is
appropriately given. I recorded the whole gamut of delicts and offences
brought to public notice in this way, from the semi-legendary, *nibai*-
creating homicides of the past, to the most recent and seemingly trivial
quarrels. In random order, the range of delicts included: adultery, abuse
of hospitality, theft, borrowing without permission, insult, beating another's
child, vindictive behaviour, lying to achieve advantage, land disputation,
arrogance, meanness, unfulfilled obligations, breach of mourning taboos,
uncomradely behaviour in migrant labour situations, etc. (see Appendix
for actual instances).

THE SIGNIFICANCE OF 'KETOWAI'

It will be clear that if such a wide range of offences is susceptible to a form
of redress by shaming prestations given through the medium of a festival,
then this institution is, like *abutu*, an instrument of social control. Not only

is the *ketowai* recipient subject to the sanction of a public shaming, he is also put under an obligation to repay the gift. He is open to the recriminations of his kinsmen – who may apply sanctions of their own – for causing them to share his shame and, to some extent, the inconvenient obligation to pay back. Its limitations as a mode of redress are also obvious, however. The initiative for a 'proceedings' lies entirely with one side at any festival; counter-offences cannot be redressed simultaneously. In contrast to the patrol officer's court, for instance, recourse to redress through *ketowai*-giving cannot be immediate, and a number of offences have to be 'accumulated' over a long period. Indeed, it is this fact which lends suspense and entertainment value to a large distribution. Very fine discriminations can be made, however, as to what constitute actionable offences – an advantage which the formal court lacks. The subtler sanctions of *ketowai*-giving are of a kind which no court would be able to enforce.

More than redress is involved, of course, for there is a crucial political motivation behind many of the *ketowai* gifts. Thus, insignificant 'offences' may be recalled by *inuba* as pretexts for giving *ketowai* to political rivals within the community. It is important to note that the shaming gifts of this category given at Malawidiya's festival in 1966, and at Bwanakovi's in 1967, were all directed across the major political cleavage in Kalauna (see Chapter 4 and Appendix). While the actual recipients were not necessarily personal rivals of the donors, the groups they represented were in general political opposition as, for instance, Lulauvile is to Iwaoyana. The broadest pattern of *nibai* relationships within the community is thus thrown into relief by *ketowai* distributions.

In the long term, by the principles of the perpetual festival cycle, access to this mode of redress and expression of political rivalry is available sooner or later to every individual and every group. *Abutu* is a complementary mode which solves some of the shortcomings of the *ketowai* distribution. It is at once more specific and more suited to immediate invocation or appeal, and permits simultaneous and reciprocal response. The concentrated barrage of *abutu* on a single target contrasts with the shot-gun effect of the *ketowai* distribution at which targets are many; and whereas *abutu* generally involves the mutual confrontation of two enemies, the festival climax involves the unilateral confrontation of numerous enemies. *Abutu* would appear to be the more flexible instrument of aggrandizement, competition, coercion and redress.

I suggested in the last chapter that the role of leaders has been crucial in the development of *abutu* during the post-contact era. I suggested also that the use of *abutu* as a mode of attempted redress, or of establishing political *détente* were developments characteristic of the intravillage context, and probably secondary to its intervillage role as an arena for competing big-men. Festivals might also be supposed to have grown in scale and ramified in function along similar lines. More abundant food surpluses permitted grander festivals, while certain peace permitted more visitors, and thus the interlocking of neighbouring festival cycles through the mutual interchange of visitors and the network of debt and credit relationships arising therefrom. Appealing though a 'peace in the feud' theory would be for the functional role of Modawa and Fakili in pre-contact times (see Gluckman 1956), there is no evidence that mutually hostile communities visited each other's festivals (but cf. Seligman 1910, p. 589). Informants were explicit that had they done so they would have expected to be attacked. It is even more inconceivable that *ketowai* prestations could have been given to enemies or token offenders from beyond the village as they are today. Expectations of repayment would have been minimal, and if *ketowai* recipients are sometimes prepared to fight today, how much more so in the past? In short, I think it is necessary to attribute much of the sociological content of festivals to relatively recent social and economic changes on Goodenough.

THE SYMBOL OF THE 'KAIWABU'

We are now in a position to interpret *kaiwabu* behaviour and understand the force of its symbolism. In Chapter 5, I stated that although in common usage *kaiwabu* refers to any leader who is by dress or demeanour 'lording it' over others, its specific referent is, in Jenness and Ballantyne's phrase, 'the chief person(s) at a feast' (1928, p. 239). The most significant factor in the use of the term is that no-one is entitled to be called *kaiwabu* all the time, not even the most highly esteemed leaders such as the Lulauvile *toitavealata*. *Kaiwabu* is not a permanent role within a system of social relationships, but rather the title of a temporary role enacted in a ceremonial and highly structured situation – the climax of a festival. Let us examine the properties of the role by considering the conduct of an ideal actor and the qualifications necessary for its adoption.

On the predetermined day of the festival's conclusion, the *kaiwabu* bathes, oils and paints himself, having spent the whole of the previous night at the final dancing or singing celebrations. The patterns of body-painting and the types of adornments he uses need not concern us here, though it might be noted that the Fakili *kaiwabu* wears different designs and ornaments from those worn by his Modawa counterpart. Before the first visitors arrive for the distribution, the *kaiwabu* will have joined his fellows on the chest-high sitting platform which has been constructed to one side of the hamlet, and from which can be viewed the other platforms piled high with food and butchered pigs. From the moment of seating himself cross-legged on the platform at mid-morning to the time of the departure of the final guests at dusk, the *kaiwabu* should not be seen to move, speak, eat, drink or do anything except gaze fixedly at the crowd and vigorously chew betel.

That the *kaiwabu* is a symbolic role is indicated by the openness of recruitment for the part. Any member of the *inuba* who is physically capable of performing the role adequately may be a *kaiwabu*, though there are rarely more than four or five at any one festival distribution. As with symbolic roles in many societies, there should be a close fit between ideal and actual, and expectations of role-performance are accordingly high. The prescribed behaviour, therefore, normally disqualifies those known to be incapable of it. In this respect the continuous betel chewing is an important criterion; youngsters and many women have not the capacity to consume a great deal,[1] while old people frequently lack the dental equipment. Women with very young children, furthermore, are often unable to leave them unattended for as long as the event requires, while many older people consider themselves incapable of restraining their natural functions for so long. Clearly, then, *kaiwabu* are partly self-selected for what is in fact a considerable physical ordeal of self-discipline. Sanctions are informal but they bite deep in this shame-conscious culture. A man masquerading as a *kaiwabu* who has to leave the platform to urinate, or to combat the heady effects of an excess of betel with food or water, would be the laughing-stock of the watchful guests. *Kaiwabu* who forget themselves enough to laugh or argue would also be subjects of the crowd's derision, which amounts to a rejection of the actors as unsuited for the role. Young Vatako, who was a *kaiwabu* at Bwanakovi's Fakili distribution in 1967 (see above pp. 104–5), acquitted himself well despite his tender age, and observers could find no fault except that, predictably, he was unable to consume much betel.

There are yet other qualifications for selection of *kaiwabu*. When Bwanakovi invited Dibele (a member of the Ukevakeva *inuba*) to be one of the *kaiwabu*, the latter refused on the grounds that he had just returned from working abroad and his gardens were in poor shape. Were he to be *kaiwabu* he would expose himself to the contempt of those who were aware of the fact. Nor would a *tonima'avilana*, a bad gardener, risk the public scorn that would be the response to his adoption of the *kaiwabu* role. The

---

[1] It should be noted that it is usual to swallow betel spittle in this part of the Massim, a practice which undoubtedly increases the intoxicating effects of the betel chewed (see Conklin 1958, pp. 23–7).

discrepancy between ideal role and imperfect actor would be too wide to create a convincing symbol for the onlooker. Eligibility, therefore, is limited to a great extent by the personal attributes and qualities of the individual.

The native interpretation of the *kaiwabu*'s prescribed behaviour is suggestive but not fully illuminating. Asked why *kaiwabu* wear so many traditional valuables, informants replied: 'Because we have to "know" them – whether they are wealthy men or poor'. Asked why they cannot move during the distribution, the answer was: 'Because they must not get angry and want to fight.' Likewise, they cannot speak: 'Because then they might get angry and start to quarrel with the visitors.' As to why they should neither eat nor drink: 'Because *kaiwabu* do not eat; it is their *tabu*.' As to why they chew so much betel: 'Because they are proud and want us to respect them. They are giving us food.'[1]

With some amplification these statements prove to be highly significant, and if interpreted in the light of Kalauna attitudes and values the conduct of *kaiwabu* becomes meaningful. The statements refer to values concerned with wealth, egalitarianism, peaceful social relations and, of course, food. Firstly, the ostentatious material wealth of the *kaiwabu*, and to some extent also the conspicuous consumption of betel nut, are marks of status above the ordinary – visible evidence of superiority and rank, which is reinforced by the physical position of the *kaiwabu* seated above the crowd. Other men paint themselves and chew betel, but they do not compete in ostentation by wearing so many valuables nor do they seat themselves higher than the *kaiwabu*. The impression of rank and superiority generated by the *kaiwabu*, however, does not threaten the egalitarian ethic of the society because, by a paradox, the *kaiwabu* also symbolizes egalitarianism itself. His individuality is minimized, his personal identity muted and masked by the highly standardized behaviour and by the proscriptions forbidding him to move or speak. For the period of his act, the *kaiwabu* is socially isolated, set apart and almost superhuman. It is said that even if a *kaiwabu* saw his house burning down or his wife sexually assaulted before his eyes, he would be unable to (i.e. expected not to) leave the platform. It is mandatory for him to preserve the fiction of his social non-involvement.

---

[1] There is also among certain down-to-earth informants what might be called a pragmatic level of interpretation. According to this, the *kaiwabu* are said to chew great quantities of betel in order to suppress their hunger, which could be partly true. The same informants say that *kaiwabu* neither eat nor drink to avoid the necessity of relieving themselves while they are on the platform, which may also be partly true. However, the appeal to pragmatic motives is undermined by the contention that *kaiwabu* do not eat after the act is over because they have eaten so much betel that food would make them vomit. This is probably the truest statement of all, but taken together a circular argument results, and none of the proscriptions are explained.

Moreover, the fact that there can be several *kaiwabu* present and that they can be of either sex, assorted ages, and of differing individual statuses in ordinary life, conveys the idea that if wealth and rank are being symbolized it is not the individual actors who necessarily possess these things.[1] The values that a *kaiwabu* represents are thus put beyond the possibility of contradiction with the egalitarian ethic, by permitting a fairly wide range of persons to participate in the symbol. Here, perhaps, lies the clue to the revulsion felt against the Mataita *kaiwabu* mentioned in an earlier chapter (p. 158), who was not content to be a mere cipher but wanted also to be himself. By wearing banknotes pinned to his chest, he stressed his individual status and personal wealth. This departure from the customary adornment with traditional shell wealth denied the values of egalitarianism, by drawing attention to a particular individual's particular achievement.

We have seen that only the food-distributing clan (or moiety in the case of Kwaiaudili) is entitled to supply the *kaiwabu*. The values of food-giving are thus conspicuously linked with superiority and rank in the symbol of the *kaiwabu*. He represents the food-givers, and this political aspect of his role is the one most immediately apparent to the people present at the distribution. The symbolism at this level is expressed succinctly by the answers to my questions about the *kaiwabu*'s appearance and conduct. He wears many shell valuables because the group he repre-sents has to demonstrate its wealth and by implication its power. The actor cannot move or speak because he should not fight or show anger – an empirical possibility in the highly charged atmosphere of the *ketowai* distributions. The *fofofo* insults the recipients on behalf of his *inuba*, some of whom are watching with studied indifference from their platform. Enemies are provoked but quarrels are denied expression by the prescribed non-participation of the *inuba* in general and the *kaiwabu* in particular. It is said that an angry *kaiwabu* will 'spoil' his food. Emotional self-restraint is here symbolically valued as a positive mode of preserving peaceful relations between enemies; without enemies the festival distribution would lack flavour and even point, but without peaceful conduct the event would be impossible to sustain. Only the *fofofo*, who insulates the givers from the receivers, can show enmity and behave aggressively. On the other hand, the mode of betel chewing practiced by the *kaiwabu* might be interpreted

[1] The notional as distinct from specific referents are more convincingly demonstrated by the Kwaiaudili people's approach to the Modawa and Fakili festivals. In contrast to Kalauna (and the remainder of Goodenough), Kwaiaudili regard the entire sponsoring moiety as *kaiwabu*, and anyone who is by birth a member of the food-giving moiety can assume the role of *kaiwabu* during a festival distribution. The idea that the *kaiwabu* is a 'ceremonial chief' (a concept which appealed to me initially) is stultified by the possibility of there being upwards of a hundred of them at the same event!

10

as the redirection of aggression. The *kaiwabu* sits rigid, staring straight
ahead while rattling his limestick noisily in the gourd and thrusting it
vigorously between his teeth, followed by persistent and forceful chomping
of his jaws – a display which gives a distinct impression of controlled,
aggressive power. Thus my informant's comment: 'they are proud and
want us to respect them' (i.e. for their 'strength'), and 'they are giving us
food.' Food-giving, it must be remembered, is an aggressive act when it
involves unrelated men, and it is not surprising that onlookers are reminded
of this when they watch the histrionic performance of the *kaiwabu*.

   As wife-giving is a corollary of incest taboos, so is food-giving a corollary
of eating prohibitions. For Modawa *kaiwabu* at least there is a supernatural
sanction, for just as his wristlet of spondylus discs (*nimakabubu*) will
break if the wearer behaves violently, it will also break if the wearer should
eat. The axiom that '*kaiwabu* do not eat', however, has a more profound
implication than the political one immediately perceived by actors and
observers. The values implicit in *sisikwana* and *lokona* concerning the
virtues of conservation over consumption find their highest expression,
their apotheosis almost, in the symbol of the *kaiwabu*. On the one hand,
since there cannot be *kaiwabu* (because there cannot be festivals) in times
of general food shortage, so the visible symbol of the *kaiwabu* is evidence
of *malia*, prosperity – a forceful reminder that gardens are producing well
and that society is functioning normally. The *kaiwabu* is to Goodenough
Islanders what the storehouse of rotting yams is to Trobrianders: a
public demonstration of general well-being. On the other hand, the axiom
that '*kaiwabu* do not eat' is a statement of the general value accorded to food
conservation by abstention from eating, and again like the Trobriander's
storehouse, the *kaiwabu* is a visible, public demonstration of this value.

   In sum, the ceremonial context of the food and pig distributions which
mark the climax of Modawa and Fakili festivals provide Goodenough
Islanders with the opportunity of seeing what they believe. In the symbol
of the *kaiwabu* many of the most profound values of the culture are
expressed, and its most pervasive ideals embodied. At the individual level
the *kaiwabu* embodies the values of the industrious food-producer, the
disciplined food-abstainer and the magnanimous food-giver. But Fakili and
Modawa festivals represent society's most successful triumph over
individualism, for without co-operative effort between kinsmen and between
inuba and *fofofo* the festivals could not take place. At the sectional level of
political opposition and competition between clans, then, the *kaiwabu*
represents the values of group strength, wealth, power and the ranking
moral superiority and prestige of the corporate food-giver. At the same
time, through the prescriptions which enjoin his self-restraint and the

devices which ensure his social insulation, he conveys the value of peaceable group relations. Although the sponsors in general and the *kaiwabu* in particular are openly expressing dominance behaviour, as is their prerogative, their ascendancy is transient and impermanent. For, by the rules of the exchange cycle, no fixed hierarchy is possible; other clans and other *kaiwabu* will get their chance. At the highest level, then, the *kaiwabu* is able to embody the value of egalitarianism. The temporary incumbent is a particular individual belonging to a specific group, but the role he enacts belongs to no permanent category of persons and no single group. An educated Kwaiaudili man expressed this in English to me when he said: 'You have only one king or one queen in England, but when we take turns to make Fakili and Modawa everyone is like a king or queen.' Although he was referring to his own Kwaiaudili variant of the custom, the principle holds for Kalauna and other Goodenough groups: over the duration of an entire festival cycle, the prestige and prerogatives of temporary rank are in theory available to all.

These aspects of the symbol of *kaiwabu* are meaningful only because the social value of food is the central, organizing referent. It mediates all other values and is the foundation on which the Modawa and Fakili festival cycle has been built. Malaveyoyo, it will be remembered, initiated a Modawa to attract Kalauna people back to the village following a famine. The legend may have reversed the actual causal sequence, but there is some significance in the notion that such festivals create or recreate community out of social fragmentation. It is fitting, therefore, that as the epitome of this supreme institutional expression of Goodenough sociality the *kaiwabu* should ultimately symbolize *malia* – prosperity and plenty.

CONCLUSION

The nature of its subject matter requires that social anthropology be the most methodologically flexible of the social sciences. It requires also a willing adaptability in its practitioners. I make no apology, therefore, for having made the main focus of this book an area of investigation which was forced upon me by the people I studied. The broad challenge they set me was simply to 'explain' their interest in food and in manipulating each other by its means. 'Fighting with food' proved to be behaviour which was fully institutionalized, and thus amenable to conventional ethnographic analysis. 'Why do they fight?' could be treated as a structural and organizational problem; 'why do they fight with food?' could be treated as a problem of social values. Although I think I have demonstrated a 'necessary' connection between the two aspects of the one problem, I am acutely aware that I have raised as many more questions as I have managed to answer. It is one thing, for instance, to have demonstrated a 'fit' between environment, settlement pattern, social structure, subsistence base, food values, leadership, and modes of social control; it is something else entirely to elucidate precisely and unambiguously the nature of the articulation.

In Chapter 10 I outlined a crude 'generative model' to account for the status of competitive food exchanges and festivals in present-day Kalauna. This, too, was suggested to me by my informants' interpretation of their local history and diagnosis of their present social ills – and also by the fact that an earlier ethnography had failed to mention these important institutions. At this point, I wish merely to recapitulate the argument, placing it in a wider ethnographic context where possible. This I do in the first section below. Secondly, it is necessary to discuss, if only very briefly, why some of the developments I documented for Kalauna failed to take place in Bwaidoga, a mere day's walk away. Finally, I wish to return to a problem which I have hitherto touched upon only in passing: the phenomenon of 'shame'.

I

Neolithic society in Goodenough rested on shaky foundations. Not only were communities mutually hostile and relations between them generally violent, but also the environment upon which they depended was inconstant. European contact brought the agents of three main changes:

steel tools which effected a minor technological revolution; superordinate government which, in suppressing warfare, resulted in a pervasive social revolution; and mission teachings which accomplished a more or less conspicuous moral revolution.[1]

Steel tools stimulated the production of subsistence crops. Despite the contention of Belshaw (1954, p. 60) and Salisbury (1962, p. 118) that the time and energy saved by the use of steel tools will tend to be spent in other ways, it appears that Goodenough Islanders chose to increase their production of subsistence foods. In the first place, gardening is for them a 'prestige' as well as a 'subsistence activity', so that Salisbury's (*ibid.* p. 119) hard distinction between the two does not appear to fit the Goodenough case. In the second place, the value configuration – which had developed certain extreme features in response to chronic ecological insecurity – welcomed and easily accommodated the new means of creating surpluses. In the third place, there were tangible social and political advantages to be gained from increased food production – and it is these rather than the original ecological factors which now maintain the system of values. Thus, it might be argued, the consequences of the technological change on Goodenough are quite different from those which Salisbury found for the Siane. 'Investment' appears to have been in 'subsistence' rather than in 'luxuries'. Capital gained from wage-labour is expended on new trade-goods with minimal exchange value, while the indigenous culture not only had weakly developed trade, but no monopolizing of 'luxury goods' and relatively scant interest in them in any case. The colonial government, moreover, had done nothing to stimulate local enterprise by offering new fields for capital investment. From the very first, wage-labour provided the only basis for a raised standard of living (and, incidentally, the only means by which to acquire steel tools), and it was one which in itself encouraged increased food production rather than otherwise – except perhaps in times of drought.

Initially parallel but later integral to this process, was the response to the banning of warfare. A fairly general statement of the nature of this response has been made by Berndt (1964, p. 184) for the New Guinea Highlands:

The official post-contact suppression of warfare provided peaceful opportunities for economic elaboration ... Where hostilities are widespread and continuous

[1] The following developmental sequence of post-contact change has some points of similarity with the more wide-ranging one proposed for the Choiseulese by Scheffler (1964). In particular, see his comments on settlement pattern, leadership, descent groups, and competitive feasting (pp. 400–2). See also Piddocke (1965) who presents an analogous, if somewhat more ethnographically remote, developmental model for the Southern Kwakiutl potlatch.

the ramifications of economic exchange are curtailed, but as warfare is brought to a standstill the economic emphases become correspondingly more prominent. The two kinds of activity are similar in respect of the pervasive themes of competition and conflict which they express, albeit in different ways. Not least, a system of economic exchange today may operate through the network of allies so vital to the pattern of traditional warfare.[1]

The relationship between conditions of peace and increased exchange activities on Goodenough was far more specific and positive than this, however, and it can be stated more precisely. Firstly, the suppression of warfare deprived indigenous leaders of an important means of gaining prestige and authority; secondly, it deprived individuals of the right to inflict physical punishment on offenders, and groups of the ability to defend their rights or assert their dominance by means of fighting. By claiming a monopoly of the use of force, the government eliminated traditional procedures of leadership formation and social control. Developed as an alternative procedure to fighting, competitive exchanging could become a true surrogate for it.[2] Indeed, peace not merely 'permitted' the elaboration of food exchanges but, given the cultural premises, virtually necessitated it.

In contrast to the central Highlands, where the most important commodities of large-scale exchange are pigs and shell valuables, the main commodities of competitive exchange on Goodenough are subsistence crops. In this fact, perhaps, lies much of the coercive and redressive potential of Goodenough exchanges (a point which I intend to develop elsewhere). Competitive food exchanges of the *abutu* type, in which one side attempts to out-give and thereby assert superiority over the other, have been frequently recorded in New Guinea.[3] Nowhere in the literature, however, have I been able to find a people who have exploited the redressive

---

[1] See also Bulmer 1960, pp. 10–11; Salisbury *ibid.* p. 119; Strathern 1966, p. 363.

[2] The observation that competitive giving can be or become a functional surrogate for warfare has been made many times, frequently by the peoples whose institutions are under study. A classic example is that presented by Codere (1950, p. 124): 'When the rivalrous character of the Kwakiutl potlatch is kept in mind, the historical shift in Kwakiutl life is tellingly expressed by their own phrases, "wars of property" instead of "wars of blood" and "fighting with wealth" instead of "with weapons".'

For Melanesia, see for example, Oliver (1949a) and Kaberry (1941, p. 344), quoted earlier. Also Malinowski (1935, p. 456): '... for the Trobrianders at least, the *kula* .. is to a large extent a surrogate and substitute for head-hunting and war'. (Although Malinowski was probably thinking mainly of the psychological satisfactions afforded by this institution.)

[3] See for example: Malinowski 1935, pp. 181–7; Williams 1936, pp. 233–4; Kaberry, *ibid.*; Groves 1954, pp. 81–2; Oosterwal 1961, pp. 80–1; Serpenti 1965, Chap. 6. Cf. especially the *ndambu* exchange of the Kimam of Frederick Hendrik Island, which has many remarkable similarities to *abutu*, not least in being a stimulus to the local economy in a precarious environment (Serpenti, *ibid.*).

possibilities of the institution (as distinct from the prestige-gaining or political possibilities) to the same extent, and with the vigour and confidence in its efficacy that Goodenough Islanders display.[1]

I have suggested that an important factor in the prevalence of 'fighting with food' in Goodenough is the problem of regulating relationships within fairly large-scale communities. Given the structural groundwork of autonomous clans, the tight residential pattern, the post-contact tendencies of growth and nucleation of communities and the continuing absence of centralized leadership, it is understandable that a regulative device such as *abutu* should have been developed. Nothing could be further from the truth as far as Goodenough is concerned than to assume with Rowley that: 'The prevention of homicide and war as a means for the discharge of tensions and as a solution of disputes makes it inevitable that the disputes will be brought to the government officer for adjudication' (1965, p. 70). Indeed, it is perhaps because *abutu* exchanges and festivals serve leaders so well as arenas of prestige-acquisition, and non-leaders, too, as modes of redress and dispute-resolution, that the government officer has had so little influence in these areas of social control.

The initial impetus in the elaboration of *abutu* and festivals would have been purposive, as leaders sought to assert themselves by these means. But the inflationary spiral brought unintended effects. Thus, the frequency and scale of contests could increase because steel tools permitted an abundance of produce for transaction; but as more food was used in competition so was more needed to best rivals, and so, therefore, did helpers need to be recruited from a wider social range. Although this process probably aided community integration, it did so at the expense of clan solidarity, resulting in the increased competitiveness and insecurity which are reflected in endemic sorcery fears. From the beginning, the recruitment-base of leadership was broadened by the increased emphasis on food-production and a more general access to the means of production. Warrior prowess was no longer the principal prerequisite for strong leadership. Magico-ritual knowledge, productive capacity and manipulative ability were more vital attributes. Wider competition between prospective leaders resulted in more frequent and more lavish *abutu* and festivals. The escalation was thus reinforced from a number of directions.

Kalauna people point to this inflationary development as a major source

[1] The Kamam would be strong contenders, however. See Serpenti *ibid.* p. 255: 'Everywhere on the island *ndambu* is a recognized procedure for solving conflicts and differences of opinion. Recently this function has gained more and more in importance in spite of missionary disapproval, for the very reason that every form of physical coercion as a means of punishment for any offence has been forbidden by the government authorities.'

of trouble between agnates. On the one hand are the neglected obligations. Abaluweya, for instance, said of her first husband's death:

People sorcerized him because of his big gardens. He had very large taro gardens, and his own brothers grew jealous and gave him tuberculosis. They wanted to eat the taro themselves but he gave it all away in *abutu*. Even when he was very sick he used his gardens for *abutu* . . . He didn't listen to them so Yaudili [his FFBSS] made sorcery to kill him.

On the other hand there is the increased competition. Nimayasi, for instance, said of his father's death:

His own group killed him. His brothers saw his big food, and heard his name called at every distribution. They wanted to take his place. They were jealous 'for *kaiwabu*', so they killed him by sorcery.

II

These developments do not appear to have occurred everywhere in the same degree on Goodenough, although as far as I can tell they apply to the communities adjacent to Kalauna with which I became fairly familiar. Bwaidoga, however, which I studied intensively to provide comparative ethnography, is an instructive contrast to Kalauna in respect of post-contact changes in general and the later development of *abutu* and festivals in particular.

Unlike Kalauna people and the majority of their neighbours, Bwaidogans are *kwana imolata*, 'people of the coast'. They possess, therefore, slightly different cultural interests from those of Kalauna people. In addition to gardening, they value fishing and canoe-making, and they conduct frequent small-scale food exchanges whenever new canoes are completed. Ecological conditions in Bwaidoga (and neighbouring Wagifa) are probably more severe than anywhere else on the island, and certainly more so than in Kalauna: rainfall is scantier (see above p. 3), top-soils are poorer, grassland is more extensive, and even sources of drinking water are few and far between. Jenness and Ballantyne remark that: 'The southern shores of Mud Bay (i.e. Bwaidoga) and Wagifa are barren districts which suffer heavily at the least approach of drought' (1920, p. 32); and they suggest that in the past Bwaidogans were often forced to plunder the gardens of their more fortunate neighbours (*ibid.*). According to my own observations in Bwaidoga, coconut palms do not produce well, little taro can be grown, and the yam crop consists predominantly of the *taitu* of which Kalauna men are so contemptuous. Diet in Bwaidoga relies more heavily upon sweet potato, bananas and manioc than in Kalauna, although thanks to fish it is probably richer in protein.

Bwaidoga has been subjected to more external influences than Kalauna, and probably more than any other community on Goodenough. It has adopted many mortuary customs – including certain food exchanges – from Fergusson Island, but it has been most profoundly affected by the seventy-year presence in its midst of a large Methodist Mission station. Leadership in Bwaidoga today retains few of the characteristics of leadership in Kalauna and other villages. Big-men, in the sense of powerful sorcerers or ritual experts, strong gardeners and shrewd exchange-initiators, no longer exist. The prominent men of this community today derive their authority from the mission or, ultimately, the colonial government. Thus, the village constable and the local government councillor (who is also the current council President), in conjunction with popularly-elected men called *komiti* (i.e. 'committee'), have a significant influence on the settlement of local disputes and the regulation of community life generally. The differences between Kalauna and Bwaidoga in this respect can be pinpointed by saying that the main impediments to 'progressive' community leadership have undergone considerable attrition in Bwaidoga: sorcery fears and the value complex concerning food have all but disappeared. Effective leadership in Bwaidoga is now to be found at the 'barrack' level, which is perhaps all the more remarkable in that the present community of Bwaidoga comprises three indigenously autonomous villages, and has a total population of over a thousand (see Young 1968).

The last *abutu* to be held in Bwaidoga was in 1964. The last festival to be sponsored by a Bwaidogan was some years before that. Both these events were linked to mortuary observances and were held ostensibly to 'honour' dead kinsmen of the initiators. I collected enough data on *abutu* and festivals of the past, however, to be satisfied that, as elsewhere on the island, they were not invariably or necessarily linked to mortuary customs. Clearly, they served leaders and social control generally in the same manner as elsewhere, though latterly the 'need' for them has disappeared. There are a number of reasons for this. In addition to the changed roles and requirements of leadership, clanship has weakened sufficiently no longer to require the form of aggrandizement provided by competitive exchanges. Despite its size, moreover, Bwaidoga appears to suffer only a fraction of the internal conflict endured by Kalauna. It would seem to be through prolonged and intensive missionary activity, however, that the greatest pressures for change have been applied; and perhaps the most convincing explanation for the demise of *abutu* can be sought in the new values of Bwaidogans themselves.

The scheme of values which I described for Kalauna in Chapters 7 and 8 would have been generally valid for Bwaidoga a few decades ago. Although

10*

Jenness and Ballantyne give very few positive clues to its existence, I managed to satisfy myself through my own enquiries that Bwaidogans once valued food conservation over consumption, and once subscribed to most of the other ideals characteristic of Kalauna attitudes. Indeed, in view of Bwaidoga's even greater propensity to drought, it would have been remarkable had I found otherwise.

An informant phrased the modern shift in values as follows:

Our ancestors looked after the customs of *abutu* well. Each hamlet had its *tofaha* [strong gardener], its *tolokona* [one who conserves by self-restraint], and its *tosisikwana* [one who dulls appetite with magic]. They made *abutu* all the time. Today we are a new generation. Today is the time of children. We reject and throw away, little by little, the old customs. Every Sunday we hear the Bible, and we want to enter Heaven. So we learn not to care too much about our gardens and the things of *kaiwabu*. Those ways were bad.

The Mission has successfully implanted the idea that *lokona* is wasting food, that *sisikwana* is an unnatural and pagan practice which, like crop magic, is incompatible with trust and faith in God, while the total value system which the *kaiwabu* personifies ('the things of *kaiwabu*') is discredited as vain, worldly, selfish and ultimately damning. 'It is easier for a camel to pass through the eye of a needle than it is for a *kaiwabu* to enter the kingdom of God' was the text of one sermon delivered by a respected Bwaidogan church leader.

'The time of children' (*biabiama yadi tova*) is an apt designation for this new moral order. Attitudes towards children are never begrudging in Bwaidoga as they sometimes are in Kalauna – yet there are far more of them. Since the establishment of an infant and maternity hospital by the Mission about ten years ago, the population has soared spectacularly. Men say they are no longer prepared to give food competitively in case it is not returned and their children suffer. 'That is why we are forgetting our *fofofo*', they explain. They are also forgetting their *nibai*, for it has been the policy of the village leaders to discourage all expressions of *nibai* enmity in the interests of 'barrack' unity. Finally, associated with considerably reduced competition over food-getting, food-sharing and food-giving, sorcery has all but disappeared. I didn't hear of a single sorcery accusation in modern Bwaidoga, and the old men were adamant that they had 'thrown away' all their sorcery paraphernalia many years ago. Social amity is far more conspicuous in Bwaidoga than it is in Kalauna. The values of kinship are here no longer threatened by the encroachment of practices, attitudes and values appropriate only to the political domain.

The rapidly expanding population and the apparent concern for children suggest that there may well be sound ecological and economic reasons for the Bwaidogans' renunciation of *abutu*, festivals and 'the things of *kaiwabu*'. To some extent, perhaps, Bwaidogans are making a virtue out of necessity in denying themselves what they cannot really afford. But this is not to say that they are unaware of it, or that their pious rejection of 'pagan' values is all sour grapes and rationalization. They know, for instance, that their puny yams and stunted taro ill-equips them for *abutu* with neighbouring villages, and now that they no longer keep pigs, they cannot fail to notice (with some shame and regret) that they receive only small token *taladidika* gifts when they visit festival climaxes in other communities. While they have forsworn crop magic and the techniques of *sisikwana* from what appear to be genuine religious and moral convictions, their rejection of the practice of *lokona* is sensibly pragmatic: it no longer confers prestige, it wastes food which might otherwise be used to nourish children, and it is nowadays (with the diversification of crops) an inadequate defence against times of hunger. Better indeed to eat all the yams and trust in manioc and the government – which, after all, sent a boatload of yams to Bwaidoga during the 1958 famine, thereby inspiring the famous local joke, rich in pathos and irony: 'We thought the Government had come to make *abutu* against us.'

Other things being equal, it has perhaps been 'easier' for Bwaidoga than it would be for any other community on Goodenough to abandon this part of its cultural heritage, and to 'throw away the things of *kaiwabu*'. Whether the principal impulse to do so has come from ecological and economic circumstances or from the purely ideological source of missionary teaching, pressures have been mutually reinforcing, and the fact remains that in modern Bwaidoga *abutu* and festivals no longer have any major functions to perform. They are no longer appropriate modes of prestige-acquisition for leaders, and *abutu* is no longer an effective means of obtaining redress for offences. The structure of social values which we found to be integral to the way of life in Kalauna is no longer operative in Bwaidoga; and this, after all, is today the most conspicuous difference between the two communities.

III

Turning from problems of social change, I wish finally to indicate a problem of social psychology which I have thus far chosen to neglect. In writing about a syndrome of behaviour which I called 'food-giving-to-shame', I said much about 'food-giving' but very little about 'to-shame'. Writers dealing with social control and social conformity in New Guinea find it impossible to avoid mentioning 'shame', though this term is usually an inadequate translation of an indigenous concept which tends to embrace a wide range of affect (see for example, Berndt 1962, pp. 195–200). From my own limited and partial understanding of the feelings and behaviour of Goodenough Islanders, I would endorse Langness's observation (1965, p. 268) that 'shame for the natives of New Guinea is an exceedingly powerful emotion', as close to guilt and 'losing face' as it is to the Western concept of shame 'which is trivial by comparison'. *Wowomumu*, which I have translated as 'shame', covers the emotional spectrum from shyness and mild embarrassment to something akin to guilt and morbid self-hatred. At the latter extreme it frequently shades into, or triggers, a state called *veumaiyiyi* – a category of emotion which is even harder to define, though like 'shame' it would appear to be an important component of the total system of social control.

Abutu is motivated by an impulse to 'shame' another. At first sight the transaction appears to defy rational psychology, for the gift seem to be going the wrong way. Instead of striking a person who offends you, you give him a yam; instead of killing an enemy, you present him with a pig. The gift is indeed in one sense an act of self-deprivation, for the object given must be of value to the donor for it to have a shaming effect upon the recipient. It is this element of self-deprivation which *abutu* behaviour appears to have in common with *veumaiyiyi*. This is the mixture of anger, resentment and self-pity which is expressed in the subject's self-punishment – a course he takes to shame or elicit sympathy from the person who offended him.[1] The simplest example is the man who cut down his own betel palm to shame another who stole from it.

What Reay has termed 'the masochistic sanction of self-injury' (1953, p. 117) is particularly common among the Orokaiva, whose equivalent of *veumaiyiyi* is *sisira* (Williams 1930, pp. 91, 116, 331–3). Williams himself defines the attitude as 'not so much "I'll make you sorry for what you have done" as "I'll make you sorry for me"' (*ibid.* p. 332). A person in a state of *sisira* 'takes the revenge of being injured':

Accordingly we find a person under a sense of wrong going to extraordinary lengths of self-castigation, from merely fasting or running away from home for a while, to delivering himself up to an enemy tribe or hanging himself from a tree (*ibid.*).

[1] Jenness and Ballantyne (1928, p. 260) translate *veumagigi* (i.e. Bwaidogan for *veumaiyiyi*) as 'jealousy: to be jealous', but they appear to have missed the point completely. They do give an example of what would be *veumaiyiyi* under *yalidi* (*ibid.* p. 264), which appears to mean 'imbalance': 'used of a present of food made by some Sabbath-breakers to those who had informed on them. The word was said to imply doubt as to receiving a return present.'

Suicide in Goodenough is 'deviant' rather than 'normal' behaviour,[1] and I managed to learn of no more than half-a-dozen attempts (successful or otherwise). Most of them were by women and most of them involved self-administered doses of derris root fish poison (cf. Fortune 1932, p. 50; Malinowski 1926, p. 94). Although suicide is rare in Goodenough, it would be possible to document numerous incidents of 'self-castigation' similar to those described by Williams for the Orokaiva. In short, Goodenough Islanders, too, commonly punish themselves in order to cause shame, sympathy and contrition in those who have wronged them.[2]

The problem, then, is the relation of this form of coercive sanction to 'food-giving-to-shame'. Goodenough Islanders acknowledge a connection between them, between the self-injury of *veumaiyiyi* and the self-deprivation of *abutu* – though they are uninterested in defining it. Both appear to be indirect forms of aggression, and it is likely that all such behaviours are culturally-directed alternatives to violent coercion or direct aggression. There is certainly something to be said for the positive value of the self-punitive sanction in face-to-face communities; and the importance of 'shame' in Melanesian societies generally is probably to be related to their small scale, their lack of formal juridical institutions, and their lateral rather than hierarchical systems of authority – in short, to their egalitarian bases. It should not be surprising, therefore, that techniques are developed and elaborated for the infliction of shame as a means of redress or coercion. Aggressive food-giving would be at one end of a continuum of such techniques of non-violent coercion, and suicide (the ultimate form of protest) at the other. Their selective use by any individual would depend upon a range of circumstantial factors, among the most crucial of which would be the status relationship between the person acting and the object of his or her attack. There is a corollary to this kind of system of social control: an undue reliance on internalized sanctions might be expected to generate heavy emotional burdens for the members of these societies; their susceptibility to shaming is related to their quickness to slight, and perhaps also to their readiness to project persecution fantasies into sorcery accusations.

These are merely speculations, however. Whatever the psychological

[1] That is to say there are no circumstances under which the culture 'expects' persons to attempt suicide. Contrast, for example, the situation in Dobu (Fortune 1932, pp. 3, 49–50, 91–2), the Trobriands (Malinowski 1926, pp. 94–8), and the eastern Highlands (Berndt 1962, pp. 179–207).
[2] See M. Strathern's fascinating analysis of *popokl*, a state analogous to *veumaiyiyi*, which is conceived by the Hageners of the Highlands to be a form of supernatural punishment inflicted out of 'pity'. Strathern suggests that *popokl* 'operates in the absence of other means of coercion or where such means have failed' (1968, p. 554). See also A. Strathern 1968.

impulses behind *abutu* behaviour, I have been mainly concerned in this book to explore its sociological significance. For *abutu* is a phenomenon of a highly complex and institutionalized nature: in ethological terms a collective displacement activity, in historical terms a surrogate for feud and warfare, in legal terms a mode of dispute settlement, and an alternative to physical coercion as a means of redress, in political terms a mode of conflict resolution and a peaceful means of achieving leader-status, and finally, in economic terms *abutu* is a stimulus to the production of a surplus which as a capital asset can be converted into prestige and used to boost the cultural standard of living. Although varying locally in emphasis and form, competitive food exchange is also a phenomenon of fairly general occurrence, as Marcel Mauss showed in his famous essay on the gift. A work of detailed comparison and careful synthesis is now required on competitive exchange systems in Melanesia. Towards this end, I have in this book simply undertaken to demonstrate the local adaptation of a general model to a set of specific social, cultural, environmental and historical conditions.

APPENDIX

PIG DISTRIBUTIONS AT FOUR FESTIVALS

I. FAKILI, Kalauna village. 1966

Leading inuba: Malawidiya, Iyahalina (Lulauvile II).

Leading fofofo: Kimaola, Didiala (Lulauvile I).

10 pigs were distributed as follows:

Taladidika: 3½ pigs distributed among visitors from about 8 villages plus Kalauna *tabotabo*.

Tutula:, 3 pigs distributed among 5 men, all *nibai*, to whom debts were owing from their festivals. All were from other villages.

Ketowai: 3½ pigs distributed among 5 men as follows:

1. *Kalauna village*

   1 to Adiwai of Iwaoyana, because he joined the Fakili celebrations before *tabotabo* were invited.

   ½ to Ilukwalukwa of Iwaoyana, because he is Siboboya's (*inuba*) *nibai*.

   1 to Kafataudi of Nouneya, because he quarrelled with Iyahalina over food.

   ½ to Bwanakovi of Iwaoyana, because he is Malawidiya's *nibai*.

2. *Wailolo village*

   ½ to Nibogana, because he had just begun his Sagali festival, and was *yakaikai* (hubristic).

II. SAGALI, Wailolo village.[1] 1967

Leading inuba: Nibogana.

Leading fofofo: Walibuwa.

19 pigs were distributed as follows:

Taladidika: 10 pigs distributed among visitors from some 20 villages, including two parties from Fergusson Island.

Tutula: 3 pigs distributed among 6 men to whom debts were owing. All were from neighbouring villages.

Ketowai: 6 pigs distributed among 12 persons as follows:

1. *Kalauna village*

   ¼ to Adifaiweya, because his dog bit a Wailolo pig.

---

[1] Wailolo is a small village of 99 persons, divided into three clans which occupy three hamlets. Over two-thirds of the village belong to the Modawa moiety. Nibogana, the *inuba* of this festival, is a 'real' big-man of considerable fame, and has no competitors within his village – which he appears to rule like a benevolent despot. He is also village constable for Belebele 'barrack' of which Wailolo is a part. On account of its small size and its leader's stature, there is no real festival 'cycle' in Wailolo. Nibogana was himself the last person to sponsor a festival here – a Modawa about six years ago.

$\frac{1}{2}$ to Didiala, because he is Kwabua's (Wailolo) *nibai*.

$\frac{1}{4}$ to Iyahalina, because he is Kayaluwa's (Wailolo) *nibai*.

$\frac{1}{2}$ to Manawadi, because he borrowed a canoe bailer without the owner's permission.

$\frac{1}{2}$ to Kunakuna, because he speared a Wailolo pig.

$\frac{1}{4}$ to Tabwaika, because his son fished in a prohibited stream.

$\frac{1}{4}$ to Neyeuli, a young girl, because she stole almonds from a tree on Wailolo land.

1 to Kimaola, because he is Uweya's (Wailolo) *nibai* (but also because he had just begun his own festival).

2. *Belebele village*

$\frac{1}{2}$ to Kwayaya, because he is Nibogana's *nibai*.

1 to Bokeya, because of his adultery with an *inuba*'s wife.

$\frac{1}{2}$ to Nauneya, because he is Walibuwa's *nibai*.

3. *Mataita village*

$\frac{1}{2}$ to ?, because he stole Nibogana's knife when they were living abroad in a labour camp.

III. FAKILI, Kalauna village. 1967

Leading inuba: Bwanakovi, Tomoadikuyau, Tomolaiyoko (Iwaoyana).

Leading fofofo: Kafataudi (Nouneya), Ilukwalukwa (Iwaoyana).

10 pigs were distributed as follows:

Taladidika: 4 pigs distributed among visitors from about 5 villages, plus Kalauna *tabotabo*.

Tutula: 2 pigs distributed among 4 men (2 from within Kalauna) to whom debts were owing from previous festivals, or in one case, from an *abutu*.

Ketowai: 4 pigs distributed among 7 men, all from within the village as follows:

1 to Adiyaleyale of Lulauvile II, for adultery with an *inuba*'s wife.

1 to Kiyodi of Lulauvile I, because he is *inuba*'s *nibai*.

$\frac{1}{2}$ to Malawidiya of Lulauvile II, because he is *inuba*'s *nibai*.

$\frac{1}{4}$ to Iyahalina of Lulauvile II, for quarrelling with his daughter-in-law, a natal $\frac{1}{4}$ member of the Iwaoyana *inuba*.

to Kawanaba of Lulauvile II, for making advances to an *inuba*'s wife.

$\frac{1}{2}$ to Wakasilele of Malabuabua, whose brother seduced Kafataudi's wife some years before.

$\frac{1}{2}$ to Adikunuwala of Ainaona, for adultery with an *inuba*'s wife.

NOTE: 22 frames of vegetable food were also distributed in roughly the same proportions as pigs were given. Kiyodi, for example, was given one whole frame of yams from Madiaiwao's gardens. (Madiaiwao was the youth who died and in whose memory the Fakili was said to have been held. The *inuba*, being his close agnates, are prohibited by custom from eating the food from his gardens.)

IV. SAGALI, Mataita II village. 1968

Leading inuba: Taboyega, Legiya, Kwanalulu.

Leading fofofo: Kalumana, Adoka, Bunaleya.

26 pigs were distributed as follows:

Taladidika: Some 10 pigs were distributed among visitors from about 20 villages, including several parties from Fergusson Island.

Tutula: About 4 pigs were distributed among 10 men, all from other villages, to whom pig debts were owing from previous festivals.

Ketowai: Some 12 pigs were distributed among 25 persons from 9 different villages. Their villages and offences were as follows:

1. (Kalokalo, Fergusson Island). Man who incited an *inuba*'s daughter to elope with him to his own island, an incident which almost led to an armed battle between the villages concerned, and caused 40 men to serve jail sentences for riotous behaviour.
2. (Mataita I). Bunaleya's *nibai*.
3. (Mataita I). Man who vindictively reported Kalumana to patrol officer for allowing his pig to break into recipient's manioc garden.
4. (Mataita I). Man who breached a fishing prohibition set on Bunaleya's stream.
5. (Mataita I). Woman who obscenely insulted a Mataita II woman during a Sagali dance.
6. (Mataita I). *Inuba's nibai.*
7. (Ufufu). Man who obstructed Mataita II men from catching a boat to Samarai by inducing the captain to refuse them a passage.
8. (Mataita I). Man who disputed ownership of a pig with a member of *inuba*.
9. (Ufufu). Man who neglected to give Legiya *taladidika* when he visited an Ufufu festival.
10. (Mataita II). Taboyega's wife, who refused to cook for her husband on one occasion.
11. (Mataita I). Woman who swore obscenely at a Sagali dance, insulting the hosts.
12. (Mataita I). Man who killed Kalumana's pig in error.
13. (Kilia). Youth who abused an *inuba*'s hospitality by seducing his host's wife.
14. (Galasea). Man who beat some Mataita II children who were annoying him in their play.
15. (Mataita I). Man who broke Legiya's plate.
16. (Wailolo). Man who churlishly refused an *inuba* woman permission to pick chestnuts from a tree on Wailolo land.
17. (Wailolo). Man who churlishly refused an *inuba* member's request for a few banana suckers to plant.
18. (Kilia). Man who abused an *inuba*'s hospitality by stealing his host's money.
19. (Mataita I). Man who stole some money from an *inuba* member while they were in a labour camp.
20. (Wailolo). Man who fired grass on Mataita II land, thereby destroying several coconut trees.
21. (Bwaidoga). Man who made a greedy and ungenerous division of his son's trade goods earned abroad. His daughter, who was married to a member of the Mataita *inuba*, was neglected in the distribution, which angered her affines.

22. (Mataita I). *Inuba's nibai*, who was rude enough to ask for pig to be given him.
23. (Mataita I). Man who took sides in a children's fight and beat Mataita II children.
24. (Wagifa). Man who abused *fofofo* Adoka's hospitality by chewing betel nut with his host's wife.
25. (Mataita I). Adultery with a Mataita II woman.

BIBLIOGRAPHY

Allied Geographical Section (1942). Terrain Study No. 23: 'Area Study of D'Entrecasteaux and Trobriand Islands'.

Barnes, J. A. (1949). 'Measures of Divorce Frequency in Simple Societies', *Journal of the Royal Anthropological Institute*, vol. 79: 37–62.

(1962). 'African Models in the New Guinea Highlands', *Man*, vol. 62: 5–9.

(1967). 'The Frequency of Divorce', in Epstein, A. L. (ed.), *The Craft of Social Anthropology*, Tavistock, London.

Barth, F. (1966). *Models of Social Organization*, Occasional Paper No. 23, Royal Anthropological Institute, London.

Bateson, G. (1936). *Naven*, Cambridge University Press.

Bell, F. L. S. (1948–9). 'The Place of Food in the Social Life of the Tanga', *Oceania*, vol. 19: 51–74.

Belshaw, C. S. (1954). *Changing Melanesia: Social Economics of Culture Contact*, Oxford University Press, Melbourne.

Berndt, R. M. (1962). *Excess and Restraint*, Chicago University Press.

(1964). 'Warfare in the New Guinea Highlands', *American Anthropologist*, vol. 66, no. 4, pt 2: 183–203.

Brass, L. J. (1959). 'Summary of the Fifth Archbold Expedition to New Guinea (1956–7)', *Bulletin of the American Museum of Natural History*, vol. 118, article 1: 1–24.

British New Guinea: Annual Reports, (1888–1903). Government Printer.

Brookfield, H. C. (1961). 'The Highland Peoples of New Guinea: a Study of Distribution and Localization', *Geographical Journal*, vol. 127: 436–48.

Bulmer, R. N. H. (1960). 'Political Aspects of the Moka Ceremonial Exchange System Among the Kyaka People', *Oceania*, vol. 31: 1–13.

Burridge, K. O. L. (1965–6). 'Tangu Political Relations', *Anthropological Forum*, vol. 1: 393–411.

Chowning, A. (1959). 'Witchcraft Among the Molima of Fergusson Island', *Philadelphia Anthropological Society Bulletin*, vol. 12 (2): 1–2.

(1960). 'Canoe Making Among the Molima of Fergusson Island', *Expedition: Bulletin of the University Museum, Pennsylvania*, vol. 3 (1): 32–9.

(1961). 'Amok and Aggression in the D'Entrecasteaux', *Proceedings of Annual Spring Meeting of American Ethnological Society*, Seattle, 78–83.

(1962). 'Cognatic Kin Groups Among the Molima of Fergusson Island', *Ethnology*, vol. 1: 92–101.

(1966). 'Lakalai Kinship', *Anthropological Forum*, vol. 1: 476–501.

(1969). 'The Fertility of Melanesian Girls, Laboratory Mice, and Prostitutes: a Comment on the "Bruce Effect"', *American Anthropologist*, vol. 71: 1122–5.

Codere, H. (1950). *Fighting With Property: a Study of Kwakiutl Potlatching and Warfare 1792–1930*. American Ethnological Society Monographs, no. 18, New York.

Cole, K. S. (1958). Agricultural Officer's Patrol Report, 10/1957-58, Administration Files, Esa'ala.

Conklin, H. C. (1958). 'Betel Chewing among the Hanunóo', *Proceedings of the Fourth Far-Eastern Prehistory Congress*, Paper No. 56, University of the Philippines.

Epstein, A. L. (1964). 'Variation and Social Structure: Local Organization on the Island of Matupit, New Britain', *Oceania*, vol. 35: 1–25.

(1968). 'Sanctions', in *Encyclopaedia of the Social Sciences*, Macmillan Company and The Free Press, New York.

Firth, R. (1959). *Social Change in Tikopia*, Allen and Unwin, London.

Fortes, M. (1945). *The Dynamics of Clanship among the Tallensi*, Oxford University Press, London.

Fortune, R. F. (1932). *Sorcerers of Dobu*, Routledge and Kegan Paul, London.

Glasse, R. M. (1963). 'Bingi at Tari', *Journal of the Polynesian Society*, vol. 72: 270–1.

Gluckman, M. (1956). *Custom and Conflict in Africa*, Blackwell, Oxford.

Gostin, O., Tomasetti, W. and Young, M. W. (1971). 'Personalities *versus* Policies', in *The Politics of Dependence*, ed. by A. L. Epstein, R. S. Parker and M. Reay, Australian National University Press, Canberra.

Groves, M. (1954). 'Dancing in Poreporena', *Journal of the Royal Anthropological Institute*, vol. 84: 75–90.

Gulliver, P. H. (1969). 'Introduction to Case Studies of Law in Non-Western Societies', in *Law in Culture and Society*, ed. by L. Nader, Chicago University Press.

Guy, A. W. (1937). 'People of the D'Entrecasteaux Group', *Walkabout*, vol. 3: 24–7.

Hogbin, H. I. (1951). *Transformation Scene*, Routledge and Kegan Paul, London.

Hogbin, H. I. and Wedgwood, C. H. (1953). 'Local Grouping in Melanesia', *Oceania*, vol. 23: 241–76; vol. 24: 58–76.

Jenness, D. and Ballantyne, A. (1920). *The Northern D'Entrecasteaux*, Clarendon Press, Oxford.

(1928). *Language, Mythology, and Songs of Bwaidoga*, Avery and Sons, New Plymouth, New Zealand.

Kaberry, P. M. (1941). 'Law and Political Organization in the Abelam Tribe, New Guinea', *Oceania*, vol. 12: 79–95, 209–25, 331–63.

(1965–6). 'Political Organization among the Northern Abelam', *Anthropological Forum*, vol. 1: 344–72.

Koch, K.-F. (1968). 'On "Possession" Behaviour in New Guinea', *Journal of the Polynesian Society*, vol. 77: 135–46.

Langness, L. L. (1964). 'Some Problems in the Conceptualization of Highlands Social Structure', *American Anthropologist*, vol. 66, no. 4, pt 2: 162–82.

(1965). 'Hysterical Psychosis in the New Guinea Highlands: A Bena Bena Example', *Psychiatry*, vol. 28: 258–77.

Lawrence, P. and Meggitt, M. J. (eds.) (1965). *Gods, Ghosts and Men in Melanesia*, Oxford University Press, Melbourne.

Lea, D. A. M. (1966). 'Yam Growing in the Maprik Area', *Papua–New Guinea Agricultural Journal*, vol. 18: 5–15.

McCarthy, D. (1959). *Southwest Pacific Area First Year: Kokoda to Wau, Australia in the War of 1939–45*, Series One: Army, vol. 5, Canberra War Memorial.

Mair, L. P. (1948). *Australia in New Guinea*, Christophers, London.

Malinowski, B. (1922). *Argonauts of the Western Pacific*, Routledge and Kegan Paul, London.

(1926). *Crime and Custom in Savage Society*, Routledge and Kegan Paul, London.

(1929). *The Sexual Life of Savages in North-Western Melanesia* (3rd ed.), Routledge and Kegan Paul, London.

(1935). *Coral Gardens and their Magic*, vol. 1, Allen and Unwin, London.

(1948). *Magic, Science and Religion and Other Essays*, The Free Press, Glencoe (Illinois).

Marwick, M. G. (1964). 'Witchcraft as a Social Strain-Gauge', *Australian Journal of Science*, vol. 26: 263–8. Repr. in: Marwick, M. G. (ed.), *Witchcraft and Sorcery*, Penguin Modern Sociology Readings, Harmondsworth, 1970.

Massal, E. and Barrau, J. (1956). *Food Plants of the South Sea Islands*, South Pacific Commission Technical Papers No. 94, Noumea.

Mauss, M. (1966). *The Gift* (trans. I. Cunnison), Cohen and West, London.

Mead, M. (1935). *Sex and Temperament in Three Primitive Societies*, Routledge, London.

Monckton, C. A. W. (1921). *Some Experiences of a New Guinea Resident Magistrate*, Bodley Head, London.

Moresby, Capt. J. (1875). 'Discoveries in Eastern New Guinea by Captain Moresby and the Officers of H.M.S. Basilisk', *Journal of the Royal Geographical Society*, vol. 45: 153–70.

Nadel, S. F. (1953). 'Social Control and Self-Regulation', *Social Forces*, vol. 31: 265–73.

Nader, L. (1965). 'The Anthropological Study of Law', *American Anthropologist*, Special Publication, vol. 67, no. 6, pt 2: 3–32.

Odgers, G. (1957). *Air War Against Japan, 1943–45. Australia in the War of 1939–45*, Series Three: Air, vol. II, Canberra War Memorial.

Oliver, D. L. (1949a). 'Human Relations and Language in a Papuan-Speaking Tribe of Southern Bougainville, Solomon Islands', *Papers of the Peabody Museum of American Archaeology and Ethnology*, vol. 29: 1–38.

(1949b). 'Economic and Social Uses of Domestic Pigs in Siuai, Southern Bougainville, Solomon Islands', *Papers of the Peabody Museum of American Archaeology and Ethnology*, vol. 29: 1–29.

(1955). *A Solomon Island Society*, Harvard University Press, Cambridge (Mass.).

Oosterwal, G. (1961). *People of the Tor: a Cultural-Anthropological Study of the Tribes of the Tor Territory* (Northern Netherlands New Guinea), Royal Van Gorcum Ltd, Assen.

Papua Annual Reports (1911–50), Government Printer. Port Moresby.

Patrol Reports (1910–66). *Official Files: Esa'ala, Port Moresby and Canberra*.

Peristiany, J. G. (1965). *Honour and Shame: the Values of Mediterranean Society*, Weidenfeld and Nicolson, London.

Piddocke, S. (1965). 'The Potlatch System of the Southern Kwakiutl: a new perspective', *Southwestern Journal of Anthropology*, vol. 21: 244–64.

Pospisil, L. (1958). *The Kapauku Papuans and their Law*, Yale University Publications in Anthropology, no. 54, Yale University Press, New Haven.

Powell, H. A. (1960). 'Competitive Leadership in Trobriand Political Organization', *Journal of the Royal Anthropological Institute*, vol. 90: 118–45.

(1969). 'Territory, Hierarchy and Kinship in Kiriwina', *Man* (N.S.), vol. 4: 580–604.

Read, K. E. (1959). 'Leadership and Consensus in a New Guinea Society', *American Anthropologist*, vol. 61: 425–36.

Reay, M. (1953). 'Social Control amongst the Orokaiva', *Oceania*, vol. 24: 110–18.

(1959). *The Kuma*, Melbourne University Press.

Roheim, G. (1945–6). 'Yaboaine, a War God of Normanby Island', *Oceania*, vol. 16: 210–33, 319–36.

(1946). 'Ceremonial Prostitution in Duau (Normanby Island)', *Journal of Clinical Psychopathology and Psychotherapy*, vol. 7: 753–64.

(1948). 'Witches of Normanby Island', *Oceania*, vol. 18: 279–308.

Rowley, C. D. (1965). *The New Guinea Villager*, Cheshire, Melbourne.

Sahlins, M. D. (1962). 'Poor Man, Rich Man, Big-Man, Chief: Political Types in Melanesia and Polynesia', *Comparative Studies in Society and History*, vol. 5: 285–303.

(1965). 'On the Sociology of Primitive Exchange', in Banton, M. (ed.), *The Relevance of Models for Social Anthropology*, A.S.A. Monographs No. 1, Tavistock, London.

Salisbury, R. F. (1962). *From Stone to Steel*, Melbourne University Press.

(1964). 'Despotism and Australian Administration in the New Guinea Highlands', *American Anthropologist*, vol. 66, no. 4, pt 2: 225–39.

Scheffler, H. W. (1964). 'The Social Consequences of Peace on Choiseul Island', *Ethnology*, vol. 3: 398–403.

(1965). *Choiseul Island Social Structure*, University of California Press.

Seligman, C. G. (1910). *The Melanesians of British New Guinea*, Cambridge University Press.

Serpenti, L. M. (1965). *Cultivators in the Swamps: Social Structure and Horticulture in a New Guinea Society* (Frederick-Hendrik Island, West New Guinea), Royal Van Gorcum Ltd, Assen.

Spencer, M. (1964). *Doctor's Wife in Papua*. Robert Hale, London.

Stanner, W. E. H. (1958). 'On the Interpretation of Cargo Cults', *Oceania*, vol. 29: 1–25.

(1959). 'Continuity and Schism in an African Tribe: A Review', *Oceania*, vol. 29: 208–17.

(1963). *On Aboriginal Religion*, Oceania Monograph No. 11, University of Sydney.

Strathern, A. (1966). 'Despots and Directors in the New Guinea Highlands', *Man* (N.S.), vol. 1: 356–67.

(1968). 'Sickness and Frustration: Variations in Two New Guinea Highlands Societies', *Mankind*, vol. 6: 545–51.

Strathern, M. (1968). '*Popokl*: the Question of Morality', *Mankind*, vol. 6: 553–62.

Tambiah, S. J. (1968). 'The Magical Power of Words', *Man* (N.S.), vol. 3: 175–208.

Van Deusen, H. M. (1957). 'A New Species of Wallaby from Goodenough Island, Papua', *American Museum Novitates*, no.1826: 1–23.

Vivian, R. A. (1921). 'Report of a Census Patrol on Goodenough Island', Commonwealth Archives, Canberra.

Watson, J. B. (1963). 'Krakatoa's Echo?', *Journal of the Polynesian Society*, 5212: 5v .–ol.7

Williams, F. E. (1930). *Orokaiva Society*, Oxford University Press, London.
 (1936). *Papuans of the Trans-Fly*, Clarendon Press, Oxford.

Young, M. W. (1968). 'Bwaidogan Descent Groups', *American Anthropologist*, vol. 70: 333–6.
 (1971). 'Goodenough Island Cargo Cults', *Oceania*: in press.

GLOSSARY OF NATIVE TERMS

aba'aiyala – digging stick.
abutu – competitive food exchange.
afo'a – crop magic, garden spell.
atuaha – stone sitting circle.
au'a – vegetable or subsistence food.
aveyau – eating companion(ship).

dala – children of *tubuya*.
deudeu – yam display platform.
dewa – distinctive customs, habits, etc., of individuals or groups.
doke – woman's skirt; man's disease caused by adulterous wife.

eda – path, kinship link.

faiyeya – foster parent.
fakili – comb; name of a ceremonial moiety.
fofofo – group food exchange partner(ship).
foya – payment of pig to secure land rights from *susu*.

hiyo – spear; ceremonial moiety.

inainala – ancestral spirits.
inuba – initiators, sponsors of exchanges.

kabisona – small.
kaiwabu – ceremonial 'chief' of a festival.
kaliva lakaina – big man, elder.
kamoabi – compensatory food provided for *inuba*.
ketowai – shaming gift of pork given at festival climax.
kuvi – large yam (*Dioscorea alata*).
kwahala – agent of mystical attack, 'familiar'.
kwamana – child, foster child.
kwava – madness, amuck.

lakaina – big.
lauhiwaiya – cooked food exchange during festival.
liva – vine or twine measure used in *abutu*.
loka – foodless state, famine.
lokoloko – traditional (shell) valuables, possessions.
lokona – practice of food hoarding by self-denial.

maiyau – spirit of person or thing.
manumanua – ritual to banish famine.
matagina – 'credit' food or pig in *abutu*.
melala – hamlet, community.
modawa – drum; ceremonial moiety.

nau'a – wooden food bowl.
nibai – traditional enemy.
niune – food received in exchanges which recipient cannot eat.

sefaiya – stylized war-dance, threat display.
seli – song form.
sisikwana – clan spells; magic of hunger supression.
solama – inherited 'trade partner(ship)'; intervillage protector.
susu – mother's *unuma*.

tabotabo – residual helpers in *abutu*; the 'public' at a festival.
taitu – small yam (*Dioscorea esculenta*).
taladidika – nominal gifts of pork to visitors at festival climax.
talahaiyi – secret clan totem invoked in curse.
tofaha – strong, skilful gardener.
toitavealata – 'guardians' who 'look after' the community by prospering the
     crops.
tokweli – singer of garden spells.
toleme – 'helpers', followers of a leader.
tolokona – man who practises *lokona* well.
tonagona – traditional warrior leader.
tonima'avilana – man despised for his lazy, ineffectual gardening.
tonuakoyo – man feared for his bad temper, 'angry man'.
tovemeiya – 'bossman', hamlet leader, 'man who gives instructions'.
tubuya – sister's child.
tufo'a – hunger-producing sorcery.
tutula – pork debts paid back at festival climax.

unuma – patrilineage, minimal descent group.

valeimu'imu – weather and crop sorcery.
vebiala – event to honour special guest during festival.
venima'abi – member of *fofofo* group with whom *niune* food is exchanged;
     individual *fofofo* partner(ship).

veo'owana – matrilineal kinsmen of *inuba* who pledge their full support during
     latters' *abutu* or festival.
veumaiyiyi – state of mind which induces self-punishment to shame an offender.
veyaina – malicious gossip.

weyo – children of *dala*.

yabu – clan, maximal descent group.
yafuna – agent of mystical attack, evil spirit.
yakaikai – 'hubris', arrogant pride.
yaleyale – spell to give fortitude while gardening.

INDEX

Abela 123, 126–7, 132, 134–5
Abelam 157n, 189, 212n
Abutu (competitive food exchange) xii–
xiii, xix, 24, 40, 43, 47, 62, 88, 113, 146,
155, 162, 186–8, ch.9 and 10 *passim*, 235,
242, 243, conclusion *passim*; in Bwaidoga
258–61; development of 222–7, 229,
256–8; intervillage 123–4, 158, 190, 198,
208–11, 219, 221, 224, 247; intravillage
74, 111, 117, 190, 204, 209, 211–19, 224,
247; and leadership 78–9, 89, 95, 96, 105,
179, 188, 193–4, 197–206 *passim*, 256–7;
structure of 197–205; status sets in 69–
72, 190–4; threats of 85, 118, 211; and
social control ('food-giving-to-shame')
xix, 114–15, 117, 119, 121, 123–4, 145,
157, ch.9 and 10 *passim*, 232, 241, 246–7,
256–7, 262–3
Adiwai 68, 235, 265
Adiyaleyale 44, 82, 84, 179, 192, 266
Administration ch.1 *passim*, 31–2, 75,
90, 114, 128n, 138–42, 171–3, 224, 255–6,
261; officers 7, 9, 17, 30–1, 32, 33, 123,
128n, 138–42, 144, 171–3, 215, 223, 257,
267
Adoption 41–3, 44, 70, 99, 102, 153, 160,
238; fosterage ('feeding') 40–3, 44, 56,
99–100, 110, 123
Adultery 53–5, 57, 91, 115, 123, 127,
131n, 138, 179, 211–22 *passim*, 237,
240–1, 266–8
Affines 51–3, 55, 95, 110, 126, 131, 217,
220–1, 267; relations between 23, 43, 53,
83, 85, 93, 238; role in *abutu* 191–4, 224,
227
Aggression 79, 109, 158, 195, 218, 220,
251–2, 263; ritualized (*sefaiya*) 64, 125,
198–9, 202, 203, 210, 219, 245
Agnates 22–8 *passim*, ch.3 *passim*, 77, 86,
94–5, 98–9, 100, 106, 110, 111, 148,
190–1, 213–20 *passim*, 225–7, 240, 266;
quarrels between 28, 43–6, 60, 78, 91,
105, 108, 169, 218–20; sorcery between
43, 91, 132–3, 169, 226–7, 257–8
Ainaona clan 31, 61, 62, 66, 71, 219, 266
Amphlett Islands 5n, 6n, 21, 241n
Amuck 134–6, 142n, 219
Ancestors 22, 23, 29–30, 34, 50, 61–6
passim, 69, 71, 76, 83, 134–5, 148, 150,
154, 186, 224, 228; ancestral spirits
66–7, 150, 152, 154, 160, 163, 173, 183,
198, 245
Arapesh 36, 56n
Atuaha (sitting circle) 22–4, 28, 35, 37,
45, 68, 164, 234
Aveyau (eating companionship) 46–7, 69,
194
Awaiya village 29, 62, 183, 218

Bananas (plantain) 6, 30, 44, 63, 81, 89,
147, 151, 156, 159, 164, 167, 168, 173,
174, 242, 258; in *abutu* 195–6, 199, 219
Barnes, J. 28, 54
'Barrack' 15–18, 19, 225, 259, 260
Barth, F. 190
Bateson, G. xxii, 69
Belebele village xviii, 5, 14, 16, 20, 21n,
23, 24, 26, 29, 30, 33, 34n, 48, 49, 64,
66, 105, 123, 126, 172, 183, 214, 219,
225, 265–6
Bell, F. L. S. 41n
Belshaw, C. 255
Berndt, R. xx, 144n, 255, 262, 263n
Betel nut, chewing 51, 53, 104, 163, 245,
249–52 *passim*; ritual control of 66, 84
Big-men (*see also* Leadership, *Tofaha*)
xix, 6, ch.5 *passim*, 164, 166, 206, 224–6,
239, 248, 259, 265n
Binamina 106, 218, 220, 232
Bolubolu (patrol post) xvii, xviii, 1, 7, 31,
87, 138, 168
Brideprice 38–42 *passim*, 51–2, 55, 56, 57,
78, 87, 123, 124, 127, 178; brideservice
52–3, 57
Burridge, K. 113, 207
Busama 141
Bush (forest) 4, 34, 80, 174, 184, 186, 188
Bwaidoga village xvii, xviii, xxi, 3, 5, 6,
8, 16, 18, 26, 59n, 64, 76, 80, 112, 123,
136, 155, 164–5, 166n, 172, 175, 181n,
229n, 233, 254, 262n, 267; contrasts
with Kalauna xix, 258–61
Bwanakovi 80, 87, 93, 98n, 103–5, 233,
247, 249, 265–6

Calendar 148, 175, 224
Cannibalism 7, 14, 33, 49, 50, 71–2, 79,
113, 172–4, 186–8, 211, 216, 223n, 224
Canoe-complex 5, 6n, 258
Cargo cult (rumours) xviii, 9, 11
Cash, crops 10; in brideprice 52–3, 57;
earnings 10, 11, 52, 57, 86–8, 106, 158–
9; needs 11, 77
Change (social and cultural) xiii, xxi,
6–11, 15–18, 56–8, 59, 124, 128–9,
137–45, 165–6, 169–70, 183, 223–9,
247–8, 254–61
Childbearing 40, 47, 51, 53, 67, 94
Children (attitudes towards) 41, 55, 93,
99, 161, 172, 174, 186, 188, 260
Choiseul 78n, 255n
Chowning, A. 5n, 27, 28n, 50n, 54, 76n,
136n, 137n, 223n, 232
Christian values 8, 79–80, 115, 178, 183,
187, 259–61
Clans (*yabu*) 24–6, 29–34 *passim*, 37, 43,
46, ch.4 *passim*, 94–5, 111, 148; in *abutu*

277